1,000,000 Books

are available to read at

www.ForgottenBooks.com

Read online
Download PDF
Purchase in print

ISBN 978-1-331-30056-4
PIBN 10171134

This book is a reproduction of an important historical work. Forgotten Books uses state-of-the-art technology to digitally reconstruct the work, preserving the original format whilst repairing imperfections present in the aged copy. In rare cases, an imperfection in the original, such as a blemish or missing page, may be replicated in our edition. We do, however, repair the vast majority of imperfections successfully; any imperfections that remain are intentionally left to preserve the state of such historical works.

Forgotten Books is a registered trademark of FB &c Ltd.
Copyright © 2018 FB &c Ltd.
FB &c Ltd, Dalton House, 60 Windsor Avenue, London, SW19 2RR.
Company number 08720141. Registered in England and Wales.

For support please visit www.forgottenbooks.com

1 MONTH OF FREE READING

at

www.ForgottenBooks.com

By purchasing this book you are eligible for one month membership to ForgottenBooks.com, giving you unlimited access to our entire collection of over 1,000,000 titles via our web site and mobile apps.

To claim your free month visit:

www.forgottenbooks.com/free171134

* Offer is valid for 45 days from date of purchase. Terms and conditions apply.

English
Français
Deutsche
Italiano
Español
Português

www.forgottenbooks.com

Mythology Photography **Fiction**
Fishing Christianity **Art** Cooking
Essays Buddhism Freemasonry
Medicine **Biology** Music **Ancient Egypt** Evolution Carpentry Physics
Dance Geology **Mathematics** Fitness
Shakespeare **Folklore** Yoga Marketing
Confidence Immortality Biographies
Poetry **Psychology** Witchcraft
Electronics Chemistry History **Law**
Accounting **Philosophy** Anthropology
Alchemy Drama Quantum Mechanics
Atheism Sexual Health **Ancient History**
Entrepreneurship Languages Sport
Paleontology Needlework Islam
Metaphysics Investment Archaeology
Parenting Statistics Criminology
Motivational

POEMS OF RURAL LIFE

IN THE DORSET DIALECT.

BY

WILLIAM BARNES.

LONDON:
KEGAN PAUL, TRENCH, TRÜBNER & CO., Ltd.
1893.

The Rights of Translation and of Reproduction are Reserved.

TO THE READER.

Kind Reader,

Two of the three Collections of these Dorset Poems have been, for some time, out of print, and the whole of the three sets are now brought out in one volume.

I have little more to say for them, than that the writing of them as glimpses of life and landscape in Dorset, which often open to my memory and mindsight, has given me very much pleasure; and my happiness would be enhanced if I could believe that you would feel my sketches to be so truthful and pleasing as to give you even a small share of pleasure, such as that of the memories from which I have written them.

This edition has a list of such Dorset words as are found in the Poems, with some hints on Dorset word shapes, and I hope that they will be found a fully good key to the meanings of the verse.

Yours kindly,

W. BARNES.

June 1879.

CONTENTS.

FIRST COLLECTION.

SPRING.

	PAGE		PAGE
The Spring	3	Bringèn Woone Gwaïn o' Zundays	1
The Woodlands	4	Evenèn Twilight	1
Leädy-Day, an' Riddèn House	5	Evenèn in the Village	2
Easter Zunday	8	May	2
Easter Monday	9	Bob the Fiddler	2
Dock-Leaves	9	Hope in Spring	2
The Blackbird	10	The White Road up athirt the Hill	2
Woodcom' Feäst	12	The Woody Hollow	2
The Milk-Maid o' the Farm	13	Jenny's Ribbons	2
The Girt Woak Tree that's in the Dell	15	Eclogue:—The 'Lotments	2
Vellèn o' the Tree	16	Eclogue:—A Bit o' Sly Coortèn	3

SUMMER.

Evenèn, an' Maïdens out at Door	34	Where we did keep our Flagon	5
The Shepherd o' the Farm	35	Week's End in Zummer, in the Wold Vo'k's Time	5
Vields in the Light	36	The Meäd a-mow'd	6
Whitsuntide an' Club Walkèn	37	The Sky a-cleärèn	6
Woodley	39	The Evenèn Star o' Zummer	6
The Brook that Ran by Gramfer's	41	The Clote	6
Sleep did come wi' the Dew	42	I got two Vields	6
Sweet Music in the Wind	43	Polly be-èn upzides wi' Tom	6
Uncle an' Aunt	44	Be'mi'ster	6
Havèn Woones Fortune a-twold	46	Thatchèn o' the Rick	6
Jeäne's Weddèn Day in Mornèn	47	Bees a-Zwarmèn	6
Rivers don't gi'e out	49	Readèn ov a Head-stwone	7
Meäken up a Miff	50	Zummer Evenèn Dance	7
Haÿ-Meäken	51	Eclogue:—The Veäiries	7
Haÿ-Carrèn	52		
Eclogue:—The Best Man in the Vield	54		

FALL.

	PAGE		PAGE
Corn a-turnèn Yollow	76	Out a-Nuttèn	90
A-Haulèn o' the Corn	77	Teäkèn in Apples	91
Harvest Hwome:—The vu'st Peärt	78	Meäple Leaves be Yollow	92
Harvest Hwome:—Second Peärt	79	Night a-zettèn in	93
A Zong ov Harvest Hwome	80	The Weather-beäten Tree	94
Poll's Jack-Daw	82	Shrodon Feäir:—The vu'st Peärt	95
The Ivy	83	Shrodon Feäir:—The rest o't	96
The Welshnut Tree	84	Martin's Tide	97
Jenny out vrom Hwome	86	Guy Faux's Night	99
Grenley Water	86	Eclogue:—The Common a-took in	100
The Veäiry Veet that I do meet	87	Eclogue:—Two Farms in Woone	102
Mornèn	88		

WINTER.

The Vrost	105	The Settle an' the Girt Wood Vire	117
A Bit o' Fun	106	The Carter	118
Fanny's Be'th-day	107	Chris'mas Invitation	120
What Dick an' I did	109	Keepèn up o' Chris'mas	121
Grammer's Shoes	111	Zittèn out the Wold Year	122
Zunsheen in the Winter	112	Woak wer Good Enough Woonce	123
The Weepèn Leädy	113	Lullaby	124
The Happy Days when I wer Young	115	Meäry-Ann's Child	125
In the Stillness o' the Night	116	Eclogue:—Father Come Hwome	126
		Eclogue:—A Ghost	129

SUNDRY PIECES.

A Zong	133	The Rwose that Deck'd her Breast	145
The Maïd vor my Bride	134	Nanny's Cow	147
The Hwomestead	135	The Shep'erd Bwoy	148
The Farmer's Woldest Dā'ter	136	Hope a-left Behind	149
Uncle out o' Debt an' out o' Danger	137	A Good Father	150
The Church an' Happy Zunday	140	The Beam in Grenley Church	151
The Wold Waggon	141	The Vaïces that be Gone	152
The Drèven o' the Common	142	Poll	153
The Common a-took in	143	Looks a-know'd Avore	154
A Wold Friend	145	The Music o' the Dead	155

CONTENTS.

	PAGE		PAGE
The Pleäce a Teäle's a-twold o'	156	The Guide Post	166
Aunt's Tantrums	158	Gwain to Feäir	167
The Stwonèn Pworch	159	Jeäne o' Grenley Mill	168
Farmer's Sons	160	The Bells ov Alderburnham	169
Jeäne	161	The Girt Wold House o' Mossy	
The Dree Woaks	162	Stwone	170
The Hwomestead a-vell into Hand	164	A Witch	173
		Eclogue :—The Times	175

SECOND COLLECTION.

Blackmwore Maïdens	185	The Poplars	232
My Orcha'd in Lindèn Lea	186	The Linden on the Lawn	233
Bishop's Caundle	187	Our abode in Arby Wood	235
Hay Meäkèn—Nunchen Time	189	Slow to come, quick agone	236
A Father out an' Mother Hwome	191	The Vier-zide	236
Riddles	192	Knowlwood	238
Day's Work a-done	196	Hallowed Pleäces	240
Light or Sheäde	197	The Wold Wall	242
The Waggon a-stooded	197	Bleäke's House	423
Gwain down the Steps	201	John Bleake at Hwome	245
Ellen Brine ov Allenburn	202	Milkèn Time	247
The Motherless Child	203	When Birds be Still	248
The Leädy's Tower	204	Ridèn Hwome at Night	249
Fatherhood	208	Zun-zet	250
The Maid o' Newton	211	Spring	252
Childhood	212	The Zummer Hedge	253
Meäry's Smile	213	The Water Crowvoot	254
Meäry Wedded	214	The Lilac	255
The Stwonèn Bwoy	215	The Blackbird	256
The Young that died in Beauty	217	The Slantèn light o' Fall	257
Fair Emily of Yarrow Mill	218	Thissledown	259
The Scud	219	The May-tree	259
Mindèn House	221	The Lydlinch Bells	260
The Lovely Maid ov Elwell Meäd	222	The Stage Coach	261
Our Fathers' Works	224	Wayfearèn	263
The Wold vo'k Dead	225	The Leäne	265
Culver Dell and the Squire	227	The Railroad	267
Our Be'thplace	229	The Railroad	268
The Window freämed wi' Stwone	230	Seats	268
The Waterspring in the Leäne	231	Sound o' Water	270

	PAGE		PAGE
Trees be Company	270	Herrènston	302
A Pleäce in Zight	272	Out at Plough	304
Gwain to Brookwell	273	The Bwoat	306
Brookwell	275	The Pleäce our own ageän	307
The Shy Man	277	Eclogue :—John an' Thomas	308
The Winter's Willow	279	Pentridge by the River	310
I know Who	281	Wheat	311
Jessie Lee	282	The Meäd in June	313
True Love	283	Early risén	315
The Beän-vield	284	Zelling woone's Honey	316
Wold Friends a-met	286	Dobbin Dead	317
Fifehead	288	Happiness	319
Ivy Hall	289	Gruffmoody Grim	320
False Friends-like	290	The Turn o' the Days	322
The Bachelor	290	The Sparrow Club	323
Married Peair's Love-walk	292	Gammony Gay	325
A Wife a-praïs'd	293	The Heäre	327
The Wife a-lost	295	Nanny Gill	329
The Thorns in the Geäte	296	Moonlight on the Door	330
Angels by the Door	297	My Love's Guardian Angel	331
Vo'k a-comèn into Church	298	Leeburn Mill	332
Woone Rule	299	Praise o' Do'set	333
Good Meäster Collins	300		

THIRD COLLECTION.

Woone Smile Mwore	339	Early Playmeäte	359
The Echo	340	Pickèn o' Scroff	360
Vull a Man	341	Good Night	361
Naighbour Playmeätes	343	Went Hwome	362
The Lark	345	The Hollow Woak	363
The Two Churches	345	Childern's Childern	364
Woak Hill	347	The Rwose in the Dark	365
The Hedger	348	Come	366
In the Spring	349	Zummer Winds	367
The Flood in Spring	350	The Neäme Letters	368
Comen Hwome	351	The New House a-gettèn Wold	370
Grammer a-crippled	352	Zunday	370
The Castle Ruins	354	The Pillar'd Geäte	371
Eclogue :—John jealous	355	Zummer Stream	373

CONTENTS.

	PAGE		PAGE
Linda Deäne	374	Went vrom Hwome	412
Eclogue :—Come an' zee us	376	The Fancy Feäir	412
Lindenore	377	Things do Come Round	414
Me'th below the Tree	378	Zummer Thoughts in Winter Time	415
Treat well your Wife	379	I'm out o' Door	416
The Child an' the Mowers	381	Grief an' Gladness	417
The Love Child	382	Slidèn	418
Hawthorn Down	383	Lwonesomeness	420
Oben Vields	385	A Snowy Night	421
What John wer a-tellèn	386	The Year-clock	421
Sheädes	387	Not goo Hwome To-night	424
Times o' Year	387	The Humstrum	426
Eclogue :—Racketèn Joe	388	Shaftesbury Feäir	427
Zummer an' Winter	391	The Beäten Path	429
To Me	392	Ruth a-ridèn	430
Two an' Two	393	Beauty Undecked	432
The Lew o' the Rick	394	My love is good	432
The Wind in Woone's Feäce	395	Heedless o' my love	434
Tokens	396	The Do'set Militia	435
Tweil	396	A Do'set Sale	437
Fancy	398	Don't ceäre	437
The Broken Heart	399	Changes	439
Evenèn Light	400	Kindness	440
Vields by Watervalls	401	Withstanders	441
The Wheel Routs	402	Daniel Dwithen	442
Nanny's new Abode	403	Turnèn things off	444
Leaves a-vallèn	404	The Giants in Treädes	445
Lizzie	405	The Little Worold	447
Blessens a-left	406	Bad News	448
Fall Time	407	The Turnstile	449
Fall	408	The Better vor zeèn o' you	450
The Zilver-weed	409	Pity	451
The Widow's House	409	John Bloom in Lon'on	453
The Child's Greäve	410	A Lot o' Maidens	456

POEMS OF RURAL LIFE.

FIRST COLLECTION.

SPRING.

THE SPRING.

When wintry weather's all a-done,
An' brooks do sparkle in the zun,
An' nâisy-buildèn rooks do vlee
Wi' sticks toward their elem tree;
When birds do zing, an' we can zee
   Upon the boughs the buds o' spring,—
   Then I'm as happy as a king,
      A-vield wi' health an' zunsheen.

Vor then the cowslip's hangèn flow'r
A-wetted in the zunny show'r,
Do grow wi' vi'lets, sweet o' smell,
Bezide the wood-screen'd grægle's bell;
Where drushes' aggs, wi' sky-blue shell,
   Do lie in mossy nest among
   The thorns, while they do zing their zong
      At evenèn in the zunsheen.

An' God do meäke his win' to blow
An' raïn to vall vor high an' low,
An' bid his mornèn zun to rise
Vor all alike, an' groun' an' skies
Ha' colors vor the poor man's eyes:
   An' in our trials He is near,
   To hear our mwoan an' zee our tear,
      An' turn our clouds to zunsheen.

An' many times when I do vind
Things all goo wrong, an' vo'k unkind,
To zee the happy veedèn herds,
An' hear the zingèn o' the birds,
Do soothe my sorrow mwore than words;
   Vor I do zee that 'tis our sin
    Do meäke woone's soul so dark 'ithin,
     When God would gi'e woone zunsheen.

THE WOODLANDS.

O SPREAD ageän your leaves an' flow'rs,
  Lwonesome woodlands! zunny woodlands!
Here underneath the dewy show'rs
  O' warm-aïr'd spring-time, zunny woodlands!
As when, in drong or open ground,
Wi' happy bwoyish heart I vound
The twitt'rèn birds a-buildèn round
  Your high-bough'd hedges, zunny woodlands!

You gie'd me life, you gie'd me jay,
  Lwonesome woodlands! zunny woodlands.
You gie'd me health, as in my play
  I rambled through ye, zunny woodlands!
You gie'd me freedom, vor to rove
In aïry meäd or sheädy grove;
You gie'd me smilèn Fannèy's love,
  The best ov all o't, zunny woodlands!

My vu'st shrill skylark whiver'd high,
  Lwonesome woodlands! zunny woodlands!
To zing below your deep-blue sky
  An' white spring-clouds, O zunny woodlands!
An' boughs o' trees that woonce stood here,
Wer glossy green the happy year

That gie'd me woone I lov'd so dear,
  An' now ha' lost, O zunny woodlands!

O let me rove ageän unspied,
  Lwonesome woodlands! zunny woodlands!
Along your green-bough'd hedges' zide,
  As then I rambled, zunny woodlands!
An' where the missèn trees woonce stood,
Or tongues woonce rung among the wood,
My memory shall meäke em good,
  Though you've a-lost em, zunny woodlands!

LEÄDY-DAY, AN' RIDDEN HOUSE.

Aye, back at Leädy-Day, you know,
I come vrom Gullybrook to Stowe;
At Leädy-Day I took my pack
O' rottletraps, an' turn'd my back
Upon the weather-beäten door,
That had a-screen'd, so long avore,
The mwost that theäse zide o' the greäve,
I'd live to have, or die to seäve!
My childern, an' my vier-pleäce,
Where Molly wi' her cheerful feäce,
When I'd a-trod my wat'ry road
Vrom night-bedarken'd vields abrode,
Wi' nimble hands, at evenèn, blest
Wi' vire an' vood my hard-won rest;
The while the little woones did clim',
So sleek-skinn'd, up from lim' to lim',
Till, strugglèn hard an' clingèn tight,
They reach'd at last my feäce's height.
All tryèn which could soonest hold
My mind wi' little teäles they twold.

An' riddèn house is such a caddle,
I shan't be over keen vor mwore ō't,
Not yet a while, you mid be sure ō't,—
I'd rather keep to woone wold staddle.

Well, zoo, avore the east begun
To redden wi' the comèn zun,
We left the beds our mossy thatch
Wer never mwore to overstratch,
An' borrow'd uncle's wold hoss *Dragon*,
To bring the slowly lumbrèn waggon,
An' when he come, we vell a-packèn
The bedsteads, wi' their rwopes an' zackèn;
An' then put up the wold eärm-chair,
An' cwoffer vull ov e'then-ware,
An' vier-dogs, an' copper kittle,
Wi' crocks an' saucepans, big an' little;
An' fryèn-pan, vor aggs to slide
In butter round his hissèn zide,
An' gridire's even bars, to bear
The drippèn steäke above the gleäre
O' brightly-glowèn coals. An' then,
All up o' top o' them ageän
The woaken bwoard, where we did eat
Our croust o' bread or bit o' meat,—
An' when the bwoard wer up, we tied
Upon the reäves, along the zide,
The woaken stools, his glossy meätes,
Bwoth when he's beäre, or when the pleätes
Do clatter loud wi' knives, below
Our merry feäces in a row.
An' put between his lags, turn'd up'ard,
The zalt-box an' the corner cupb'ard.
An' then we laid the wold clock-ceäse,
All dumb, athirt upon his feäce,
Vor we'd a-left, I needen tell ye,

Noo works 'ithin his head or belly.
An' then we put upon the pack
The settle, flat upon his back;
An' after that, a-tied in pairs
In woone another, all the chairs,
An' bits o' lumber wo'th a ride,
An' at the very top a-tied,
The childern's little stools did lie,
Wi' lags a-turn'd towärd the sky:
Zoo there we lwoaded up our scroff,
An' tied it vast, an' started off.
An',—as the waggon cooden car all
We had to teäke,—the butter-barrel
An' cheese-wring, wi' his twinèn screw,
An' all the pails an' veäts, an' blue
Wold milk leads, and a vew things mwore,
Wer all a-carr'd the day avore,
And when the mwost ov our wold stuff
Wer brought outside o' thik brown ruf,
I rambled roun' wi' narrow looks,
In fusty holes an' darksome nooks,
To gather all I still mid vind,
O' rags or sticks a-left behind.
An' there the unlatch'd doors did creak,
A-swung by winds, a-streamèn weak
Drough empty rooms, an' meäkèn sad
My heart, where me'th woonce meäde me glad.
Vor when a man do leäve the he'th
An' ruf where vu'st he drew his breath,
Or where he had his bwoyhood's fun,
An' things wer woonce a-zaid an' done
That took his mind, do touch his heart
A little bit, I'll answer vor't.
Zoo riddèn house is such a caddle,
That I would rather keep my staddle.

EASTER ZUNDAY.

Last Easter Jim put on his blue
Frock cwoat, the vu'st time—vier new;
Wi' yollow buttons all o' brass,
That glitter'd in the zun lik' glass;
An' pok'd 'ithin the button-hole
A tutty he'd a-begg'd or stole.
A span-new wes'co't, too, he wore,
Wi' yollow stripes all down avore;
An' tied his breeches' lags below
The knee, wi' ribbon in a bow;
An' drow'd his kitty-boots azide,
An' put his laggèns on, an' tied
His shoes wi' strings two vingers wide,
    Because 'twer Easter Zunday.

An' after mornèn church wer out
He come back hwome, an' stroll'd about
All down the vields, an' drough the leäne,
Wi' sister Kit an' cousin Jeäne,
A-turnèn proudly to their view
His yollow breast an' back o' blue.
The lambs did play, the grounds wer green,
The trees did bud, the zun did sheen;
The lark did zing below the sky,
An' roads wer all a-blown so dry,
As if the zummer wer begun;
An' he had sich a bit o' fun!
He meäde the maïdens squeäl an' run,
    Because 'twer Easter Zunday.

EASTER MONDAY.

An' zoo o' Monday we got drough
Our work betimes, an ax'd a vew
Young vo'k vrom Stowe an' Coom, an' zome
Vrom uncle's down at Grange, to come.
An' they so spry, wi' merry smiles,
Did beät the path an' leäp the stiles,
Wi' two or dree young chaps bezide,
To meet an' keep up Easter tide:
Vor we'd a-zaid avore, we'd git
Zome friends to come, an' have a bit
O' fun wi' me, an' Jeäne, an' Kit,
  Because 'twer Easter Monday.

An' there we play'd away at quaïts,
An' weigh'd ourzelves wi' sceäles an' waïghts;
An' jump'd to zee who jump'd the spryest,
An' sprung the vurdest an' the highest;
An' rung the bells vor vull an hour,
An' play'd at vives ageän the tower.
An' then we went an' had a tait,
An' cousin Sammy, wi' his waight,
Broke off the bar, he wer so fat!
An' toppled off, an' vell down flat
Upon his head, an' squot his hat,
  Because 'twer Easter Monday.

DOCK-LEAVES.

The dock-leaves that do spread so wide
Up yonder zunny bank's green zide,
Do bring to mind what we did do
At play wi' dock-leaves years agoo:

How we,—when nettles had a-stung
Our little hands, when we wer young,—
Did rub em wi' a dock, an' zing
"*Out nettl', in dock. In dock, out sting.*"
An' when your feäce, in zummer's het,
Did sheen wi' tricklèn draps o' zweat,
How you, a-zot bezide the bank,
Didst toss your little head, an' pank,
An' teäke a dock-leaf in your han',
An' whisk en lik' a leädy's fan;
While I did hunt, 'ithin your zight,
Vor streaky cockle-shells to fight.

In all our play-geämes we did bruise
The dock-leaves wi' our nimble shoes;
Bwoth where we merry chaps did fling
You maïdens in the orcha'd swing,
An' by the zaw-pit's dousty bank,
Where we did taït upon a plank.
—(D'ye mind how woonce, you cou'den zit
The bwoard, an' vell off into pit?)
An' when we hunted you about
The grassy barken, in an' out
Among the ricks, your vlèe-èn frocks
An' nimble veet did strik' the docks.
An' zoo they docks, a-spread so wide
Up yonder zunny bank's green zide,
Do bring to mind what we did do,
Among the dock-leaves years agoo.

THE BLACKBIRD.

Ov all the birds upon the wing
Between the zunny show'rs o' spring,—
Vor all the lark, a-swingèn high,
Mid zing below a cloudless sky.

THE BLACKBIRD.

An' sparrows, clust'rèn roun' the bough,
Mid chatter to the men at plough,—
The blackbird, whisslèn in among
The boughs, do zing the gayest zong.

Vor we do hear the blackbird zing
His sweetest ditties in the spring,
When nippèn win's noo mwore do blow
Vrom northern skies, wi' sleet or snow,
But drēve light doust along between
The leäne-zide hedges, thick an' green;
An' zoo the blackbird in among
The boughs do zing the gayest zong.

'Tis blithe, wi' newly-open'd eyes,
To zee the mornèn's ruddy skies;
Or, out a-haulèn frith or lops
Vrom new-plēsh'd hedge or new-vell'd copse,
To rest at noon in primrwose beds
Below the white-bark'd woak-trees' heads;
But there's noo time, the whole däy long,
Lik' evenèn wi' the blackbird's zong.

Vor when my work is all a-done
Avore the zettèn o' the zun,
Then blushèn Jeäne do walk along
The hedge to meet me in the drong,
An' staÿ till all is dim an' dark
Bezides the ashen tree's white bark;
An' all bezides the blackbird's shrill
An' runnèn evenèn-whissle's still.

An' there in bwoyhood I did rove
Wi' pryèn eyes along the drove
To vind the nest the blackbird meäde
O' grass-stalks in the high bough's sheäde:

Or clim' aloft, wi' clingèn knees,
Vor crows' aggs up in swayèn trees,
While frighten'd blackbirds down below
Did chatter o' their little foe.
An' zoo there's noo pleäce lik' the drong,
Where I do hear the blackbird's zong.

WOODCOM' FEAST.

Come, Fanny, come! put on thy white,
'Tis Woodcom' feäst, good now! to-night.
Come! think noo mwore, you silly maïd,
O' chickèn drown'd, or ducks a-stray'd;
Nor mwope to vind thy new frock's tail
A-tore by hitchèn in a naïl;
Nor grieve an' hang thy head azide,
A-thinkèn o' thy lam' that died.
The flag's a-vleèn wide an' high,
An' ringèn bells do sheäke the sky;
The fifes do play, the horns do roar,
An' boughs be up at ev'ry door:
They'll be a-dancèn soon,—the drum
'S a-rumblèn now. Come, Fanny, come!
Why father's gone, an' mother too.
They went up leäne an hour agoo;
An' at the green the young and wold
Do stan' so thick as sheep in vwold:
The men do laugh, the bwoys do shout,—
Come out you mwopèn wench, come out,
An' go wi' me, an' show at leäst
Bright eyes an' smiles at Woodcom' feäst.

Come, let's goo out, an' fling our heels
About in jigs an' vow'r-han' reels;
While äll the stiff-lagg'd wolder vo'k,
A-zittèn roun', do talk an' joke

An' smile to zee their own wold rigs.
A-show'd by our wild geämes an' jigs.
Vor ever since the vwold church speer
Vu'st prick'd the clouds, vrom year to year,
When grass in meäd did reach woone's knees,
An' blooth did kern in apple-trees,
Zome merry day 'v' a-broke to sheen
Above the dance at Woodcom' green,
An' all o' they that now do lie
So low all roun' the speer so high,
Woonce, vrom the biggest to the leäst,
Had merry hearts at Woodcom' feäst.

Zoo keep it up, an' gi'e it on
To other vo'k when we be gone.
Come out; vor when the zettèn zun
Do leäve in sheäde our harmless fun,
The moon a-risèn in the east
Do gi'e us light at Woodcom' feäst.
Come, Fanny, come! put on thy white,
'Tis merry Woodcom' feäst to night:
There's nothèn vor to mwope about,—
Come out, you leäzy jeäde, come out!
An' thou wult be, to woone at leäst,
The prettiest maïd at Woodcom' feäst.

THE MILK-MAID O' THE FARM.

O Poll's the milk-maïd o' the farm!
   An' Poll's so happy out in groun',
Wi' her white païl below her eärm
   As if she wore a goolden crown.

An' Poll don't zit up half the night,
   Nor lie vor half the day a-bed;
An' zoo her eyes be sparklèn bright,
   An' zoo her cheäks be bloomèn red.

In zummer mornèns, when the lark
   Do rouse the litty lad an' lass
To work, then she's the vu'st to mark
   Her steps along the dewy grass.

An' in the evenèn, when the zun
   Do sheen ageän the western brows
O' hills, where bubblèn brooks do run,
   There she do zing bezide her cows.

An' ev'ry cow of hers do stand,
   An' never overzet her pail;
Nor try to kick her nimble hand,
   Nor switch her wi' her heavy taïl.

Noo leädy, wi' her muff an' vaïl,
   Do walk wi' sich a steätely tread
As she do, wi' her milkèn païl
   A-balanc'd on her comely head.

An' she, at mornèn an' at night,
   Do skim the yollow cream, an' mwold
An' wring her cheeses red an' white,
   An' zee the butter vetch'd an' roll'd.

An' in the barken or the ground,
   The chaps do always do their best
To milk the vu'st their own cows round,
   An' then help her to milk the rest.

Zoo Poll's the milk-maïd o' the farm!
   An' Poll's so happy out in groun',
Wi' her white pail below her eärm,
   As if she wore a goolden crown.

THE GIRT WOAK TREE THAT'S IN THE DELL.

The girt woak tree that's in the dell!
There's noo tree I do love so well;
Vor times an' times when I wer young,
I there've a-climb'd, an' there've a-zwung,
An' pick'd the eäcorns green, a-shed
In wrestlèn storms vrom his broad head.
An' down below's the cloty brook
Where I did vish with line an' hook,
An' beät, in playsome dips and zwims,
The foamy stream, wi' white-skinn'd lim's.
An' there my mother nimbly shot
Her knittèn-needles, as she zot
At evenèn down below the wide
Woak's head, wi' father at her zide.
An' I've a-played wi' many a bwoy,
That's now a man an' gone awoy;
  Zoo I do like noo tree so well
  'S the girt woak tree that's in the dell.

An' there, in leäter years, I roved
Wi' thik poor maïd I fondly lov'd,—
The maïd too feäir to die so soon,—
When evenèn twilight, or the moon,
Cast light enough 'ithin the pleäce
To show the smiles upon her feäce,
Wi' eyes so clear 's the glassy pool,
An' lips an' cheäks so soft as wool.
There han' in han', wi' bosoms warm,
Wi' love that burn'd but thought noo harm,
Below the wide-bough'd tree we past
The happy hours that went too vast;
An' though she'll never be my wife,
She's still my leäden star o' life.

She's gone : an' she 've a-left to me
Her mem'ry in the girt woak tree;
  Zoo I do love noo tree so well
  'S the girt woak tree that's in the dell.

An' oh ! mid never ax nor hook
Be brought to spweil his steätely look;
Nor ever roun' his ribby zides
Mid cattle rub ther heäiry hides;
Nor pigs rout up his turf, but keep
His lwonesome sheäde vor harmless sheep;
An' let en grow, an' let en spread,
An' let en live when I be dead.
But oh ! if men should come an' vell
The girt woak tree that's in the dell,
An' build his planks 'ithin the zide
O' zome girt ship to plough the tide,
Then, life or death ! I'd goo to sea,
A sailèn wi' the girt woak tree :
An' I upon his planks would stand,
An' die a-fightèn vor the land,—
The land so dear,—the land so free,—
The land that bore the girt woak tree;
  Vor I do love noo tree so well
  'S the girt woak tree that's in the dell.

VELLEN O' THE TREE.

AYE, the girt elem tree out in little hwome groun'
Wer a-stannèn this mornèn, an' now's a-cut down.
Aye, the girt elem tree, so big roun' an' so high,
Where the mowers did goo to their drink, an' did lie
In the sheäde ov his head, when the zun at his heighth
Had a-drove em vrom mowèn, wi' het an' wi' drîth,

Where the hay-meäkers put all their picks an' their reäkes,
An' did squot down to snabble their cheese an' their ceäkes,
An' did vill vrom their flaggons their cups wi' their eäle,
An' did meäke theirzelves merry wi' joke an' wi' teäle.

Ees, we took up a rwope an' we tied en all round
At the top o'n, wi' woone end a-hangèn to ground,
An' we cut, near the ground, his girt stem a'most drough,
An' we bent the wold head o'n wi' woone tug or two;
An' he sway'd all his limbs, an' he nodded his head,
Till he vell away down like a pillar o' lead:
An' as we did run vrom en, there, clwose at our backs,
Oh! his boughs come to groun' wi' sich whizzes an' cracks;
An' his top wer so lofty that, now he is down,
The stem o'n do reach a-most over the groun'.
Zoo the girt elem tree out in little hwome groun'
Wer a-stannèn this mornèn, an' now's a-cut down.

BRINGEN WOONE GWAÏN * O' ZUNDAYS.

AH! John! how I do love to look
At theäse green hollor, an' the brook
Among the withies that do hide
The stream, a-growèn at the zide;
An' at the road athirt the wide
   An' shallow vword, where we young bwoys
   Did peärt, when we did goo half-woys,
     To bring ye gwaïn o' Zundays.

Vor after church, when we got hwome,
In evenèn you did always come
To spend a happy hour or two
Wi' us, or we did goo to you;

---

* "To bring woone gwain,"— to bring one going; to bring one on his way.

B

An' never let the comers goo
    Back hwome alwone, but always took
    A stroll down wi' em to the brook
        To bring em gwaïn o' Zundays.

How we did scote all down the groun',
A-pushèn woone another down!
Or challengèn o' zides in jumps
Down over bars, an' vuzz, an' humps;
An' peärt at last wi' slaps an' thumps,
    An' run back up the hill to zee
    Who'd get hwome soonest, you or we,
        That brought ye gwaïn o' Zundays.

O' leäter years, John, you've a-stood
My friend, an' I've a-done you good;
But tidden, John, vor all that you
Be now, that I do like ye zoo,
But what you wer vor years agoo:
    Zoo if you'd stir my heart-blood now,
    Tell how we used to play, an' how
        You brought us gwaïn o' Zundays.

EVENÈN TWILIGHT.

AH! they vew zummers brought us round
The happiest days that we've a-vound,
When in the orcha'd, that did stratch
To westward out avore the patch
Ov high-bough'd wood, an' shelve to catch
    The western zun-light, we did meet
    Wi' merry tongues an' skippèn veet
        At evenèn in the twilight.

The evenèn aïr did fan, in turn,
The cheäks the midday zun did burn.

EVENÈN TWILIGHT.

An' zet the russlèn leaves at play,
An' meäke the red-stemm'd brembles sway
In bows below the snow-white may;
   An' whirlèn roun' the trees, did sheäke
   Jeäne's raven curls about her neck,
     They evenèns in the twilight.

An' there the yollow light did rest
Upon the bank towárd the west,
An' twitt'rèn birds did hop in drough
The hedge, an' many a skippèn shoe
Did beät the flowers, wet wi' dew,
   As underneäth the tree's wide limb
   Our merry sheäpes did jumpy, dim,
     They evenèns in the twilight.

How sweet's the evenèn dusk to rove
Along wi' woone that we do love!
When light enough is in the sky
To sheäde the smile an' light the eye
'Tis all but heaven to be by;
   An' bid, in whispers soft an' light
   'S the ruslèn ov a leaf, " Good night,"
     At evenèn in the twilight.

An' happy be the young an' strong,
That can but work the whole day long
So merry as the birds in spring;
An' have noo ho vor any thing
Another day mid teäke or bring;
   But meet, when all their work's a-done,
   In orcha'd vor their bit o' fun
     At evenèn in the twilight.

EVENÈN IN THE VILLAGE.

Now the light o' the west is a-turn'd to gloom,
　　An' the men be at hwome vrom ground;
An' the bells be a-zeudèn all down the Coombe
　　From tower, their mwoansome sound.
　　　　An' the wind is still,
　　　An' the house-dogs do bark,
An' the rooks be a-vled to the elems high an' dark,
　　An' the water do roar at mill.

An' the flickerèn light drough the window-peäne
　　Vrom the candle's dull fleäme do shoot,
An' young Jemmy the smith is a-gone down leäne,
　　A-playèn his shrill-vaïced flute.
　　　　An' the miller's man
　　　Do zit down at his ease
On the seat that is under the cluster o' trees,
　　Wi' his pipe an' his cider can.

MAY.

Come out o' door, 'tis Spring! 'tis May
The trees be green, the vields be gay;
The weather's warm, the winter blast,
Wi' all his traïn o' clouds, is past;
The zun do rise while vo'k do sleep,
To teäke a higher daily zweep,
Wi' cloudless feäce a-flingèn down
His sparklèn light upon the groun'.

The aïr's a-streamèn soft,—come drow
The windor open; let it blow

MAY.

In drough the house, where vire, an' door
A-shut, kept out the cwold avore.
Come, let the vew dull embers die,
An' come below the open sky;
An' wear your best, vor fear the groun'
In colours gay mid sheäme your gown:
An' goo an' rig wi' me a mile
Or two up over geäte an' stile,
Drough zunny parrocks that do leäd,
Wi' crooked hedges, to the meäd,
Where elems high, in steätely ranks,
Do rise vrom yollow cowslip-banks,
An' birds do twitter vrom the spray
O' bushes deck'd wi' snow-white may;
An' gil'cups, wi' the deäisy bed,
Be under ev'ry step you tread.

We'll wind up roun' the hill, an' look
All down the thickly-timber'd nook,
Out where the squier's house do show
His grey-wall'd peaks up drough the row
O' sheädy elems, where the rook
Do build her nest; an' where the brook
Do creep along the meäds, an' lie
To catch the brightness o' the sky;
An' cows, in water to theïr knees,
Do stan' a-whiskèn off the vlees.

Mother o' blossoms, and ov all
That's feäir a-vield vrom Spring till Fall,
The gookoo over white-weäv'd seas
Do come to zing in thy green trees,
An' buttervlees, in giddy flight,
Do gleäm the mwost by thy gay light.
Oh! when, at last, my fleshly eyes
Shall shut upon the vields an' skies,

Mid zummer's zunny days be gone,
An' winter's clouds be comèn on:
Nor mid I draw upon the e'th,
O' thy sweet aïr my leätest breath;
Alassen I mid want to stay
Behine' for thee, O flow'ry May!

BOB THE FIDDLER.

Oh! Bob the fiddler is the pride
O' chaps an' maïdens vur an' wide;
They can't keep up a merry tide,
   But Bob is in the middle.
If merry Bob do come avore ye,
He'll zing a zong, or tell a story;
But if you'd zee en in his glory,
   Jist let en have a fiddle.

Aye, let en tuck a crowd below
His chin, an' gi'e his vist a bow,
He'll dreve his elbow to an' fro',
   An' play what you do please.
At Maypolèn, or feäst, or feäir,
His eärm wull zet off twenty peäir,
An' meäke em dance the groun' dirt-beäre,
   An' hop about lik' vlees.

Long life to Bob! the very soul
O' me'th at merry feäst an' pole;
Vor when the crowd do leäve his jowl,
   They'll all be in the dumps.
Zoo at the dance another year,
At *Shillinston* or *Hazelbur'*,
Mid Bob be there to meäke em stir,
   In merry jigs, their stumps!

HOPE IN SPRING.

In happy times a while agoo,
   My lively hope, that's now a-gone
Did stir my heart the whole year drough,
   But mwost when green-bough'd spring come on :
When I did rove, wi' litty veet,
Drough deäisy-beds so white's a sheet,
But still avore I us'd to meet
   The blushèn cheäks that bloom'd vor me!

An' afterward, in lightsome youth,
   When zummer wer a-comèn on,
An' all the trees wer white wi' blooth,
   An' dippèn zwallows skimm'd the pon';
Sweet hope did vill my heart wi' jay,
An' tell me, though thik spring wer gay,
There still would come a brighter May,
   Wi' blushèn cheäks to bloom vor me!

An' when, at last, the time come roun',
   An' brought a lofty zun to sheen
Upon my smilèn Fanny, down
   Drough nēsh young leaves o' yollow green;
How charmèn wer the het that glow'd,
How charmèn wer the sheäde a-drow'd,
How charmèn wer the win' that blow'd
   Upon her cheäks that bloom'd vor me!

But hardly did they times begin,
   Avore I vound em short to stay :
An' year by year do now come in,
   To peärt me wider vrom my jay,
Vor what's to meet, or what's to peärt,
Wi' maïdens kind, or maïdens smart,
When hope's noo longer in the heart,
   An' cheäks noo mwore do bloom vor me?

But there's a worold still to bless
　　The good, where zickness never rose;
An' there's a year that's winterless,
　　Where glassy waters never vroze;
An' there, if true but e'thly love
Do seem noo sin to God above,
'S a smilèn still my harmless dove,
　　So feäir as when she bloom'd vor me!

THE WHITE ROAD UP ATHIRT THE HILL.

WHEN hot-beam'd zuns do strik right down,
An' burn our zweaty feäzen brown;
An' zunny slopes, a-lyèn nigh,
Be back'd by hills so blue's the sky;
Then, while the bells do sweetly cheem
Upon the champèn high-neck'd team,
How lively, wi' a friend, do seem
　　The white road up athirt the hill.

The zwellèn downs, wi' chalky tracks
A-climmèn up their zunny backs,
Do hide green meäds an' zedgy brooks,
An' clumps o' trees wi' glossy rooks,
An' hearty vo'k to laugh an' zing,
An' parish-churches in a string,
Wi' tow'rs o' merry bells to ring,
　　An' white roads up athirt the hills

At feäst, when uncle's vo'k do come
To spend the day wi' us at hwome,
An' we do lay upon the bwoard
The very best we can avvword,
The wolder woones do talk an' smoke,
An' younger woones do play an' joke,
An' in the evenèn all our vo'k
　　Do bring em gwain athirt the hill.

An' while the green do zwarm wi' wold
An' young, so thick as sheep in vwold,
The bellows in the blacksmith's shop,
An' miller's moss-green wheel do stop,
An' lwonesome in the wheelwright's shed
'S a-left the wheelless waggon-bed;
While zwarms o' comèn friends do tread
   The white road down athirt the hill.

An' when the windèn road so white,
A-climmèn up the hills in zight,
Do leäd to pleäzen, east or west,
The vu'st a-known, an' lov'd the best,
How touchèn in the zunsheen's glow,
Or in the sheädes that clouds do drow
Upon the zunburnt downs below,
   'S the white road up athirt the hill.

What peaceful hollows here the long
White roads do windy round among!
Wi' deäiry cows in woody nooks,
An' haymeäkers among their pooks,
An' housen that the trees do screen
From zun an' zight by boughs o' green!
Young blushèn beauty's hwomes between
   The white roads up athirt the hills.

THE WOODY HOLLOW.

If mem'ry, when our hope's a-gone,
Could bring us dreams to cheat us on,
Ov happiness our hearts voun' true
In years we come too quickly drough;
What days should come to me, but you,
   That burn'd my youthvul cheäks wi' *zuns*
   O' zummer, in my playsome runs
     About the woody hollow.

When evenèn's risèn moon did peep
Down drough the hollow dark an' deep,
Where gigglèn sweethearts meäde their vows
In whispers under waggèn boughs;
When whisslèn bwoys, an' rott'lèn ploughs
  Wer still, an' mothers, wi' their thin
  Shrill vaïces, call'd their daughters in,
    From walkèn in the hollow;

What souls should come avore my zight,
But they that had your zummer light?
The litsome younger woones that smil'd
Wi' comely feäzen now a-spweil'd;
Or wolder vo'k, so wise an' mild,
  That I do miss when I do goo
    To zee the pleäce, an' walk down drough
      The lwonesome woody hollow?

When wrongs an' overbearèn words
Do prick my bleedèn heart lik' swords,
Then I do try, vor Christes seäke,
To think o' you, sweet days! an' meäke
My soul as 'twer when you did weäke
  My childhood's eyes, an' when, if spite
  Or grief did come, did die at night
    In sleep 'ithin the hollow.

JENNY'S RIBBONS.

JEAN ax'd what ribbon she should wear
'Ithin her bonnet to the feäir?
She had woone white, a-gi'ed her when
She stood at Meäry's chrissenèn;
She had woone brown, she had woone red,
A keepseäke vrom her brother dead,

JENNY'S RIBBONS.

That she did like to wear, to goo
To zee his greäve below the yew.

She had woone green among her stock,
That I'd a-bought to match her frock;
She had woone blue to match her eyes,
The colour o' the zummer skies,
An' thik, though I do like the rest,
Is he that I do like the best,
Because she had en in her heäir
When vu'st I walk'd wi' her at feäir

The brown, I zaid, would do to deck
Thy heäir; the white would match thy neck;
The red would meäke thy red cheäk wan
A-thinkèn o' the gi'er gone;
The green would show thee to be true;
But still I'd sooner zee the blue,
Because 'twer he that deck'd thy heäir
When vu'st I walk'd wi' thee at feäir.

Zoo, when she had en on, I took
Her han' 'ithin my elbow's crook,
An' off we went athirt the weir
An' up the meäd toward the feäir;
The while her mother, at the geäte,
Call'd out an' bid her not stay leäte,
An' she, a-smilèn wi' her bow
O' blue, look'd roun' and nodded, *No*.

Eclogue.

THE 'LOTMENTS.

John and Richard.

JOHN.

Zoo you be in your groun' then, I do zee,
A-workèn and a-zingèn lik' a bee.
How do it answer? what d'ye think about it?
D'ye think 'tis better wi' it than without it?
A-recknèn rent, an' time, an' zeed to stock it,
D'ye think that you be any thing in pocket?

RICHARD.

O', 'tis a goodish help to woone, I'm sure o't.
If I had not a-got it, my poor bwones
Would now ha' eäch'd a-crackèn stwones
Upon the road; I wish I had zome mwore o't.

JOHN.

I wish the girt woones had a-got the greäce
To let out land lik' this in ouer pleäce;
But I do fear there'll never be nwone vor us,
An' I can't tell whatever we shall do:
We be a-most starvèn, an' we'd goo
To 'merica, if we'd enough to car us

RICHARD.

Why 'twer the squire, good now! a worthy man,
That vu'st brought into ouer pleäce the plan,
He zaid he'd let a vew odd eäcres
O' land to us poor leäb'rèn men;

An', faïth, he had enough o' teäkers
Vor that, an' twice so much ageän.
Zoo I took zome here, near my hovel,
To exercise my speäde an' shovel;
An' what wi' dungèn, diggèn up, an' zeedèn,
A-thinnèn, cleänèn, howèn up an' weedèn,
I, an' the biggest o' the childern too,
Do always vind some useful jobs to do.

JOHN.

Aye, wi' a bit o' ground, if woone got any,
Woone's bwoys can soon get out an' eärn a penny;
An' then, by workèn, they do learn the vaster
The way to do things when they have a meäster;
Vor woone must know a deäl about the land
Bevore woone's fit to lend a useful hand,
In geärden or a-vield upon a farm.

RICHARD.

An' then the work do keep em out o' harm;
Vor vo'ks that don't do nothèn wull be vound
Soon doèn woorse than nothèn, I'll be bound.
But as vor me, d'ye zee, with theäse here bit
O' land, why I have ev'ry thing a'mwost:
Vor I can fatten vowels for the spit,
Or zell a good fat goose or two to rwoast;
An' have my beäns or cabbage, greens or grass,
Or bit o' wheat, or, sich my happy feäte is,
That I can keep a little cow, or ass,
An' a vew pigs to eat the little teäties.

JOHN.

An' when your pig's a-fatted pretty well
Wi' teäties, or wi' barley an' some bran,
Why you've a-got zome vlitches vor to zell,
Or hang in chimney-corner, if you can.

RICHARD.

Aye, that's the thing; an' when the pig do die,
We got a lot ov offal for to fry,
An' netlèns for to bwoil; or put the blood in,
An' meäke a meal or two o' good black-pudden.

JOHN.

I'd keep myzelf from parish, I'd be bound,
If I could get a little patch o' ground.

Eclogue.
A BIT O' SLY COORTEN.

John and Fanny.

JOHN.

Now, Fanny, 'tis too bad, you teazèn maïd!
How leäte you be a' come! Where have ye stay'd?
How long you have a-meäde me waït about!
I thought you werden gwaïn to come ageän:
I had a mind to goo back hwome ageän.
This idden when you promis'd to come out.

FANNY.

Now 'tidden any good to meäke a row,
Upon my word, I cooden come till now.
Vor I've a-been kept in all day by mother,
At work about woone little job an' t'other.
If you do want to goo, though, don't ye stay
Vor me a minute longer, I do pray.

JOHN.

I thought you mid be out wi' Jemmy Bleäke,

FANNY.

An' why be out wi' him, vor goodness' seäke?

JOHN.

You walk'd o' Zunday evenèn wi'n, d'ye know,
You went vrom church a-hitch'd up in his eärm.

FANNY.

Well, if I did, that werden any harm.
Lauk! that *is* zome'at to teäke notice o'.

JOHN.

He took ye roun' the middle at the stile,
An' kiss'd ye twice 'ithin the ha'f a mile.

FANNY.

Ees, at the stile, because I shoulden vall,
He took me hold to help me down, that's all;
An' I can't zee what very mighty harm
He could ha' done a-lendèn me his eärm.
An' as vor kissèn o' me, if he did,
I didden ax en to, nor zay he mid:
An' if he kiss'd me dree times, or a dozen,
What harm wer it? Why idden he my cousin?
An' I can't zee, then, what there is amiss
In cousin Jem's jist gi'èn me a kiss.

JOHN.

Well, he shan't kiss ye, then; you shan't be kiss'd
By his girt ugly chops, a lanky houn'!
If I do zee'n, I'll jist wring up my vist
An' knock en down.
I'll squot his girt pug-nose, if I don't miss en;
I'll warn I'll spweil his pretty lips vor kissèn!

FANNY.

Well, John, I'm sure I little thought to vind
That you had ever sich a jealous mind.
What then! I s'pose that I must be a dummy,
An' mussen goo about nor wag my tongue
To any soul, if he's a man, an' young;
Or else you'll work yourzelf up mad wi' passion,
An' talk away o' gi'èn vo'k a drashèn,
An' breakèn bwones, an' beäten heads to pummy!
If you've a-got sich jealous ways about ye,
I'm sure I should be better off 'ithout ye.

JOHN.

Well, if girt Jemmy have a-won your heart,
We'd better break the coortship off, an' peärt.

FANNY.

He won my heart! There, John, don't talk sich stuff;
Don't talk noo mwore, vor you've a-zaid enough.
If I'd a-lik'd another mwore than you,
I'm sure I shoulden come to meet ye zoo;
Vor I've a-twold to father many a storry,
An' took o' mother many a scwoldèn vor ye.
[weeping.]
But 'twull be over now, vor you shan't zee me
Out wi' ye noo mwore, to pick a quarrel wi' me.

JOHN.

Well, Fanny, I woon't zay noo mwore, my dear.
Let's meäke it up. Come, wipe off thik there tear.
Let's goo an' zit o' top o' theäse here stile,
An' rest, an' look about a little while.

FANNY.

Now goo away, you crabbed jealous chap!
You shan't kiss me,—you shan't! I'll gi' ye a slap.

JOHN.

Then you look smilèn ; don't you pout an' toss
Your head so much, an' look so very cross.

FANNY.

Now, John ! don't squeeze me roun' the middle zoo.
I woon't stop here noo longer, if you do.
Why, John ! be quiet, wull ye ? Fie upon it !
Now zee how you've a-wrumpl'd up my bonnet !
Mother 'ill zee it after I'm at hwome,
An' gi'e a guess directly how it come.

JOHN.

Then don't you zay that I be jealous, Fanny.

FANNY.

I wull : vor you *be* jealous, Mister Jahnny.
There's zomebody a-comèn down the groun'
Towards the stile. Who is it ? Come, get down.
I must run hwome, upon my word then, now ;
If I do stay, they'll kick up sich a row.
Good night. I can't stay now.

JOHN.

Then good night, Fanny !
Come out a-bit to-morrow evenèn, can ye ?

SUMMER.

EVENÈN, AN' MAIDENS OUT AT DOOR.

Now the sheädes o' the elems do stratch mwore an' mwore,
Vrom the low-zinkèn zun in the west o' the sky;
An' the maïdens do stand out in clusters avore
The doors, vor to chatty an' zee vo'k goo by.

An' their cwombs be a-zet in their bunches o' heäir,
An' their currels do hang roun' their necks lily-white,
An' their cheäks they be rwosy, their shoulders be beäre,
Their looks they be merry, their limbs they be light.

An' the times have a-been—but they cant be noo mwore—
When I had my jay under evenèn's dim sky,
When my Fanny did stan' out wi' others avore
Her door, vor to chatty an' zee vo'k goo by.

An' up there, in the green, is her own honey-zuck,
That her brother traïn'd up roun' her window; an' there
Is the rwose an' the jessamy, where she did pluck
A fiow'r vor her bosom or bud vor her heäir.

An' zoo smile, happy maïdens! vor every feäce,
As the zummers do come, an' the years do roll by,
Will soon sadden, or goo vur away vrom the pleäce,
Or else, lik' my Fanny, will wither an' die.

But when you be a-lost vrom the parish, zome mwore
Will come on in your pleäzen to bloom an' to die;
An' the zummer will always have maïdens avore
Their doors, vor to chatty an' zee vo'k goo by.

Vor daughters ha' mornèn when mothers ha' night,
An' there's beauty alive when the feäirest is dead;
As when woone sparklèn weäve do zink down vrom the light,
Another do come up an' catch it instead.

Zoo smile on, happy maïdens! but I shall noo mwore
Zee the maïd I do miss under evenèn's dim sky;
An' my heart is a-touch'd to zee you out avore
The doors, vor to chatty an' zee vo'k goo by.

THE SHEPHERD O' THE FARM.

OH! I be shepherd o' the farm,
    Wi' tinklèn bells an' sheep-dog's bark,
An' wi' my crook a-thirt my eärm,
    Here I do rove below the lark.

An' I do bide all day among
    The bleäten sheep, an' pitch their vwold;
An' when the evenèn sheädes be long,
    Do zee em all a-penn'd an' twold.

An' I do zee the friskèn lam's,
    Wi' swingèn taïls an' woolly lags,
A-playèn roun' their veedèn dams,
    An' pullèn o' their milky bags.

An' I bezide a hawthorn tree,
    Do' zit upon the zunny down,
While sheädes o' zummer clouds do vlee
    Wi' silent flight along the groun'.

An' there, among the many cries
    O' sheep an' lambs, my dog do pass
A zultry hour, wi' blinkèn eyes,
    An' nose a-stratch'd upon the grass;

But, in a twinklèn, at my word,
    He's all awake, an' up, an' gone
Out roun' the sheep lik' any bird,
    To do what he's a-zent upon.

An' I do goo to washèn pool,
    A-sousèn over head an' ears,
The shaggy sheep, to cleän their wool
    An' meäke em ready vor the sheärs.

An' when the shearèn time do come,
    Then we do work vrom dawn till dark;
Where zome do shear the sheep, and zome
    Do mark their zides wi' meästers mark.

An' when the shearèn's all a-done,
    Then we do eat, an' drink, an' zing,
In meäster's kitchen till the tun
    Wi' merry sounds do sheäke an' ring.

Oh! I be shepherd o' the farm,
    Wi' tinklèn bells an' sheep dog's bark,
An' wi' my crook a-thirt my eärm,
    Here I do rove below the lark.

YIELDS IN THE LIGHT.

Woone's heart mid leäp wi' thoughts o' jay
In comèn manhood light an' gay
When we do teäke the worold on
Vrom our vore-elders dead an' gone;

But days so feäir in hope's bright eyes
Do often come wi' zunless skies:
Woone's fancy can but be out-done,
Where trees do sway an' brooks do run,
By risèn moon or zettèn zun.

Vor when at evenèn I do look
All down theäse hangèn on the brook,
Wi' weäves a-leäpèn clear an' bright,
Where boughs do sway in yollow light;
Noo hills nor hollows, woods nor streams,
A-voun' by day or zeed in dreams,
Can ever seem so fit to be
Good angel's hwomes, though they do gi'e
But païn an' tweil to such as we.

An' when by moonlight darksome sheädes
Do lie in grass wi' dewy bleädes,
An' worold-hushèn night do keep
The proud an' angry vast asleep,
When I can think, as I do rove,
Ov only souls that I do love;
Then who can dream a dream to show,
Or who can think o' moons to drow,
A sweeter light to rove below?

WHITSUNTIDE AN' CLUB WALKEN.

EES, last Whit-Monday, I an' Meäry
Got up betimes to mind the deäiry;
An' gi'ed the milkèn païls a scrub,
An' dress'd, an' went to zee the club.
Vor up at public-house, by ten
O'clock the pleäce wer vull o' men,
A-dress'd to goo to church, an' dine,
An' walk about the pleäce in line.

Zoo off they started, two an' two,
Wi' painted poles an' knots o' blue,
An' girt silk flags,—I wish my box
'D a-got em all in ceäpes an' frocks,—
A-weävèn wide an' flappèn loud
In playsome winds above the crowd;
While fifes did squeak an' drums did rumble,
An' deep beäzzoons did grunt an' grumble,
An' all the vo'k in gath'rèn crowds
Kick'd up the doust in smeechy clouds,
That slowly rose an' spread abrode
In streamèn aïr above the road.
An' then at church there wer sich lots
O' hats a-hangèn up wi' knots,
An' poles a-stood so thick as iver,
The rushes stood beside a river.
An' Mr Goodman gi'ed em warnèn
To spend their evenèn lik' their mornèn;
An' not to pray wi' mornèn tongues,
An' then to zwear wi' evenèn lungs;
Nor vu'st sheäke hands, to let the wrist
Lift up at last a bruisèn vist:
Vor clubs were all a-meän'd vor friends,
He twold em, an' vor better ends
Than twitèn vo'k an' pickèn quarrels,
An' tipplèn cups an' emptèn barrels,—
Vor meäkèn woone man do another
In need the kindness ov a brother.

An' after church they went to dine
'Ithin the long-wall'd room behine
The public-house, where you remember,
We had our dance back last December.
An' there they meäde sich stunnèn clatters
Wi' knives an' forks, an' pleätes an' platters;

An' waïters ran, an' beer did pass
Vrom tap to jug, vrom jug to glass:
An' when they took away the dishes,
They drink'd good healths, an' wish'd good wishes,
To all the girt vo'k o' the land,
An' all good things vo'k took in hand;
An' woone cried *hip, hip, hip!* an' hollow'd,
An' tothers all struck in, an' vollow'd;
An' grabb'd their drink wi' eager clutches,
An' swigg'd it wi' sich hearty glutches,
As vo'k, stark mad wi' pweison stuff,
That thought theirzelves not mad enough.

An' after that they went all out
In rank ageän, an' walk'd about,
An' gi'ed zome parish vo'k a call;
An', then went down to Narley Hall
An' had zome beer, an' dauc'd between
The elem trees upon the green.
An' down along the road they done
All sorts o' mad-cap things vor fun;
An' danc'd, a-pokèn out their poles,
An' pushèn bwoys down into holes:
An' Sammy Stubbs come out o' rank,
An' kiss'd me up ageän the bank,
A saucy chap; I ha'nt vor'gied en
Not yet,—in short, I han't a-zeed en.
Zoo in the dusk ov evenèn, zome
Went back to drink, an' zome went hwome.

WOODLEY.

Sweet Woodley! oh! how fresh an' gay
Thy leänes an' vields be now in May,
The while the broad-leav'd clotes do zwim
In brooks wi' gil'cups at the brim;

An' yollow cowslip-beds do grow
By thorns in blooth so white as snow;
An' win' do come vrom copse wi' smells
O' grægles wi' their hangèn bells!

Though time do dreve me on, my mind
Do turn in love to thee behind,
The seäme's a bulrush that's a-shook
By wind a-blowèn up the brook:
The curlèn stream would dreve en down,
But playsome aïr do turn en roun',
An' meäke en seem to bend wi' love
To zunny hollows up above.

Thy tower still do overlook
The woody knaps an' windèn brook,
An' leäne's wi' here an' there a hatch,
An' house wi' elem-sheäded thatch,
An' vields where chaps do vur outdo
The Zunday sky, wi' cwoats o' blue;
An' maïdens' frocks do vur surpass
The whitest deäsies in the grass.

What peals to-day from thy wold tow'r
Do strike upon the zummer flow'r,
As all the club, wi' dousty lags,
Do walk wi' poles an' flappèn flags,
An' wind, to music, roun' between
A zwarm o' vo'k upon the green!
Though time do dreve me on, my mind
Do turn wi' love to thee behind.

THE BROOK THAT RAN BY GRAMFER'S.

WHEN snow-white clouds wer thin an' vew
Avore the zummer sky o' blue,
An' I'd noo ho but how to vind
Zome play to entertaïn my mind;
Along the water, as did wind
   Wi' zedgy shoal an' hollow crook,
   How I did ramble by the brook
   That ran all down vrom gramfer's.

A-holdèn out my line beyond
The clote-leaves, wi' my withy wand,
How I did watch, wi' eager look,
My zwimmèn cork, a-zunk or shook
By minnows nibblèn at my hook,
   A-thinkèn I should catch a breäce
   O' perch, or at the leäst some deäce,
   A-zwimmèn down vrom gramfer's.

Then ten good deäries wer a-ved
Along that water's windèn bed,
An' in the lewth o' hills an' wood
A half a score farm-housen stood:
But now,—count all o'm how you would,
   So many less do hold the land,—
   You'd vind but vive that still do stand,
   A-comèn down vrom gramfer's.

There, in the midst ov all his land,
The squier's ten-tunn'd house did stand,
Where he did meäke the water clim'
A bank, an' sparkle under dim
Bridge arches, villèn to the brim
   His pon', an' leäpèn, white as snow,
   Vrom rocks a-glitt'rèn in a bow,
   An' runnèn down to gramfer's.

An' now woone wing is all you'd vind
O' thik girt house a-left behind;
An' only woone wold stwonen tun
'S a-stannèn to the raïn an' zun,—
An' all's undone that he'd a-done;
    The brook ha' now noo call to stay
    To vill his pon' or clim' his bay,
    A-runnèn down to gramfer's.

When woonce, in heavy raïn, the road
At Grenley bridge wer overflow'd,
Poor Sophy White, the pleäces pride,
A-gwaïn vrom market, went to ride
Her pony droo to tother zide;
    But vound the strëam so deep an' strong,
    That took her off the road along
    The hollow down to gramfer's.

'Twer dark, an' she went on too vast
To catch hold any thing she pass'd;
Noo bough hung over to her hand,
An' she could reach noo stwone nor land,
Where woonce her little voot could stand;
    Noo ears wer out to hear her cries,
    Nor wer she woonce a-zeen by eyes,
    Till took up dead at gramfer's.

SLEEP DID COME WI' THE DEW.

O WHEN our zun's a-zinkèn low,
How soft's the light his feäce do drow
Upon the backward road our mind
Do turn an' zee a-left behind;
When we, in childhood's days did vind
Our jay among the gil'cup flow'rs,
All drough the zummer's zunny hours;
    An' sleep did come wi' the dew.

An' afterwards, when we did zweat
A tweilèn in the zummer het,
An' when our daily work wer done
Did meet to have our evenèn fun:
Till up above the zettèn zun
The sky wer blushèn in the west,
An' we laid down in peace to rest,
   An' sleep did come wi' the dew.

Ah! zome do turn—but tidden right—
The night to day, an' day to night;
But we do zee the vu'st red streak
O' mornèn, when the day do break;
Zoo we don't grow up peäle an' weak,
But we do work wi' health an' strength,
Vrom mornèn drough the whole day's length,
   An' sleep do come wi' the dew.

An' when, at last, our e'thly light
Is jist a-drawèn in to night,
We mid be sure that God above,
If we be true when he do prove
Our stedvast faïth an' thankvul love,
Wull do vor us what mid be best,
An' teäke us into endless rest,
   As sleep do come wi' the dew.

SWEET MUSIC IN THE WIND.

When evenèn is a-drawèn in,
I'll steal vrom others' naïsy din;
An' where the whirlèn brook do roll
Below the walnut-tree, I'll stroll
An' think o' thee wi' all my soul,
Dear Jenny; while the sound o' bells
Do vlee along wi' mwoansome zwells,
   Sweet music in the wind!

I'll think how in the rushy leäze
O' zunny evenèns jis' lik' theäse,
In happy times I us'd to zee
Thy comely sheäpe about the tree,
Wi' païl a-held avore thy knee;
An' lissen'd to thy merry zong
That at a distance come along,
   Sweet music in the wind!

An' when wi' me you walk'd about
O' Zundays, after church wer out.
Wi' hangèn eärm an' modest look;
Or zittèn in some woody nook
We lissen'd to the leaves that shook
Upon the poplars straïght an' tall,
Or rottle o' the watervall,
   Sweet music in the wind!

An' when the playvul aïr do vlee,
O' moonlight nights, vrom tree to tree,
Or whirl upon the sheäkèn grass,
Or rottle at my window glass:
Do seem,— as I do hear it pass,—
As if thy vaïce did come to tell
Me where thy happy soul do dwell,
   Sweet music in the wind!

UNCLE AN' AUNT.

How happy uncle us'd to be
O' zummer time, when aunt an' he
O' Zunday evenèns, cärm in eärm,
Did walk about their tiny farm,
While birds did zing an' gnats did zwarm,
Drough grass a'most above their knees,
An' roun' by hedges an' by trees
   Wi' leafy boughs a-swayèn.

His hat wer broad, his cwoat wer brown,
Wi' two long flaps a-hangèn down;
An' vrom his knee went down a blue
Knit stockèn to his buckled shoe;
An' aunt did pull her gown-tail drough
Her pocket-hole, to keep en neat,
As she mid walk, or teäke a seat
   By leafy boughs a-zwayèn.

An' vu'st they'd goo to zee their lots
O' pot-eärbs in the geärden plots;
An' he, i'-may-be, by the hatch,
Would zee aunt's vowls upon a patch
O' zeeds, an' vow if he could catch
Em wi' his gun, they shoudden vlee
Noo mwore into their roostèn tree,
   Wi' leafy boughs a-swayèn.

An' then vrom geärden they did pass
Drough orcha'd out to zee the grass,
An' if the apple-blooth, so white,
Mid be at all a-touch'd wi' blight;
An' uncle, happy at the zight,
Did guess what cider there mid be
In all the orcha'd, tree wi' tree,
   Wi' tutties all a-swayèn.

An' then they stump'd along vrom there
A-vield, to zee the cows an' meäre;
An' she, when uncle come in zight,
Look'd up, an' prick'd her ears upright,
An' whicker'd out wi' all her might;
An' he, a-chucklèn, went to zee
The cows below the sheädy tree,
   Wi' leafy boughs a-swayen.

An' last ov all, they went to know
How vast the grass in meäd did grow

An' then aunt zaid 'twer time to goo
In hwome,—a-holdèn up her shoe,
To show how wet he wer wi' dew.
An' zoo they toddled hwome to rest,
Lik' doves a-vleèn to their nest
    In leafy boughs a-swayen.

HAVEN WOONES FORTUNE A-TWOLD.

In leäne the gipsies, as we went
A-milkèn, had a-pitch'd their tent,
Between the gravel-pit an' clump
O' trees, upon the little hump:
An' while upon the grassy groun'
    Their smokèn vire did crack an' bleäze,
    Their shaggy-cwoated hoss did greäze
Among the bushes vurder down.

An' zoo, when we brought back our païls,
The woman met us at the raïls,
An' zaid she'd tell us, if we'd show
Our han's, what we should like to know.
Zoo Poll zaid she'd a mind to try
    Her skill a bit, if I would vu'st;
    Though, to be sure, she didden trust
To gipsies any mwore than I.

Well; I agreed, an' off all dree
O's went behind an elem tree,
An' after she'd a-zeed 'ithin
My han' the wrinkles o' the skin,
She twold me—an' she must a-know'd
    That Dicky met me in the leäne,—
    That I'd a-walk'd, an' should ageän,
Wi' zomebody along thik road.

An' then she twold me to bewar
O' what the letter *M* stood vor.
An' as I walk'd, o' *M*onday night,
Drough *M*eäd wi' Dicky overright
The *M*ill, the *M*iller, at the stile,
   Did stan' an' watch us teäke our stroll,
   An' then, a blabbèn dousty-poll!
'Twold *M*other o't. Well wo'th his while!

An' Poll too wer a-bid bewar
O' what the letter *F* stood vor;
An' then, because she took, at *F*eäir,
A bosom-pin o' Jimmy Heäre,
Young *F*ranky beät en black an' blue.
   'Tis *F* vor *F*eäir; an' 'twer about
   A *F*earèn *F*rank an' Jimmy foüght,
Zoo I do think she twold us true.

In short, she twold us all about
What had a-vell, or would vall out;
An' whether we should spend our lives
As maïdens, or as wedded wives;
But when we went to bundle on,
   The gipsies' dog were at the raïls
   A-lappèn milk vrom ouer pails,—
A pretty deäl o' Poll's wer gone.

JEANE'S WEDDEN DAY IN MORNEN.

At last Jeäne come down stairs, a-drest
Wi' weddèn knots upon her breast,
A-blushèn, while a tear did lie
Upon her burnèn cheäk half dry;
An' then her Robert, drawèn nigh
Wi' tothers, took her han' wi' pride,
To meäke her at the church his bride,
   Her weddèn day in mornèn.

Wi' litty voot an' beatèn heart
She stepp'd up in the new light cart,
An' took her bridemaïd up to ride
Along wi' Robert at her zide:
An' uncle's meäre look'd roun' wi' pride
To zee that, if the cart wer vull,
'Twer Jenny that he had to pull,
   Her weddèn day in mornèn.

An' aunt an' uncle stood stock-still,
An' watch'd em trottèn down the hill;
An' when they turn'd off out o' groun'
Down into leäne, two tears run down
Aunt's feäce; an' uncle, turnèn roun',
Sigh'd woonce, an' stump'd off wi' his stick,
Because did touch en to the quick
   To peärt wi' Jeäne thik mornèn.

"Now Jeäne's agone," Tom mutter'd, "we
Shall mwope lik' owls 'ithin a tree;
Vor she did zet us all agog
Vor fun, avore the burnèn log."
An' as he zot an' talk'd, the dog
Put up his nose athirt his thighs,
But coulden meäke en turn his eyes,
   Jeäne's weddèn day in mornèn.

An' then the naïghbours round us, all
By woones an' twos begun to call,
To meet the young vo'k, when the meäre
Mid bring em back a married peäir:
An' all o'm zaid, to Robert's sheäre,
There had a-vell the feärest feäce,
An' kindest heart in all the pleäce,
   Jeäne's weddèn day in mornèn.

RIVERS DON'T GI'E OUT.

The brook I left below the rank
Ov alders that do sheäde his bank,
A-runnèn down to dreve the mill
Below the knap, 's a runnèn still;
The creepèn days an' weeks do vill
    Up years, an' meäke wold things o' new,
    An' vok' do come, an' live, an' goo,
    But rivers don't gi'e out, John.

The leaves that in the spring do shoot
Zo green, in fall be under voot;
May flow'rs do grow vor June to burn,
An' milk-white blooth o' trees do kern,
An' ripen on, an' vall in turn;
    The miller's moss-green wheel mid rot,
    An' he mid die an' be vorgot,
    But rivers don't gi'e out, John.

A vew short years do bring an' rear
A maïd—as Jeäne wer—young an' feäir,
An' vewer zummer-ribbons, tied
In Zunday knots, do feäde bezide
Her cheäk avore her bloom ha' died:
    Her youth won't stay,—her rwosy look
    'S a feädèn flow'r, but time's a brook
    To run an' not gi'e out, John.

An' yet, while things do come an' goo,
God's love is steadvast, John, an' true;
If winter vrost do chill the ground,
'Tis but to bring the zummer round.
All's well a-lost where He's a-vound,

Vor if 'tis right, vor Christes seäke
He'll gi'e us mwore than he do teäke,—
His goodness don't gi'e out, John.

MEAKEN UP A MIFF.

VORGI'E me, Jenny, do! an' rise
Thy hangèn head an' teary eyes,
An' speak, vor I've a-took in lies,
   An' I've a-done thee wrong;
But I wer twold,—an' thought 'twer true,—
That Sammy down at Coome an' you
Wer at the feäir, a-walkèn drough
   The pleäce the whole day long.

An' tender thoughts did melt my heart,
An' zwells o' viry pride did dart
Lik' lightnèn drough my blood; a-peärt
   Ov your love I should scorn,
An' zoo I vow'd, however sweet
Your looks mid be when we did meet,
I'd trample ye down under veet,
   Or let ye goo forlorn.

But still thy neäme would always be
The sweetest, an' my eyes would zee
Among all maïdens nwone lik' thee
   Vor ever any mwore;
Zoo by the walks that we've a-took
By flow'ry hedge an' zedgy brook,
Dear Jenny, dry your eyes, an' look
   As you've a-look'd avore.

Look up, an' let the evenèn light
But sparkle in thy eyes so bright,
As they be open to the light

O' zunzet in the west;
An' let's stroll here vor half an hour,
Where hangèn boughs do meäke a bow'r
Above theäse bank, wi' eltrot flow'r
　An' robinhoods a-drest.

HAY-MEAKEN.

'Tis merry ov a zummer's day,
Where vo'k be out a-meäkèn haÿ;
Where men an' women, in a string,
Do ted or turn the grass, an' zing,
Wi' cheemèn vaïces, merry zongs,
A-tossèn o' their sheenèn prongs
Wi' eärms a-zwangèn left an' right,
In colour'd gowns an' shirtsleeves white;
Or, wider spread, a reäkèn round
The rwosy hedges o' the ground,
Where Sam do zee the speckled sneäke,
An' try to kill en wi' his reäke;
An' Poll do jump about an' squall,
To zee the twistèn slooworm crawl.

'Tis merry where a gaÿ-tongued lot
Ov haÿ-meäkers be all a-squot,
On lightly-russlèn haÿ, a-spread
Below an elem's lofty head,
To rest their weary limbs an' munch
Their bit o' dinner, or their nunch;
Where teethy reäkes do lie all round
By picks a-stuck up into ground.
An' wi' their vittles in their laps,
An' in their hornen cups their draps
O' cider sweet, or frothy eäle,
'Their tongues do run wi' joke an' teäle.

An' when the zun, so low an' red,
Do sheen above the leafy head
O' zome broad tree, a-rizèn high
Avore the vi'ry western sky,
'Tis merry where all han's do goo
Athirt the groun', by two an' two,
A-reäkèn, over humps an' hollors,
The russlèn grass up into rollers.
An' woone do row it into line,
An' woone do clwose it up behine;
An' after them the little bwoys
Do stride an' fling their eärms all woys,
Wi' busy picks, an' proud young looks
A-meäkèn up their tiny pooks.
An' zoo 'tis merry out among
The vo'k in haÿ-vield all day long.

HAY-CARREN.

'Tis merry ov a zummer's day,
When vo'k be out a-haulèn haÿ,
Where boughs, a-spread upon the ground,
Do meäke the staddle big an' round;
An' grass do stand in pook, or lie
In long-back'd weäles or parsels, dry.
There I do vind it stir my heart
To hear the frothèn hosses snort,
A-haulèn on, wi' sleek heäir'd hides,
The red-wheel'd waggon's deep-blue zides.
Aye; let me have woone cup o' drink,
An' hear the linky harness clink,
An' then my blood do run so warm,
An' put sich strangth 'ithin my eärm,
That I do long to toss a pick,
A-pitchèn or a-meäkèn rick.

HAY-CARREN.

The bwoy is at the hosse's head,
An' up upon the waggon bed
The lwoaders, strong o' eärm do stan',
At head, an' back at taïl, a man,
Wi' skill to build the lwoad upright
An' bind the vwolded corners tight;
An' at each zide ō'm, sprack an' strong,
A pitcher wi' his long-stem'd prong,
Avore the best two women now
A-call'd to reäky after plough.

When I do pitchy, 'tis my pride
Vor Jenny Hine to reäke my zide,
An' zee her fling her reäke, an' reach
So vur, an' teäke in sich a streech;
An' I don't shatter hay, an' meäke
Mwore work than needs vor Jenny's reäke.
I'd sooner zee the weäles' high rows
Lik' hedges up above my nose,
Than have light work myzelf, an' vind
Poor Jeäne a-beät an' left behind;
Vor she would sooner drop down dead.
Than let the pitchers get a-head.

'Tis merry at the rick to zee
How picks do wag, an' hay do vlee.
While woone's unlwoadèn, woone do teäke
The pitches in; an' zome do meäke
The lofty rick upright an' roun',
An' tread en hard, an' reäke en down,
An' tip en, when the zun do zet.
To shoot a sudden vall o' wet.
An' zoo 'tis merry any day
Where vo'k be out a-carrèn hay.

Eclogue.

THE BEST MAN IN THE YIELD.

Sam and Bob.

SAM.

That's slowish work, Bob. What'st a-been about?
Thy pookèn don't goo on not over sprack.
Why I've a-pook'd my weäle, lo'k zee, clear out,
An' here I be ageän a-turnèn back.

BOB.

I'll work wi' thee then, Sammy, any day,
At any work dost like to teäke me at,
Vor any money thou dost like to lay.
Now, Mister Sammy, what dost think o' that?
My weäle is nearly twice so big as thine,
Or else, I warnt, I shouldden be behin'.

SAM.

Ah! hang thee, Bob! don't tell sich whoppèn lies.
My weäle's the biggest, if do come to size.
'Tis jist the seäme whatever bist about;
Why, when dost goo a-teddèn grass, you sloth,
Another hand's a-fwo'c'd to teäke thy zwath,
An' ted a half way back to help thee out;
An' then a-reäkèn rollers, bist so slack,
Dost keep the very bwoys an' women back.
An' if dost think that thou canst challenge I
At any thing,—then, Bob, we'll teäke a pick a-picce,
An' woonce theäse zummer, goo an' try
To meäke a rick a-piece.

A rick o' thine wull look a little funny,
When thou'st a-done en, I'll bet any money.

BOB.

You noggerhead! last year thou meäd'st a rick,
An' then we had to trig en wi' a stick.
An' what did John that tipp'd en zay? Why zaid
He stood a-top o'en all the while in dread,
A-thinkèn that avore he should a-done en
He'd tumble over slap wi' him upon en.

SAM.

You yoppèn dog! I warnt I meäde my rick
So well's thou meäd'st thy lwoad o' haÿ last week.
They hadden got a hundred yards to haul en,
An' then they vound 'twer best to have en boun',
Vor if they hadden, 'twould a-tumbl'd down;
An' after that I zeed en all but vallèn,
An' trigg'd en up wi' woone o'm's pitchèn pick,
To zee if I could meäke en ride to rick;
An' when they had the dumpy heap unboun',
He vell to pieces flat upon the groun'.

BOB.

Do shut thy lyèn chops! What dosten mind
Thy pitchèn to me out in Gully-plot,
A-meäkèn o' me waït (wast zoo behind)
A half an hour vor ev'ry pitch I got?
An' how didst groun' thy pick? an' how didst quirk
To get en up on end? Why hadst hard work
To rise a pitch that wer about so big
'S a goodish crow's nest, or a wold man's wig!
Why bist so weak, dost know, as any roller:
Zome o' the women vo'k will beät thee hollor.

SAM.

You snub-nos'd flopperchops! I pitch'd so quick,
That thou dost know thou hadst a hardish job
To teäke in all the pitches off my pick;
An' dissèn zee me groun' en, nother, Bob.
An' thou bist stronger, thou dost think, than I?
Girt bandy-lags! I jist should like to try.
We'll goo, if thou dost like, an' jist zee which
Can heave the mwost, or car the biggest nitch.

BOB.

There, Sam, do meäke me zick to hear thy braggèn!
Why bissèn strong enough to car a flagon.

SAM.

You grinnèn fool! why I'd zet thee a-blowèn,
If thou wast wi' me vor a day a-mowèn.
I'd wear my cwoat, an' thou midst pull thy rags off,
An' then in half a zwath I'd mow thy lags off.

BOB.

Thee mow wi' me! Why coossen keep up wi' me:
Why bissèn fit to goo a-vield to skimmy,
Or mow down docks an' thistles! Why I'll bet
A shillèn, Samel, that thou cassen whet.

SAM.

Now don't thee zay much mwore than what'st a-zaid,
Or else I'll knock thee down, heels over head.

BOB.

Thou knock me down, indeed! Why cassen gi'e
A blow half hard enough to kill a bee.

SAM.

Well, thou shalt veel upon thy chops and snout.

BOB.

Come on, then, Samel; jist let's have woone bout.

WHERE WE DID KEEP OUR FLAGON.

When we in mornèn had a-drow'd
The grass or russlèn hay abrode,
The lit'some maïdens an' the chaps,
Wi' bits o' nunchèns in their laps,
Did all zit down upon the knaps
　　Up there, in under hedge, below
　　The highest elem o' the row,
　　　　Where we did keep our flagon.

There we could zee green vields at hand,
Avore a hunderd on beyand,
An' rows o' trees in hedges roun'
Green meäds, an' zummerleäzes brown,
An' thorns upon the zunny down,
　　While aïer, vrom the rockèn zedge
　　In brook, did come along the hedge,
　　　　Where we did keep our flagon.

There laughèn chaps did try in play
To bury maïdens up in hay,
As gigglèn maïdens tried to roll
The chaps down into zome deep hole,
Or sting wi' nettles woone o'm's poll;
　　While John did hele out each his drap
　　O' eäle or cider, in his lap
　　　　Where he did keep the flagon.

Woone day there spun a whirlwind by
Where Jenny's clothes wer out to dry;
An' off vled frocks, a'most a-catch'd
By smock-frocks wi' their sleeves outstratch'd,
An' caps a-frill'd an' eäperns patch'd;

> An' she a-steärèn in a fright,
> Wer glad enough to zee em light
>   Where we did keep our flagon.
>
> An' when white clover wer a-sprung
> Among the eegrass, green an' young,
> An' elder-flowers wer a-spread
> Among the rwosen white an' red,
> An' honeyzucks wi' hangèn head,—
>   O' Zunday evenèns we did zit
>   To look all roun' the grounds a bit,
>   Where we'd a-kept our flagon.

WEEK'S END IN ZUMMER, IN THE WOLD VO'K'S TIME.

> His aunt an' uncle,—ah! the kind
> Wold souls be often in my mind:
> A better couple never stood
> In shoes, an' vew be voun' so good.
> *She* cheer'd the work-vo'k in their tweils
> Wi' timely bits an' draps, an' smiles;
> An' *he* païd all o'm at week's end,
> Their money down to goo an' spend.
>
> In zummer, when week's end come roun'
> The hay-meäkers did come vrom groun',
> An' all zit down, wi' weary bwones,
> Within the yard a-peäved wi' stwones,
> Along avore the peäles, between
> The yard a-steän'd an' open green.
> There women zot wi' bare-neck'd chaps,
> An' maïdens wi' their sleeves an' flaps
> To screen vrom het their eärms an' polls,
> An' men wi' beards so black as coals:

Girt stocky Jim, an' lanky John,
An' poor wold Betty dead an' gone;
An' cleän-grown Tom so spry an' strong,
An' Liz the best to pitch a zong,
That now ha' nearly half a score
O' childern zwarmèn at her door;
An' whindlen Ann, that cried wi' fear
To hear the thunder when 'twer near,—
A zickly maïd, so peäle's the moon,
That voun' her zun goo down at noon;
An' blushèn Jeäne so shy an' meek,
That seldom let us hear her speak,
That wer a-coorted an' undone
By Farmer Woodley's woldest son;
An' after she'd a-been vorzook,
Wer voun' a-drown'd in Longmeäd brook.

An' zoo, when *he*'d a-been all roun',
An' païd em all their wages down,
She us'd to bring vor all, by teäle
A cup o' cider or ov eäle,
An' then a tutty meäde o' lots
O' blossoms vrom her flower-nots,
To wear in bands an' button-holes
At church, an' in their evenèn strolls.
The pea that rangled to the oves,
An' columbines an' pinks an' cloves,
Sweet rwosen vrom the prickly tree,
An' jilliflow'rs, an' jessamy;
An' short-liv'd pinies, that do shed
Their leaves upon a eärly bed.
She didden put in honeyzuck:
She'd nwone, she zaïd, that she could pluck
Avore wild honeyzucks, a-vound
In ev'ry hedge ov ev'ry ground.

Zoo maïd an' woman, bwoy an' man,
Went off, while zunzet aïr did fan
Their merry zunburnt feäzen; zome
Down leäne, an' zome drough parrocks hwome.

Ah! who can tell, that ha'nt a-vound,
The sweets o' week's-end comèn round!
When Zadurday do bring woone's mind
Sweet thoughts o' Zunday clwose behind;
The day that's all our own to spend
Wi' God an' wi' an e'thly friend.
The worold's girt vo'k, wi' the best
O' worldly goods mid be a-blest;
But Zunday is the poor man's peärt,
To seäve his soul an' cheer his heart.

THE MEAD A-MOW'D.

WHEN sheädes do vall into ev'ry hollow,
  An' reach vrom trees half athirt the groun';
An' banks an' walls be a-lookèn yollow,
  That be a-turn'd to the zun gwaïn down;
    Drough hay in cock, O,
    We all do vlock, O,
Along our road vrom the meäd a-mow'd.

An' when the last swayèn lwoad's a-started
  Up hill so slow to the lofty rick,
Then we so weary but merry-hearted,
  Do shoulder each ō's a reäke an' pick,
    Wi' empty flagon,
    Behind the waggon,
To teäke our road vrom the meäd a-mow'd.

When church is out, an' we all so slowly
  About the knap be a-spreadèn wide,

How gay the paths be where we do strolly
　Along the leäne an' the hedge's zide;
　　But nwone's a voun', O,
　　Up hill or down, O,
So gay's the road drough the meäd a-mow'd.

An' when the visher do come, a-drowèn
　His flutt'ren line over bleädy zedge,
Drough groun's wi' red thissle-heads a-blowèn,
　An' watchèn o't by the water's edge;
　　Then he do love, O,
　　The best to rove, O,
Along his road drough the meäd a-mow'd.

THE SKY A-CLEAREN.

The drevèn scud that overcast
The zummer sky is all a-past,
An' softer aïr, a-blowèn drough
The quiv'rèn boughs, do sheäke the vew
Last raïn drops off the leaves lik' dew;
　An' peäviers, now a-gettèn dry,
　Do steam below the zunny sky
　　That's now so vast a-cleärèn.

The sheädes that wer a-lost below
The stormy cloud, ageän do show
Their mockèn sheäpes below the light;
An' house-walls be a-lookèn white,
An' vo'k do stir woonce mwore in zight,
　An' busy birds upon the wing
　Do whiver roun' the boughs an' zing,
　　To zee the sky a-clearèn.

Below the hill's an ash; below
The ash, white elder-flow'rs do blow:

Below the elder is a bed
O' robinhoods o' blushèn red;
An' there, wi' nunches all a-spread,
  The haÿ-meäkers, wi' each a cup
    O' drink, do smile to zee hold up
      The raïn, an' sky a-cleärèn.

'Mid blushèn maïdens, wi' their zong,
Still draw their white-stemm'd reäkes among
The long-back'd weäles an' new-meäde pooks,
By brown-stemm'd trees an' cloty brooks;
But have noo call to spweil their looks
  By work, that God could never meäke
    Their weaker han's to underteäke,
      Though skies mid be a-cleärèn.

'Tis wrong vor women's han's to clips
The zull an' reap-hook, speädes an' whips;
An' men abroad, should leäve, by right,
Woone faïthful heart at hwome to light
Their bit o' vier up at night,
  An' hang upon the hedge to dry
    Their snow-white linen, when the sky
      In winter is a-cleärèn.

THE EVENÈN STAR O' ZUMMER.

WHEN vu'st along theäse road vrom mill,
I zeed ye hwome all up the hill,
The poplar tree, so straïght an' tall,
Did rustle by the watervall;
An' in the leäze the cows wer all
  A-lyèn down to teäke their rest.
    An' slowly zunk towárd the west
      The evenèn star o' zummer.

In parrock there the hay did lie
In weäle below the elems, dry;
An' up in hwome-groun' Jim, that know'd
We all should come along thik road,
ᵃD a-tied the grass in knots that drow'd
    Poor Poll, a-watchèn in the West
    Woone brighter star than all the rest,—
        The evenèn star o' zummer.

The stars that still do zet an' rise,
Did sheen in our forefather's eyes;
They glitter'd to the vu'st men's zight,
The last will have em in their night;
But who can vind em half so bright
    As I thought thik peäle star above
    My smilèn Jeäne, my zweet vu'st love,
        The evenèn star o' zummer.

How sweet's the mornèn fresh an' new,
Wi' sparklèn brooks an' glitt'rèn dew;
How sweet's the noon wi' sheädes a-drow'd
Upon the groun' but leätely mow'd,
An' bloomèn flowers all abrode;
    But sweeter still, as I do clim',
    Theäse woody hill in evenèn dim
        'S the evenèn star o' zummer.

THE CLOTE.
(*Water-lily.*)

O zummer clote! when the brook's a-glidèn
    So slow an' smooth down his zedgy bed,
Upon thy broad leaves so scäfe a-ridèn
    The water's top wi' thy yollow head,
        By alder's heads, O,
        An' bulrush beds, O.
Thou then dost float, goolden zummer clote!

The grey-bough'd withy's a-leänèn lowly
    Above the water thy leaves do hide;
The bendèn bulrush, a-swayèn slowly,
    Do skirt in zummer thy river's zide.
        An' perch in shoals, O,
        Do vill the holes, O,
Where thou dost float, goolden zummer clote!

Oh! when thy brook-drinkèn flow'r 's a-blowèn,
    The burnèn zummer's a-zettèn in;
The time o' greenness, the time o' mowèn,
    When in the hay-vield, wi' zunburnt skin,
        The vo'k do drink, O,
        Upon the brink, O,
Where thou dost float, goolden zummer clote!

Wi' eärms a-spreadèn, an' cheäks a-blowèn,
    How proud wer I when I vu'st could zwim
Athirt the pleäce where thou bist a-growèn,
    Wi' thy long more vrom the bottom dim;
        While cows, knee-high, O,
        In brook, wer nigh, O,
Where thou dost float, goolden zummer clote!

Ov all the brooks drough the meäds a-windèn,
    Ov all the meäds by a river's brim,
There's nwone so feäir o' my own heart's vindèn,
    As where the maïdens do zee thee swim,
        An' stan' to teäke, O,
        Wi' long-stemm'd reäke, O,
Thy flow'r afloat, goolden zummer clote!

I GOT TWO VIELDS.

I got two vields, an' I don't ceäre
What squire mid have a bigger sheäre.
My little zummer-leäze do stratch
All down the hangèn, to a patch
O' meäd between a hedge an' rank
Ov elems, an' a river bank.
Where yollow clotes, in spreadèn beds
O' floatèn leaves, do lift their heads
By bendèn bulrushes an' zedge
A-swayèn at the water's edge,
Below the withy that do spread
Athirt the brook his grey-leav'd head.
An' eltrot flowers, milky white,
Do catch the slantèn evenèn light;
An' in the meäple boughs, along
The hedge, do ring the blackbird's zong;
Or in the day, a-vleèn drough
The leafy trees, the whoa'se gookoo
Do zing to mowers that do zet
Their zives on end, an' stan' to whet.
From my wold house among the trees
A leäne do goo along the leäze
O' yollow gravel, down between
Two mossy banks vor ever green.
An' trees, a-hangèn overhead,
Do hide a trinklèn gully-bed,
A-cover'd by a bridge vor hoss
Or man a-voot to come across.
Zoo wi' my hwomestead, I don't ceäre
What squire mid have a bigger sheäre!

POLLY BE-EN UPZIDES WI' TOM.

Ah! yesterday, d'ye know, I voun'
Tom Dumpy's cwoat an' smock-frock, down
Below the pollard out in groun';
    An' zoo I slyly stole
An' took the smock-frock up, an' tack'd
The sleeves an' collar up, an' pack'd
Zome nice sharp stwones, all fresh a-crack'd
    'Ithin each pocket-hole.

An' in the evenèn, when he shut
Off work, an' come an' donn'd his cwoat,
Their edges gi'ed en sich a cut,
    How we did stan' an' laugh!
An' when the smock-frock I'd a-zow'd
Kept back his head an' hands, he drow'd
Hizzelf about, an' teäv'd, an' blow'd,
    Lik' any up-tied calf.

Then in a veag away he flung
His frock, an' after me he sprung,
An' mutter'd out sich dreats, an' wrung
    His vist up sich a size!
But I, a-runnèn, turn'd an' drow'd
Some doust, a-pick'd up vrom the road,
Back at en wi' the wind, that blow'd
    It right into his eyes.

An' he did blink, an' vow he'd catch
Me zomehow yet, an' be my match.
But I wer nearly down to hatch
    Avore he got vur on;
An' up in chammer, nearly dead
Wi' runnèn, lik' a cat I vled,
An' out o' window put my head
    To zee if he wer gone.

An' there he wer, a-prowlèn roun'
Upon the green; an' I look'd down
An' told en that I hoped he voun'
    He mussen think to peck
Upon a body zoo, nor whip
The meäre to drow me off, nor tip
Me out o' cart ageän, nor slip
    Cut hoss-heäir down my neck.

BE'MI'STER.

Sweet Be'mi'ster, that bist a-bound
By green an' woody hills all round,
Wi' hedges, reachèn up between
A thousan' vields o' zummer green,
Where elems' lofty heads do drow
Their sheädes vor hay-meakers below,
An' wild hedge-flow'rs do charm the souls
O' maïdens in their evenèn strolls.

When I o' Zunday nights wi' Jeäne
Do saunter drough a vield or leäne,
Where elder-blossoms be a-spread
Above the eltrot's milk-white head,
An' flow'rs o' blackberries do blow
Upon the brembles, white as snow,
To be outdone avore my zight
By Jeän's gay frock o' dazzlèn white;

Oh! then there's nothèn that's 'ithout
Thy hills that I do ho about,—
Noo bigger pleäce, noo gayer town,
Beyond thy sweet bells' dyèn soun',
As they do ring, or strike the hour,
At evenèn vrom thy wold red tow'r.
No: shelter still my head, an' keep
My bwones when I do vall asleep.

THATCHEN O' THE RICK.

As I wer out in meäd last week,
A-thatchèn o' my little rick,
There green young ee-grass, ankle-high,
Did sheen below the cloudless sky;
An' over hedge in tother groun',
Among the bennets dry an' brown,
My dun wold meäre, wi' neck a-freed
Vrom Zummer work, did snort an' veed;
An' in the sheäde o' leafy boughs,
My vew wold ragged-cwoated cows
Did rub their zides upon the raïls,
Or switch em wi' their heäiry taïls.

An' as the mornèn zun rose high
Above my mossy roof clwose by,
The blue smoke curreled up between
The lofty trees o' feädèn green:
A zight that's touchèn when do show
A busy wife is down below,
A-workèn hard to cheer woone's tweil
Wi' her best feäre, an' better smile.
Mid women still in wedlock's yoke
Zend up, wi' love, their own blue smoke,
An' husbands vind their bwoards a-spread
By faïthvul hands when I be dead,
An' noo good men in ouer land
Think lightly o' the weddèn band.
True happiness do bide alwone
Wi' them that ha' their own he'th-stwone
To gather wi' their childern roun',
A-smilèn at the worold's frown.

My bwoys, that brought me thatch an' spars,
Wer down a-taïtèn on the bars,
Or zot a-cuttèn wi' a knife,
Dry eltrot-roots to meäke a fife;
Or drevèn woone another round
The rick upon the grassy ground.
An', as the aïer vrom the west
Did fan my burnèn feäce an' breast,
An' hoppèn birds, wi' twitt'rèn beaks,
Did show their sheenèn spots an' streaks,
Then, wi' my heart a-vill'd wi' love
An' thankvulness to God above,
I didden think ov anything
That I begrudg'd o' lord or king;
Vor I ha' round me, vur or near,
The mwost to love an' nwone to fear,
An' zoo can walk in any pleäce,
An' look the best man in the feäce.
What good do come to eächèn heads,
O' lièn down in silken beds?
Or what's a coach, if woone do pine
To zee woone's naïghbour's twice so fine?
Contentment is a constant feäst,
He's richest that do want the leäst.

BEES A-ZWARMEN.

Avore we went a-milkèn, vive
Or six o's here wer all alive
A-teäkèn bees that zwarm'd vrom hive;
   An' we'd sich work to catch
The hummèn rogues, they led us sich
A dance all over hedge an' ditch;
An' then at last where should they pitch,
   But up in uncle's thatch?

Dick rung a sheep-bell in his han',
Liz beät a cannister, an' Nan
Did bang the little fryèn-pan
   Wi' thick an' thumpèn blows ;
An' Tom went on, a-carrèn roun'
A bee-pot up upon his crown,
Wi' all his edge a-reachèn down
   Avore his eyes an' nose.

An' woone girt bee, wi' spitevul hum,
Stung Dicky's lip, an' meäde it come
All up amost so big's a plum ;
   An' zome, a-vleèn on,
Got all roun' Liz, an' meäde her hop
An' scream, a-twirlèn lik' a top,
An' spring away right backward, flop
   Down into barken pon' :

An' Nan' gi'ed Tom a roguish twitch
Upon a bank, an' meäde en pitch
Right down, head-voremost, into ditch,—
   Tom couldèn zee a wink.
An' when the zwarm wer scäfe an' sound
In mother's bit o' bee-pot ground,
She meäde us up a treat all round
   O' sillibub to drink.

READEN OV A HEAD-STWONE.

As I wer readèn ov a stwone
In Grenley church-yard all alwone,
A little maïd ran up, wi' pride
To zee me there, an' push'd a-zide
A bunch o' bennets that did hide
   A verse her father, as she zaïd,
   Put up above her mother's head,
      To tell how much he loved her:

The verse wer short, but very good,
I stood an' larn'd en where I stood :—
"Mid God, dear Meäry, gi'e me greäce
To vind, lik' thee, a better pleäce,
Where I woonce mwore mid zee thy feäce;
  An' bring thy childern up to know
    His word, that they mid come an' show
      Thy soul how much I lov'd thee."

"Where's father, then," I zaid, "my chile?"
"Dead too," she answer'd wi' a smile;
"An' I an' brother Jim do bide
At Betty White's, o' tother zide
O' road." "Mid He, my chile," I cried,
  "That's father to the fatherless,
    Become thy father now, an' bless,
      An' keep, an' leäd, an' love thee."

Though she've a-lost, I thought, so much,
Still He don't let the thoughts o't touch
Her litsome heart by day or night;
An' zoo, if we could teäke it right,
Do show He'll meäke his burdens light
  To weaker souls, an' that his smile
    Is sweet upon a harmless chile,
      When they be dead that lov'd it.

ZUMMER EVENÈN DANCE.

Come out to the parrock, come out to the tree,
The maïdens an' chaps be a-waïtèn vor thee;
There's Jim wi' his fiddle to play us some reels,
Come out along wi' us, an' fling up thy heels.

Come, all the long grass is a-mow'd an' a-carr'd,
An' the turf is so smooth as a bwoard an' so hard;

There's a bank to zit down, when y'ave danced a reel drough,
An' a tree over head vor to keep off the dew.

There be rwoses an' honeyzucks hangèn among
The bushes, to put in thy weäst; an' the zong
O' the nightingeäle's heärd in the hedges all roun';
An' I'll get thee a glow-worm to stick in thy gown.

There's Meäry so modest, an' Jenny so smart,
An' Mag that do love a good rompse to her heart;
There's Joe at the mill that do zing funny zongs,
An' short-lagged Dick, too, a-waggèn his prongs.

Zoo come to the parrock, come out to the tree,
The maïdens an' chaps be a-waïtèn vor thee;
There's Jim wi' his fiddle to play us some reels,—
Come out along wi' us, an' fling up thy heels.

Eclogue.
THE VEAIRIES.

Simon an' Samel.

SIMON.

There's what the vo'k do call a veäiry ring
Out there, lo'k zee. Why, 'tis an oddish thing.

SAMEL.

Ah! zoo do seem. I wunder how do come!
What is it that do meäke it, I do wonder?

SIMON.

Be hang'd if I can tell, I'm sure! But zome
Do zay do come by lightnèn when do thunder;
An' zome do say sich rings as thik ring there is,
Do grow in dancèn-tracks o' little veäiries,
That in the nights o' zummer or o' spring
Do come by moonlight, when noo other veet
Do tread the dewy grass, but their's, an' meet
An' dance away together in a ring.

SAMEL.

An' who d'ye think do work the fiddlestick?
A little veäiry too, or else wold Nick!

SIMON.

Why, they do zay, that at the veäiries' ball,
There's nar a fiddle that's a-heär'd at all;
But they do play upon a little pipe
A-meäde o' kexes or o' straws, dead ripe,
A-stuck in row (zome short an' longer zome)
Wi' slime o' snaïls, or bits o' plum-tree gum,
An' meäke sich music that to hear it sound,
You'd stick so still's a pollard to the ground.

SAMEL.

What do em dance? 'Tis plaïn by theäse green wheels,
They don't frisk in an' out in dree-hand reels;
Vor else, instead o' theäse here girt round O,
They'd cut us out a figure aïght (8), d'ye know.

SIMON.

Oh! they ha' jigs to fit their little veet.
They woulden dance, you know, at their fine ball,
The dree an' vow'r han' reels that we do sprawl
An' kick about in, when we men do meet.

SAMEL.

An' zoo have zome vo'k, in their midnight rambles,
A-catch'd the veäiries, then, in theäsem gambols.

SIMON.

Why, yes; but they be off lik' any shot,
So soon's a man's a-comèn near the spot.

SAMEL.

But in the day-time where do veäiries hide?
Where be their hwomes, then? where do veäiries bide

SIMON.

Oh! they do get away down under ground,
In hollow pleäzen where they can't be vound.
But still my gramfer, many years agoo,
(He liv'd at Grenley-farm, an milk'd a deäiry),
If what the wolder vo'k do tell is true,
Woone mornèn eärly vound a veäiry.

SAMEL.

An' did he stop, then, wi' the good wold bwoy?
Or did he soon contrive to slip awoy?

SIMON.

Why, when the vo'k were all asleep, a-bed,
The veäiries us'd to come, as 'tis a-zaid,
Avore the vire wer cwold, an' dance an hour
Or two at dead o' night upon the vloor;
Var they, by only utterèn a word
Or charm, can come down chimney lik' a bird;
Or draw their bodies out so long an' narrow,
That they can vlee drough keyholes lik' an arrow.
An' zoo woone midnight, when the moon did drow
His light drough window, roun' the vloor below,
An' crickets roun' the bricken he'th did zing,
They come an' danced about the hall in ring;

THE VEAIRIES.

An' tapp'd, drough little holes noo eyes could spy,
A kag o' poor aunt's meäd a-stannèn by.
An' woone o'm drink'd so much, he couldn mind
The word he wer to zay to meäke en small;
He got a-dather'd zoo, that after all
Out tothers went an' left en back behind.
An' after he'd a-beät about his head,
Ageän the keyhole till he wer half dead,
He laid down all along upon the vloor
Till gramfer, comen down, unlocked the door:
An' then he zeed en ('twer enough to frighten èn)
Bolt out o' door, an' down the road lik' lightenèn.

FALL.

CORN A-TURNEN YOLLOW.

The windless copse ha' sheädy boughs,
    Wi' blackbirds' evenèn whistles;
The hills ha' sheep upon their brows,
    The zummerleäze ha' thistles :
The meäds be gay in grassy May,
    But, oh ! vrom hill to hollow,
Let me look down upon a groun'
    O' corn a-turnèn yollow.

An' pease do grow in tangled beds,
    An' beäns be sweet to snuff, O ;
The teäper woats do bend their heads,
    The barley's beard is rough, O.
The turnip green is fresh between
    The corn in hill or hollow,
But I'd look down upon a groun'
    O' wheat a-turnèn yollow.

'Tis merry when the brawny men
    Do come to reap it down, O,
Where glossy red the poppy head
    'S among the stalks so brown, O.
'Tis merry while the wheat's in hile,
    Or when, by hill or hollow,
The leäzers thick do stoop to pick
    The ears so ripe an' yollow.

A-HAULEN O' THE CORN.

Ah! yesterday, you know, we carr'd
    The piece o' corn in Zidelèn Plot,
An' work'd about it pretty hard,
    An' vound the weather pretty hot.
'Twer all a-tied an' zet upright
In tidy hile o' Monday night;
Zoo yesterday in afternoon
We zet, in eärnest, ev'ry woone
      A-haulèn o' the corn.

The hosses, wi' the het an' lwoad,
    Did froth, an' zwang vrom zide to zide,
A-gwaïn along the dousty road,
    An' seem'd as if they would a-died.
An' wi' my collar all undone,
An' neck a-burnèn wi' the zun,
I got, wi' work, an' doust, an' het,
So dry at last, I couden spet,
      A-haulèn o' the corn.

At uncle's orcha'd, gwaïn along,
    I begged some apples, vor to quench
My drith, o' Poll that wer among
    The trees: but she, a saucy wench,
Toss'd over hedge some crabs vor fun.
I squaïl'd her, though, an' meäde her run;
An' zoo she gie'd me, vor a treat,
A lot o' stubberds vor to eat.
      A-haulèn o' the corn.

An' up at rick, Jeäne took the flagon,
    An' gi'ed us out zome eäle; an' then
I carr'd her out upon the waggon,
    Wi' bread an' cheese to gi'e the men.

An' there, vor fun, we dress'd her head
Wi' noddèn poppies bright an' red,
As we wer catchèn vrom our laps,
Below a woak, our bits an' draps,
    A-haulèn o' the corn.

HARVEST HWOME.

The vu'st peärt. The Supper.

SINCE we wer striplèns naïghbour John,
The good wold merry times be gone:
But we do like to think upon
    What we've a-zeed an' done.
When I wer up a hardish lad,
At harvest hwome the work-vo'k had
Sich suppers, they wer jumpèn mad
    Wi' feästèn an' wi' fun.

At uncle's, I do mind, woone year,
I zeed a vill o' hearty cheer;
Fat beef an' puddèn, eäle an' beer,
    Vor ev'ry workman's crop
An' after they'd a-gie'd God thanks,
They all zot down, in two long ranks,
Along a teäble-bwoard o' planks,
    Wi' uncle at the top.

An' there, in platters, big and brown,
Wer red fat beäcon, an' a roun'·
O' beef wi' gravy that would drown
    A little rwoastèn pig;
Wi' beäns an' teäties vull a zack,
An' cabbage that would meäke a stack,
An' puddèns brown, a-speckled black
    Wi' figs, so big's my wig.

An' uncle, wi' his elbows out,
Did carve, an' meäke the gravy spout;
An' aunt did gi'e the mugs about
    A-frothèn to the brim.
Pleätes werden then ov e'then ware,
They ate off pewter, that would bear
A knock; or wooden trenchers, square,
    Wi' zalt-holes at the rim.

An' zoo they munch'd their hearty cheer,
An' dipp'd their beards in frothy-beer,
An' laugh'd, an' jok'd—they couldden hear
    What woone another zaid.
An' all o'm drink'd, wi' woone accword,
The wold vo'k's health: an' beät the bwoard,
An' swung their eärms about, an' roar'd,
    Enough to crack woone's head.

HARVEST HWOME.

Second Peärt. What they did after Supper.

Zoo after supper wer a-done,
They clear'd the teäbles, an' begun
To have a little bit o' fun,
    As long as they mid stop.
The wold woones took their pipes to smoke,
An' tell their teäles, an' laugh an' joke,
A-lookèn at the younger vo'k,
    That got up vor a hop.

Woone screäp'd away, wi' merry grin,
A fiddle stuck below his chin;
An' woone o'm took the rollèn pin,
    An' beät the fryèn pan.

An' tothers, dancèn to the soun',
Went in an' out, an' droo an' roun',
An' kick'd, an' beät the tuèn down,
    A-laughèn, maïd an' man.

An' then a maïd, all up tip-tooe,
Vell down; an' woone o'm wi' his shoe
Slit down her pocket-hole in two,
    Vrom top a-most to bottom.
An' when they had a-danc'd enough,
They got a-playèn blindman's buff,
An' sard the maïdens pretty rough,
    When woonce they had a-got em.

An' zome did drink, an' laugh, an' roar,
An' lots o' teäles they had in store,
O' things that happen'd years avore
    To them, or vo'k they know'd.
An' zome did joke, an' zome did zing,
An' meäke the girt wold kitchen ring;
Till uncle's cock, wi' flappèn wing,
    Stratch'd out his neck an' crow'd.

A ZONG OV HARVEST HWOME.

THE ground is clear. There's nar a ear
  O' stannèn corn a-left out now,
Vor win' to blow or raïn to drow;
  'Tis all up seäfe in barn or mow.
    Here's health to them that plough'd an' zow'd;
    Here's health to them that reap'd an' mow'd,
    An' them that had to pitch an' lwoad,
    Or tip the rick at Harvest Hwome.
The happy zight,—the merry night,
The men's delight,—the Harvest Hwome.

A ZONG OV HARVEST HWOME.

An' mid noo harm o' vire or storm
   Beval the farmer or his corn;
An' ev'ry zack o' zeed gi'e back
   A hunderd-vwold so much in barn.
   An' mid his Meäker bless his store,
   His wife an' all that she've a-bore,
   An' keep all evil out o' door.
   Vrom Harvest Hwome to Harvest Hwome.
The happy zight,—the merry night,
The men's delight,—the Harvest Hwome.

Mid nothèn ill betide the mill,
   As day by day the miller's wheel
Do dreve his clacks, an' heist his zacks,
   An' vill his bins wi' show'rèn meal:
   Mid's water never overflow
   His dousty mill, nor zink too low,
   Vrom now till wheat ageän do grow,
   An' we've another Harvest Hwome.
The happy zight,—the merry night,
The men's delight,—the Harvest Hwome.

Drough cisterns wet an' malt-kil's het,
   Mid barley pay the malter's pains;
An' mid noo hurt bevall the wort,
   A-bweilèn vrom the brewer's graïns.
   Mid all his beer keep out o' harm
   Vrom bu'sted hoop or thunder storm,
   That we mid have a mug to warm
   Our merry hearts nex' Harvest Hwome.
The happy zight,—the merry night,
The men's delight,—the Harvest Hwome.

Mid luck an' jay the beäker pay,
   As he do hear his vier roar,
Or nimbly catch his hot white batch,
   A-reekèn vrom the oven door.

  An' mid it never be too high
  Vor our vew zixpences to buy,
  When we do hear our childern cry
  Vor bread, avore nex' Harvest Hwome.
The happy zight,—the merry night,
The men's delight,—the Harvest Hwome.

Wi' jay o' heart mid shooters start
  The whirrèn pa'tridges in vlocks;
While shots do vlee drough bush an' tree,
  An' dogs do stan' so still as stocks.
  An' let em ramble round the farms
  Wi' guns 'ithin their bended eärms,
  In goolden zunsheen free o' storms,
  Rejaïcèn vor the Harvest Hwome.
The happy zight,—the merry night,
The men's delight,—the Harvest Hwome.

POLL'S JACK-DAW.

AH! Jimmy vow'd he'd have the law
Ov ouer cousin Poll's Jack-daw,
That had by day his withy jaïl
A-hangèn up upon a nail,
Ageän the elem tree, avore
The house, jist over-right the door.
An' twitted vo'k a-passèn by
A-most so plaïn as you or I;
Vor hardly any day did pass
'Ithout Tom's teachèn o'm zome sa'ce;
Till by-an'-by he call'd em all
'Soft-polls' an' 'gawkeys,' girt an' small.

An' zoo, as Jim went down along
The leäne a-whisslèn ov a zong,
The saucy Daw cried out by rote
"Girt Soft-poll!" lik' to split his droat.

Jim stopp'd an' grabbled up a clot,
An' zent en at en lik' a shot;
An' down went Daw an' cage avore
The clot, up thump ageän the door.
Zoo out run Poll an' Tom, to zee
What all the meänèn o't mid be;
"Now who did that?" zaid Poll. "Who whurr'd
Theäse clot?" "Girt Soft-poll!" cried the bird.

An' when Tom catch'd a glimpse o' Jim,
A-lookèn all so red an' slim,
An' slinkèn on, he vled, red hot,
Down leäne to catch en, lik' a shot;
But Jim, that thought he'd better trust
To lags than vistes, tried em vu'st.
An' Poll, that zeed Tom woulden catch
En, stood a-smilèn at the hatch.
An' zoo he vollow'd en for two
Or dree stwones' drows, an' let en goo.

THE IVY.

UPON theäse knap I'd sooner be
The ivy that do climb the tree,
Than bloom the gaÿest rwose a-tied
An' trimm'd upon the house's zide.
The rwose mid be the maïdens' pride,
  But still the ivy's wild an' free;
  An' what is all that life can gi'e,
    'Ithout a free light heart, John?

The creepèn sheäde mid steal too soon
Upon the rwose in afternoon;
But here the zun do drow his het
Vrom when do rise till when do zet,

To dry the leaves the raïn do wet.
   An' evenèn aïr do bring along
   The merry deäiry-maïden's zong,
     The zong of free light hearts, John.

Oh! why do vo'k so often chaïn
Their pinèn minds vor love o' gaïn,
An' gi'e their innocence to rise
A little in the woroıd's eyes?
If pride could lift us to the skies,
   What man do value God do slight,
   An' all is nothèn in his zight
     'Ithout an honest heart, John.

An ugly feäce can't bribe the brooks
To show it back young han'some looks,
Nor crooked vo'k intice the light
To cast their zummer sheädes upright:
Noo goold can blind our Meäker's zight.
   An' what's the odds what cloth do hide
   The bosom that do hold inside
     A free an' honest heart, John?

THE WELSHNUT TREE.

When in the evenèn the zun's a-zinkèn,
   A-drowèn sheädes vrom the yollow west,
An' mother, weary, 's a-zot a thinkèn,
   Wi' vwolded eärms by the vire at rest,
     Then we do zwarm, O,
     Wi' such a charm, O,
So vull o' glee by the welshnut tree.

A-leävèn father in-doors, a-leinèn
   In his girt chair in his easy shoes,

Or in the settle so high behine en,
　　While down bezide en the dog do snooze,
　　　　Our tongues do run, O,
　　　　Enough to stun, O,
　　Your head wi' glee by the welshnut tree.

There we do play 'thread the woman's needle.'
　　An' slap the maïdens a-dartèn drough :
Or try who'll ax em the hardest riddle,
　　Or soonest tell woone a-put us, true ;
　　　　Or zit an' ring, O,
　　　　The bells, ding, ding, O,
　　Upon our knee by the welshnut tree.

An' zome do goo out, an' hide in orcha't,
　　An' tothers, slily a-stealèn by,
Where there's a dark cunnèn pleäce, do sarch it,
　　Till they do zee em an' cry, "I spy,"
　　　　An' thik a-vound, O,
　　　　Do gi'e a bound, O,
　　To get off free to the welshnut tree.

Poll went woone night, that we midden vind her,
　　Inzide a woak wi' a hollow moot,
An' drough a hole near the groun' behind her,
　　I pok'd a stick in, an' catch'd her voot ;
　　　　An' out she scream'd, O,
　　　　An' jump'd, an' seem'd, O,
　　A-móst to vlee to the welshnut tree.

An' when, at last, at the drashel, mother
　　Do call us, smilèn, in-door to rest,
Then we do cluster by woone another,
　　To zee hwome them we do love the best :
　　　　An' then do sound, O,
　　　　"Good night," all round, O,
　　To end our glee by the welshnut tree.

JENNY OUT VROM HWOME.

O wild-reävèn west winds; as you do roar on,
   The elems do rock an' the poplars do ply,
An' weäve do dreve weäve in the dark-water'd pon',—
   Oh! where do ye rise vrom, an' where do ye die?

O wild-reävèn winds I do wish I could vlee
   Wi' you, lik' a bird o' the clouds, up above
The ridge o' the hill an' the top o' the tree,
   To where I do long vor, an' vo'k I do love.

Or else that in under theäse rock I could hear,
   In the soft-zwellèn sounds you do leäve in your road,
Zome words you mid bring me, vrom tongues that be dear,
   Vrom friends that do love me, all scatter'd abroad.

O wild-reävèn winds! if you ever do roar
   By the house an' the elems vrom where I'm a-come,
Breathe up at the window, or call at the door,
   An' tell you've a-voun' me a-thinkèn o' hwome.

GRENLEY WATER.

The sheädeless darkness o' the night
Can never blind my mem'ry's zight;
An' in the storm, my fancy's eyes
Can look upon their own blue skies.
The laggèn moon mid fail to rise,
   But when the daylight's blue an' green
   Be gone, my fancy's zun do sheen
     At hwome at Grenley Water.

As when the work-vo'k us'd to ride
In waggon, by the hedge's zide,

Drough evenèn sheädes that trees cast down
Vrom lofty stems athirt the groun';
An' in at house the mug went roun',
   While ev'ry merry man praïs'd up
     The pretty maïd that vill'd his cup,
       The maïd o' Grenley Water.

There I do seem ageän to ride
The hosses to the water-zide,
An' zee the visher fling his hook
Below the withies by the brook;
Or Fanny, wi' her blushèn look,
   Car on her païl, or come to dip
     Wi' ceäreful step, her pitcher's lip
       Down into Grenley Water.

If I'd a farm wi' vower ploughs,
An' vor my deäiry fifty cows;
If Grenley Water winded down
Drough two good miles o' my own groun';
If half ov Ashknowle Hill wer brown
   Wi' my own corn,—noo growèn pride
     Should ever meäke me cast azide
       The maïd o' Grenley Water.

THE VEAIRY VEET THAT I DO MEET.

When dewy fall's red leaves do vlee
Along the grass below the tree,
Or lie in yollow beds a-shook
Upon the shallow-water'd brook,
Or drove 'ithin a sheädy nook;
   Then softly, in the evenèn, down
     The knap do steal along the groun'
       The veäiry veet that I do meet
       Below the row o' beech trees.

'Tis jist avore the candle-light
Do redden windows up at night,
An' peäler stars do light the vogs
A-risèn vrom the brooks an' bogs,
An' when in barkens yoppèn dogs
  Do bark at vo'k a-comèn near,
  Or growl a-lis'enèn to hear
    The veäiry veet that I do meet
    Below the row o' beech trees.

Dree times a-year do bless the road
O' womanhood a-gwaïn abrode:
When vu'st her litty veet do tread
The eärly May's white deäisy bed:
When leaves be all a-scattered dead;
  An' when the winter's vrozen grass
  Do glissen in the zun lik' glass
    Vor veäiry veet that I do meet
    Below the row o' beech trees.

MORNÈN.

When vu'st the breakèn day is red,
  An' grass is dewy wet,
An' roun' the blackberry's a-spread
  The spider's gliss'nèn net,
Then I do dreve the cows across
  The brook that's in a vog,
While they do trot, an' bleäre, an' toss
  Their heads to hook the dog;
Vor the cock do gi'e me warnèn,
    An' light or dark,
    So brisk's a lark,
I'm up at break o' mornèn.

Avore the maïden's sleep's a-broke
  By window-strikèn zun,

MORNÈN.

Avore the busy wife's vu'st smoke
   Do curl above the tun,
My day's begun. An' when the zun
   'S a-zinkèn in the west,
The work the mornèn brought's a-done,
   An' I do goo to rest,
Till the cock do gi'e me warnèn;
     An' light or dark,
     So brisk's a lark,
I'm up ageän nex' mornèn.

We can't keep back the daily zun,
   The wind is never still,
An' never ha' the streams a-done
   A-runnèn down at hill.
Zoo they that ha' their work to do,
   Should do't so soon's they can;
Vor time an' tide will come an' goo,
   An' never waït vor man,
As the cock do gi'e me warnèn;
     When, light or dark,
     So brisk's a lark,
I'm up so rathe in mornèn.

We've leäzes where the aïr do blow,
   An' meäds wi' deäiry cows,
An' copse wi' lewth an' sheäde below
   The overhangèn boughs.
An' when the zun, noo time can tire,
   'S a-quench'd below the west,
Then we've, avore the bleäzèn vire,
   A settle vor to rest,—
To be up ageän nex' mornèr.
     So brisk's a lark,
     When, light or dark,
The cock do gi'e us warnèn.

OUT A-NUTTÈN.

Last week, when we'd a haul'd the crops,
We went a-nuttèn out in copse,
Wi' nuttèn-bags to bring hwome vull,
An' beaky nuttèn-crooks to pull
The bushes down; an' all o's wore
Wold clothes that wer in rags avore,
An' look'd, as we did skip an' zing,
Lik' merry gipsies in a string,
    A-gwaïn a-nuttèn.

Zoo drough the stubble, over rudge
An' vurrow, we begun to trudge;
An' Sal an' Nan agreed to pick
Along wi' me, an' Poll wi' Dick;
An' they went where the wold wood, high
An' thick, did meet an' hide the sky;
But we thought we mid vind zome good
Ripe nuts among the shorter wood,
    The best vor nuttèn.

We voun' zome bushes that did feäce
The downcast zunlight's highest pleäce,
Where clusters hung so ripe an' brown,
That some slipp'd shell an' vell to groun'.
But Sal wi' me zoo hitch'd her lag
In brembles, that she coulden wag;
While Poll kept clwose to Dick, an' stole
The nuts vrom's hinder pocket-hole,
    While he did nutty.

An' Nanny thought she zaw a sneäke,
An' jump'd off into zome girt breäke,
An' tore the bag where she'd a-put
Her sheäre, an' shatter'd ev'ry nut.

An' out in vield we all zot roun'
A white-stemm'd woak upon the groun',
Where yollor evenèn light did strik'
Drough yollow leaves, that still wer thick
    In time o' nuttèn,

An' twold ov all the luck we had
Among the bushes, good an' bad!
Till all the maïdens left the bwoys,
An' skipp'd about the leäze all woys
Vor musherooms, to car back zome,
A treat vor father in at hwome.
Zoo off we trudg'd wi' clothes in slents
An' libbets, jis' lik' Jack-o'-lents,
    Vrom copse a-nuttèn.

TEAKEN IN APPLES.

WE took the apples in last week,
An' got, by night, zome eächèn backs
A-stoopèn down all day to pick
So many up in mawns an' zacks.
An' there wer Liz so proud an' prim,
An' dumpy Nan, an' Poll so sly;
An' dapper Tom, an' loppèn Jim,
An' little Dick, an' Fan, an' I.

An' there the lwoaded tree bent low,
Behung wi' apples green an' red;
An' springèn grass could hardly grow,
Drough windvalls down below his head.
An' when the maïdens come in roun'
The heavy boughs to vill their laps,
We slily shook the apples down
Lik' haïl, an' gi'ed their backs some raps.

An' zome big apple, Jimmy flung
To squaïl me, gi'ed me sich a crack;
But very shortly his ear rung,
Wi' woone I zent to pay en back.
An' after we'd a-had our squaïls,
Poor Tom, a-jumpèn in a bag,
Wer pinch'd by all the maïden's naïls,
An' rolled down into hwome-groun' quag.

An' then they carr'd our Fan all roun',
'Ithin a mawn, till zome girt stump
Upset en over on the groun',
An' drow'd her out along-straïght, plump.
An' in the cider-house we zot
Upon the windlass Poll an' Nan,
An' spun 'em roun' till they wer got
So giddy that they coulden stan'.

MEAPLE LEAVES BE YOLLOW.

Come, let's stroll down so vur's the poun',
Avore the sparklèn zun is down:
The zummer's gone, an' days so feäir
As theäse be now a-gettèn reäre.
The night, wi' mwore than daylight's sheäre
  O' wat'ry sky, do wet wi' dew
    The ee-grass up above woone's shoe,
      An' meäple leaves be yollow.

The last hot doust, above the road,
An' vu'st dead leaves ha' been a-blow'd
By playsome win's where spring did spread
The blossoms that the zummer shed;
An' near blue sloos an' conkers red
  The evenèn zun, a zettèn soon,
    Do leäve a-quiv'rèn to the moon,
      The meäple leaves so yollow.

Zoo come along, an' let's injay
The last fine weather while do stay;
While thou canst hang, wi' ribbons slack,
Thy bonnet down upon thy back,
Avore the winter, cwold an' black,
   Do kill thy flowers, an' avore
    Thy bird-cage is a-took in door,
      Though meäple leaves be yollow.

NIGHT A-ZETTEN IN.

When leäzers wi' their laps o' corn
   Noo longer be a-stoopèn,
An' in the stubble, all vorlorn,
   Noo poppies be a-droopèn;
When theäse young harvest-moon do weäne,
   That now've his horns so thin, O,
We'll leäve off walkèn in the leäne,
   While night's a zettèn in, O.

When zummer doust is all a-laïd
   Below our litty shoes, O;
When all the raïn-chill'd flow'rs be dead,
   That now do drink the dews, O;
When beauty's neck, that's now a-show'd,
   'S a-muffled to the chin, O;
We'll leäve off walkèn in the road,
   When night's a-zettèn in, O.

But now, while barley by the road
   Do hang upon the bough, O,
A-pull'd by branches off the lwoad
   A-ridèn hwome to mow, O;
While spiders roun' the flower-stalks
   Ha' cobwebs yet to spin, O,
We'll cool ourzelves in out-door walks,
   When night's a-zettèn in, O.

While down at vword the brook so small,
   That leätely wer so high, O,
Wi' little tinklèn sounds do vall
   In roun' the stwones half dry, O ;
While twilight ha' sich aïr in store,
   To cool our zunburnt skin, O,
We'll have a ramble out o' door,
   When night's a-zettèn in, O.

THE WEATHER-BEATEN TREE.

THE woaken tree, a-beät at night
By stormy winds wi' all their spite,
Mid toss his lim's, an' ply, an' mwoan,
Wi' unknown struggles all alwone ;
An' when the day do show his head,
A-stripp'd by winds at last a-laid,
How vew mid think that didden zee,
How night-time had a-tried thik tree.

An' happy vo'k do seldom know
How hard our unknown storms do blow,
The while our heads do slowly bend
Below the trials God do zend,
Like shiv'rèn bennets, beäre to all
The drevèn winds o' dark'nèn fall.
An' zoo in tryèn hardships we
Be lik' the weather beäten tree.

But He will never meäke our sheäre
O' sorrow mwore than we can bear,
But meäke us zee, if 'tis His will,
That He can bring us good vrom ill ;
As after winter He do bring,
In His good time, the zunny spring,
An' leaves, an' young vo'k vull o' glee
A-dancèn roun' the woaken tree.

True love's the ivy that do twine
Unwith'rèn roun' his mossy rine,
When winter's zickly zun do sheen
Upon its leaves o' glossy green,
So patiently a-holdèn vast
Till storms an' cwold be all a-past,
An' only livèn vor to be
A-meäted to the woaken tree.

SHRODON FEÄIR.

The vu'st Peärt.

An' zoo's the day wer warm an' bright,
An' nar a cloud wer up in zight,
We wheedled father vor the meäre
An' cart, to goo to Shrodon feäir.
An' Poll an' Nan run off up stairs,
To shift their things, as wild as heäres;
An' pull'd out, each o'm vrom her box,
Their snow-white leäce an' newest frocks,
An' put their bonnets on, a-lined
Wi' blue an' sashes tied behind;
An' turn'd avore the glass their feäce
An' back, to zee their things in pleäce;
While Dick an' I did brush our hats
An' cwoats, an' cleän ourzelves lik' cats.
At woone or two o'clock, we vound
Ourzelves at Shrodon seäfe an' sound,
A-struttèn in among the rows
O' tilted stannèns an' o' shows,
An' girt long booths wi' little bars
Chock-vull o' barrels, mugs, an' jars,
An' meat a-cookèn out avore
The vier at the upper door;

Where zellers bwold to buyers shy
Did hollow round us, "What d'ye buy?"
An' scores o' merry tongues did speak
At woonce, an' childern's pipes did squeak,
An' horns did blow, an' drums did rumble,
An' bawlèn merrymen did tumble;
An' woone did all but want an edge
To peärt the crowd wi', lik' a wedge.

We zaw the dancers in a show
Dance up an' down, an' to an' fro,
Upon a rwope, wi' chalky zoles,
So light as magpies up on poles;
An' tumblers, wi' their streaks an' spots,
That all but tied theirzelves in knots.
An' then a conjurer burn'd off
Poll's han'kerchief so black's a snoff,
An' het en, wi' a single blow,
Right back ageän so white as snow.
An' after that, he fried a fat
Girt ceäke inzide o' my new hat;
An' yet, vor all he did en brown,
He didden even zweal the crown.

SHRODON FEÄR.

The rest o't.

An' after that we met wi' zome
O' Mans'on vo'k, but jist a-come,
An' had a raffle vor a treat
All roun', o' gingerbread to eat;
An' Tom meäde leäst, wi' all his sheäkes,
An' païd the money vor the ceäkes,
But wer so lwoth to put it down
As if a penny wer a poun'.

Then up come zidelèn Sammy Heäre,
That's fond o' Poll, an' she can't bear,
A-holdèn out his girt scram vist,
An' ax'd her, wi' a grin an' twist,
To have zome nuts; an' she, to hide
Her laughèn, turn'd her head azide,
An' answer'd that she'd rather not,
But Nancy mid. An' Nan, so hot
As vier, zaid 'twer quite enough
Vor Poll to answer vor herzuf:
She had a tongue, she zaid, an' wit
Enough to use en, when 'twer fit.
An' in the dusk, a-ridèn round
Drough Okford, who d'ye think we vound
But Sam ageän, a-gwäin vrom feäir
Astride his broken-winded meäre.
An' zoo, a-hettèn her, he tried
To keep up clwose by ouer zide:
But when we come to Hayward-brudge,
Our Poll gi'ed Dick a meänèn nudge,
An' wi' a little twitch our meäre
Flung out her lags so lights a heäre,
An' left poor Sammy's skin an' bwones
Behind, a-kickèn o' the stwones.

MARTIN'S TIDE.

COME, bring a log o' cleft wood, Jack,
An' fling en on ageän the back,
An' zee the outside door is vast,—
The win' do blow a cwoldish blast.
Come, so's! come, pull your chairs in roun'
Avore the vire; an' let's zit down,
An' keep up Martin's-tide, vor I
Shall keep it up till I do die.

G

'Twer Martinmas, and ouer feäir,
When Jeäne an' I, a happy peäir,
Vu'st walk'd, a-keepèn up the tide,
Among the stan'ens, zide by zide;
An' thik day twel'month, never failèn,
She gi'ed me at the chancel railèn
A heart—though I do sound her praise—
As true as ever beät in stays.
How vast the time do goo! Do seem
But yesterday,—'tis lik' a dream!

Ah, sō's! 'tis now zome years agoo
You vu'st knew me, an' I knew you;
An' we've a-had zome bits o' fun,
By winter vire an' zummer zun.
Aye; we've a-prowl'd an' rigg'd about
Lik' cats, in harm's way mwore than out,
An' busy wi' the tricks we play'd
In fun, to outwit chap or maïd.
An' out avore the bleäzèn he'th,
Our naïsy tongues, in winter me'th,
'V a-shook the warmèn-pan, a-hung
Bezide us, till his cover rung.
There, 'twer but tother day thik chap,
Our Robert, wer a child in lap;
An' Poll's two little lags hung down
Vrom thik wold chair a span vrom groun',
An' now the saucy wench do stride
About wi' steps o' dree veet wide.
How time do goo! A life do seem
As 'twer a year; 'tis lik' a dream!

GUY FAUX'S NIGHT.

Guy Faux's night, dost know, we chaps,
A-putten on our woldest traps,
Went up the highest o' the knaps,
    An' meäde up such a vier!
An' thou an' Tom wer all we miss'd,
Vor if a sarpent had a-hiss'd
Among the rest in thy sprack vist,
    Our fun 'd a-been the higher.

We chaps at hwome, an' Will our cousin,
Took up a half a lwoad o' vuzzen;
An' burn'd a barrel wi' a dozen
    O' faggots, till above en
The fleämes, arisèn up so high
'S the tun, did snap, an' roar, an' ply,
    Lik' vier in an' oven.

An' zome wi' hissèn squibs did run,
To pay off zome what they'd a-done,
An' let em off so loud's a gun
    Ageän their smokèn polls;
An' zome did stir their nimble pags
Wi' crackers in between their lags,
While zome did burn their cwoats to rags,
    Or wes'cots out in holes.

An' zome o'm's heads lost half their locks,
An' zome o'm got their white smock-frocks
Jist fit to vill the tinder-box,
    Wi' half the backs o'm off;
An' Dick, that all o'm vell upon,
Vound woone flap ov his cwoat-tail gone,
An' tother jist a-hangèn on,
    A-zweal'd so black's a snoff.

Eclogue.

THE COMMON A-TOOK IN.

Thomas an' John.

THOMAS.

Good morn t'ye, John. How b'ye? how b'ye?
Zoo you be gwaïn to market, I do zee.
Why, you be quite a-lwoaded wi' your geese.

JOHN.

Ees, Thomas, ees.
Why, I'm a-gettèn rid ov ev'ry goose
An' goslèn I've a-got: an' what is woose,
I fear that I must zell my little cow.

THOMAS.

How zoo, then, John? Why, what's the matter now?
What, can't ye get along? B'ye run a-ground?
An' can't pay twenty shillèns vor a pound?
What can't ye put a lwoaf on shelf?

JOHN.

Ees, now;
But I do fear I shan't 'ithout my cow.
No; they do mëan to teäke the moor in, I do hear,
An' 'twill be soon begun upon;
Zoo I must zell my bit o' stock to-year,
Because they woon't have any groun' to run upon.

THOMAS.

Why, what d'ye tell o'? I be very zorry
To hear what they be gwaïn about;
But yet I s'pose there 'll be a 'lotment vor ye,
When they do come to mark it out.

JOHN.

No; not vor me, I fear. An' if there should,
Why 'twoulden be so handy as 'tis now;
Vor 'tis the common that do do me good,
The run for my vew geese, or vor my cow.

THOMAS.

Ees, that's the job; why 'tis a handy thing
To have a bit o' common, I do know,
To put a little cow upon in Spring,
The while woone's bit ov orcha'd grass do grow.

JOHN.

Aye, that's the thing, you zee. Now I do mow
My bit o' grass, an' meäke a little rick;
An' in the zummer, while do grow,
My cow do run in common vor to pick
A bleäde or two o' grass, if she can vind em,
Vor tother cattle don't leäve much behind em.
Zoo in the evenèn, we do put a lock
O' nice fresh grass avore the wicket;
An' she do come at vive or zix o'clock,
As constant as the zun, to pick it.
An' then, bezides the cow, why we do let
Our geese run out among the emmet hills;
An' then when we do pluck em, we do get
Vor zeäle zome veathers an' zome quills;
An' in the winter we do fat em well,
An' car em to the market vor to zell
To gentlevo'ks, vor we don't oft avvword
To put a goose a-top ov ouer bwoard;
But we do get our feäst,—vor we be eäble
To clap the giblets up a-top o' teäble.

THOMAS.

An' I don't know o' many better things,
Than geese's heads and gizzards, lags an' wings.

JOHN.

An' then, when I ha' nothèn else to do,
Why I can teäke my hook an' gloves, an' goo
To cut a lot o' vuzz and briars
Vor hetèn ovens, or vor lightèn viers.
An' when the childern be too young to eärn
A penny, they can g'out in zunny weather,
An' run about, an' get together
A bag o' cow-dung vor to burn.

THOMAS.

'Tis handy to live near a common;
But I've a-zeed, an' I've a-zaid,
That if a poor man got a bit o' bread,
They'll try to teäke it vrom en.
But I wer twold back tother day,
That they be got into a way
O' lettèn bits o' groun' out to the poor.

JOHN.

Well, I do hope 'tis true, I'm sure;
An' I do hope that they will do it here,
Or I must goo to workhouse, I do fear.

Eclogue.

TWO FARMS IN WOONE.

Robert an' Thomas.

ROBERT.

You'll lose your meäster soon, then, I do vind;
He's gwain to leäve his farm, as I do larn,
At Mielmas; an' I be zorry vor'n.
What, is he then a little bit behind?

THOMAS.

O no! at Miëlmas his time is up,
An' thik there sly wold fellow, Farmer Tup,
A-fearèn that he'd get a bit o' bread,
'V a-been an' took his farm here over 's head.

ROBERT.

How come the Squire to treat your meäster zoo?

THOMAS.

Why, he an' meäster had a word or two.

ROBERT.

Is Farmer Tup a-gwaïn to leäve his farm?
He han't a-got noo young woones vor to zwarm.
Poor over-reachèn man! why to be sure
He don't want all the farms in parish, do er?

THOMAS.

Why ees, all ever he can come across,
Last year, you know, he got away the eäcre
Or two o' ground a-rented by the beäker,
An' what the butcher had to keep his hoss;
An' vo'k do beänhan' now, that meäster's lot
Will be a-drowd along wi' what he got.

ROBERT.

That's it. In theäse here pleäce there used to be
Eight farms avore they wer a-drowd together,
An' eight farm-housen. Now how many be there?
Why after this, you know there'll be but dree.

THOMAS.

An' now they don't imploy so many men
Upon the land as work'd upon it then,
Vor all they midden crop it worse, nor stock it.
The lan'lord, to be sure, is into pocket;
Vor half the housen beën down, 'tis clear,
Don't cost so much to keep em up, a-near.

But then the jobs o' work in wood an' morter
Do come I 'spose, you know, a little shorter;
An' many that wer little farmers then,
Be now a-come all down to leäb'rèn men;
An' many leäb'rèn men, wi' empty hands,
Do live lik' drones upon the worker's lands.

ROBERT.

Aye, if a young chap, woonce, had any wit
To try an' scrape together zome vew pound,
To buy some cows an' teäke a bit o' ground,
He mid become a farmer, bit by bit.
But, hang it! now the farms be all so big,
An' bits o' groun' so skeä'ce, woone got no scope;
If woone could seäve a poun', woone couldden hope
To keep noo live stock but a little pig.

THOMAS.

Why here wer vourteen men, zome years agoo,
A-kept a-drashèn half the winter drough;
An' now, woone's drashels be'n't a bit o' good.
They got machines to drashy wi', plague teäke em!
An' he that vu'st vound out the way to meäke em,
I'd drash his busy zides vor'n if I could!
Avore they took away our work, they ought
To meäke us up the bread our leäbour bought.

ROBERT.

They hadden need meäke poor men's leäbour less,
Vor work a'ready is uncommon skeä'ce.

THOMAS.

Ah! Robert! times be badish vor the poor;
An' worse will come, I be a-fear'd, if Moore
In theäse year's almanick do tell us right.

ROBERT.

Why then we sartainly must starve. Good night!

WINTER.

THE VROST.

Come, run up hwome wi' us to night,
Athirt the vield a-vroze so white,
Where vrosty sheädes do lie below
The winter ricks a-tipp'd wi' snow,
An' lively birds, wi' waggèn taïls,
Do hop upon the icy raïls,
An' rime do whiten all the tops
O' bush an' tree in hedge an' copse,
   In wind's a-cuttèn keen.

Come, maïdens, come: the groun's a-vroze
Too hard to-night to spweil your clothes.
You got noo pools to waddle drough,
Nor clay a-pullèn off your shoe:
An' we can trig ye at the zide,
To keep ye up if you do slide:
Zoo while there's neither wet nor mud,
'S the time to run an' warm your blood,
   In winds a-cuttèn keen.

Vor young men's hearts an' maïden's eyes
Don't vreeze below the cwoldest skies,
While they in twice so keen a blast
Can wag their brisk lim's twice so vast!

Though vier-light, a-flick'rèn red
Drough vrosty window-peänes, do spread
Vrom wall to wall, vrom he'th to door,
Vor us to goo an' zit avore,
    Vrom winds a-cuttèn keen.

A BIT O' FUN.

WE thought you woulden leäve us quite
So soon as what you did last night;
Our fun jist got up to a height
    As you about got hwome.
The friskèn chaps did skip about,
An' cou'se the maïdens in an' out,
A-meäkèn such a randy-rout,
    You coulden hear a drum.

An' Tom, a-springèn after Bet
Blind-vwolded, whizz'd along, an' het
Poor Grammer's zide, an' overzet
    Her chair, at blind-man's buff;
An' she, poor soul, as she did vall,
Did show her snags o' teeth an' squall,
An' what, she zaid, wer wo'se than all,
    She shatter'd all her snuff.

An' Bet, a-hoppèn back vor fear
O' Tom, struck uncle zomewhere near,
An' meäde his han' spill all his beer
    Right down her poll an' back;
An' Joe, in middle o' the din,
Slipt out a bit, an' soon come in
Wi' all below his dapper chin
    A-jumpèn in a zack.

An' in a twinklèn tother chaps
Jist hung en to a crook wi' straps,

An' meäde en bear the maïdens' slaps,
   An' prickens wi' a pin.
An' Jim, a-catchèn Poll, poor chap,
In back-house in the dark, vell slap
Athirt a tub o' barm,—a trap
   She set to catch en in.

An' then we zot down out o' breath,
An' meäde a circle roun' the he'th,
A-keepèn up our harmless me'th,
   Till supper wer a-come.
An' after we'd a-had zome prog,
All tother chaps begun to jog,
Wi' sticks to lick a thief or dog,
   To zee the maïdens hwome.

FANNY'S BE'TH-DAY.

How merry, wi' the cider cup,
We kept poor Fanny's be'th-day up!
An' how our busy tongues did run
An' hands did wag, a-meäkèn fun!
What playsome anticks zome ō's done!
   An' how, a-reelèn roun' an' roun',
   We beät the merry tuèn down,
     While music wer a-soundèn!

The maïdens' eyes o' black an' blue
Did glisten lik' the mornèn dew;
An' while the cider-mug did stand
A-hissèn by the bleäzèn brand,
An' uncle's pipe wer in his hand,
   How little he or we did think
   How peäle the zettèn stars did blink
     While music wer a-soundèn.

An' Fanny's last young *teen* begun,
Poor maïd, wi' thik day's risèn zun,
An' we all wish'd her many mwore
Long years wi' happiness in store;
An' as she went an' stood avore
 The vier, by her father's zide,
  Her mother dropp'd a tear o' pride
   While music wer a-soundèn.

An' then we did all kinds o' tricks
Wi' han'kerchicfs, an' strings, an' sticks:
An' woone did try to overmatch
Another wi' zome cunnèn catch,
While tothers slyly tried to hatch
 Zome geäme; but yet, by chap an' maïd,
  The dancèn wer the mwost injay'd,
   While music wer a-soundèn.

The briskest chap ov all the lot
Wer Tom, that danc'd hizzelf so hot,
He doff'd his cwoat an' jump'd about,
Wi' girt new shirt-sleeves all a-strout,
Among the maïdens screamèn out,
 A-thinkèn, wi' his strides an' stamps,
  He'd squot their veet wi' his girt clamps,
   While music wer a-soundèn.

Then up jump'd uncle vrom his chair,
An' pull'd out aunt to meäke a peäir;
An' off he zet upon his tooe.
So light's the best that beät a shoe,
Wi' aunt a-crièn "Let me goo:"
 While all ov us did laugh so loud,
  We drown'd the tuèn o' the croud,
   While music wer a-soundèn.

A-comèn out o' passage, Nan,
Wi' pipes an' cider in her han',

An' watchèn uncle up so sprack,
Vorgot her veet, an' vell down smack
Athirt the house-dog's shaggy back,
   That wer in passage vor a snooze,
   Beyond the reach o' dancers' shoes,
     While music wer a-soundèn.

WHAT DICK AN' I DID.

LAST week the Browns ax'd nearly all
   The naïghbours to a randy,
An' left us out o't, girt an' small,
   Vor all we liv'd so handy;
An' zoo I zaid to Dick, "We'll trudge,
   When they be in their fun, min;
An' car up zome'hat to the rudge,
   An' jis' stop up the tun, min."

Zoo, wi' the ladder vrom the rick,
   We stole towards the house,
An' crope in roun' behind en, lik'
   A cat upon a mouse.
Then, lookèn roun', Dick whisper'd "How
   Is theäse job to be done, min:
Why we do want a faggot now,
   Vor stoppèn up the tun, min."

"Stan' still," I answer'd; "I'll teäke ceäre
   O' that: why dussen zee
The little grindèn stwone out there,
   Below the apple-tree?
Put up the ladder; in a crack
   Shalt zee that I wull run, min,
An' teäke en up upon my back,
   An' soon stop up the tun, min."

Zoo up I clomb upon the thatch,
   An' clapp'd en on; an' slided
Right down ageän, an' run drough hatch,
   Behind the hedge, an' hided.
The vier that wer clear avore,
   Begun to spweil their fun, min;
The smoke all roll'd toward the door,
   Vor I'd a-stopp'd the tun, min.

The maïdens cough'd or stopp'd their breath,
   The men did hauk an' spet;
The wold vo'k bundled out from he'th
   Wi' eyes a-runnèn wet.
" 'T'ool choke us all," the wold man cried,
   "Whatever's to be done, min?
Why zome'hat is a-vell inside
   O' chimney drough the tun, min."

Then out they scamper'd all, vull run,
   An' out cried Tom, " I think
The grindèn-stwone is up on tun,
   Vor I can zee the wink.
This is some kindness that the vo'k
   At Woodley have a-done, min;
I wish I had em here, I'd poke
   Their numskulls down the tun, min."

Then off he zet, an' come so quick
   'S a lamplighter, an' brote
The little ladder in vrom rick,
   To clear the chimney's droat.
While I, a-chucklèn at the joke,
   A-slided down, to run, min,
To hidelock, had a-left the vo'k
   As bad as na'r a tun, min.

GRAMMER'S SHOES.

I do seem to zee Grammer as she did use
Vor to show us, at Chris'mas, her weddèn shoes,
An' her flat spreadèn bonnet so big an' roun'
As a girt pewter dish a-turn'd upside down;
    When we all did draw near
      In a cluster to hear
O' the merry wold soul how she did use
To walk an' to dance wi' her high-heel shoes.

She'd a gown wi' girt flowers lik' hollyhocks,
An' zome stockèns o' gramfer's a-knit wi' clocks,
An' a token she kept under lock an' key,—
A small lock ov his heäir off avore 't wer grey.
    An' her eyes wer red,
      An' she shook her head,
When we'd all a-look'd at it, an' she did use
To lock it away wi' her weddèn shoes.

She could tell us such teäles about heavy snows,
An' o' raïns an' o' floods when the waters rose
All up into the housen, an' carr'd awoy
All the bridge wi' a man an' his little bwoy;
    An' o' vog an' vrost,
      An' o' vo'k a-lost,
An' o' peärties at Chris'mas, when she did use
Vor to walk hwome wi' gramfer in high-heel shoes.

Ev'ry Chris'mas she lik'd vor the bells to ring,
An' to have in the zingers to heär em zing
The wold carols she heärd many years a-gone,
While she warm'd em zome cider avore the bron';
    An' she'd look an' smile
      At our dancèn, while
She did tell how her friends now a-gone did use
To reely wi' her in their high-heel shoes.

Ah! an' how she did like vor to deck wi' red
Holly-berries the window an' wold clock's head,
An' the clavy wi' boughs o' some bright green leaves,
An' to meäke twoast an' eäle upon Chris'mas eves;
    But she's now, drough greäce,
    In a better pleäce,
Though we'll never vorget her, poor soul, nor lose
Gramfer's token ov heäir, nor her weddèn shoes.

ZUNSHEEN IN THE WINTER.

The winter clouds, that long did hide
The zun, be all a-blown azide,
An' in the light, noo longer dim,
Do sheen the ivy that do clim'
The tower's zide an' elem's stim;
    An' holmen bushes, in between
    The leafless thorns, be bright an' green
        To zunsheen o' the winter.

The trees, that yesterday did twist
In wind's a-drevèn raïn an' mist,
Do now drow sheädes out, long an' still;
But roarèn watervals do vill
Their whirlèn pools below the hill,
    Where, wi' her païl upon the stile,
    A-gwaïn a-milkèn Jeäne do smile
        To zunsheen o' the winter.

The birds do sheäke, wi' playsome skips,
The raïn-drops off the bushes' tips,
A-chirripèn wi' merry sound;
While over all the grassy ground
The wind's a-whirlèn round an' round
    So softly, that the day do seem
    Mwore lik' a zummer in a dream,
        Than zunsheen in the winter.

The wold vo'k now do meet abrode,
An' tell o' winter's they've a-know'd;
When snow wer long above the groun',
Or floods broke all the bridges down,
Or wind unheal'd a half the town,—
　　The teäles o' wold times long a-gone,
　　But ever dear to think upon,
　　　　The zunsheen o' their winter.

Vor now to them noo brook can run,
Noo hill can feäce the winter zun,
Noo leaves can vall, noo flow'rs can feäde,
Noo snow can hide the grasses bleäde,
Noo vrost can whiten in the sheäde,
　　Noo day can come, but what do bring
　　To mind ageän their early spring,
　　　　That's now a-turn'd to winter.

THE WEEPEN LEÄDY.

When, leäte o' nights, above the green
By thik wold house, the moon do sheen,
A leädy there, a-hangèn low
Her head, 's a-walkèn to an' fro
In robes so white's the driven snow,
　　Wi' woone cärm down, while woone do rest
　　All lily-white athirt the breast
　　　　O' thik poor weepèn leädy.

The whirlèn wind an' whis'lèn squall
Do sheäke the ivy by the wall,
An' meäke the plyèn tree-tops rock,
But never ruffle her white frock;
An' slammèn door an' rattlèn lock,
　　That in thik empty house do sound,
　　Do never seem to meäke look round
　　　　Thik ever downcast leädy.

A leädy, as the teäle do goo,
That woonce liv'd there, an' lov'd too true,
Wer by a young man cast azide.
A mother sad, but not a bride;
An' then her father, in his pride
   An' anger, offer'd woone o' two
   Vull bitter things to undergoo
     To thik poor weepèn leädy:

That she herzelf should leäve his door,
To darken it ageän noo mwore;
Or that her little playsome chile,
A-zent away a thousand mile,
Should never meet her eyes to smile
   An' play ageän; till she, in sheäme,
   Should die an' leäve a tarnish'd neäme,
     A sad vorseäken leädy.

"Let me be lost," she cried, "the while
I do but know vor my poor chile;"
An' left the hwome ov all her pride,
To wander drough the worold wide,
Wi' grief that vew but she ha' tried:
   An' lik' a flow'r a blow ha' broke,
   She wither'd wi' the deadly stroke,
     An' died a weepèn leädy.

An' she do keep a-comèn on
To zee her father dead an' gone,
As if her soul could have noo rest
Avore her teäry cheäk's a-prest
By his vorgivèn kiss. Zoo blest
   Be they that can but live in love,
   An' vind a pleäce o' rest above
     Unlik' the weepèn leädy.

THE HAPPY DAYS WHEN I WER YOUNG.

In happy days when I wer young,
An' had noo ho, an' laugh'd an' zung,
The maïd wer merry by her cow,
An' men wer merry wi' the plough;
But never talk'd, at hwome or out
O' doors, o' what's a-talk'd about
By many now,—that to despise
The laws o' God an' man is wise.
Wi' daïly health, an' daïly bread,
An' thatch above their shelter'd head,
They velt noo fear, an' had noo spite,
To keep their eyes awake at night;
But slept in peace wi' God on high
An' man below, an' fit to die.

O' grassy meäd an' woody nook,
An' waters o' the windèn brook,
That sprung below the vu'st dark sky
That rain'd, to run till seas be dry;
An' hills a-stannèn on while all
The works o' man do rise an' vall;
An' trees the toddlèn child do vind
At vu'st, an' leäve at last behind;
I wish that you could now unvwold
The peace an' jäy o' times o' wold;
An' tell, when death do still my tongue,
O' happy days when I wer young.
Vrom where wer all this venom brought,
To kill our hope an' taint our thought?
Clear brook! thy water coulden bring
Such venom vrom thy rocky spring;
Nor could it come in zummer blights,
Or reävèn storms o' winter nights.

Or in the cloud an' viry stroke
O' thunder that do split the woak.

O valley dear! I wish that I
'D a-liv'd in former times, to die
Wi' all the happy souls that trod
Thy turf in peäce, an' died to God;
Or gone wi' them that laugh'd an' zung
In happy days when I wer young!

IN THE STILLNESS O' THE NIGHT.

Ov all the housen o' the pleäce,
  There 's woone where I do like to call
  By day or night the best ov all,
To zee my Fanny's smilèn feäce;
An' there the steätely trees do grow,
A-rockèn as the win' do blow,
While she do sweetly sleep below,
  In the stillness o' the night.

An' there, at evenèn, I do goo
  A-hoppèn over geätes an' bars,
  By twinklèn light o' winter stars,
When snow do clumper to my shoe;
An' zometimes we do slyly catch
A chat an hour upon the stratch,
An' peärt wi' whispers at the hatch
  In the stillness o' the night.

An' zometimes she do goo to zome
  Young naïghbours' housen down the pleäce,
  An' I do get a clue to treäce
Her out, an' goo to zee her hwome;
An' I do wish a vield a mile,
As she do sweetly chat an' smile
Along the drove, or at the stile,
  In the stillness o' the night.

THE SETTLE AN' THE GIRT WOOD VIRE.

AH! naïghbour John, since I an' you
Wer youngsters, ev'ry thing is new.
My father's vires wer all o' logs
O' cleft-wood, down upon the dogs
Below our clavy, high, an' brode
Enough to teäke a cart an' lwoad,
Where big an' little all zot down
At bwoth zides, an' bevore, all roun'.
An' when I zot among em, I
Could zee all up ageän the sky
Drough chimney, where our vo'k did hitch
The zalt-box an' the beäcon-vlitch,
An' watch the smoke on out o' vier,
All up an' out o' tun, an' higher.
An' there wer beäcon up on rack,
An' pleätes an' dishes on the tack;
An' roun' the walls wer heärbs a-stowed
In peäpern bags, an' blathers blowed.
An' just above the clavy-bwoard
Wer father's spurs, an' gun, an' sword;
An' there wer then, our girtest pride,
The settle by the vier zide.
 Ah! gi'e me, if I wer a squier,
 The settle an' the girt wood vier.

But they've a-wall'd up now wi' bricks
The vier pleäce vor dogs an' sticks,
An' only left a little hole
To teäke a little greäte o' coal,
So small that only twos or drees
Can jist push in an' warm their knees.
An' then the carpets they do use,
Bēn't fit to tread wi' ouer shoes;

An' chairs an' couches be so neat,
You mussen teäke em vor a seat:
They be so fine, that vo'k mus' pleäce
All over em an' outer ceäse,
An' then the cover, when 'tis on,
Is still too fine to loll upon.
 Ah! gi'e me, if I wer a squier,
 The settle an' the girt wood vier.

Carpets, indeed! You coulden hurt
The stwone-vloor wi' a little dirt;
Vor what wer brought in doors by men,
The women soon mopp'd out ageän.
Zoo we did come vrom muck an' mire,
An' walk in straïght avore the vier;
But now, a man's a-kept at door
At work a pirty while, avore
He's screäp'd an' rubb'd, an' cleän and fit
To goo in where his wife do zit.
An' then if he should have a whiff
In there, 'twould only breed a miff:
He cānt smoke there, vor smoke woon't goo
'Ithin the footy little flue.
 Ah! gi'e me, if I wer a squier,
 The settle an' the girt wood vier.

THE CARTER.

O, I be a carter, wi' my whip
 A-smackèn loud, as by my zide,
Up over hill, an' down the dip,
 The heavy lwoad do slowly ride.

An' I do haul in all the crops,
 An' I do bring in vuzz vrom down;
An' I do goo vor wood to copse,
 An' car the corn an' straw to town.

THE CARTER.

An' I do goo vor lime, an' bring
   Hwome cider wi' my sleek-heäir'd team,
An' smack my limber whip an' zing,
   While all their bells do gaily cheeme.

An' I do always know the pleäce
   To gi'e the hosses breath, or drug;
An' ev'ry hoss do know my feäce,
   An' mind my *'mether ho!* an' *whug!*

An' merry hay-meäkers do ride
   Vrom vield in zummer wi' their prongs,
In my blue waggon, zide by zide
   Upon the reäves, a-zingèn zongs.

An' when the vrost do catch the stream,
   An' oves wi' icicles be hung,
My pantèn hosses' breath do steam
   In white-grass'd vields, a-haulèn dung.

An' mine's the waggon fit vor lwoads,
   An' mine be lwoads to cut a rout;
An' mine's a team, in routy rwoads,
   To pull a lwoaded waggon out.

A zull is nothèn when do come
   Behind their lags; an' they do teäke
A roller as they would a drum,
   An' harrow as they would a reäke.

O! I be a carter, wi' my whip
   A-smackèn loud, as by my zide,
Up over hill, an' down the dip,
   The heavy lwoad do slowly ride.

CHRIS'MAS INVITATION.

Come down to-morrow night; an' mind,
Don't leäve thy fiddle-bag behind;
We'll sheäke a lag, an' drink a cup
O' eäle, to keep wold Chris'mas up.

An' let thy sister teäke thy eärm,
The walk won't do her any harm;
There's noo dirt now to spweil her frock,
The ground's a-vroze so hard's a rock.

You won't meet any stranger's feäce,
But only naïghbours o' the pleäce,
An' Stowe, an' Combe; an' two or dree
Vrom uncle's up at Rookery.

An' thou wu'lt vind a rwosy feäce,
An' peäir ov eyes so black as sloos,
The prettiest woones in all the pleäce,—
I'm sure I needen tell thee whose.

We got a back-bran', dree girt logs
So much as dree ov us can car;
We'll put em up athirt the dogs,
An' meäke a vier to the bar.

An' ev'ry woone shall tell his teäle,
An' ev'ry woone shall zing his zong,
An' ev'ry woone wull drink his eäle
To love an' frien'ship all night long.

We'll snap the tongs, we'll have a ball,
We'll sheäke the house, we'll lift the ruf,
We'll romp an' meäke the maïdens squall,
A catchèn o'm at blind-man's buff.

Zoo come to-morrow night; an' mind,
Don't leäve thy fiddle-bag behind;
We'll sheäke a lag, an' drink a cup
O' eäle, to keep wold Chris'mas up.

KEEPEN UP O' CHRIS'MAS.

An' zoo you didden come athirt,
To have zome fun last night: how wer't?
Vor we'd a-work'd wi' all our might
To scour the iron things up bright,
An' brush'd an' scrubb'd the house all drough;
An' brought in vor a brand, a plock
O' wood so big's an uppèn-stock,
An' hung a bough o' misseltoo,
An' ax'd a merry friend or two,
    To keepèn up o' Chris'mas.

An' there wer wold an' young; an' Bill,
Soon after dark, stalk'd up vrom mill.
An' when he wer a-comèn near,
He whissled loud vor me to hear;
Then roun' my head my frock I roll'd,
An' stood in orcha'd like a post,
To meäke en think I wer a ghost.
But he wer up to't, an' did scwold
To vind me stannèn in the cwold,
    A keepèn up o' Chris'mas.

We play'd at forfeits, an' we spun
The trencher roun', an' meäde such fun!
An' had a geäme o' dree-ceärd loo,
An' then begun to hunt the shoe.
An' all the wold vo'k zittèn near,
A-chattèn roun' the vier pleäce,
Did smile in woone another's feäce,

An' sheäke right hands wi' hearty cheer,
An' let their left hands spill their beer,
　A keepèn up o' Chris'mas.

ZITTEN OUT THE WOLD YEAR.

WHY, raïn or sheen, or blow or snow,
　I zaid, if I could stand so's,
I'd come, vor all a friend or foe,
　To sheäke ye by the hand, so's;
An' spend, wi' kinsvo'k near an' dear,
A happy evenèn, woonce a year,
　　　A-zot wi' me'th
　　　Avore the he'th
　To zee the new year in, so's.

There's Jim an' Tom, a-grown the size
　O' men, girt lusty chaps, so's,
An' Fanny wi' her sloo-black eyes,
　Her mother's very dap's, so's;
An' little Bill, so brown's a nut,
An' Poll a gigglèn little slut.
　　　I hope will shoot
　　　Another voot
　The year that's comèn in, so's.

An' there, upon his mother's knee,
　So peärt do look about, so's,
The little woone ov all, to zee
　His vu'st wold year goo out, so's
An' zoo mid God bless all o's still,
Gwaïn up or down along the hill,
　　　To meet in glee
　　　Ageän to zee
　A happy new year in, so's.

The wold clock's han' do softly steal
　　Up roun' the year's last hour, so's ;
Zoo let the han'-bells ring a peal,
　　Lik' them a-hung in tow'r, so's.
Here, here be two vor Tom, an' two
Vor Fanny, an' a peäir vor you ;
　　　We'll meäke em swing,
　　　An' meäke em ring,
The merry new year in, so's.

Tom, mind your time there ; you be wrong.
　　Come, let your bells all sound, so's :
A little clwoser, Poll ; ding, dong !
　　There, now 'tis right all round, so's.
The clock's a-strikèn twelve, d'ye hear?
Ting, ting, ding, dong ! Farewell, wold year !
　　　'Tis gone, 'tis gone !—
　　　Goo on, goo on,
An' ring the new woone in, so's !

WOAK WER GOOD ENOUGH WOONCE.

Ees : now mahogany's the goo,
An' good wold English woak won't do.
I wish vo'k always mid avvword
Hot meals upon a woakèn bwoard.
As good as thik that took my cup
An' trencher all my growèn up.
Ah ! I do mind en in the hall,
A-reachèn all along the wall,
Wi' us at father's end, while tother
Did teäke the maïdens wi' their mother ,
An' while the risèn steam did spread
In curlèn clouds up over head,
Our mouths did wag, an' tongues did run,
To meäke the maïdens laugh o' fun.

A woaken bedstead, black an' bright,
Did teäke my weary bwones at night,
Where I could stratch an' roll about
Wi' little fear o' vallèn out;
An' up above my head a peäir
Ov ugly heads a-carv'd did steäre,
An' grin avore a bright vull moon
A'most enough to frighten woone.
An' then we had, vor cwoats an' frocks,
Woak cwoffers wi' their rusty locks
An' neämes in naïls, a-left behind
By kinsvo'k dead an' out o' mind;
Zoo we did get on well enough
Wi' things a-meäde ov English stuff.
But then, you know, a woaken stick
Wer cheap, vor woaken trees wer thick.
When poor wold Gramfer Green wer young,
He zaid a squirrel mid a-sprung
Along the dell, vrom tree to tree,
Vrom Woodcomb all the way to Lea;
An' woak wer all vo'k did avvword,
Avore his time, vor bed or bwoard.

LULLABY.

The rook's nest do rock on the tree-top
Where vew foes can stand;
The martin's is high, an' is deep
In the steep cliff o' zand.
But thou, love, a-sleepèn where vootsteps
Mid come to thy bed,
Hast father an' mother to watch thee
An' shelter thy head.
   Lullaby, Lilybrow. Lie asleep;
  Blest be thy rest.

An' zome birds do keep under ruffèn
　　Their young vrom the storm,
An' zome wi' nest-hoodèns o' moss
　　And o' wool, do lie warm.
An' we wull look well to the houseruf
　　That o'er thee mid leäk,
An' the blast that mid beät on thy winder
　　Shall not smite thy cheäk.
　　　　Lullaby, Lilibrow.　Lie asleep ;
　　　　Blest be thy rest.

MEARY-ANN'S CHILD.

Meary-Ann wer alwone wi' her beäby in eärms,
　　In her house wi' the trees over head,
Vor her husban' wer out in the night an' the storms,
　　In his business a-tweilèn vor bread ;
An' she, as the wind in the elems did roar,
Did grievy vor Robert all night out o' door.

An' her kinsvo'k an' naï'bours did zay ov her chile,
　　(Under the high elem tree),
That a prettier never did babble or smile
　　Up o' top ov a proud mother's knee ;
An' his mother did toss en, an' kiss en, an' call
En her darlèn, an' life, an' her hope, an' her all.

But she vound in the evenèn the chile werden well,
　　(Under the dark elem tree),
An' she thought she could gi'e all the worold to tell,
　　Vor a truth what his aïlèn mid be ;
An' she thought o'en last in her praÿers at night,
An' she look'd at en last as she put out the light.

An' she vound en grow wo'se in the dead o' the night,
　　(Under the dark elem tree).

An' she press'd en ageän her warm bosom so tight,
   An' she rock'd en so sorrowfully;
An' there laid a-nestlèn the poor little bwoy,
Till his struggles grew weak, an' his cries died awoy.

An' the moon wer a-sheenèn down into the pleäce,
    (Under the dark elem tree),
An' his mother could zee that his lips an' his feäce
   Wer so white as cleän axen could be;
An' her tongue wer a-tied an' her still heart did zwell,
Till her senses come back wi' the vu'st tear that vell.

Never mwore can she veel his warm feäce in her breast,
    (Under the green elem tree),
Vor his eyes be a-shut, an' his hands be at rest,
   An' he's now vrom his païn a-zet free;
Vor his soul, we do know, is to heaven a-vled,
Where noo païn is a-known, an' noo tears be a-shed.

Eclogue.

FATHER COME HWOME.

John, Wife, an' Child.

CHILD.

O MOTHER, mother! be the teäties done?
Here's father now a-comèn down the track.
Hes got his nitch o' wood upon his back,
An' such a speäker in en! I'll be bound,
He's long enough to reach vrom ground
Up to the top ov ouer tun;
'Tis jist the very thing vor Jack an' I
To goo a-colepecksèn wi', by an' by.

WIFE.

The teäties must be ready pretty nigh;
Do teäke woone up upon the fork' an' try.
The ceäke upon the vier, too, 's a-burnèn,
I be afeärd: do run an' zee, an' turn en.

JOHN.

Well, mother! here I be woonce mwore, at hwome.

WIFE.

Ah! I be very glad you be a-come.
You be a-tired an' cwold enough, I s'pose;
Zit down an' rest your bwones, an' warm your nose.

JOHN.

Why I be nippy: what is there to eat?

WIFE.

Your supper's nearly ready. I've a got
Some teäties here a-doèn in the pot;
I wish wi' all my heart I had some meat.
I got a little ceäke too, here, a-beäken o'n
Upon the vier. 'Tis done by this time though.
He's nice an' moist; vor when I wer a-meäken o'n
I stuck some bits ov apple in the dough.

CHILD.

Well, father; what d'ye think? The pig got out
This mornèn; an' avore we zeed or heärd en,
He run about, an' got out into geärden,
An' routed up the groun' zoo wi' his snout!

JOHN.

Now only think o' that! You must contrive
To keep en in, or else he'll never thrive.

CHILD.

An' father, what d'ye think? I voun' to-day
The nest where thik wold hen ov our's do lay:
'Twer out in orcha'd hedge, an' had vive aggs.

WIFE.

Lo'k there: how wet you got your veet an' lags!
How did ye get in such a pickle, Jahn?

JOHN.

I broke my hoss, an' been a-fwo'ced to stan'
All's day in mud an' water vor to dig,
An' meäde myzelf so wetshod as a pig.

CHILD.

Father, teäke off your shoes, then come, and I
Will bring your wold woones vor ye, nice an' dry.

WIFE.

An' have ye got much hedgèn mwore to do?

JOHN.

Enough to last vor dree weeks mwore or zoo.

WIFE.

An' when y'ave done the job you be about,
D'ye think you'll have another vound ye out?

JOHN.

O ees, there'll be some mwore: vor after that,
I got a job o' trenchèn to goo at;
An' then zome trees to shroud, an' wood to vell,—
Zoo I do hope to rub on pretty well
Till zummer time; an' then I be to cut
The wood an' do the trenchèn by the tut.

CHILD.

An' nex' week, father, I'm a-gwaïn to goo
A-pickèn stwones, d'ye know, vor Farmer True.

WIFE.

An' little Jack, you know, 's a-gwaïn to eärn
A penny too, a-keepèn birds off corn.

JOHN.

O brave! What wages do 'e meän to gi'e?

WIFE.

She dreppence vor a day, an' twopence he.

JOHN.

Well, Polly; thou must work a little spracker
When thou bist out, or else thou wu'ten pick
A dungpot lwoad o' stwones up very quick.

CHILD.

Oh! yes I shall. But Jack do want a clacker:
An' father, wull ye teäke an' cut
A stick or two to meäke his hut.

JOHN.

You wench! why you be always up a-baggèn.
I be too tired now to-night, I'm sure,
   To zet a-doèn any mwore:
Zoo I shall goo up out o' the waÿ o' the waggon.

Eclogue.

A GHOST.

Jem an' Dick.

JEM.

This is a darkish evenèn; b'ye a-feärd
O' zights? Theäse leäne's a-haunted, I've a heärd.

DICK.

No, I be'nt much a-feär'd. If vo'k don't strive
To over-reach me while they be alive,
I don't much think the dead wull ha' the will
To come back here to do me any ill.
An' I've a-been about all night, d'ye know,
Vrom candle-lightèn till the cock did crow;
But never met wi' nothèn bad enough
To be much wo'se than what I be myzuf;
Though I, lik' others, have a-heärd vo'k zay
The girt house is a-haunted, night an' day.

JEM.

Aye; I do mind woone winter 'twer a-zaid
The farmer's vo'k could hardly sleep a-bed,
They heärd at night such scuffèns an' such jumpèns,
Such ugly naïses an' such rottlèn thumpèns.

DICK.

Aye, I do mind I heärd his son, young Sammy,
Tell how the chairs did dance an' doors did slammy;
He stood to it—though zome vo'k woulden heed en—
He didden only hear the ghost, but zeed en;
An', hang me! if I han't a'most a-shook,
To hear en tell what ugly sheäpes it took.
Did zometimes come vull six veet high, or higher,
In white, he zaid, wi' eyes lik' coals o' vier;
An' zometimes, wi' a feäce so peäle as milk,
A smileless leädy, all a-deck'd in silk.
His heäir, he zaid, did use to stand upright,
So stiff's a bunch o' rushes, wi' his fright.

JEM.

An' then you know that zome'hat is a-zeed
Down there in leäne, an' over in the meäd,
A-comèn zometimes lik' a slinkèn hound,
Or rollèn lik' a vleece along the ground.

An' woonce, when gramfer wi' his wold grey meäre
Wer ridèn down the leäne vrom Shroton feäir,
It roll'd so big's a pack ov wool across
The road just under en, an' leäm'd his hoss.

DICK.

Aye; did ye ever hear—vo'k zaid 'twer true—
O' what bevell Jack Hine zome years agoo?
Woone vrosty night, d'ye know, at Chris'mas tide,
Jack, an' another chap or two bezide,
'D a-been out, zomewhere up at tother end
O' parish, to a naïghbour's house to spend
A merry hour, an' mid a-took a cup
Or two o' eäle a-keepèn Chris'mas up;
Zoo I do lot 'twer leäte avore the peärty
'D a-burnt their bron out; I do lot, avore
They thought o' turnèn out o' door
'Twer mornèn, vor their friendship then wer hearty.
Well; clwose ageän the vootpath that do leäd
Vrom higher parish over withy-meäd,
There's still a hollow, you do know: they tried there,
In former times, to meäke a cattle-pit,
But gie'd it up, because they coulden get
The water any time to bide there.
Zoo when the merry fellows got
Just overright theäse lwonesome spot,
Jack zeed a girt big house-dog wi' a collar,
A-stannèn down in thik there hollor.
Lo'k there, he zaïd, there's zome girt dog a-prowlèn:
I'll just goo down an' gi'e'n a goodish lick
Or two wi' theäse here groun'-ash stick,
An' zend the shaggy rascal hwome a-howlèn.
Zoo there he run, an' gi'ed en a good whack
Wi' his girt ashen stick a-thirt his back;
An', all at woonce, his stick split right all down
In vower pieces; an' the pieces vled

Out ov his hand all up above his head,
An' pitch'd in vower corners o' the groun'.
An' then he velt his han' get all so num',
He coulden veel a vinger or a thum';
An' after that his eärm begun to zwell,
An' in the night a-bed he vound
  The skin o't peelèn off all round.
'Twer near a month avore he got it well.

JEM.

That wer vor hettèn ō'n. He should a let en
Alwone d'ye zee : 'twer wicked vor to het en.

SUNDRY PIECES.

A ZONG.

O JENNY, don't sobby! vor I shall be true;
Noo might under heaven shall peärt me vrom you.
My heart will be cwold, Jenny, when I do slight
The zwell o' thy bosom, thy eyes' sparklèn light.

My kinsvo'k would faïn zee me teäke vor my meäte
A maïd that ha' wealth, but a maïd I should heäte;
But I'd sooner leäbour wi' thee vor my bride,
Than live lik' a squier wi' any bezide.

Vor all busy kinsvo'k, my love will be still
A-zet upon thee lik' the vir in the hill;
An' though they mid worry, an' dreaten, an' mock,
My head's in the storm, but my root's in the rock.

Zoo, Jenny, don't sobby! vor I shall be true;
Noo might under heaven shall peärt me vrom you.
My heart will be cwold, Jenny, when I do slight
The zwell o' thy bosom, thy eyes' sparklèn light.

THE MAID VOR MY BRIDE.

Ah! don't tell o' maïdens! the woone vor my bride
Is little lik' too many maïdens bezide,—
Not brantèn, nor spitevul, nor wild; she've a mind
To think o' what's right, an' a heart to be kind.

She's straïght an' she's slender, but not over tall,
Wi' lim's that be lightsome, but not over small;
The goodness o' heaven do breathe in her feäce,
An' a queen, to be steätely, must walk wi' her peäce.

Her frocks be a-meäde all becomèn an' plaïn,
An' cleän as a blossom undimm'd by a staïn;
Her bonnet ha' got but two ribbons, a-tied
Up under her chin, or let down at the zide.

When she do speak to woone, she don't steäre an' grin;
There's sense in her looks, vrom her eyes to her chin,
An' her words be so kind, an' her speech is so meek,
As her eyes do look down a-beginnèn to speak.

Her skin is so white as a lily, an' each
Ov her cheäks is so downy an' red as a peach;
She's pretty a-zittèn; but oh! how my love
Do watch her to madness when woonce she do move.

An' when she do walk hwome vrom church drough the
    groun',
Wi' woone eärm in mine, an' wi' woone a-hung down,
I do think, an' do veel mwore o' sheäme than o' pride,
That do meäke me look ugly to walk by her zide.

Zoo don't talk o' maïden's! the woone vor my bride
Is but little lik' too many maïdens bezide,—
Not brantèn, nor spitevul, nor wild; she've a mind
To think o' what's right, an' a heart to be kind.

THE HWOMESTEAD.

If I had all the land my zight
   Can overlook vrom Chalwell hill,
Vrom Sherborn left to Blanvord right,
   Why I could be but happy still.
An' I be happy wi' my spot
O' freehold ground an' mossy cot,
An' shoulden get a better lot
   If I had all my will.

My orcha'd's wide, my trees be young;
   An' they do bear such heavy crops,
Their boughs, lik' onion-rwopes a-hung,
   Be all a-trigg'd to year, wi' props.
I got some geärden groun' to dig,
A parrock, an' a cow an' pig;
I got zome cider vor to swig,
   An' eäle o' malt an' hops.

I'm landlord o' my little farm,
   I'm king 'ithin my little pleäce;
I don't break laws, an' don't do harm,
   An' bent a-feär'd o' noo man's feäce.
When I'm a-cover'd wi' my thatch,
Noo man do deäre to lift my latch;
Where honest han's do shut the hatch,
   There fear do leäve the pleäce.

My lofty elem trees do screen
   My brown-ruf'd house, an' here below,
My geese do strut athirt the green,
   An' hiss an' flap their wings o' snow;
As I do walk along a rank
Ov apple trees, or by a bank,
Or zit upon a bar or plank,
   To see how things do grow.

THE FARMER'S WOLDEST DĀ'TER.

No, no! I ben't a-runnèn down
The pretty maïden's o' the town,
   Nor wishèn o'm noo harm;
But she that I would marry vu'st,
To sheäre my good luck or my crust,
   'S a-bred up at a farm.
In town, a maïd do zee mwore life,
   An' I don't under-reäte her;
But ten to woone the sprackest wife
   'S a farmer's woldest dā'ter.

Vor she do veed, wi' tender ceärc,
The little woones, an' peärt their heäir,
   An' keep em neat an' pirty;
An' keep the saucy little chaps
O' bwoys in trim wi' dreats an' slaps,
   When they be wild an' dirty.
Zoo if you'd have a bus'lèn wife,
   An' childern well look'd after,
The maïd to help ye all drough life
   'S a farmer's woldest dā'ter.

An' she can iorn up an' vwold
A book o' clothes wï' young or wold,
   An' zalt an' roll the butter;
An' meäke brown bread, an' elder wine,
An' zalt down meat in pans o' brine,
   An' do what you can put her.
Zoo if you've wherewi', an' would vind
   A wife wo'th lookèn ā'ter,
Goo an' get a farmer in the mind
   To gi'e ye his woldest dā'ter.

Her heart's so innocent an' kind,
She idden thoughtless, but do mind
   Her mother an' her duty;
An' livèn blushes, that do spread
Upon her healthy feäce o' red,
   Do heighten all her beauty;
So quick's a bird, so neat's a cat,
   So cheerful in her neätur,
The best o' maïdens to come at
   'S a farmer's woldest dā'ter.

UNCLE OUT O' DEBT AN' OUT O' DANGER.

Ees; uncle had thik small hwomestead,
The leäzes an' the bits o' mead,
Besides the orcha'd in his prime,
An' copse-wood vor the winter time.
His wold black meäre, that draw'd his cart,
An' he, wer seldom long apeärt;
Vor he work'd hard an' païd his woy,
An' zung so litsom as a bwoy,
   As he toss'd an' work'd,
   An' blow'd an' quirk'd,
"I'm out o' debt an' out o' danger,
   An' I can feäce a friend or stranger;
I've a vist vor friends, an' I'll vind a peäir
Vor the vu'st that do meddle wi' me or my meäre.

His meäre's long vlexy vetlocks grow'd
Down roun' her hoofs so black an' brode;
Her head hung low, her tail reach'd down
A-bobbèn nearly to the groun'.
The cwoat that uncle mwostly wore
Wer long behind an' straïght avore,

An' in his shoes he had girt buckles,
An' breeches button'd round his huckles;
   An' he zung wi' pride,
   By's wold meäre's zide,
"I'm out o' debt an' out o' danger,
An' I can feäce a friend or stranger;
I've a vist vor friends, an' I'll vind a peäir
Vor the vu'st that do meddle wi' me or my meare."

An' he would work,—an' lwoad, an' shoot,
An' spur his heaps o' dung or zoot;
Or car out hay, to sar his vew
Milch cows in corners dry an' lew;
Or dreve a zyve, or work a pick,
To pitch or meäke his little rick;
Or thatch en up wi' straw or zedge,
Or stop a shard, or gap, in hedge;
   An' he work'd an' flung
   His eärms, an' zung
"I'm out o' debt an' out o' danger,
An' I can feäce a friend or stranger;
I've a vist vor friends, an' I'll vind a peäir
Vor the vu'st that do meddle wi' me or my meare."

An' when his meäre an' he'd a-done
Their work, an' tired ev'ry bwone,
He zot avore the vire, to spend
His evenèn wi' his wife or friend;
An' wi' his lags out-stratch'd vor rest,
An' woone hand in his wes'coat breast,
While burnèn sticks did hiss an' crack,
An' fleämes did bleäzy up the back,
   There he zung so proud
   In a bakky cloud,
"I'm out o' debt an' out o' danger,
An' I can feäce a friend or stranger;

I've a vist vor friends, an' I'll vind a peäir
Vor the vu'st that do meddle wi' me or my meare."

  From market how he used to ride,
  Wi' pot's a-bumpèn by his zide
  Wi' things a-bought—but not vor trust,
  Vor what he had he païd vor vu'st;
  An' when he trotted up the yard,
  The calves did bleäry to be sar'd,
  An' pigs did scoat all drough the muck,
  An' geese did hiss, an' hens did cluck;
   An' he zung aloud,
   So pleased an' proud,
  " I'm out o' debt an' out o' danger,
  An' I can feäce a friend or stranger;
I've a vist vor friends, an' I'll vind a peair
Vor the vu'st that do meddle wi' me or my meare."

  When he wer joggèn hwome woone night
  Vrom market, after candle-light,
  (He mid a-took a drop o' beer,
  Or midden, vor he had noo fear,)
  Zome ugly, long-lagg'd, herrèn ribs,
  Jump'd out an' ax'd en vor his dibs;
  But he soon gi'ed en such a mawlèn,
  That there he left en down a-sprawlèn,
   While he jogg'd along
   Wi' his own wold zong,
  " I'm out o' debt an' out o' danger,
  An' I can feäce a friend or stranger;
I've a vist vor friends, an' I'll vind a peair
Vor the vu'st that do meddle wi' me or my meare."

THE CHURCH AN' HAPPY ZUNDAY.

Ah! ev'ry day mid bring a while
O' eäse vrom all woone's ceäre an' tweil,
The welcome evenèn, when 'tis sweet
Vor tired friends wi' weary veet,
But litsome hearts o' love, to meet:
An' yet while weekly times do roll,
The best vor body an' vor soul
  'S the church an' happy Zunday.

Vor then our loosen'd souls do rise
Wi' holy thoughts beyond the skies,
As we do think o' *Him* that shed
His blood vor us, an' still do spread
His love upon the live an' dead;
An' how He gi'ed a time an' pleäce
To gather us, an' gi'e us greäce,—
  The church an' happy Zunday.

There, under leänen mossy stwones,
Do lie, vorgot, our fathers' bwones,
That trod this groun' vor years agoo,
When things that now be wold wer new;
An' comely maïdens, mild an' true,
That meäde their sweet-hearts happy brides,
An' come to kneel down at their zides
  At church o' happy Zundays.

'Tis good to zee woone's naïghbours come
Out drough the churchyard, vlockèn hwome,
As woone do nod, an' woone do smile,
An' woone do toss another's chile;
An' zome be sheäken han's, the while
Poll's uncle, chuckèn her below
Her chin, do tell her she do grow,
  At church o' happy Zundays.

Zoo while our blood do run in vaïns
O' livèn souls in theäsum plains,
Mid happy housen smoky round
The church an' holy bit o' ground;
An' while their weddèn bells do sound,
Oh! mid em have the meäns o' greäce,
The holy day an' holy pleäce,
   The church an' happy Zunday.

THE WOLD WAGGON.

The girt wold waggon uncle had,
When I wer up a hardish lad,
Did stand, a-screen'd vrom het an' wet,
In zummer at the barken geäte,
Below the elems' spreädèn boughs,
A-rubb'd by all the pigs an' cows.
An' I've a-clom his head an' zides,
A-riggèn up or jumpèn down
A-playèn, or in happy rides
Along the leäne or drough the groun'.
An' many souls be in their greäves,
That rod' together on his reäves;
An' he, an' all the hosses too,
'V a-ben a-done vor years agoo.

Upon his head an' taïl wer pinks,
A-painted all in tangled links;
His two long zides wer blue,—his bed
Bent slightly upward at the head;
His reäves rose upward in a bow
Above the slow hind-wheels below.
Vour hosses wer a-kept to pull
The girt wold waggon when 'twer vull :
The black meäre *Smiler*, strong enough
To pull a house down by herzuf,

So big, as took my widest strides
To straddle halfway down her zides;
An' champèn *Vi'let*, sprack an' light,
That foam'd an' pull'd wi' all her might:
An' *Whitevoot*, leäzy in the treäce,
Wi' cunnèn looks an' show-white feäce;
Bezides a bay woone, short-taïl *Jack*,
That wer a treäce-hoss or a hack.

How many lwoads o' vuzz, to scald
The milk, thik waggon have a-haul'd!
An' wood vrom copse, an' poles vor raïls,
An' bavèns wi' their bushy taïls;
An' loose-ear'd barley, hangèn down
Outzide the wheels a'móst to groun',
An' lwoads o' hay so sweet an' dry,
A-builded straïght, an' long, an' high;
An' hay-meäkers, a-zittèn roun'
The reäves, a-ridèn hwome vrom groun',
When Jim gi'ed Jenny's lips a-smack,
An' jealous Dicky whipp'd his back,
An' maïdens scream'd to veel the thumps
A-gi'ed by trenches an' by humps.
But he, an' all his hosses too,
'V a-ben a-done vor years agoo.

THE DRÈVEN O' THE COMMON.*

In the common by our hwome
There wer freely-open room,
Vor our litty veet to roam
By the vuzzen out in bloom.
That wi' prickles kept our lags
Vrom the skylark's nest ov aggs;

---

* The Driving of the Common was by the *Hayward* who, whenever he thought fit, would drive all the cattle into a corner and impound all heads belonging to owners without a right of commonage for them, so that they had to ransom them by a fine.

While the peewit wheel'd around
Wi' his cry up over head,
Or he sped, though a-limpèn, o'er the ground.

There we heärd the whickr'èn meäre
Wi' her vaïce a-quiv'rèn high;
Where the cow did loudly bleäre
By the donkey's vallèn cry.
While a-stoopèn man did zwing
His bright hook at vuzz or ling
Free o' fear, wi' wellglov'd hands,
O' the prickly vuzz he vell'd,
Then sweet-smell'd as it died in faggot bands.

When the hayward drove the stock
In a herd to zome oone pleäce,
Thither vo'k begun to vlock,
Each to own his beästes feäce.
While the geese, bezide the stream,
Zent vrom gapèn bills a scream,
An' the cattle then avound,
Without right o' greäzen there,
Went to bleäre bray or whicker in the pound.

THE COMMON A-TOOK IN.

OH! no, Poll, no! Since they've a-took
The common in, our lew wold nook
Don't seem a-bit as used to look
   When we had runnèn room;
Girt banks do shut up ev'ry drong,
An' stratch wi' thorny backs along
Where we did use to run among
   The vuzzen an' the broom.

Ees ; while the ragged colts did crop
The nibbled grass, I used to hop
The emmet-buts, vrom top to top,
   So proud o' my spry jumps :
Wi' thee behind or at my zide,
A-skippèn on so light an' wide
'S thy little frock would let thee stride,
   Among the vuzzy humps.

Ah while the lark up over head
Did twitter, I did search the red
Thick bunch o' broom, or yollow bed
   O' vuzzen vor a nest ;
An' thou di'st hunt about, to meet
Wi' strawberries so red an' sweet,
Or clogs or shoes off hosses veet,
   Or wild thyme vor thy breast ;

Or when the cows did run about
A-stung, in zummer, by the stout,
Or when they play'd, or when they foüght,
   Di'st stand a-lookèn on :
An' where white geese, wi' long red bills,
Did veed among the emmet-hills,
There we did goo to vind their quills
   Alongzide o' the pon'.

What fun there wer among us, when
The hayward come, wi' all his men,
To drève the common, an' to pen
   Strange cattle in the pound ;
The cows did bleäre, the men did shout
An' toss their eärms an' sticks about,
An' vo'ks, to own their stock, come out
   Vrom all the housen round.

A WOLD FRIEND.

OH! when the friends we us'd to know,
   'V a-been a-lost vor years; an' when
Zome happy day do come, to show
   Their feäzen to our eyes ageän,
Do meäke us look behind, John,
Do bring wold times to mind, John,
   Do meäke hearts veel, if they be steel,
All warm, an' soft, an' kind, John.

When we do lose, still gay an' young,
   A vaïce that us'd to call woone's neäme,
An' after years ageän his tongue
   Do sound upon our ears the seäme,
Do kindle love anew, John,
Do wet woone's eyes wi' dew, John,
   As we do sheäke, vor friendship's seäke,
His vist an' vind en true, John.

What tender thoughts do touch woone's soul,
   When we do zee a meäd or hill
Where we did work, or play, or stroll,
   An' talk wi' vaices that be still;
'Tis tonchèn vor to treäce, John,
Wold times drough ev'ry pleäce, John;
   But that can't touch woone's heart so much,
As zome wold long-lost feäce, John.

THE RWOSE THAT DECK'D HER BREAST.

POOR Jenny wer her Robert's bride
Two happy years, an' then he died;
An' zoo the wold vo'k meäde her come,
Vorseäken, to her maiden hwome.

But Jenny's merry tongue wer dum';
  An' round her comely neck she wore
  A murnèn kerchif, where avore
    The rwose did deck her breast.

She walk'd alwone, wi' eye-balls wet,
To zee the flow'rs that she'd a-zet;
The lilies, white's her maïden frocks,
The spike, to put 'ithin her box,
Wi' columbines an' hollyhocks;
  The jilliflow'r an' noddèn pink,
  An' rwose that touch'd her soul to think
    Ov woone that deck'd her breast.

Vor at her weddèn, just avore
Her maïden hand had yet a-wore
A wife's goold ring, wi' hangèn head
She walk'd along thik flower-bed,
Where stocks did grow, a-staïned wi' red,
  An' meärygoolds did skirt the walk,
  An' gather'd vrom the rwose's stalk
    A bud to deck her breast.

An' then her cheäk, wi' youthvul blood
Wer bloomèn as the rwoses bud;
But now, as she wi' grief do pine,
'Tis peäle 's the milk-white jessamine.
But Robert have a-left behine
  A little beäby wi' his feäce,
  To smile, an' nessle in the pleäce
    Where the rwose did deck her breast.

NANNY'S COW.

Ov all the cows, among the rest
Wer woone that Nanny lik'd the best;
An' after milkèn us'd to stan'
A-veedèn o' her, vrom her han',
   Wi' grass or hay; an' she know'd Ann,
   An' in the evenèn she did come
    The vu'st, a-beätèn up roun' hwome
      Vor Ann to come an' milk her.

Her back wer hollor as a bow,
Her lags wer short, her body low;
Her head wer small, her horns turn'd in
Avore her feäce so sharp's a pin:
   Her eyes wer vull, her ears wer thin,
   An' she wer red vrom head to taïl,
    An' didden start nor kick the pail,
      When Nanny zot to milk her.

But losses zoon begun to vall
On Nanny's fàther, that wi' all
His tweil he voun', wi' breakèn heart,
That he mus' leäve his ground, an' peärt
   Wi' all his beäst an' hoss an' cart;
   An', what did touch en mwost, to zell
    The red cow Nanny lik'd so well,
      An' lik'd vor her to milk her.

Zalt tears did run vrom Nanny's eyes,
To hear her restless father's sighs.
But as vor me, she mid be sure
I wont vorzeäke her now she's poor,
Vor I do love her mwore. an' mwore;
   An' if I can but get a cow
   An' parrock, I'll vulvil my vow,
      An' she shall come an' milk her.

THE SHEP'ERD BWOY.

When the warm zummer breeze do blow over the hill,
   An' the vlock 's a-spread over the ground;
When the vaïce o' the busy wold sheep dog is still,
   An' the sheep-bells do tinkle all round;
   Where noo tree vor a sheäde but the thorn is a-vound,
      There, a zingèn a zong,
      Or a-whislèn among
The sheep, the young shep'erd do bide all day long.

When the storm do come up wi' a thundery cloud
   That do shut out the zunlight, an' high
Over head the wild thunder do rumble so loud,
   An' the lightnèn do flash vrom the sky,
   Where noo shelter's a-vound but his hut, that is nigh,
      There out ov all harm,
      In the dry an' the warm,
The poor little shep'erd do smile at the storm.

When the cwold winter win' do blow over the hill,
   An' the hore-vrost do whiten the grass,
An' the breath o' the no'th is so cwold, as to chill
   The warm blood ov woone's heart as do pass;
   When the ice o' the pond is so slipp'ry as glass,
      There, a-zingèn a zong,
      Or a-whislèn among
The sheep, the poor shep'erd do bide all day long.

When the shearèn's a-come, an' the shearers do pull
   In the sheep, hangèn back a-gwaïn in,
Wi' their roun' zides a-heavèn in under their wool,
   To come out all a-clipp'd to the skin;
   When the feästèn, an' zingèn, an fun do begin,
      Vor to help em, an' sheäre
      All their me'th an' good feäre,
The poor little shep'erd is sure to be there.

HOPE A-LEFT BEHIND.

Don't try to win a maïden's heart,
  To leäve her in her love,—'tis wrong:
'Tis bitter to her soul to peärt
  Wi' woone that is her sweetheart long.
  A maïd's vu'st love is always strong;
An' if do faïl, she'll linger on,
Wi' all her best o' pleasure gone,
  An' hope a-left behind her.

Thy poor lost Jenny wer a-grow'd
  So kind an' thoughtvul vor her years,
When she did meet wi' vo'k a-know'd
  The best, her love did speak in tears.
  She walk'd wi' thee, an' had noo fears
O' thy unkindness, till she zeed
Herzelf a-cast off lik' a weed,
  An' hope a-left behind her.

Thy slight turn'd peäle her cherry lip;
  Her sorrow, not a-zeed by eyes,
Wer lik' the mildew, that do nip
  A bud by darksome midnight skies.
  The day mid come, the zun mid rise,
But there's noo hope o' day nor zun;
The storm ha' blow'd, the harm's a-done,
  An' hope's a-left behind her.

The time will come when thou wouldst gi'e
  The worold vor to have her smile,
Or meet her by the parrock tree,
  Or catch her jumpèn off the stile;
  Thy life's avore thee vor a while,
But thou wilt turn thy mind in time,
An' zee the deèd as 'tis,—a crime,
  An' hope a-left behind thee.

Zoo never win a maïden's heart,
   But her's that is to be thy bride,
An' play drough life a manly peärt,
   An' if she's true when time ha' tried
     Her mind, then teäke her by thy zide.
True love will meäke thy hardships light,
True love will meäke the worold bright,
     When hope's a-left behind thee.

A GOOD FATHER.

No; mind thy father. When his tongue
   Is keen, he's still thy friend, John,
Vor wolder vo'k should warn the young
   How wickedness will end, John;
An' he do know a wicked youth
   Would be thy manhood's beäne,
An' zoo would bring thee back ageän
   'Ithin the ways o' truth.

An' mind en still when in the end
   His leäbour's all a-done, John,
An' let en vind a steadvast friend
   In thee his thoughtvul son, John;
Vor he did win what thou didst lack
   Avore couldst work or stand,
     An' zoo, when time do num' his hand,
       Then pay his leäbour back.

An' when his bwones be in the dust,
   Then honour still his neäme, John;
An' as his godly soul wer just,
   Let thine be voun' the seäme, John.
Be true, as he wer true, to men,
   An' love the laws o' God;
     Still tread the road that he've a-trod,
       An' live wi' him ageän.

THE BEAM IN GRENLEY CHURCH.

In church at Grenley woone mid zee
A beam vrom wall to wall; a tree
That's longer than the church is wide,
An' zoo woone end o'n's drough outside,—
Not cut off short, but bound all round
Wi' lead, to keep en seäfe an' sound.

Back when the builders vu'st begun
The church,—as still the teäle do run,—
A man work'd wi' em; no man knew
Who 'twer, nor whither he did goo.
He wer as harmless as a chile,
An' work'd 'ithout a frown or smile,
Till any woaths or strife did rise
To overcast his sparklèn eyes:

An' then he'd call their minds vrom strife,
To think upon another life.
He wer so strong, that all alwone
He lifted beams an' blocks o' stwone,
That others, with the girtest païns,
Could hardly wag wi' bars an' chaïns;
An' yet he never used to stay
O' Zaturdays, to teäke his pay.

Woone day the men wer out o' heart,
To have a beam a-cut too short;
An' in the evenèn, when they shut
Off work, they left en where 'twer put;
An' while dumb night went softly by
Towárds the vi'ry western sky,
A-lullèn birds, an' shuttèn up
The deäisy an' the butter cup,

They went to lay their heavy heads
An' weary bwones upon their beds.

An' when the dewy mornèn broke,
An' show'd the worold, fresh awoke,
Their godly work ageän, they vound
The beam they left upon the ground
A-put in pleäce, where still do bide,
An' long enough to reach outzide.
But he unknown to tother men
Wer never there at work ageän:
Zoo whether he mid be a man
Or angel, wi' a helpèn han',
Or whether all o't wer a dream,
They didden deäre to cut the beam.

THE VAÏCES THAT BE GONE.

WHEN evenèn sheädes o' trees do hide
A body by the hedge's zide,
An' twitt'rèn birds, wi' playsome flight,
Do vlee to roost at comèn night,
Then I do saunter out o' zight
   In orcha'd, where the pleäce woonce rung
   Wi' laughs a-laugh'd an' zongs a-zung
     By vaïces that be gone.

There's still the tree that bore our swing,
An' others where the birds did zing;
But long-leav'd docks do overgrow
The groun' we trampled beäre below,
Wi' merry skippèns to an' fro
   Bezide the banks, where Jim did zit
    A-playèn o' the clarinit
     To vaïces that be gone.

How mother, when we us'd to stun
Her head wi' all our naïsy fun,
Did wish us all a-gone vrom hwome:
An' now that zome be dead, an' zome
A-gone, an' all the pleäce is dum',
   How she do wish, wi' useless tears,
   To have ageän about her ears
      The vaïces that be gone.

Vor all the maïdens an' the bwoys
But I, be marri'd off all woys,
Or dead an' gone; but I do bide
At hwome, alwone, at mother's zide,
An' often, at the evenèn-tide,
   I still do saunter out, wi' tears,
   Down drough the orcha'd, where my ears
      Do miss the vaïces gone.

POLL.

When out below the trees, that drow'd
Their scraggy lim's athirt the road,
While evenèn zuns, a'móst a-zet,
Gi'ed goolden light, but little het,
The merry chaps an' maïdens met,
   An' look'd to zomebody to neäme
   Their bit o' fun, a dance or geäme,
      'Twer Poll they cluster'd round.

An' after they'd a-had enough
O' snappèn tongs, or blind-man's buff,
O' winter nights, an' went an' stood
Avore the vire o' bleäzen wood,
Though there wer maïdens kind an' good,
   Though there wer maïdens feäir an' tall,
   'Twer Poll that wer the queen o'm all,
      An' Poll they cluster'd round.

An' when the childern used to catch
A glimpse o' Poll avore the hatch,
The little things did run to meet
Their friend wi' skippèn tott'rèn veet.
An' thought noo other kiss so sweet
 As hers; an' nwone could vind em out
  Such geämes to meäke em jump an' shout,
   As Poll they cluster'd round.

An' now, since she've a-left em, all
The pleäce do miss her, girt an' small.
In vaïn vor them the zun do sheen
Upon the lwonesome rwoad an' green;
Their zwing do hang vorgot between
 The leänen trees, vor they've a-lost
  The best o' maïdens, to their cost,
   The maïd they cluster'd round.

LOOKS A-KNOW'D AVORE.

WHILE zome, a-gwaïn from pleäce to pleäce,
Do daily meet wi' zome new feäce,
When my day's work is at an end,
Let me zit down at hwome, an' spend
A happy hour wi' zome wold friend,
 An' by my own vire-zide rejaïce
  In zome wold naïghbour's welcome vaïce,
   An' looks I know'd avore, John.

Why is it, friends that we've a-met
By zuns that now ha' long a-zet,
Or winter vires that bleäzed for wold
An' young vo'k, now vor ever cwold,
Be met wi' jay that can't be twold?
 Why, 'tis because they friends have all
  Our youthvul spring ha' left our fall,—
   The looks we know'd avore, John.

'Tis lively at a feäir, among
The chattèn, laughèn, shiften drong,
When wold an' young, an' high an' low,
Do streamy round, an' to an' fro;
But what new feäce that we don't know,
 Can ever meäke woone's warm heart dance
  Among ten thousan', lik' a glance
   O' looks we know'd avore, John.

How of'en have the wind a-shook
The leaves off into yonder brook,
Since vu'st we two, in youthvul strolls,
Did ramble roun' them bubblèn shoals!
An' oh! that zome o' them young souls,
 That we, in jäy, did play wi' then
  Could come back now, an' bring ageän
   The looks we know'd avore, John.

So soon's the barley's dead an' down,
The clover-leaf do rise vrom groun',
An' wolder feäzen do but goo
To be a-vollow'd still by new;
But souls that be a-tried an' true
 Shall meet ageän beyond the skies,
  An' bring to woone another's eyes
   The looks they know'd avore, John.

THE MUSIC O' THE DEAD.

When music, in a heart that's true,
Do kindle up wold loves anew,
An' dim wet eyes, in feäirest lights,
Do zee but inward fancy's zights;
When creepèn years, wi' with'rèn blights,
 'V a-took off them that wer so dear,
  How touchèn 'tis if we do hear
   The tuèns o' the dead, John.

When I, a-stannèn in the lew
O' trees a storm's a-beätèn drough,
Do zee the slantèn mist a-drove
By spitevul winds along the grove,
An' hear their hollow sounds above
   My shelter'd head, do seem, as I
    Do think o' zunny days gone by,
     Lik' music vor the dead, John.

Last night, as I wer gwaïn along
The brook, I heärd the milk-maïd's zong
A-ringèn out so clear an' shrill
Along the meäds an' roun' the hill.
I catch'd the tuèn, an' stood still
   To hear 't ; 'twer woone that Jeäne did zing
    A-vield a-milkèn in the spring,—
     Sweet music o' the dead, John.

Don't tell o' zougs that be a-zung
By young chaps now, wi' sheämeless tongue:
Zing me wold ditties, that would start
The maïden's tears, or stir my heart
To teäke in life a manly peärt,—
   The wold vo'k's zongs that twold a teäle,
    An' vollow'd round their mugs o' eäle,
     The music o' the dead, John.

THE PLEÄCE A TEÄLE'S A-TWOLD O'.

Why tidden vields an' runnèn brooks,
  Nor trees in Spring or fall ;
An' tidden woody slopes an' nooks,
  Do touch us mwost ov all ;
An' tidden ivy that do cling
  By housen big an' wold, O,
But this is, after all, the thing,—
  The pleäce a teäle's a-twold o'.

At Burn, where mother's young friends know'd
  The vu'st her maïden neäme,
The zunny knaps, the narrow road
  An' green, be still the seäme;
The squier's house, an' ev'ry ground
  That now his son ha' zwold, O,
An' ev'ry wood he hunted round
  'S a pleäce a teäle's a-twold o'.

The maïd a-lov'd to our heart's core,
  The dearest of our kin,
Do meäke us like the very door
  Where they went out an' in.
'Tis zome'hat touchèn that bevel
  Poor flesh an' blood o' wold, O,
Do meäke us like to zee so well
  The pleäce a teäle's a-twold o'.

When blushèn Jenny vu'st did come
  To zee our Poll o' nights,
An' had to goo back leätish hwome,
  Where vo'k did zee the zights,
A-chattèn loud below the sky
  So dark, an' winds so cwold, O,
How proud wer I to zee her by
  The pleäce the teäle's a-twold o'.

Zoo whether 'tis the humpy ground
  That wer a battle viel',
Or mossy house, all ivy-bound,
  An' vallèn down piece-meal;
Or if 'tis but a scraggy tree,
  Where beauty smil'd o' wold, O,
How dearly I do like to zee
  The pleäce a teäle's a-twold o'.

AUNT'S TANTRUMS.

Why ees, aunt Anne's a little staïd,
But kind an' merry, poor wold maid!
If we don't cut her heart wi' slights,
She'll zit an' put our things to rights,
Upon a hard day's work, o' nights;
   But zet her up, she's jis' lik' vier,
   An' woe betide the woone that's nigh 'er.
     When she is in her tantrums.

She'll toss her head, a-steppèn out
Such strides, an' fling the pails about;
An' slam the doors as she do goo,
An' kick the cat out wi' her shoe,
Enough to het her off in two.
   The bwoys do bundle out o' house,
   A-lassen they should get a towse,
     When aunt is in her tantrums.

She whurr'd, woone day, the wooden bowl
In such a veag at my poor poll;
It brush'd the heäir above my crown,
An' whizz'd on down upon the groun',
An' knock'd the bantam cock right down;
   But up he sprung, a-teäkèn flight
   Wi' tothers, cluckèn in a fright,
     Vrom aunt in such a tantrum!

But Dick stole in, an' reach'd en down
The biggest blather to be voun',
An' crope an' put en out o' zight
Avore the vire, an' plimm'd en tight
An crack'd en wi' the slice thereright.
   She scream'd, an' bundled out o' house,
   An' got so quiet as a mouse,—
     It frighten'd off her tantrum.

THE STWONÈN PWORCH

A NEW house! Ees, indeed! a small
Straïght, upstart thing, that, after all,
Do teäke in only half the groun'
The wold woone did avore 'twer down;
Wi' little windows straïght an' flat,
Not big enough to zun a-cat,
An' dealèn door a-meäde so thin,
A puff o' wind would blow en in,
Where woone do vind a thing to knock
So small's the hammer ov a clock,
That wull but meäke a little click
About so loud's a clock do tick!
Gi'e me the wold house, wi' the wide
An' lofty-lo'ted rooms inside;
An' wi' the stwonèn pworch avore
The naïl-bestudded woaken door,
That had a knocker very little
Less to handle than a bittle,
That het a blow that vled so loud
Drough house as thunder drough a cloud,
An' meäde the dog behind the door
Growl out so deep's a bull do roar.

In all the house, o' young an' wold,
There werden woone but could a-twold
When he'd noo wish to seek abrode
Mwore jay than thik wold pworch bestow'd!
For there, when yollow evenèn shed
His light ageän the elem's head,
An' gnots did whiver in the zun,
An' uncle's work wer all a-done,
His whiffs o' meltèn smoke did roll
Above his bendèn pipe's white bowl,

While he did chat, or, zittèn dumb,
Injay his thoughts as they did come.

An' Jimmy, wi' his crowd below
His chin, did dreve his nimble bow
In tuèns vor to meäke us spring
A-reelèn, or in zongs to zing,
An' there, between the dark an' light,
Zot Poll by Willy's zide at night
A-whisp'rèn, while her eyes did zwim
In jay avore the twilight dim;
An' when (to know if she wer near)
Aunt call'd, did cry, "Ees, mother; here."

No, no; I woulden gi'e thee thanks
Vor fine white walls an' vloors o' planks,
Nor doors a-päinted up so fine.
If I'd a wold grey house o' mine,
Gi'e me vor all it should be small,
A stwonèn pworch instead ō't all.

FARMER'S SONS.

Ov all the chaps a-burnt so brown
   By zunny hills an' hollors,
Ov all the whindlèn chaps in town
   Wi' backs so weak as rollers,
There's narn that's half so light o' heart,
   (I'll bet, if thou't zay "done," min,)
An' narn that's half so strong an' smart,
   'S a merry farmer's son, min.

He'll fling a stwone so true's a shot,
   He'll jump so light's a cat;
He'll heave a waïght up that would squot
   A weakly fellow flat.

He wont gi'e up when things don't fay,
   But turn em into fun, min;
An' what's hard work to zome, is play
   Avore a farmer's son, min.

His bwony eärm an' knuckly vist
   ('Tis best to meäke a friend o't)
Would het a fellow, that's a-miss'd,
   Half backward wi' the wind o't.
Wi' such a chap at hand, a maïd
   Would never goo a nun, min;
She'd have noo call to be afraid
   Bezide a farmer's son, min.

He'll turn a vurrow, drough his langth,
   So straïght as eyes can look,
Or pitch all day, wi' half his strangth,
   At ev'ry pitch a pook;
An' then goo vower mile, or vive,
   To vind his friends in fun, min,
Vor maïden's be but dead alive
   'Ithout a farmer's son, min.

Zoo jay be in his heart so light,
   An' manly feäce so brown;
An' health goo wi' en hwome at night,
   Vrom meäd, or wood, or down.
O' rich an' poor, o' high an' low,
   When all's a-said an' done, min,
The smartest chap that I do know,
   'S a workèn farmer's son, min.

JEÄNE.

WE now mid hope vor better cheer,
My smilèn wife o' twice vive year.
Let others frown, if thou bist near
   Wi' hope upon thy brow, Jeäne;

Vor I vu'st lov'd thee when thy light
Young sheäpe vu'st grew to woman's height;
I loved thee near, an' out o' zight,
   An' I do love thee now, Jeäne.

An' we've a-trod the sheenèn bleäde
Ov eegrass in the zummer sheäde,
An' when the leäves begun to feäde
   Wi' zummer in the weäne, Jeäne;
An' we've a-wander'd drough the groun'
O' swayèn wheat a-turnèn brown,
An' we've a-stroll'd together roun'
   The brook an' drough the leäne, Jeane.

An' nwone but I can ever tell
Ov all thy tears that have a·vell
When trials meäde thy bosom zwell,
   An' nwone but thou o' mine, Jeäne;
An' now my heart, that heav'd wi' pride
Back then to have thee at my zide,
Do love thee mwore as years do slide,
   An' leäve them times behine, Jeäne.

THE DREE WOAKS.

By the brow o' thik hangèn I spent all my youth,
   In the house that did peep out between
The dree woaks, that in winter avworded their lewth,
   An' in zummer their sheäde to the green;
An' there, as in zummer we play'd at our geämes,
     We ēach own'd a tree,
     Vor we wer but dree,
An' zoo the dree woaks wer a-call'd by our neämes.

THE DREE WOAKS.

An' two did grow scraggy out over the road,
   An' they wer call'd Jimmy's an' mine;
An' tother wer Jeännet's, much kindlier grow'd,
   Wi' a knotless an' white ribbèd rine.
An' there, o' fine nights avore gwäin in to rest,
     We did dance, vull o' life,
     To the sound o' the fife,
Or play at some geäme that poor Jeännet lik'd best.

Zoo happy wer we by the woaks o' the green,
   Till we lost sister Jeännet, our pride;
Vor when she wer come to her last blushèn *teen*,
   She suddenly zicken'd an' died.
An' avore the green leaves in the fall wer gone by,
     The lightnèn struck dead
     Her woaken tree's head,
An' left en a-stripp'd to the wintery sky.

But woone ov his eäcorns, a-zet in the Fall,
   Come up the Spring after, below
The trees at her head-stwone 'ithin the church-wall,
   An' mother, to see how did grow,
Shed a tear; an' when father an' she wer bwoth dead.
     There they wer laid deep,
     Wi' their Jeännet, to sleep,
Wi' her at his zide, an' her tree at her head.

An' vo'k do still call the wold house the dree woaks,
   Vor thik is a-reckon'd that's down,
As mother, a-neämèn her childern to vo'ks,
   Meäde dree when but two wer a-voun';
An' zaid that hereafter she knew she should zee
     Why God, that's above,
     Vound fit in his love
To strike wi' his han' the poor maïd an' her tree.

THE HWOMESTEAD A-VELL INTO HAND.

The house where I wer born an' bred,
　　Did own his woaken door, John,
When vu'st he shelter'd father's head,
　　An' gramfer's long avore, John.
An' many a ramblèn happy chile,
　　An' chap so strong an' bwold,
An' bloomèn maïd wi' playsome smile,
　　Did call their hwome o' wold
　　　　Thik ruf so warm,
　　　　A kept vrom harm
By elem trees that broke the storm.

An' in the orcha'd out behind,
　　The apple-trees in row, John,
Did sway wi' moss about their rind
　　Their heads a-noddèn low, John.
An' there, bezide zome groun' vor corn,
　　Two strips did skirt the road;
In woone the cow did toss her horn,
　　While tother wer a-mow'd,
　　　　In June, below
　　　　The lofty row
Ov trees that in the hedge did grow.

A-workèn in our little patch
　　O' parrock, rathe or leäte, John,
We little ho'd how vur mid stratch
　　The squier's wide esteäte, John.
Our hearts, so honest an' so true,
　　Had little vor to fear;
Vor we could pay up all their due,
　　An' gi'e a friend good cheer
　　　　At hwome, below
　　　　The lofty row
O' trees a-swayèn to an' fro.

An' there in het, an' there in wet,
   We tweil'd wi' busy hands, John;
Vor ev'ry stroke o' work we het,
   Did better our own lands, John.
But after me, ov all my kin,
   Not woone can hold em on;
Vor we can't get a life put in
   Vor mine, when I'm a-gone
      Vrom thik wold brown
      Thatch ruf, a-boun'
By elem trees a-growèn roun'.

Ov eight good hwomes, where, I can mind
   Vo'k liv'd upon their land, John,
But dree be now a-left behind;
   The rest ha' vell in hand, John,
An' all the happy souls they ved
   Be scatter'd vur an' wide.
An' zome o'm be a-wantèn bread,
   Zome, better off, ha' died,
      Noo mwore to ho,
      Vor homes below
The trees a-swayen to an' fro.

An' I could lead ye now all round
   The parish, if I would, John,
An' show ye still the very ground
   Where vive good housen stood, John.
In broken orcha'ds near the spot,
   A vew wold trees do stand;
But dew do vall where vo'k woonce zot
   About the burnèn brand
      In housen warm,
      A-kept vrom harm
By elems that did break the storm.

THE GUIDE POST.

Why thik wold post so long kept out,
Upon the knap, his eärms astrout,
A-zendèn on the weary veet
By where the dree cross roads do meet;
An' I've a-come so much thik woy,
Wi' happy heart, a man or bwoy,
That I'd a-meäde, at last, a'móst
A friend o' thik wold guidèn post.

An' there, wi' woone white eärm he show'd,
Down over bridge, the Leyton road;
Wi' woone, the leäne a-leädèn roun'
By Bradlinch Hill, an' on to town;
An' wi' the last, the way to turn
Drough common down to Rushiburn,—
The road I lik'd to goo the mwost
Ov all upon the guidèn post.

The Leyton road ha' lofty ranks
Ov elem trees upon his banks;
The woone athirt the hill do show
Us miles o' hedgy meäds below;
An' he to Rushiburn is wide
Wi' strips o' green along his zide,
An' ouer brown-ruf'd house a-móst
In zight o' thik wold guidèn post.

An' when the hay-meäkers did zwarm
O' zummer evenèns out vrom farm,
The merry maïdens an' the chaps,
A-peärtèn there wi' jokes an' slaps,

Did goo, zome woone way off, an' zome
Another, all a-zingèn hwome;
Vor vew o'm had to goo, at mwost,
A mile beyond the guidèn post.

Poor Nanny Brown, woone darkish night,
When he'd a-been a-païnted white,
Wer frighten'd, near the gravel pits,
So dead's a hammer into fits,
A-thinkèn 'twer the ghost she know'd
Did come an' haunt the Leyton road;
Though, after all, poor Nanny's ghost
Turn'd out to be the guidèn post.

GWAIN TO FEÄIR.

To morrow stir so brisk's you can,
An' get your work up under han';
Vor I an' Jim, an' Poll's young man,
   Shall goo to feäir; an' zoo,
If you wull let us gi'e ye a eärm
Along the road, or in the zwarm
O' vo'k, we'll keep ye out o' harm,
   An' gi'e ye a feäirèn too.

We won't stay leäte there, I'll be boun';
We'll bring our sheädes off out o' town
A mile, avore the zun is down,
   If he's a sheenèn clear.
Zoo when your work is all a-done,
Your mother can't but let ye run
An' zee a little o' the fun,
   There's nothèn there to fear.

JEÄNE O' GRENLEY MILL.

When in happy times we met,
   Then by look an' deed I show'd,
How my love wer all a-zet
   In the smiles that she bestow'd.
She mid have, o' left an' right,
Maïdens feäirest to the zight;
I'd a-chose among em still,
Pretty Jeäne o' Grenley Mill.

She wer feäirer, by her cows
   In her work-day frock a-drest,
Than the rest wi' scornvul brows
   All a-flantèn in their best.
Gaÿ did seem, at feäst or feäir,
Zights that I had her to sheäre;
Gaÿ would be my own heart still,
But vor Jeäne o' Grenley Mill.

Jeäne—a-checkèn ov her love—
   Leän'd to woone that, as she guess'd,
Stood in worldly wealth above
   Me she know'd she lik'd the best.
He wer wild, an' soon run drough
All that he'd a-come into,
Heartlessly a-treatèn ill
Pretty Jeäne o' Grenley Mill.

Oh! poor Jenny! thou'st a-tore
   Hopèn love vrom my poor heart,
Losèn vrom thy own small store,
   All the better, sweeter peärt.
Hearts a-slighted must vorseäke
Slighters, though a-doom'd to break;
I must scorn, but love thee still,
Pretty Jeäne o' Grenley Mill.

Oh! if ever thy soft eyes
  Could ha' turn'd vrom outward show,
To a lover born to rise
  When a higher woone wer low;
If thy love, when zoo a-tried,
Could ha' stood ageän thy pride,
How should I ha' lov'd thee still,
Pretty Jeäne o' Grenley Mill.

THE BELLS OV ALDERBURNHAM.

WHILE now upon the win' do zwell
  The church-bells' evenèn peal, O,
Along the bottom, who can tell
  How touch'd my heart do veel, O.
To hear ageän, as woonce they rung
In holidays when I wer young,
    Wi' merry sound
    A-ringèn round,
  The bells ov Alderburnham.

Vor when they rung their gaÿest peals
  O' zome sweet day o' rest, O,
We all did ramble drough the viels,
  A-dress'd in all our best, O;
An' at the bridge or roarèn weir,
Or in the wood, or in the gleäre
    Ov open ground,
    Did hear ring round
  The bells ov Alderburnham.

They bells, that now do ring above
  The young brides at church-door, O,
Woonce rung to bless their mother's love,
  When they were brides avore, O.

An' sons in tow'r do still ring on
The merry peals o' fathers gone,
  Noo mwore to sound,
  Or hear ring round,
 The bells ov Alderburnham.

Ov happy peäirs, how soon be zome
 A-wedded an' a-peärted!
Vor woone ov jay, what peals mid come
 To zome o's broken-hearted!
The stronger mid the sooner die,
The gayer mid the sooner sigh;
  An' who do know
  What grief's below
 The bells ov Alderburnham!

But still 'tis happiness to know
 That there's a God above us;
An' he, by day an' night, do ho
 Vor all ov us, an' love us,
An' call us to His house, to heal
Our hearts, by his own Zunday peal
  Ov bells a-rung
  Vor wold an' young,
 The bells ov Alderburnham.

THE GIRT WOLD HOUSE O' MOSSY STWONE.

The girt wold house o' mossy stwone,
Up there upon the knap alwone,
Had woonce a bleäzèn kitchèn-vier,
That cook'd vor poor-vo'k an' a squier.
The very last ov all the reäce
That liv'd the squier o' the pleäce,
Died off when father wer a-born,
An' now his kin be all vorlorn

Vor ever,—vor he left noo son
To teäke the house o' mossy stwone.
An' zoo he vell to other hands,
An' gramfer took en wi' the lands :
An' there when he, poor man, wer dead,
My father shelter'd my young head.
An' if I wer a squier, I
Should like to spend my life, an' die
In thik wold house o' mossy stwone,
Up there upon the knap alwone.

Don't talk ov housen all o' brick,
Wi' rockèn walls nine inches thick,
A-trigg'd together zide by zide
In streets, wi' fronts a straddle wide,
Wi' yards a-sprinkled wi' a mop,
Too little vor a vrog to hop ;
But let me live an' die where I
Can zee the ground, an' trees, an' sky.
The girt wold house o' mossy stwone
Had wings vor either sheäde or zun :
Woone where the zun did glitter drough,
When vu'st he struck the mornèn dew ;
Woone feäced the evenèn sky, an' woone
Push'd out a pworch to zweaty noon :
Zoo woone stood out to break the storm,
An' meäde another lew an' warm.
An' there the timber'd copse rose high,
Where birds did build an' heäres did lie,
An' beds o' grægles in the lew,
Did deck in May the ground wi' blue.
An' there wer hills an' slopèn grounds,
That they did ride about wi' hounds ;
An' drough the meäd did creep the brook
Wi' bushy bank an' rushy nook,

Where perch did lie in sheädy holes
Below the alder trees, an' shoals
O' gudgeon darted by, to hide
Theirzelves in hollows by the zide.
An' there by leänes a-windèn deep,
Wer mossy banks a-risèn steep;
An' stwonèn steps, so smooth an' wide,
To stiles an' vootpaths at the zide.
An' there, so big's a little ground,
The geärden wer a-wall'd all round:
An' up upon the wall wer bars
A-sheäped all out in wheels an' stars,
Vor vo'k to walk, an' look out drough
Vrom trees o' green to hills o' blue.
An' there wer walks o' peävement, broad
Enough to meäke a carriage-road,
Where steätely leädies woonce did use
To walk wi' hoops an' high-heel shoes,
When yonder hollow woak wer sound,
Avore the walls wer ivy-bound,
Avore the elems met above
The road between em, where they drove
Their coach all up or down the road
A-comèn hwome or gwaïn abroad.
The zummer aïr o' theäse green hill
'V a-heav'd in bosoms now all still,
An' all their hopes an' all their tears
Be unknown things ov other years.
But if, in heaven, souls be free
To come back here; or there can be
An e'thly pleäce to meäke em come
To zee it vrom a better hwome,—
Then what's a-twold us mid be right,
That still, at dead o' tongueless night,
Their gauzy sheäpes do come an' glide
By vootways o' their youthvul pride,

An' while the trees do stan' that grow'd
Vor them, or walls or steps they know'd
Do bide in pleäce, they'll always come
To look upon their e'thly hwome.
Zoo I would always let alwone
The girt wold house o' mossy stwone
I woulden pull a wing o'n down,
To meäke ther speechless sheädes to frown;
Vor when our souls, mid woonce become
Lik' their's, all bodiless an' dumb,
How good to think that we mid vind
Zome thought vrom them we left behind,
An' that zome love mid still unite
The hearts o' blood wi' souls o' light.
Zoo, if 'twer mine, I'd let alwone
The girt wold house o' mossy stwone.

A WITCH.

There's thik wold hag, Moll Brown, look zee, jus' past!
I wish the ugly sly wold witch
Would tumble over into ditch;
I woulden pull her out not very vast.
No, no. I don't think she's a bit belied,
No, she's a witch, aye, Molly's evil-eyed.
Vor I do know o' many a-withrèn blight
A-cast on vo'k by Molly's mutter'd spite;
She did, woone time, a dreadvul deäl o' harm
To Farmer Gruff's vo'k, down at Lower Farm.
Vor there, woone day, they happened to offend her,
An' not a little to their sorrow,
Because they woulden gi'e or lend her
Zome'hat she come to bag or borrow;
An' zoo, they soon began to vind
That she'd agone an' left behind

Her evil wish that had such pow'r,
That she did meäke their milk an' eäle turn zour,
An' addle all the aggs their vowls did lay;
They coulden vetch the butter in the churn,
An' all the cheese begun to turn
All back ageän to curds an' whey;
The little pigs, a-runnèn wi' the zow,
Did zicken, zomehow, noobody know'd how,
An' vall, an' turn their snouts towärd the sky.
An' only gi'e woone little grunt, and die;
An' all the little ducks an' chickèn
Wer death-struck out in yard a-pickèn
Their bits o' food, an' vell upon their head,
An' flapp'd their little wings an' drapp'd down dead.
They coulden fat the calves, they woulden thrive;
They coulden seäve their lambs alive;
Their sheep wer all a-coath'd, or gi'ed noo wool;
The hosses vell away to skin an' bwones,
An' got so weak they coulden pull
A half a peck o' stwones:
The dog got dead-alive an' drowsy,
The cat vell zick an' woulden mousy;
An' every time the vo'k went up to bed,
They wer a-hag-rod till they wer half dead.
They us'd to keep her out o' house, 'tis true,
A-naïlèn up at door a hosses shoe;
An' I've a-heärd the farmer's wife did try
To dawk a needle or a pin
In drough her wold hard wither'd skin,
An' draw her blood, a-comèn by:
But she could never vetch a drap,
For pins would ply an' needless snap
Ageän her skin; an' that, in coo'se,
Did meäke the hag bewitch em woo'se.

Eclogue.

THE TIMES.

John an' Tom.

JOHN.

Well, Tom, how be'st? Zoo thou'st a-got thy neäme
Among the leaguers, then, as I've a heärd.

TOM.

Aye, John, I have, John; an' I ben't afeärd
To own it. Why, who woulden do the seäme?
We shant goo on lik' this long, I can tell ye.
Bread is so high an' wages be so low,
That, after workèn lik' a hoss, you know,
A man can't eärn enough to vill his belly.

JOHN.

Ah! well! Now there, d'ye know, if I wer sure
That theäsem men would gi'e me work to do
All drough the year, an' always pay me mwore
Than I'm a-eärnèn now, I'd jein em too.
If I wer sure they'd bring down things so cheap,
That what mid buy a pound o' mutton now
Would buy the hinder quarters, or the sheep,
Or what wull buy a pig would buy a cow:
In short, if they could meäke a shillèn goo
In market just so vur as two,
Why then, d'ye know, I'd be their man;
But, hang it! I don't think they can.

TOM.

Why ees they can, though you don't know't,
An' theäsem men can meäke it clear.
Why vu'st they'd zend up members ev'ry year
To Parli'ment, an' ev'ry man would vote;
Vor if a fellow midden be a squier,
He mid be just so fit to vote, an' goo
To meäke the laws at Lon'on, too,
As many that do hold their noses higher.
Why shoulden fellows meäke good laws an' speeches
A-dressed in fusti'n cwoats an' cord'roy breeches?
Or why should hooks an' shovels, zives an' axes,
Keep any man vrom votèn o' the taxes?
An' when the poor've a-got a sheäre
In meäkèn laws, they'll teäke good ceäre
To meäke some good woones vor the poor.
Do stan' by reason, John; because
The men that be to meäke the laws,
Will meäke em vor theirzelves, you mid be sure.

JOHN.

Ees, that they wull. The men that you mid trust
To help you, Tom, would help their own zelves vu'st.

TOM.

Aye, aye. But we would have a better plan
O' votèn, than the woone we got. A man,
As things be now, d'ye know, can't goo an' vote
Ageän another man, but he must know't.
We'll have a box an' balls, vor votèn men
To pop their hands 'ithin, d'ye know; an' then,
If woone don't happen vor to lik' a man,
He'll drop a little black ball vrom his han',
An' zend en hwome ageän. He woon't be led
To choose a man to teäke away his bread.

JOHN.

But if a man you midden like to 'front,
Should chance to call upon ye, Tom, zome day,
An' ax ye vor your vote, what could ye zay?
Why if you woulden answer, or should grunt
Or bark, he'd know you'd meän "I won't."
To promise woone a vote an' not to gi'e't,
Is but to be a liar an' a cheat.
An' then, bezides, when he did count the balls,
An' vind white promises a-turn'd half black;
Why then he'd think the voters all a pack
O' rogues together,—ev'ry woone o'm false.
An' if he had the power, very soon
Perhaps he'd vall upon em, ev'ry woone.
The times be pinchèn me, so well as you,
But I can't tell what ever they can do.

TOM.

Why meäke the farmers gi'e their leäbourèn men
Mwore wages,—half or twice so much ageän
As what they got.

JOHN.

But, Thomas, you can't meäke
A man pay mwore away than he can teäke.
If you do meäke en gi'e, to till a vield,
So much ageän as what the groun' do yield,
He'll shut out farmèn—or he'll be a goose—
An' goo an' put his money out to use.
Wages be low because the hands be plenty;
They mid be higher if the hands wer skenty.
Leäbour, the seäme's the produce o' the vield,
Do zell at market price—jist what 'till yield.
Thou wouldsten gi'e a zixpence, I do guess,
Vor zix fresh aggs, if zix did zell for less.

If theäsem vo'k could come an' meäke mwore lands,
If they could teäke wold England in their hands
An' stratch it out jist twice so big ageän,
They'd be a-doèn some'hat vor us then.

TOM.

But if they wer a-zent to Parli'ment
To meäke the laws, dost know, as I've a-zaid,
They'd knock the corn-laws on the head;
An' then the landlards must let down their rent,
An' we should very soon have cheaper bread:
Farmers would gi'e less money vor their lands.

JOHN.

Aye, zoo they mid, an' prices mid be low'r
Vor what their land would yield; an' zoo their hands
Would be jist where they wer avore.
An' if theäse men wer all to hold together,
They coulden meäke new laws to change the weather!
They ben't so mighty as to think o' frightenèn
The vrost an' raïn, the thunder an' the lightenèn!
An' as vor me, I don't know what to think
O' them there fine, big-talkèn, cunnèn,
Strange men, a-comèn down vrom Lon'on.
Why they don't stint theirzelves, but eat an' drink
The best at public-house where they do stay;
They don't work gratis, they do get their pay.
They woulden pinch theirzelves to do us good,
Nor gi'e their money vor to buy us food.
D'ye think, if we should meet em in the street
Zome day in Lon'on, they would stand a treat?

TOM.

They be a-païd, because they be a-zent
By corn-law vo'k that be the poor man's friends,
To tell us all how we mid gaïn our ends,
A-zeudèn peäpers up to Parli'ment.

JOHN.

Ah ! teäke ceäre how dost trust em.   Dost thou know
The funny feäble o' the pig an' crow?
Woone time a crow begun to strut an' hop
About some groun' that men'd a-been a-drillèn
Wi' barley or some wheat, in hopes o' villèn
Wi' good fresh corn his empty crop.
But lik' a thief, he didden like the païns
O' workèn hard to get en a vew graïns ;
Zoo while the sleeky rogue wer there a-huntèn,
Wi' little luck, vor corns that mid be vound
A-peckèn vor, he heärd a pig a-gruntèn
Just tother zide o' hedge, in tother ground.
" Ah ! " thought the cunnèn rogue, an' gi'ed a hop,
" Ah ! that's the way vor me to vill my crop ;
Aye, that's the plan, if nothèn don't defeät it.
If I can get thik pig to bring his snout
In here a bit an' turn the barley out,
Why, hang it ! I shall only have to eat it."
Wi' that he vled up straïght upon a woak,
An' bowèn, lik' a man at hustèns, spoke :
" My friend," zaid he, " that's poorish livèn vor ye
In thik there leäze.   Why I be very zorry
To zee how they hard-hearted vo'k do sarve ye.
You can't live there.   Why ! do they meän to starve ye?"
" Ees," zaid the pig, a-gruntèn, " ees ;
What wi' the hosses an' the geese,
There's only docks an' thissles here to chaw.
Instead o' livèn well on good warm straw,
I got to grub out here, where I can't pick
Enough to meäke me half an ounce o' flick."
" Well," zaid the crow, " d'ye know, if you'll stan' that,
You mussen think, my friend, o' gettèn fat.
D'ye want some better keep?   Vor if you do,
Why, as a friend, I be a-come to tell ye,

That if you'll come an' jus' get drough
Theäse gap up here, why you mid vill your belly.
Why, they've a-been a-drillèn corn, d'ye know,
In theäse here piece o' groun' below;
An' if you'll just put in your snout,
An' run en up along a drill,
Why, hang it! you mid grub it out,
An' eat, an' eat your vill.
Their idden any fear that vo'k mid come,
Vor all the men be jist a-gone in hwome."
The pig, believèn ev'ry single word
That wer a-twold en by the cunnèn bird
Wer only vor his good, an' that 'twer true,
Just gi'ed a grunt, an' bundled drough,
An' het his nose, wi' all his might an' maïn,
Right up a drill, a-routèn up the graïn;
An' as the cunnèn crow did gi'e a caw
A-praisèn ō'n, oh! he did veel so proud!
An' work'd, an' blow'd, an' toss'd, an' ploughed
The while the cunnèn crow did vill his maw.
An' after workèn till his bwones
Did eäche, he soon begun to veel
That he should never get a meal,
Unless he dined on dirt an' stwones.
"Well," zaid the crow, "why don't ye eat?"
"Eat what, I wonder!" zaid the heäiry plougher,
A-brislèn up an' lookèn rather zour;
"I don't think dirt an' flints be any treat."
"Well," zaid the crow, "why you be blind.
What! don't ye zee how thick the corn do lie
Among the dirt? An' don't ye zee how I
Do pick up all that you do leäve behind?
I'm zorry that your bill should be so snubby."
"No," zaid the pig, "methinks that I do zee
My bill will do uncommon well vor thee,
Vor thine wull peck, an' mine wull grubby."

An' just wi' this a-zaid by mister Flick
To mister Crow, wold John the farmer's man
Come up, a-zwingèn in his han'
A good long knotty stick,
An' laid it on, wi' all his might,
The poor pig's vlitches, left an' right;
While mister Crow, that talk'd so fine
O' friendship, left the pig behine,
An' vled away upon a distant tree,
Vor pigs can only grub, but crows can vlee.

TOM.

Aye, thik there teäle mid do vor childern's books;
But you wull vind it hardish for ye
To frighten me, John, wi' a storry
O' silly pigs an' cunnèn rooks.
If we be grubbèn pigs, why then, I s'pose,
The farmers an' the girt woones be the crows.

JOHN.

'Tis very odd there idden any friend
To poor-vo'k hereabout, but men mus' come
To do us good away from tother end
Ov England! Han't we any frien's near hwome?
I mus' zay, Thomas, that 'tis rather odd
That strangers should become so very civil,—
That ouer vo'k be childern o' the Devil,
An' other vo'k be all the vo'k o' God!
If we've a-got a friend at all,
Why who can tell—I'm sure thou cassen—
But that the squier, or the pa'son,
Mid be our friend, Tom, after all?
The times be hard, 'tis true! an' they that got
His blessèns, shoulden let theirzelves vorget
How 'tis where the vo'k do never zet
A bit o' meat within their rusty pot.

The man a-zittèn in his easy chair
To flesh, an' vowl, an' vish, should try to speäre
The poor theäse times, a little vrom his store;
An' if he don't, why sin is at his door.

TOM.

Ah! we won't look to that; we'll have our right,—
If not by feäir meäns, then we wull by might.
We'll meäke times better vor us; we'll be free
Ov other vo'k an' others' charity.

JOHN.

Ah! I do think you mid as well be quiet;
You'll meäke things wo'se, i'-ma'-be, by a riot.
You'll get into a mess, Tom, I'm afeärd;
You'll goo vor wool, an' then come hwome a-sheär'd.

POEMS OF RURAL LIFE.

SECOND COLLECTION.

BLACKMWORE MAIDENS.

The primrwose in the sheäde do blow,
The cowslip in the zun,
The thyme upon the down do grow,
The clote where streams do run;
An' where do pretty maïdens grow
An' blow, but where the tow'r
Do rise among the bricken tuns,
In Blackmwore by the Stour.

If you could zee their comely gaït,
An' pretty feäces' smiles,
A-trippèn on so light o' waïght,
An' steppèn off the stiles;
A-gwaïn to church, as bells do swing
An' ring 'ithin the tow'r,
You'd own the pretty maïdens' pleäce
Is Blackmwore by the Stour.

If you vrom Wimborne took your road,
To Stower or Paladore,
An' all the farmers' housen show'd
Their daughters at the door;
You'd cry to bachelors at hwome—
" Here, come : 'ithin an hour
You'll vind ten maïdens to your mind,
In Blackmwore by the Stour."

An' if you look'd 'ithin their door,
To zee em in their pleäce,

A-doèn housework up avore
Their smilèn mother's feäce;
You'd cry—" Why, if a man would wive
An' thrive, 'ithout a dow'r,
Then let en look en out a wife
In Blackmwore by the Stour."

As I upon my road did pass
A school-house back in May,
There out upon the beäten grass
Wer maïdens at their play;
An' as the pretty souls did tweil
An' smile, I cried, " The flow'r
O' beauty, then, is still in bud
In Blackmwore by the Stour."

MY ORCHA'D IN LINDEN LEA.

'Ithin the woodlands, flow'ry gleäded,
  By the woak tree's mossy moot,
The sheenèn grass-bleädes, timber-sheäded,
  Now do quiver under voot;
An' birds do whissle over head,
An' water's bubblèn in its bed,
An' there vor me the apple tree
Do leän down low in Linden Lea.

When leaves that leätely wer a-springèn
  Now do feäde 'ithin the copse,
An' païnted birds do hush their zingèn
  Up upon the timber's tops;
An' brown-leav'd fruit's a-turnèn red,
In cloudless zunsheen, over head,
Wi' fruit vor me, the apple tree
Do leän down low in Linden Lea.

Let other vo'k meäke money vaster
   In the aïr o' dark-room'd towns,
I don't dread a peevish meäster;
   Though noo man do heed my frowns,
I be free to goo abrode,
Or teäke ageän my hwomeward road
To where, vor me, the apple tree
Do leän down low in Linden Lea.

BISHOP'S CAUNDLE.

At peace day, who but we should goo
To Caundle vor an' hour or two
As gaÿ a day as ever broke
Above the heads o' Caundle vo'k,
Vor peace, a-come vor all, did come
To them wi' two new friends at hwome.
Zoo while we kept, wi' nimble peäce,
The wold dun tow'r avore our feäce,
The aïr, at last, begun to come
Wi' drubbèns ov a beäten drum;
An' then we heärd the horns' loud droats
Plaÿ off a tuen's upper notes;
An' then ageän a-risèn cheärm
Vrom tongues o' people in a zwarm·
An' zoo, at last, we stood among
The merry feäces o' the drong.
An' there, wi' garlands all a-tied
In wreaths an' bows on every zide,
An' color'd flags, a fluttrèn high
An' bright avore the sheenèn sky,
The very guide-post wer a-drest
Wi' posies on his eärms an' breast.
At last, the vo'k zwarm'd in by scores

An' hundreds droo the high barn-doors,
To dine on English feäre, in ranks,
A-zot on chairs, or stools, or planks,
By bwoards a-reachèn, row an' row,
Wi' cloths so white as driven snow.
An' while they took, wi' merry cheer,
Their pleäces at the meat an' beer,
The band did blow an' beät aloud
Their merry tuèns to the crowd;
An' slowly-zwingèn flags did spread
Their hangèn colors over head.
An' then the vo'k, wi' jay an' pride,
Stood up in stillness, zide by zide,
Wi' downcast heads, the while their friend
Rose up avore the teäble's end,
An' zaid a timely greäce, an' blest
The welcome meat to every guest.
An' then arose a mingled naïse
O' knives an' pleätes, an' cups an' traÿs,
An' tongues wi' merry tongues a-drown'd
Below a deaf'nèn storm o' sound.
An' zoo, at last, their worthy host
Stood up to gi'e em all a twoast,
That they did drink, wi' shouts o' glee,
An' whirlèn eärms to dree times dree.
An' when the bwoards at last wer beäre
Ov all the cloths an' goodly feäre,
An' froth noo longer rose to zwim
Within the beer-mugs sheenèn rim,
The vo'k, a-streamèn drough the door,
Went out to geämes they had in store.
An' on the blue-reäv'd waggon's bed,
Above his vower wheels o' red,
Musicians zot in rows, an' play'd
Their tuèns up to chap an' maïd,
That beät, wi' playsome tooes an' heels,

The level ground in nimble reels.
An' zome ageän, a-zet in line,
An' startèn at a given sign,
Wi' outreach'd breast, a-breathèn quick
Droo op'nèn lips, did nearly kick
Their polls, a-runnèn sich a peäce,
Wi' streamèn heäir, to win the reäce.
An' in the house, an' on the green,
An' in the shrubb'ry's leafy screen,
On ev'ry zide we met sich lots
O' smilèn friends in happy knots,
That I do think, that drough the feäst
In Caundle, vor a day at leäst,
You woudden vind a scowlèn feäce
Or dumpy heart in all the pleäce.

HAY MEAKEN—NUNCHEN TIME.

Anne an' John a-ta'kèn o't.

A. Back here, but now, the jobber John
   Come by, an' cried, "Well done, zing on,
   I thought as I come down the hill,
   An' heärd your zongs a-ringèn sh'ill,
   Who woudden like to come, an' fling
   A peäir o' prongs where you did zing?"

J. Aye, aye, he woudden vind it play,
   To work all day a-meäkèn hay,
   Or pitchèn o't, to eärms a-spread
   By lwoaders, yards above his head,
   'T'ud meäke en wipe his drippèn brow.

A. Or else a-reäken after plow.

J. Or workèn, wi' his nimble pick,
   A-stiffled wi' the hay, at rick.

A. Our Company would suit en best,
   When we do teäke our bit o' rest,
   At nunch, a-gather'd here below
   The sheäde theäse wide-bough'd woak do drow,
   Where hissèn froth mid rise, an' float
   In horns o' eäle, to wet his droat.

J. Aye, if his zwellèn han' could drag
   A meat-slice vrom his dinner bag.
   'T'ud meäke the busy little chap
   Look rather glum, to zee his lap
   Wi' all his meal ov woone dry croust,
   An' vinny cheese so dry as doust.

A. Well, I don't grumble at my food,
   'Tis wholesome, John, an' zoo 'tis good.

J. Whose reäke is that a-lyèn there?
   Do look a bit the woo'se vor wear.

A. Oh! I mus' get the man to meäke
   A tooth or two vor thik wold reäke,
   'Tis leäbour lost to strik a stroke
   Wi' him, wi' half his teeth a-broke.

J. I should ha' thought your han' too fine
   To break your reäke, if I broke mine.

A. The ramsclaws thin'd his wooden gum
   O' two teeth here, an' here were zome
   That broke when I did reäke a patch
   O' groun' wi' Jimmy, vor a match:
   An' here's a gap ov woone or two
   A-broke by Simon's clumsy shoe,
   An' when I gi'ed his poll a poke,
   Vor better luck, another broke.
   In what a veag have you a-swung
   Your pick, though, John? His stem's a-sprung.

J. When I an' Simon had a het
   O' pookèn, yonder, vor a bet,
   The prongs o'n gi'ed a tump a poke,
   An' then I vound the stem a-broke,
   But they do meäke the stems o' picks
   O' stuff so brittle as a kicks.

A. There's poor wold Jeäne, wi' wrinkled skin,
   A-tellèn, wi' her peakèd chin,
   Zome teäle ov her young days, poor soul.
   Do meäke the young-woones smile. 'Tis droll.
   What is it? Stop, an' let's goo near.
   I do like theäse wold teäles. Let's hear.

A FATHER OUT, AN' MOTHER HWOME.

THE snow-white clouds did float on high
In shoals avore the sheenèn sky,
An' runnèn weäves in pon' did cheäse
Each other on the water's feäce,
As hufflèn win' did blow between
The new-leav'd boughs o' sheenèn green.
An' there, the while I walked along
The path, drough leäze, above the drong,
A little maïd, wi' bloomèn feäce,
Went on up hill wi' nimble peäce,
A-leänèn to the right-han' zide,
To car a basket that did ride,
A-hangèn down, wi' all his heft,
Upon her elbow at her left.
An' yet she hardly seem'd to bruise
The grass-bleädes wi' her tiny shoes,
That pass'd each other, left an' right,
In steps a'most too quick vor zight.
But she'd a-left her mother's door
A-bearèn vrom her little store

Her father's welcome bit o' food,
Where he wer out at work in wood;
An' she wer bless'd wi' mwore than zwome—
A father out, an' mother hwome.

An' there, a-vell'd 'ithin the copse,
Below the timber's new-leav'd tops,
Wer ashèn poles, a-castèn straïght,
On primrwose beds, their langthy waïght;
Below the yollow light, a-shed
Drough boughs upon the vi'let's head,
By climèn ivy, that did reach,
A sheenèn roun' the dead-leav'd beech.
An' there her father zot, an' meäde
His hwomely meal bezide a gleäde;
While she, a-croopèn down to ground,
Did pull the flowers, where she vound
The droopèn vi'let out in blooth,
Or yollow primrwose in the lewth,
That she mid car em proudly back,
An' zet em on her mother's tack;
Vor she wer bless'd wi' mwore than zwome—
A father out, an' mother hwome.
A father out, an' mother hwome,
Be blessèns soon a-lost by zome;
A-lost by me, an' zoo I pray'd
They mid be speär'd the little maïd.

RIDDLES.

Anne an' Joey a-ta'ken.

A. A plague! theäse cow wont stand a bit,
   Noo sooner do she zee me zit
   Ageän her, than she's in a trot,
   A-runnèn to zome other spot.

J. Why 'tis the dog do sceäre the cow,
   He worried her a-vield benow.

A. Goo in, Ah! *Liplap*, where's your taïl!

J. He's off, then up athirt the raïl.
   Your cow there, Anne's a-come to hand
   A goodish milcher. A. If she'd stand,
   But then she'll steäre an' start wi' fright
   To zee a dumbledore in flight.
   Last week she het the païl a flought,
   An' flung my meal o' milk half out.

J. Ha! Ha! But Anny, here, what lout
   Broke half your small païl's bottom out?

A. What lout indeed! What, do ye own
   The neäme? What dropp'd en on a stwone?

J. Hee! Hee! Well now he's out o' trim
   Wi' only half a bottom to en;
   Could you still vill en' to the brim
   An' yit not let the milk run drough en?

A. Aye, as for nonsense, Joe, your head
   Do hold it all so tight's a blather,
   But if 'tis any good, do shed
   It all so leäky as a lather.
   Could you vill païls 'ithout a bottom,
   Yourself that be so deeply skill'd?

J. Well, ees, I could, if I'd a-got em
   Inside o' bigger woones a-vill'd.

A. La! that *is* zome'hat vor to hatch!
   Here answer me theäse little catch.
   Down under water an' o' top o't
   I went, an' didden touch a drop o't,

J. Not when at mowèn time I took
　　An' pull'd ye out o' Longmeäd brook,
　　Where you'd a-slidder'd down the edge
　　An' zunk knee-deep bezide the zedge,
　　A-tryèn to reäke out a clote.

A. Aye I do hear your chucklèn droat
　　When I athirt the brudge did bring
　　Zome water on my head vrom spring.
　　Then under water an' o' top o't,
　　Wer I an' didden touch a drop o't.

J. O Lauk! What thik wold riddle still,
　　Why that's as wold as Duncliffe Hill;
　　"A two-lagg'd thing do run avore
　　An' run behind a man,
　　An' never run upon his lags
　　Though on his lags do stan'.
　　　What's that?
　　　I don't think you do know.
　　There idden sich a thing to show.
　　Not know? Why yonder by the stall
　　'S a wheel-barrow bezide the wall,
　　Don't he stand on his lags so trim,
　　An' run on nothèn but his wheels wold rim.

A. There's *horn* vor Goodman's eye-zight seäke;
　　There's *horn* vor Goodman's mouth to teäke;
　　There's *horn* vor Goodman's ears, as well
　　As *horn* vor Goodman's nose to smell—
　　What *horns* be they, then? Do your hat
　　Hold wit enough to tell us that?

J. Oh! *horns!* but no, I'll tell ye what,
　　My cow is hornless, an' she's *knot.*

A. *Horn* vor the *mouth's* a hornèn cup.

J. An' eäle 's good stuff to vill en up.

A. An' *horn* vor *eyes* is horn vor light,
   Vrom Goodman's lantern after night;
   Horn vor the *ears* is woone to sound
   Vor hunters out wi' ho'se an' hound;
   But *horn* that vo'k do buy to smell o'
   Is *hart's-horn*. J. Is it? What d'ye tell o'
   How proud we be, vor ben't we smart?
   Aye, *horn* is *horn*, an' hart is hart.
   Well here then, Anne, while we be at it,
   'S a ball vor you if you can bat it.
   On dree-lags, two-lags, by the zide
   O' vower-lags, woonce did zit wi' pride,
   When vower-lags, that velt a prick,
   Vrom zix-lags, het two lags a kick.
   An' two an' dree-lags vell, all vive,
   Slap down, zome dead an' zome alive.

A. Tech! hech! what have ye now then, Joe,
   At last, to meäke a riddle o'?

J. Your dree-lagg'd stool woone night did bear
   Up you a milkèn wi' a peäir;
   An' there a zix-lagg'd stout did prick
   Your vow'r-lagg'd cow, an meäke her kick,
   A-hettèn, wi' a pretty pat,
   Your stool an' you so flat 's a mat.
   You scrambled up a little dirty,
   But I do hope it didden hurt ye.

A. You hope, indeed! a likely ceäse,
   Wi' thik broad grin athirt your feäce
   You saucy good-vor-nothèn chap,
   I'll gi'e your grinnèn feäce a slap,
   Your drawlèn tongue can only run
   To turn a body into fun.

J. Oh! I woont do 't ageän. Oh dear!
   Till next time, Anny. Oh my ear!
   Oh! Anne, why you've a-het my hat
   'Ithin the milk, now look at that.

A. Do sar ye right, then, I don't ceäre.
   I'll thump your noddle,—there—there—there.

DAY'S WORK A-DONE.

AND oh! the jay our rest did yield,
    At evenèn by the mossy wall,
When we'd a-work'd all day a-vield,
    While zummer zuns did rise an' vall;
        As there a-lettèn
        Goo all frettèn,
An' vorgettèn all our tweils,
We zot among our childern's smiles.

An' under skies that glitter'd white,
    The while our smoke, arisèn blue,
Did melt in aiër, out o' zight,
    Above the trees that kept us lew;
        Wer birds a-zingèn,
        Tongues a-ringèn,
Childern springèn, vull o' jay,
A-finishèn the day in play.

An' back behind, a-stannèn tall,
    The cliff did sheen to western light;
An' while avore the water-vall,
    A-rottlèn loud, an' foamèn white.
        The leaves did quiver,
        Gnots did whiver,
By the river, where the pool,
In evenèn aïr did glissen cool.

An' childern there, a-runnèn wide,
  Did play their geämes along the grove,
Vor though to us 'twer jay to bide
  At rest, to them 'twer jay to move.
    The while my smilèn
      Jeäne, beguilèn,
All my tweilèn, wi' her ceäre,
Did call me to my evenèn feäre.

LIGHT OR SHEÄDE.

A Maytide's evenèn wer a-dyèn,
Under moonsheen, into night,
Wi' a streamèn wind a-sighèn
By the thorns a-bloomèn white.
Where in sheäde, a-zinkèn deeply,
Wer a nook, all dark but lew,
By a bank, arisèn steeply,
Not to let the win' come drough.

Should my love goo out, a-showèn
All her smiles, in open light;
Or, in lewth, wi' wind a-blowèn,
Stay in darkness, dim to zight?
Stay in sheäde o' bank or wallèn,
In the warmth, if not in light;
Words alwone vrom her a-vallèn,
Would be jay vor all the night.

THE WAGGON A-STOODED.

Dree o'm a-ta'kèn o't.

(1) WELL, here we be, then, wi' the vu'st poor lwoad
  O' vuzz we brought, a-stoodèd in the road.

(2) The road, George, no.   There's na'r a road.   That's
    wrong.
    If we'd a road, we mid ha' got along.

(1) Noo road!   Ees 'tis, the road that we do goo.

(2) Do goo, George, no.   The pleäce we can't get drough.

(1) Well, there, the vu'st lwoad we 've a-haul'd to day
    Is here a-stoodèd in theäse bed o' clay.
    Here's rotten groun'! an' how the wheels do cut!
    The little woone's a-zunk up to the nut.

(3) An' yeet this rotten groun' don't reach a lug.

(1) Well, come, then, gi'e the plow another tug.

(2) They meäres wull never pull the waggon out,
    A-lwoaded, an' a-stoodèd in thik rout.

(3) We'll try.   Come, *Smiler*, come!   C' up, *Whitevoot*, gee!

(2) White-voot wi' lags all over mud!   Hee! Hee!

(3) 'Twoon't wag.   We shall but snap our gear,
    An' overstraïn the meäres.   'Twoon't wag, 'tis clear.

(1) That's your work, William.   No, in coo'se, 'twoon't wag.
    Why did ye drēve en into theäse here quag?
    The vore-wheels be a-zunk above the nuts.

(3) What then?   I coulden leäve the beäten track,
    To turn the waggon over on the back
    Ov woone o' theäsem wheel-high emmet-butts.
    If you be sich a drēver, an' do know't,
    You drēve the plow, then; but you'll overdrow 't.

(1) I drēve the plow, indeed!   Oh! ees, what, now
    The wheels woont wag, then, *I* mid drēve the plow!
    We'd better dig away the groun' below
    The wheels.   (2) There's na'r a speäde to dig wi'.

(1) An' teäke an' cut a lock o' frith, an' drow
    Upon the clay.   (2) Nor hook to cut a twig wi'.

THE WAGGON A-STOODED.

(1) Oh! here's a bwoy a-comèn. Here, my lad,
Dost know vor a'r a speäde, that can be had?

(B) At father's. (1) Well, where's that? (Bwoy) At Sam'el
Riddick's.

(1) Well run, an' ax vor woone. Fling up your heels,
An' mind: a speäde to dig out theäsem wheels,
An' hook to cut a little lock o' widdicks.

(3) Why, we shall want zix ho'ses, or a dozen,
To pull the waggon out, wi' all theäse vuzzen.

(1) Well, we mus' lighten en; come, Jeämes, then, hop
Upon the lwoad, an' jus' fling off the top.

(2) If I can clim' en; but 'tis my cousaït,
That I shall overzet en wi' my waïght.

(1) You overzet en! No, Jeämes, he won't vall,
The lwoad's a-built so firm as any wall.

(2) Here! lend a hand or shoulder vor my knee
Or voot. I'll scramble to the top an' zee
What I can do. Well, here I be, among
The fakkets, vor a bit, but not vor long.
Heigh, George! Ha! ha! Why this wull never stand.
Your firm 's a wall, is all so loose as zand;
'Tis all a-come to pieces. Oh! Teäke ceäre!
Ho! I'm a-vallèn, vuzz an' all! Haë! There!

(1) Lo'k there, thik fellor is a-vell lik' lead,
An' half the fuzzen wi 'n, heels over head!
There's all the vuzz a-lyèn lik' a staddle,
An' he a-deäb'd wi' mud. Oh! Here's a caddle!

(3) An' zoo you soon got down zome vuzzen, Jimmy.

(2) Ees, I do know 'tis down, I brought it wi' me.

(3) Your lwoad, George, wer a rather slick-built thing,
But there, 'twer prickly vor the hands! Did sting?

(1) Oh! ees, d'ye teäke me vor a nincompoop,
 No, no. The lwoad wer up so firm's a rock,
 But two o' theäsem emmet-butts would knock
 The tightest barrel nearly out o' hoop.

(3) Oh! now then, here's the bwoy a-bringèn back
 The speäde. Well done, my man. That idder slack.

(2) Well done, my lad, sha't have a ho'se to ride
 When thou'st a meäre. (Bwoy) Next never's-tide.

(3) Now let's dig out a spit or two
 O' clay, a-vore the little wheels;
 Oh! so's, I can't pull up my heels,
 I be a-stogg'd up over shoe.

(1) Come, William, dig away! Why you do spuddle
 A'most so weak's a child. How you do muddle!
 Gi'e me the speäde a-bit. A pig would rout
 It out a'most so nimbly wi' his snout.

(3) Oh! so's, d'ye hear it, then. How we can thunder!
 How big we be, then George! what next I wonder?

(1) Now, William, gi'e the waggon woone mwore twitch,
 The wheels be free, an' 'tis a lighter nitch.

(3) Come, *Smiler*, gee! C'up, *White-voot*. (1) That wull do

(2) Do wag. (1) Do goo at last. (3) Well done. 'Tis
 drough.

(1) Now, William, till you have mwore ho'ses' lags,
 Don't drēve the waggon into theäsem quags.

(3) You build your lwoads up tight enough to ride.

(1) I can't do less, d'ye know, wi' you vor guide.

GWAÏN DOWN THE STEPS VOR WATER.

WHILE zuns do roll vrom east to west
To bring us work, or leäve us rest,
There down below the steep hill-zide,
Drough time an' tide, the spring do flow;
An' mothers there, vor years a-gone,
Lik' daughters now a-comèn on,
To bloom when they be weak an' wan,
Went down the steps vor water.

An' what do yonder ringers tell
A-ringèn changes, bell by bell;
Or what's a-show'd by yonder zight
O' vo'k in white, upon the road,
But that by John o' Woodleys zide,
There's now a-blushèn vor his bride,
A pretty maïd that vu'st he spied,
Gwain down the steps vor water.

Though she, 'tis true, is feäir an' kind,
There still be mwore a-left behind;
So cleän 's the light the zun do gi'e,
So sprack's a bee when zummer's bright;
An' if I've luck, I woont be slow
To teäke off woone that I do know,
A-trippèn gaily to an' fro,
Upon the steps vor water.

Her father idden poor—but vew
In parish be so well to do;
Vor his own cows do swing their taïls
Behind his païls, below his boughs:
An' then ageän to win my love,
Why, she's as hwomely as a dove,
An' don't hold up herzelf above
Gwaïn down the steps vor water.

Gwaïn down the steps vor water ! No !
How handsome it do meäke her grow.
If she'd be straïght, or walk abrode,
To tread her road wi' comely gaït,
She coulden do a better thing
To zet herzelf upright, than bring
Her pitcher on her head, vrom spring
Upon the steps, wi' water.

No ! don't ye neäme in woone seäme breath
Wi' bachelors, the husband's he'th ;
The happy pleäce, where vingers thin
Do pull woone's chin, or pat woone's feäce.
But still the bleäme is their's, to slight
Their happiness, wi' such a zight
O' maïdens, mornèn, noon, an' night,
A-gwaïn down steps vor water.

ELLEN BRINE OV ALLENBURN.

Noo soul did hear her lips complaïn,
An' she's a-gone vrom all her païn,
An' others' loss to her is gaïn
For she do live in heaven's love ;
Vull many a longsome day an' week
She bore her aïlèn, still, an' meek ;
A-workèn while her strangth held on,
An' guidèn housework, when 'twer gone.
Vor Ellen Brine ov Allenburn,
Oh ! there be souls to murn.

The last time I'd a-cast my zight
Upon her feäce, a-feäded white,
Wer in a zummer's mornèn light
In hall avore the smwold'rèn vier,
The while the childern beät the vloor,

In play, wi' tiny shoes they wore,
An' call'd their mother's eyes to view
The feät's their little limbs could do.
Oh! Ellen Brine ov Allenburn,
They childern now mus' murn.

Then woone, a-stoppèn vrom his reäce,
Went up, an' on her knee did pleäce
His hand, a-lookèn in her feäce,
An' wi' a smilèn mouth so small,
He zaid, "You promised us to goo
To Shroton feäir, an' teäke us two!"
She heärd it wi' her two white ears,
An' in her eyes there sprung two tears,
Vor Ellen Brine ov Allenburn
Did veel that they mus' murn.

September come, wi' Shroton feäir,
But Ellen Brine wer never there!
A heavy heart wer on the meäre
Their father rod his hwomeward road.
'Tis true he brought zome feärèns back,
Vor them two childern all in black;
But they had now, wi' playthings new,
Noo mother vor to shew em to,
Vor Ellen Brine ov Allenburn
Would never mwore return.

THE MOTHERLESS CHILD

THE zun'd a-zet back tother night,
   But in the zettèn pleäce
The clouds, a-redden'd by his light,
   Still glow'd avore my feäce.
An' I've a-lost my Meäry's smile,
I thought; but still I have her chile,

Zoo like her, that my eyes can treäce
The mother's in her daughter's feäce.
  O little feäce so near to me,
An' like thy mother's gone; why need I zay
Sweet night cloud, wi' the glow o' my lost day,
  Thy looks be always dear to me.
The zun'd a-zet another night;
  But, by the moon on high,
He still did zend us back his light
  Below a cwolder sky.
My Meäry's in a better land
I thought, but still her chile's at hand,
An' in her chile she'll zend me on
Her love, though she herzelf's a-gone.
  O little chile so near to me,
An' like thy mother gone; why need I zay,
Sweet moon, the messenger vrom my lost day,
  Thy looks be always dear to me.

THE LEÄDY'S TOWER.

An' then we went along the gleädes
O' zunny turf, in quiv'rèn sheädes,
A-windèn off, vrom hand to hand,
Along a path o' yollow zand,
  An' clomb a stickle slope, an' vound
An open patch o' lofty ground,
  Up where a steätely tow'r did spring,
So high as highest larks do zing.

"Oh! Meäster Collins," then I zaid,
A-lookèn up wi' back-flung head;
Vor who but he, so mild o' feäce,
Should teäke me there to zee the pleäce.

"What is it then theäse tower do meän,
A-built so feäir, an' kept so cleän?"
"Ah! me," he zaid, wi' thoughtvul feäce,
"'Twer grief that zet theäse tower in pleäce.
The squier's e'thly life's a-blest
Wi' gifts that mwost do teäke vor best;
The lofty-pinion'd rufs do rise
To screen his head vrom stormy skies;
His land's a-spreadèn roun' his hall,
An' hands do leäbor at his call;
The while the ho'se do fling, wi' pride,
His lofty head where he do guide;
But still his e'thly jay's a-vled,
His woone true friend, his wife, is dead.
Zoo now her happy soul's a-gone,
An' he in grief's a-ling'rèn on,
Do do his heart zome good to show
His love to flesh an' blood below.
An' zoo he rear'd, wi' smitten soul,
Theäse Leädy's Tower upon the knowl.
An' there you'll zee the tow'r do spring
Twice ten veet up, as roun's a ring,
Wi' pillars under mwolded eäves,
Above their heads a-carv'd wi' leaves;
An' have to peäce, a-walkèn round
His voot, a hunderd veet o' ground.
An' there, above his upper wall,
A roundèd tow'r do spring so tall
'S a springèn arrow shot upright,
A hunderd giddy veet in height.
An' if you'd like to straïn your knees
A-climèn up above the trees,
To zee, wi' slowly wheelèn feäce,
The vur-sky'd land about the pleäce,
You'll have a flight o' steps to wear
Vor forty veet, up steäir by steäir,

That roun' the risèn tow'r do wind,
Like withwind roun' the saplèn's rind,
An' reach a landèn, wi' a seat,
To rest at last your weary veet,
'Ithin a breast be-screenèn wall,
To keep ye vrom a longsome vall.
An' roun' the windèn steäirs do spring
Aïght stwonèn pillars in a ring,
A-reachèn up their heavy strangth
Drough forty veet o' slender langth,
To end wi' carvèd heads below
 The broad-vloor'd landèn's aïry bow.
Aïght zides, as you do zee, do bound
The lower buildèn on the ground,
An' there in woone, a two-leav'd door
Do zwing above the marble vloor:
An' aÿe, as luck do zoo betide
Our comèn, wi' can goo inside.
The door is oben now. An' zoo
The keeper kindly let us drough.
There as we softly trod the vloor
O' marble stwone, 'ithin the door,
The echoes ov our vootsteps vled
Out roun' the wall, and over head;
An' there a-païnted, zide by zide,
In memory o' the squier's bride,
In zeven païntèns, true to life,
Wer zeven zights o' wedded life."

Then Meäster Collins twold me all
The teäles a-païntèd roun' the wall;
An' vu'st the bride did stan' to plight
Her weddèn vow, below the light
A-shootèn down, so bright's a fleäme,
In drough a churches window freäme.

THE LEÄDY'S TOWER.

An' near the bride, on either hand,
You'd zee her comely bridemaïds stand,
Wi' eyelashes a-bent in streäks
O' brown above their bloomèn cheäks:
An' sheenèn feäir, in mellow light,
Wi' flowèn heäir, an' frocks o' white.

"An' here," good Meäster Collins cried,
"You'll zee a creädle at her zide,
An' there's her child, a-lyèn deep
'Ithin it, an' a-gone to sleep,
Wi' little eyelashes a-met
In fellow streäks, as black as jet;
The while her needle, over head,
Do nimbly leäd the snow-white thread,
To zew a robe her love do meäke
Wi' happy leäbor vor his seäke.

"An' here a-geän's another pleäce,
Where she do zit wi' smilèn feäce,
An' while her bwoy do leän, wi' pride,
Ageän her lap, below her zide,
Her vinger tip do leäd his look
To zome good words o' God's own book.

"An' next you'll zee her in her pleäce,
Avore her happy husband's feäce,
As he do zit, at evenèn-tide,
A-restèn by the vier-zide.
An' there the childern's heads do rise,
Wi' laughèn lips, an' beamèn eyes,
Above the bwoard, where she do lay
Her sheenèn tacklèn, wi' the tea.

"An' here another zide do show
Her vinger in her scizzars' bow

Avore two daughters, that do stand,
Wi' leärnsome minds, to watch her hand
A-sheäpèn out, wi' skill an' ceäre,
A frock vor them to zew an' wear.

"Then next you'll zee her bend her head
Above her aïlèn husband's bed,
A-fannèn, wi' an inward pray'r,
His burnèn brow wi' beäten aïr;
The while the clock, by candle light,
Do show that 'tis the dead o' night.

" An' here ageän upon the wall,
Where we do zee her last ov all,
Her husband's head's a-hangèn low,
'Ithin his hands in deepest woe.
An' she, an angel ov his God,
Do cheer his soul below the rod,
A-liftèn up her han' to call
His eyes to writèn on the wall,
As white as is her spotless robe,
' Hast thou rememberèd my servant Job?'

" An' zoo the squier, in grief o' soul,
Built up the Tower upon the knowl."

FATHERHOOD.

LET en zit, wi' his dog an' his cat,
  Wi' their noses a-turn'd to the vier,
  An' have all that a man should desire;
But there idden much reädship in that.
Whether vo'k mid have childern or no,
  Wou'dden meäke mighty odds in the maïn;
They do bring us mwore jay wi' mwore ho,
  An' wi' nwone we've less jay wi' less païn.

FATHERHOOD.

We be all lik' a zull's idle sheäre out,
An' shall rust out, unless we do wear out,
  Lik' do-nothèn, rue-nothèn,
    Dead alive dumps.

As vor me, why my life idden bound
  To my own heart alwone, among men;
  I do live in myzelf, an' ageän
In the lives o' my childern all round:
I do live wi' my bwoy in his play,
  An' ageän wi' my maïd in her zongs;
An' my heart is a-stirr'd wi' their jay,
  An' would burn at the zight o' their wrongs.
I ha' nine lives, an' zoo if a half
O'm do cry, why the rèst o'm mid laugh
  All so playvully, jayvully,
    Happy wi' hope.

Tother night I come hwome a long road,
  When the weather did sting an' did vreeze;
An' the snow—vor the day had a-snow'd—
  Wer avroze on the boughs o' the trees;
An' my tooes an' my vingers wer num',
  An' my veet wer so lumpy as logs,
An' my ears wer so red's a cock's cwom';
  An' my nose wer so cwold as a dog's;
But so soon's I got hwome I vorgot
Where my limbs wer a-cwold or wer hot,
  When wi' loud cries an' proud cries
    They coll'd me so cwold.

Vor the vu'st that I happen'd to meet
  Come to pull my girtcwoat vrom my eärm,
  An' another did rub my feäce warm,
An' another hot-slipper'd my veet;
While their mother did cast on a stick,
  Vor to keep the red vier alive;

An' they all come so busy an' thick
  As the bees vlee-èn into their hive,
An' they meäde me so happy an' proud,
That my heart could ha' crow'd out a-loud;
  They did tweil zoo, an' smile zoo,
    An' coll me so cwold.

As I zot wi' my teacup, at rest,
  There I pull'd out the taÿs I did bring;
  Men a-kickèn, a-wagg'd wi' a string,
An' goggle-ey'd dolls to be drest;
An' oh! vrom the childern there sprung
  Such a charm when they handled their taÿs,
That vor pleasure the bigger woones wrung
  Their two hands at the zight o' their jaÿs;
As the bwoys' bigger vaïces vell in
Wi' the maïdens a-titterèn thin,
  An' their dancèn an' prancèn,
    An' little mouth's laughs.

Though 'tis hard stripes to breed em all up,
  If I'm only a-blest vrom above,
  They'll meäke me amends wi' their love,
Vor their pillow, their pleäte, an' their cup;
Though I shall be never a-spweil'd
  Wi' the sarvice that money can buy;
Still the hands ov a wife an' a child
  Be the blessèns ov low or ov high;
An' if there be mouths to be ved,
He that zent em can zend me their bread,
  An' will smile on the chile
    That's a-new on the knee.

THE MAID O' NEWTON.

In zummer, when the knaps wer bright
In cool-aïr'd evenèn's western light,
An' hay that had a-dried all day,
Did now lie grey, to dewy night;
I went, by happy chance, or doom,
Vrom Broadwoak Hill, athirt to Coomb,
An' met a maïd in all her bloom:
    The feaïrest maïd o' Newton.

She bore a basket that did ride
So light, she didden leän azide;
Her feäce wer oval, an' she smil'd
So sweet's a child, but walk'd wi' pride.
I spoke to her, but what I zaid
I didden know; wi' thoughts a-vled,
I spoke by heart, an' not by head,
    Avore the maïd o' Newton.

I call'd her, oh! I don't know who,
'Twer by a neäme she never knew;
An' to the heel she stood upon,
She then brought on her hinder shoe,
An' stopp'd avore me, where we met,
An' wi' a smile woone can't vorget,
She zaid, wi' eyes a-zwimmèn wet,
    "No, I be woone o' Newton."

Then on I rambled to the west,
Below the zunny hangèn's breast,
Where, down athirt the little stream,
The brudge's beam did lie at rest:
But all the birds, wi' lively glee,

Did chirp an' hop vrom tree to tree,
As if it wer vrom pride, to zee
   Goo by the maïd o' Newton.

By fancy led, at evenèn's glow,
I woonce did goo, a-rovèn slow,
Down where the elèms, stem by stem,
Do stan' to hem the grove below;
But after that, my veet vorzook
The grove, to seek the little brook
At Coomb, where I mid zometimes look,
   To meet the maïd o' Newton.

CHILDHOOD.

AYE, at that time our days wer but vew,
An' our lim's wer but small, an' a-growèn;
An' then the feäir worold wer new,
An' life wer all hopevul an' gay;
An' the times o' the sproutèn o' leaves,
An' the cheäk-burnèn seasons o' mowèn,
An' bindèn o' red-headed sheaves,
Wer all welcome seasons o' jay.

Then the housen seem'd high, that be low,
An' the brook did seem wide that is narrow,
An' time, that do vlee, did goo slow,
An' veelèns now feeble wer strong,
An' our worold did end wi' the neämes
Ov the Sha'sbury Hill or Bulbarrow;
An' life did seem only the geämes
That we play'd as the days rolled along.

Then the rivers, an' high-timber'd lands,
An' the zilvery hills, 'ithout buyèn,

Did seem to come into our hands
Vrom others that own'd em avore;
An' all zickness, an' sorrow, an' need,
Seem'd to die wi' the wold vo'k a-dyèn,
An' leäve us vor ever a-freed
Vrom evils our vorefathers bore.

But happy be childern the while
They have elders a-livèn to love em,
An' teäke all the wearisome tweil
That zome hands or others mus' do;
Like the low-headed shrubs that be warm,
In the lewth o' the trees up above em,
A-screen'd vrom the cwold blowèn storm
That the timber avore em must rue.

MEÄRY'S SMILE.

WHEN mornèn winds, a-blowèn high,
Do zweep the clouds vrom all the sky,
An' laurel-leaves do glitter bright,
The while the newly broken light
Do brighten up, avore our view,
The vields wi' green, an' hills wi' blue;
What then can highten to my eyes
The cheerful feäce ov e'th an' skies,
  But Meäry's smile, o' Morey's Mill,
  My rwose o' Mowy Lea.

An' when, at last, the evenèn dews
Do now begin to wet our shoes;
An' night's a-ridèn to the west,
To stop our work, an' gi'e us rest,
Oh! let the candle's ruddy gleäre
But brighten up her sheenèn heäir;

Or else, as she do walk abroad,
Let moonlight show, upon the road,
    My Meäry's smile, o' Morey's Mill,
    My rwose o' Mowy Lea.

An' O! mid never tears come on,
To wash her feäce's blushes wan,
Nor kill her smiles that now do play
Like sparklèn weäves in zunny May;
But mid she still, vor all she's gone
Vrom souls she now do smile upon,
Show others they can vind woone jay
To turn the hardest work to play.
    My Meäry's smile, o' Morey's Mill,
    My rwose o' Mowy Lea.

MEÄRY WEDDED.

The zun can zink, the stars mid rise,
An' woods be green to sheenèn skies;
The cock mid crow to mornèn light,
An' workvo'k zing to vallèn night;
The birds mid whissle on the spray,
An' childern leäp in merry play,
But our's is now a lifeless pleäce,
Vor we've a-lost a smilèn feäce—
    Young Meäry Meäd o' merry mood,
    Vor she's a-woo'd an' wedded.

The dog that woonce wer glad to bear
  Her fondlèn vingers down his heäir,
Do leän his head ageän the vloor,
  To watch, wi' heavy eyes, the door;
An' men she zent so happy hwome
  O' Zadurdays, do seem to come

To door, wi' downcast hearts, to miss
Wi' smiles below the clematis,
    Young Meäry Meäd o' merry mood,
    Vor she's a-woo'd an' wedded.

When they do draw the evenèn blind,
An' when the evenèn light's a-tin'd,
The cheerless vier do drow a gleäre
O' light ageän her empty chair;
An' wordless gaps do now meäke thin
Their talk where woonce her vaïce come in.
Zoo lwonesome is her empty pleäce,
An' blest the house that ha' the feäce
    O' Meäry Meäd, o' merry mood,
    Now she's a-woo'd and wedded.

The day she left her father's he'th,
Though sad, wer kept a day o' me'th,
An' dry-wheel'd waggons' empty beds
Wer left 'ithin the tree-screen'd sheds;
An' all the hosses, at their eäse,
Went snortèn up the flow'ry leäse,
But woone, the smartest for the roäd,
That pull'd away the dearest lwoad—
    Young Meäry Meäd o' merry mood,
    That wer a-woo'd an' wedded.

THE STWONEN BWOY UPON THE PILLAR.

Wi' smokeless tuns an' empty halls,
An' moss a-clingèn to the walls,
In ev'ry wind the lofty tow'rs
Do teäke the zun, an' bear the show'rs;
An' there, 'ithin a geät a-hung,
But vasten'd up, an' never swung,

Upon the pillar, all alwone,
Do stan' the little bwoy o' stwone;
'S a poppy bud mid linger on,
Vorseäken, when the wheat's a-gone.
An' there, then, wi' his bow let slack,
An' little quiver at his back,
Drough het an' wet, the little chile
Vrom day to day do stan' an' smile.
When vu'st the light, a-risèn weak,
At break o' day, do smite his cheäk,
Or while, at noon, the leafy bough
Do cast a sheäde a-thirt his brow,
Or when at night the warm-breath'd cows
Do sleep by moon-belighted boughs;
An' there the while the rooks do bring
Their scroff to build their nest in Spring,
Or zwallows in the zummer day
Do cling their little huts o' clay,
'Ithin the raïnless sheädes, below
The steadvast arches' mossy bow.
Or when, in Fall, the woak do shed
The leaves, a-wither'd, vrom his head,
An' western win's, a-blowèn cool,
Do dreve em out athirt the pool,
Or Winter's clouds do gather dark
An' wet, wi' raïn, the elem's bark,
You'll zee his pretty smile betwixt
His little sheäde-mark'd lips a-fix'd;
As there his little sheäpe do bide
Drough day an' night, an' time an' tide.
An' never change his size or dress,
Nor overgrow his prettiness.
But, oh! thik child, that we do vind
In childhood still, do call to mind
A little bwoy a-call'd by death,
Long years ago, vrom our sad he'th;

An' I, in thought, can zee en dim
The seäme in feäce, the seäme in lim'.
My heäir mid whiten as the snow,
My limbs grow weak, my step wear slow,
My droopèn head mid slowly vall
Above the han'-staff's glossy ball,
An' yeet, vor all a wid'nèn span
Ov years, mid change a livèn man,
My little child do still appear
To me wi' all his childhood's gear,
'Ithout a beard upon his chin,
'Ithout a wrinkle in his skin,
A-livèn on, a child the seäme
In look, an' sheäpe, an' size, an' neäme.

THE YOUNG THAT DIED IN BEAUTY.

If souls should only sheen so bright
In heaven as in e'thly light,
An' nothèn better wer the ceäse,
How comely still, in sheäpe an' feäce,
Would many reach thik happy pleäce,—
The hopeful souls that in their prime
Ha' seem'd a-took avore their time—
The young that died in beauty.

But when woone's lim's ha' lost their strangth
A-tweilèn drough a lifetime's langth,
An' over cheäks a-growèn wold
The slowly-weästen years ha' rolled,
The deep'nèn wrinkle's hollow vwold;
When life is ripe, then death do call
Vor less ov thought, than when do vall
On young vo'ks in their beauty.

But pinèn souls, wi' heads a-hung
In heavy sorrow vor the young,
The sister ov the brother dead,
The father wi' a child a-vled,
The husband when his bride ha' laid
Her head at rest, noo mwore to turn,
Have all a-vound the time to murn
Vor youth that died in beauty.

An' yeet the church, where prayer do rise
Vrom thoughtvul souls, wi' downcast eyes,
An' village greens, a-beät half beäre
By dancers that do meet, an' weär
Such merry looks at feäst an' feäir,
Do gather under leätest skies,
Their bloomèn cheäks an' sparklèn eyes,
Though young ha' died in beauty.

But still the dead shall mwore than keep
The beauty ov their eärly sleep;
Where comely looks shall never weär
Uncomely, under tweil an' ceäre.
The feäir at death be always feäir,
Still feäir to livers' thought an' love,
An' feäirer still to God above,
Than when they died in beauty.

FAIR EMILY OV YARROW MILL.

Dear Yarrowham, 'twer many miles
   Vrom thy green meäds that, in my walk,
I met a maïd wi' winnèn smiles,
   That talk'd as vo'k at hwome do talk;
An' who at last should she be vound,
Ov all the souls the sky do bound,
But woone that trod at vu'st thy groun'
         Fair Emily ov Yarrow Mill.

But thy wold house an' elmy nook,
　　An' wall-screen'd geärden's mossy zides,
Thy grassy meäds an' zedgy brook,
　　An' high-bank'd leänes, wi' sheädy rides,
Wer all a-known to me by light
Ov eärly days, a-quench'd by night,
Avore they met the younger zight
　　　　　　Ov Emily ov Yarrow Mill.

An' now my heart do leäp to think
　　O' times that I've a-spent in play,
Bezide thy river's rushy brink,
　　Upon a deäizybed o' May;
I lov'd the friends thy land ha' bore,
An' I do love the paths they wore,
An' I do love thee all the mwore,
　　　　　　Vor Emily ov Yarrow Mill.

When bright above the e'th below
　　The moon do spread abroad his light,
An' aïr o' zummer nights do blow
　　Athirt the vields in playsome flight,
'Tis then delightsome under all
The sheädes o' boughs by path or wall,
But mwostly thine when they do vall
　　　　　　On Emily ov Yarrow Mill.

THE SCUD.

Aye, aye, the leäne wi' flow'ry zides
A-kept so lew, by hazzle-wrides,
Wi' beds o' grægles out in bloom,
Below the timber's windless gloom
　　An' geäte that I've a-swung,
　　An' rod as he's a-hung,
When I wer young, in Woakley Coomb.

'Twer there at feäst we all did pass
The evenèn on the leänezide grass,
Out where the geäte do let us drough,
Below the woak-trees in the lew,
In merry geämes an' fun
That meäde us skip an' run,
Wi' burnèn zun, an' sky o' blue.

But still there come a scud that drove
The titt'rèn maïdens vrom the grove;
An' there a-left wer flow'ry mound,
'Ithout a vaïce, 'ithout a sound,
Unless the aïr did blow,
Drough ruslèn leaves, an' drow,
The raïn drops low, upon the ground.

I linger'd there an' miss'd the naïse;
I linger'd there an' miss'd our jaÿs;
I miss'd woone soul beyond the rest;
The maïd that I do like the best.
Vor where her vaïce is gaÿ
An' where her smiles do plaÿ,
There's always jaÿ vor ev'ry breast.

Vor zome vo'k out abroad ha' me'th,
But nwone at hwome bezide the he'th;
An' zome ha' smiles vor strangers' view;
An' frowns vor kith an' kin to rue;
But her sweet vaïce do vall,
Wi' kindly words to all,
Both big an' small, the whole day drough.

An' when the evenèn sky wer peäle,
We heärd the warblèn nightèngeäle,
A-drawèn out his lwonesome zong,
In windèn music down the drong;
An' Jenny vrom her he'th,

Come out, though not in me'th,
But held her breath, to hear his zong

Then, while the bird wi' oben bill
Did warble on, her vaïce wer still;
An' as she stood avore me, bound
In stillness to the flow'ry mound,
"The bird's a jay to zome,"
I thought, "but when he's dum,
Her vaïce will come, wi' sweeter sound."

MINDEN HOUSE

'Twer when the vo'k wer out to hawl
A vield o' hay a day in June,
An' when the zun begun to vall
Toward the west in afternoon,
Woone only wer a-left behind
To bide indoors, at hwome, an' mind
The house, an' answer vo'k avore
The geäte or door,—young Fanny Deäne.

The aïr 'ithin the geärden wall
Wer deadly still, unless the bee
Did hummy by, or in the hall
The clock did ring a-hettèn dree,
An' there, wi' busy hands, inside
The iron ceäsement, oben'd wide,
Did zit an' pull wi' nimble twitch
Her tiny stitch, young Fanny Deäne.

As there she zot she heärd two blows
A-knock'd upon the rumblèn door,
An' laid azide her work, an' rose,
An' walk'd out feäir, athirt the vloor;
An' there, a-holdèn in his hand
His bridled meäre, a youth did stand,

An' mildly twold his neäme and pleäce
Avore the feäce o' Fanny Deäne.

He twold her that he had on hand
Zome business on his father's zide,
But what she didden understand;
An' zoo she ax'd en if he'd ride
Out where her father mid be vound,
Bezide the plow, in Cowslip Ground;
An' there he went, but left his mind
Back there behind, wi' Fanny Deäne.

An' oh! his hwomeward road wer gay
In aïr a-blowèn, whiff by whiff,
While sheenèn water-weäves did play
An' boughs did sway above the cliff;
Vor Time had now a-show'd en dim
The jay it had in store vor him;
An' when he went thik road ageän
His errand then wer Fanny Deäne.

How strangely things be brought about
By Providence, noo tongue can tell,
She minded house, when vo'k wer out,
An' zoo mus' bid the house farewell;
The bees mid hum, the clock mid call
The lwonesome hours 'ithin the hall,
But in behind the woaken door,
There's now noo mwore a Fanny Deäne.

THE LOVELY MAÏD OV ELWELL MEÄD.

A MAÏD wi' many gifts o' greäce,
A maïd wi' ever-smilèn feäce,

A child o' yours my chilhood's pleäce,
   O leänèn lawns ov Allen ;
'S a-walkèn where your stream do flow,
A-blushèn where your flowers do blow,
A-smilèn where your zun do glow,
   O leänèn lawns ov Allen.
     An' good, however good's a-waïgh'd,
     'S the lovely maïd ov Elwell Meäd.

An' oh ! if I could teäme an' guide
The winds above the e'th, an' ride
As light as shootèn stars do glide,
   O leänèn lawns ov Allen,
To you I'd teäke my daily flight,
Drough dark'nèn aïr in evenèn's light,
An' bid her every night " Good night,"
   O leänèn lawns ov Allen.
     Vor good, however good's a-waïgh'd,
     'S the lovely maïd ov Elwell Meäd.

An' when your hedges' slooes be blue,
By blackberries o' dark'nèn hue,
An' spiders' webs behung wi' dew,
   O leänèn lawns ov Allen,
Avore the winter aïr's a-chill'd,
Avore your winter brook's a-vill'd
Avore your zummer flow'rs be kill'd,
   O leänèn lawns ov Allen ;
     I there would meet, in white array'd,
     The lovely maïd ov Elwell Meäd.

For when the zun, as birds do rise,
Do cast their sheädes vrom autum' skies,
A-sparklèn in her dewy eyes,
   O leänèn lawns ov Allen :

Then all your mossy paths below
The trees, wi' leaves a-vallèn slow,
Like zinkèn fleäkes o' yollow snow,
   O leänèn lawns ov Allen.
      Would be mwore teakèn where they stray'd
      The lovely maïd ov Elwell Meäd.

OUR FATHERS' WORKS.

Ah! I do think, as I do tread
Theäse path, wi' elems overhead,
A-climèn slowly up vrom Bridge,
By easy steps, to Broadwoak Ridge,
That all theäse roads that we do bruise
Wi' hosses' shoes, or heavy lwoads;
An' hedges' bands, where trees in row
Do rise an' grow aroun' the lands,
Be works that we've a-vound a-wrought
By our vorefathers' ceäre an' thought.

They clear'd the groun' vor grass to teäke
The pleäce that bore the bremble breäke,
An' draïn'd the fen, where water spread,
A-lyèn dead, a beäne to men;
An' built the mill, where still the wheel
Do grind our meal, below the hill;
An' turn'd the bridge, wi' arch a-spread,
Below a road, vor us to tread.

They vound a pleäce, where we mid seek
The gifts o' greäce vrom week to week;
An' built wi' stwone, upon the hill,
A tow'r we still do call our own;
With bells to use, an' meäke rejaïce,
Wi' giant vaïce, at our good news:

An' lifted stwones an' beams to keep
The raïn an' cwold vrom us asleep.

Zoo now mid nwone ov us vorget
The pattern our vorefathers zet;
But each be fäin to underteäke
Some work to meäke vor others' gaïn,
That we mid leäve mwore good to sheäre,
Less ills to bear, less souls to grieve,
An' when our hands do vall to rest,
It mid be vrom a work a-blest.

THE WOLD VO'K DEAD.

My days, wi' wold vo'k all but gone,
An' childern now a-comèn on,
Do bring me still my mother's smiles
In light that now do show my chile's;
An' I've a-sheär'd the wold vo'ks' me'th,
Avore the burnèn Chris'mas he'th,
At friendly bwoards, where feäce by feäce,
Did, year by year, gi'e up its pleäce,
An' leäve me here, behind, to tread
The ground a-trod by wold vo'k dead.

But wold things be a-lost vor new,
An' zome do come, while zome do goo:
As wither'd beech-tree leaves do cling
Among the nesh young buds o' Spring;
An' frettèn worms ha' slowly wound,
Droo beams the wold vo'k lifted sound,
An' trees they planted little slips
Ha' stems that noo two eärms can clips;
An' grey an' yollow moss do spread
On buildèns new to wold vo'k dead

The backs of all our zilv'ry hills,
The brook that still do dreve our mills,
The roads a-climèn up the brows
O' knaps, a-screen'd by meäple boughs,
Wer all a-mark'd in sheäde an' light
Avore our wolder fathers' zight,
In zunny days, a-gied their hands
For happy work, a-tillèn lands,
That now do yield their childern bread
Till they do rest wi' wold vo'k dead.

But livèn vo'k, a-grievèn on,
Wi' lwonesome love, vor souls a-gone,
Do zee their goodness, but do vind
All else a-stealèn out o' mind;
As air do meäke the vurthest land
Look feäirer than the vield at hand,
An' zoo, as time do slowly pass,
So still's a sheäde upon the grass,
Its wid'nèn speäce do slowly shed
A glory roun' the wold vo'k dead.

An' what if good vo'ks' life o' breath
Is zoo a-hallow'd after death,
That they mid only know above,
Their times o' faïth, an' jay, an' love,
While all the evil time ha' brought
'S a-lost vor ever out o' thought;
As all the moon that idden bright,
'S a-lost in darkness out o' zight;
And all the godly life they led
Is glory to the wold vo'k dead.

If things be zoo, an' souls above
Can only mind our e'thly love,

Why then they'll veel our kindness drown
The thoughts ov all that meäde em frown.
An' jay o' jays will dry the tear
O' sadness that do trickle here,
An' nothèn mwore o' life than love,
An' peace, will then be know'd above.
Do good, vor that, when life's a-vled,
Is still a pleasure to the dead.

CULVER DELL AND THE SQUIRE.

There's noo pleäce I do like so well,
As Elem Knap in Culver Dell,
Where timber trees, wi' lofty shouds,
Did rise avore the western clouds;
An' stan' ageän, wi' veathery tops,
A-swayèn up in North-Hill Copse.
An' on the east the mornèn broke
Above a dewy grove o' woak:
An' noontide shed its burnèn light
On ashes on the southern height;
An' I could vind zome teäles to tell,
O' former days in Culver Dell.

An' all the vo'k did love so well
The good wold squire o' Culver Dell,
That used to ramble drough the sheädes
O' timber, or the burnèn gleädes,
An' come at evenèn up the leäze
Wi' red-eär'd dogs bezide his knees.
An' hold his gun, a-hangèn drough
His eärmpit, out above his tooe.
Wi' kindly words upon his tongue,
Vor vo'k that met en, wold an' young,
Vor he did know the poor so well
'S the richest vo'k in Culver Dell.

An' while the woäk, wi' spreadèn head,
Did sheäde the foxes' verny bed;
An' runnèn heäres, in zunny gleädes,
Did beät the grasses' quiv'rèn' bleädes;
An' speckled pa'tridges took flight
In stubble vields a-feädèn white;
Or he could zee the pheasant strut
In sheädy woods, wi' painted cwoat;
Or long-tongued dogs did love to run
Among the leaves, bezide his gun;
We didden want vor call to dwell
At hwome in peace in Culver Dell.

But now I hope his kindly feäce
Is gone to vind a better pleäce;
But still, wi' vo'k a-left behind
He'll always be a-kept in mind,
Vor all his springy-vooted hounds
Ha' done o' trottèn round his grounds,
An' we have all a-left the spot,
To teäke, a-scatter'd, each his lot;
An' even Father, lik' the rest,
Ha' left our long vorseäken nest;
An' we should vind it sad to dwell,
Ageän at hwome in Culver Dell.

The aïry mornèns still mid smite
Our windows wi' their rwosy light,
An' high-zunn'd noons mid dry the dew
On growèn groun' below our shoe;
The blushèn evenèn still mid dye,
Wi' viry red, the western sky;
The zunny spring-time's quicknèn power
Mid come to oben leaf an' flower;
An' days an' tides mid bring us on
Woone pleasure when another's gone.
But we must bid a long farewell
To days an' tides in Culver Dell.

OUR BE'THPLACE.

How dear's the door a latch do shut,
An' geärden that a hatch do shut,
Where vu'st our bloomèn cheäks ha' prest
The pillor ov our childhood's rest;
Or where, wi' little tooes, we wore
The paths our fathers trod avore;
Or clim'd the timber's bark aloft,
Below the zingèn lark aloft,
The while we heärd the echo sound
Drough all the ringèn valley round.

A lwonesome grove o' woak did rise,
To screen our house, where smoke did rise,
A-twistèn blue, while yeet the zun
Did langthen on our childhood's fun;
An' there, wi' all the sheäpes an' sounds
O' life, among the timber'd grounds,
The birds upon their boughs did zing,
An' milkmaïds by their cows did zing,
Wi' merry sounds, that softly died,
A-ringèn down the valley zide.

By river banks wi' reeds a-bound,
An' sheenèn pools, wi' weeds a-bound,
The long-neck'd gander's ruddy bill
To snow-white geese did cackle sh'ill;
An' stridèn peewits heästen'd by,
O' tiptooe wi' their screamèn cry;
An' stalkèn cows a-lowèn loud,
An' struttèn cocks a-crowèn loud,
Did rouse the echoes up to mock
Their mingled sounds by hill an' rock.

The stars that clim'd our skies all dark,
Above our sleepèn eyes all dark,
An' zuns a-rollèn round to bring
The seasons on, vrom Spring to Spring,
Ha' vled, wi' never-restèn flight,
Drough green-bough'd day, an' dark-tree'd night;
Till now our childhood's pleäces there,
Be gay wi' other feäces there,
An' we ourselves do vollow on
Our own vorelivers dead an' gone.

THE WINDOW FREÄM'D WI' STWONE.

When Pentridge House wer still the nest
O' souls that now ha' better rest,
Avore the viër burnt to ground
His beams an' walls, that then wer sound,
'Ithin a naïl-bestudded door,
An' passage wi' a stwonèn vloor,
There spread the hall, where zun-light shone
In drough a window freäm'd wi' stwone.

A clavy-beam o' sheenèn woak
Did span the he'th wi' twistèn smoke,
Where fleämes did shoot in yollow streaks,
Above the brands, their flashèn peaks;
An' aunt did pull, as she did stand
O'-tip-tooe, wi' her lifted hand,
A curtain feäded wi' the zun,
Avore the window freäm'd wi' stwone.

When Hwome-ground grass, below the moon,
Wer damp wi' evenèn dew in June,
An' aunt did call the maïdens in
Vrom walkèn, wi' their shoes too thin,

They zot to rest their litty veet
Upon the window's woaken seat,
An' chatted there, in light that shone
In drough the window freäm'd wi' stwone.

An' as the seasons, in a ring,
Roll'd slowly roun' vrom Spring to Spring,
An' brought em on zome holy-tide,
When they did cast their tools azide;
How glad it meäde em all to spy
In Stwonylands their friends draw nigh,
As they did know em all by neäme
Out drough the window's stwonèn freäme.

O evenèn zun, a-ridèn drough
The sky, vrom Sh'oton Hill o' blue,
To leäve the night a-broodèn dark
At Stalbridge, wi' its grey-wall'd park;
Small jay to me the vields do bring,
Vor all their zummer birds do zing,
Since now thy beams noo mwore do fleäme
In drough the window's stwonèn freäme.

THE WATER-SPRING IN THE LEANE.

Oh! aye! the spring 'ithin the leäne,
A-leäden down to Lyddan Brook;
An' still a-nesslèn in his nook,
As weeks do pass, an' moons do weäne.
    Nwone the drier,
    Nwone the higher,
Nwone the nigher to the door
Where we did live so long avore.

An' oh! what vo'k his mossy brim
Ha' gathered in the run o' time!

The wife a-blushèn in her prime ;
The widow wi' her eyezight dim ;
  Maïdens dippèn,
  Childern sippèn,
Water drippèn, at the cool
Dark wallèn ov the little pool.

Behind the spring do lie the lands
My father till'd, vrom Spring to Spring,
Awäitèn on vor time to bring
The crops to pay his weary hands.
  Wheat a-growèn,
  Beäns a-blowèn,
Grass vor mowèn, where the bridge
Do leäd to Ryall's on the ridge.

But who do know when liv'd an' died
The squier o' the mwoldrèn hall ;
That lined en wi' a stwonèn wall,
An' steän'd so cleän his wat'ry zide ?
  We behind en,
  Now can't vind en,
But do mind en, an' do thank
His meäker vor his little tank.

THE POPLARS.

If theäse day's work an' burnèn sky
'V'a-zent hwome you so tired as I,
Let's zit an' rest 'ithin the screen
O' my wold bow'r upon the green ;
Where I do goo myself an' let
The evenèn aiër cool my het,
When dew do wet the grasses bleädes,
A-quiv'rèn in the dusky sheädes.

There yonder poplar trees do play
Soft music, as their heads do sway,
While wind, a-rustlèn soft or loud,
Do stream ageän their lofty sh'oud;
An' seem to heal the ranklèn zore
My mind do meet wi' out o' door,
When I've a-bore, in downcast mood,
Zome evil where I look'd vor good.

O' they two poplars that do rise
So high avore our naïghbours' eyes,
A-zet by gramfer, hand by hand,
Wi' grammer, in their bit o' land;
The woone upon the western zide
Wer his, an' woone wer grammer's pride,
An' since they died, we all do teäke
Mwore ceäre o'm vor the wold vo'k's seäke.

An' there, wi' stems a-growèn tall
Avore the houses mossy wall,
The while the moon ha' slowly past
The leafy window, they've a-cast
Their sheädes 'ithin the window peäne;
While childern have a-grown to men,
An' then ageän ha' left their beds,
To bear their childern's heavy heads.

THE LINDEN ON THE LAWN.

No! Jenny, there's noo pleäce to charm
My mind lik' yours at Woakland farm,
A-peärted vrom the busy town,
By longsome miles ov airy down,
Where woonce the meshy wall did gird
Your flow'ry geärden, an' the bird

Did zing in zummer wind that stirr'd
The spreäden linden on the lawn.

An' now ov all the trees wi' sheädes
A-wheelèn round in Blackmwore gleädes,
There's noo tall poplar by the brook,
Nor elem that do rock the rook,
Nor ash upon the shelvèn ledge,
Nor low-bough'd woak bezide the hedge,
Nor withy up above the zedge,
So dear's thik linden on the lawn.

Vor there, o' zummer nights, below
The wall, we zot when aïr did blow,
An' sheäke the dewy rwose a-tied
Up roun' the window's stwonèn zide.
An' while the carter rod' along
A-zingèn, down the dusky drong,
There you did zing a sweeter zong
Below the linden on the lawn.

An' while your warbled ditty wound.
Drough playsome flights o' mellow sound,
The nightèngeäle's sh'ill zong, that broke
The stillness ov the dewy woak,
Rung clear along the grove, an' smote
To sudden stillness ev'ry droat;
As we did zit, an' hear it float
Below the linden on the lawn.

Where dusky light did softly vall
'Ithin the stwonèn-window'd hall,
Avore your father's blinkèn eyes,
His evenèn whiff o' smoke did rise,

An' vrom the bedroom window's height
Your little John, a-cloth'd in white,
An' gwaïn to bed, did cry " good night "
Towards the linden on the lawn.

But now, as Dobbin, wi' a nod
Vor ev'ry heavy step he trod,
Did bring me on, to-night, avore
The geäbled house's pworchèd door,
Noo laughèn child a-cloth'd in white,
Look'd drough the stwonèn window's light,
An' noo vaïce zung, in dusky night,
Below the linden on the lawn.

An' zoo, if you should ever vind
My kindness seem to grow less kind,
An' if upon my clouded feäce
My smile should yield a frown its pleäce,
Then, Jenny, only laugh an' call
My mind 'ithin the geärden wall,
Where we did play at even-fall,
Below the linden on the lawn.

OUR ABODE IN ARBY WOOD.

Though ice do hang upon the willows
    Out bezide the vrozen brook,
An' storms do roar above our pillows,
    Drough the night, 'ithin our nook;
Our evenèn he'th's a-glowèn warm,
    Drough wringèn vrost, an' roarèn storm.
Though winds mid meäke the wold beams sheäke.
    In our abode in Arby Wood.

An' there, though we mid hear the timber
  Creake avore the windy raïn;
An' climèn ivy quiver, limber,
  Up ageän the window peäne;
Our merry vaïces then do sound,
  In rollèn glee, or dree-vaïce round;
Though wind mid roar, 'ithout the door,
  Ov our abode in Arby Wood.

SLOW TO COME, QUICK AGONE.

Ah! there's a house that I do know
Besouth o' yonder trees,
Where northern winds can hardly blow
But in a softest breeze.
An' there woonce sounded zongs an' teäles
Vrom vaïce o' maïd or youth,
An' sweeter than the nightèngeäle's
Above the copses lewth.

How swiftly there did run the brooks,
How swift wer winds in flight,
How swiftly to their roost the rooks
Did vlee o'er head at night.
Though slow did seem to us the peäce
O' comèn days a-head,
That now do seem as in a reäce
Wi' aïr-birds to ha' vled.

THE VIER-ZIDE.

'Tis zome vo'ks jay to teäke the road,
An' goo abro'd, a-wand'rèn wide,
Vrom shere to shere, vrom pleäce to pleäce,
The swiftest peäce that vo'k can ride.
But I've a jay 'ithin the door,
Wi' friends avore the vier-zide.

THE VIER-ZIDE.

An' zoo, when winter skies do lour,
An' when the Stour's a-rollèn wide,
Drough bridge-voot raïls, a-painted white,
To be at night the traveller's guide,
Gi'e me a pleäce that's warm an' dry,
A-zittèn nigh my vier-zide.

Vor where do love o' kith an' kin,
At vu'st begin, or grow an' wride,
Till souls a-lov'd so young, be wold,
Though never cwold, drough time nor tide,
But where in me'th their gather'd veet
Do often meet—the vier-zide.

If, when a friend ha' left the land,
I shook his hand a-most wet-eyed,
I velt too well the ob'nèn door
Would leäd noo mwore where he did bide,
An' where I heärd his vaïces sound,
In me'th around the vier-zide.

As I've a-zeed how vast do vall
The mwold'rèn hall, the wold vo'ks pride,
Where merry hearts wer woonce a-ved
Wi' daily bread, why I've a-sigh'd,
To zee the wall so green wi' mwold,
An' vind so cwold the vier-zide.

An' Chris'mas still mid bring his me'th
To ouer he'th, but if we tried
To gather all that woonce did wear
Gay feäces there! Ah! zome ha' died,
An' zome be gone to leäve wi' gaps
O' missèn laps, the vier-zide.

But come now, bring us in your hand,
A heavy brand o' woak a-dried,
To cheer us wi' his het an' light,
While vrosty night, so starry-skied,
Go gather souls that time do speäre
To zit an' sheäre our vier-zide.

KNOWLWOOD.

I don't want to sleep abrode, John,
I do like my hwomeward road, John;
An' like the sound o' Knowlwood bells the best.
Zome would rove vrom pleäce to pleäce, John,
Zome would goo from feäce to feäce, John,
But I be happy in my hwomely nest;
An' slight's the hope vor any pleäce bezide,
To leäve the plaïn abode where love do bide.

Where the shelvèn knap do vall, John,
Under trees a-springèn tall, John;
'Tis there my house do show his sheenèn zide,
Wi' his walls vor ever green, John,
Under ivy that's a screen, John,
Vrom wet an' het, an' ev'ry changèn tide,
An' I do little ho vor goold or pride,
To leäve the plaïn abode where love do bide.

There the bendèn stream do flow, John,
By the mossy bridge's bow, John;
An' there the road do wind below the hill;
There the miller, white wi' meal, John,
Deafen'd wi' his foamy wheel, John,
Do stan' o' times a-lookèn out o' mill:
The while 'ithin his lightly-sheäken door,
His wheatèn flour do whitèn all his floor.

KNOWLWOOD.

When my daily work's a-done, John,
At the zettèn o' the zun, John,
An' I all day 've a-plaÿ'd a good man's peärt,
I do vind my ease a-blest, John,
While my conscience is at rest, John ;
An' while noo worm's a-left to fret my heart;
An' who vor finer hwomes o' restless pride,
Would pass the plaïn abode where peace do bide?

By a windor in the west, John,
There upon my fiddle's breast, John,
The strings do sound below my bow's white heäir ;
While a zingèn drush do swaÿ, John,
Up an' down upon a spraÿ, John,
An' cast his sheäde upon the window square ;
Vor birds do know their friends, an' build their nest,
An' love to roost, where they can live at rest.

Out o' town the win' do bring, John,
Peals o' bells when they do ring, John,
An' roun' me here, at hand, my ear can catch
The maïd a-zingèn by the stream, John,
Or carter whislèn wi' his team, John,
Or zingèn birds, or water at the hatch ;
An' zoo wi' sounds o' vaïce, an' bird an' bell,
Noo hour is dull 'ithin our rwosy dell.

An' when the darksome night do hide, John,
Land an' wood on ev'ry zide, John ;
An' when the light's a-burnèn on my bwoard,
Then vor pleasures out o' door, John,
I've enough upon my vloor, John :
My Jenny's lovèn deed, an' look, an' word,
An' we be lwoth, lik' culvers zide by zide,
To leäve the plaïn abode where love do bide.

HALLOWED PLEÄCES.

At Woodcombe farm, wi' ground an' tree
Hallow'd by times o' youthvul glee,
At Chris'mas time I spent a night
Wi' feäces dearest to my zight;
An' took my wife to tread, woonce mwore,
Her maïden hwome's vorseäken vloor,
An' under stars that slowly wheel'd
Aloft, above the keen-aïr'd vield,
While night bedimm'd the rus'lèn copse,
An' darken'd all the ridges' tops,
The hall, a-hung wi' holly, rung
Wi' many a tongue o' wold an' young.

There, on the he'th's well-hetted ground,
Hallow'd by times o' zittèn round,
The brimvul mug o' cider stood
An' hiss'd avore the bleäzèn wood;
An' zome, a-zittèn knee by knee,
Did tell their teäles wi' hearty glee,
An' others gamboll'd in a roar
O' laughter on the stwonèn vloor;
An' while the moss o' winter-tide
Clung chilly roun' the house's zide,
The hall, a-hung wi' holly, rung
Wi' many a tongue o' wold an' young.

There, on the pworches bench o' stwone,
Hallow'd by times o' youthvul fun,
We laugh'd an' sigh'd to think o' neämes
That rung there woonce, in evenèn geämes;

HALLOWED PLEÄCES.

An' while the swayèn cypress bow'd,
In chilly wind, his darksome sh'oud
An' honeyzuckles, beäre o' leäves,
Still reach'd the window-sheädèn eaves
Up where the clematis did trim
The stwonèn arches mossy rim,
The hall, a-hung wi' holly, rung
Wi' many a tongue o' wold an' young.

There, in the geärden's wall-bound square,
Hallow'd by times o' strollèn there,
The winter wind, a-hufflèn loud,
Did sway the pear-tree's leafless sh'oud,
An' beät the bush that woonce did bear
The damask rwose vor Jenny's heäir;
An' there the walk o' peävèn stwone
That burn'd below the zummer zun,
Struck icy-cwold drough shoes a-wore
By maïdens vrom the hetted vloor
In hall, a-hung wi' holm, where rung
Vull many a tongue o' wold an' young.

There at the geäte that woonce wer blue
Hallow'd by times o' passèn drough,
Light strawmotes rose in flaggèn flight,
A-floated by the winds o' night,
Where leafy ivy-stems did crawl
In moonlight on the windblown wall,
An' merry maïdens' vaïces vled
In echoes sh'ill, vrom wall to shed,
As shiv'rèn in their frocks o' white
They come to bid us there "Good night,"
Vrom hall, a-hung wi' holm, that rung
Wi' many a tongue o' wold an' young.

There in the narrow leäne an' drong
Hallow'd by times o' gwaïn along,
The lofty ashes' leafless sh'ouds
Rose dark avore the clear-edged clouds,
The while the moon, at girtest height,
Bespread the pooly brook wi' light,
An' as our child, in loose-limb'd rest,
Lay peäle upon her mother's breast,
Her waxen eyelids seal'd her eyes
Vrom darksome trees, an' sheenèn skies,
An' halls a-hung wi' holm, that rung
Wi' many a tongue, o' wold an' young.

THE WOLD WALL.

HERE, Jeäne, we vu'st did meet below
The leafy boughs, a-swingèn slow,
Avore the zun, wi' evenèn glow,
Above our road, a-beamèn red;
The grass in zwath wer in the meäds,
The water gleam'd among the reeds
In aïr a-steälèn roun' the hall,
Where ivy clung upon the wall.
Ah! well-a-day! O wall adieu!
The wall is wold, my grief is new.

An' there you walk'd wi' blushèn pride,
Where softly-wheelèn streams did glide,
Drough sheädes o' poplars at my zide,
An' there wi' love that still do live,
Your feäce did wear the smile o' youth,
The while you spoke wi' age's truth,
An' wi' a rwosebud's mossy ball,
I deck'd your bosom vrom the wall.
Ah! well-a-day! O wall adieu!
The wall is wold, my grief is new.

But now when winter's raïn do vall,
An' wind do beät ageän the hall,
The while upon the wat'ry wall
In spots o' grey the moss do grow;
The ruf noo mwore shall overspread
The pillor ov our weary head,
Nor shall the rwose's mossy ball
Behang vor you the house's wall.
Ah! well-a-day! O wall adieu!
The wall is wold, my grief is new.

EÄKE'S HOUSE IN BLACKMWORE.

John Bleäke he had a bit o' ground
Come to en by his mother's zide;
An' after that, two hunderd pound
His uncle left en when he died;
"Well now," cried John, "my mind's a-bent
To build a house, an' pay noo rent."
An' Meäry gi'ed en her consent.
"Do, do,"—the maïdens cried.
"True, true,"—his wife replied.
"Done, done,—a house o' brick or stwone,"
Cried merry Bleäke o' Blackmwore.

Then John he call'd vor men o' skill,
An' builders answer'd to his call;
An' met to reckon, each his bill;
Vor vloor an' window, ruf an' wall.
An' woone did mark it on the groun',
An' woone did think, an' scratch his crown,
An' reckon work, an' write it down:
"Zoo, zoo,"—woone treädesman cried,
"True, true,"—woone mwore replied.
"Aye, aye,—good work, an' have good pay,"
Cried merry Bleäke o' Blackmwore.

The work begun, an' trowels rung,
An' up the brickèn wall did rise,
An' up the slantèn refters sprung,
Wi' busy blows, an' lusty cries!
An' woone brought planks to meäke a vloor,
An' woone did come wi' durns or door,
An' woone did zaw, an' woone did bore.
"Brick, brick,—there down below,
Quick, quick,—why b'ye so slow?"
"Lime, lime,—why we do weäste the time,
Vor merry Bleäke o' Blackmwore."

The house wer up vrom groun' to tun,
An' thatch'd ageän the raïny sky,
Wi' windows to the noonday zun,
Where rushy Stour do wander by.
In coo'se he had a pworch to screen
The inside door, when win's wer keen,
An' out avore the pworch, a green.
"Here! here!"—the childern cried:
"Dear! dear!"—the wife replied;
"There, there,—the house is perty feäir,"
Cried merry Bleäke o' Blackmwore.

Then John he ax'd his friends to warm
His house, an' they, a goodish batch,
Did come alwone, or eärm in eärm,
All roads, a-meäkèn vor his hatch:
An' there below the clavy beam
The kettle-spout did zing an' steam;
An' there wer ceäkes, an' tea wi' cream.
"Lo! lo!"—the women cried;
"Ho! ho!"—the men replied;
"Health, health,—attend ye wi' your wealth,
Good merry Bleäke o' Blackmwore."

Then John, a-praïs'd, flung up his crown,
All back a-langhèn in a roar.
They praïs'd his wife, an' she look'd down
A-simperèn towards the vloor.
Then up they sprung a-dancèn reels,
An' up went tooes, an' up went heels,
A-windèn roun' in knots an' wheels.
"Brisk, brisk,"—the maïdens cried;
"Frisk, frisk,"—the men replied;
"Quick, quick,—there wi' your fiddle-stick,"
Cried merry Bleäke o' Blackmwore.

An' when the morrow's zun did sheen,
John Bleäke beheld, wi' jay an' pride,
His brickèn house, an' pworch, an' green,
Above the Stour's rushy zide.
The zwallows left the lwonesome groves,
To build below the thatchèn oves,
An' robins come vor crumbs o' lwoaves:
"Tweet, tweet,"—the birds all cried;
"Sweet, sweet,"—John's wife replied;
"Dad, dad,"—the childern cried so glad,
To merry Bleäke o' Blackmwore.

JOHN BLEÄKE AT HWOME AT NIGHT.

No: where the woak do overspread,
The grass begloom'd below his head,
An' water, under bowèn zedge,
A-springèn vrom the river's edge,
Do ripple, as the win' do blow,
An' sparkle, as the sky do glow;
An' grey-leav'd withy-boughs do cool,
Wi' darksome sheädes, the clear-feäced pool,

My chimny smoke, 'ithin the lew
O' trees is there arisèn blue;
Avore the night do dim our zight
Or candle-light, a-sheenèn bright,
Do sparkle drough the window.

When crumpled leaves o' Fall do bound
Avore the wind, along the ground,
An' wither'd bennet-stems do stand
A-quiv'rèn on the chilly land;
The while the zun, wi' zettèn rim,
Do leäve the workman's pathway dim;
An' sweet-breath'd childern's hangèn heads
Be laid wi' kisses, on their beds;
Then I do seek my woodland nest,
An' zit bezide my vier at rest,
While night's a-spread, where day's a-vled,
An' lights do shed their beams o' red,
A-sparklèn drough the window.

If winter's whistlèn winds do vreeze
The snow a-gather'd on the trees,
An' sheädes o' poplar stems do vall
In moonlight up athirt the wall;
An' icicles do hang below
The oves, a-glitt'rèn in a row,
An' risèn stars do slowly ride
Above the ruf's upslantèn zide;
Then I do lay my weary head
Asleep upon my peaceful bed,
When middle-night ha' quench'd the light
Ov embers bright, an' candles white
A-beamèn drough the window.

MILKEN TIME.

'Twer when the busy birds did vlee,
Wi' sheenèn wings, vrom tree to tree,
To build upon the mossy lim',
Their hollow nestes' rounded rim;
The while the zun, a-zinkèn low,
Did roll along his evenèn bow,
I come along where wide-horn'd cows,
'Ithin a nook, a-screen'd by boughs,
Did stan' an' flip the white-hoop'd païls
Wi' heäiry tufts o' swingèn taïls;
An' there wer Jenny Coom a-gone
Along the path a vew steps on.
A-beärèn on her head, upstraïght,
Her païl, wi' slowly-ridèn waïght,
An' hoops a-sheenèn, lily-white,
Ageän the evenèn's slantèn light;
An' zo I took her pail, an' left
Her neck a-freed vrom all his heft;
An' she a-lookèn up an' down,
Wi' sheäpely head an' glossy crown,
Then took my zide, an' kept my peäce
A-talkèn on wi' smilèn feäce,
An' zettèn things in sich a light,
I'd faïn ha' heär'd her talk all night;
An' when I brought her milk avore
The geäte, she took it in to door,
An' if her pail had but allow'd
Her head to vall, she would ha' bow'd,
An' still, as 'twer, I had the zight
Ov her sweet smile droughout the night.

WHEN BIRDS BE STILL.

Vor all the zun do leäve the sky,
An' all the sounds o' day do die,
An' noo mwore veet do walk the dim
Vield-path to clim' the stiel's bars,
Yeet out below the rizèn stars,
The dark'nèn day mid leäve behind
Woone tongue that I shall always vind,
A-whisperèn kind, when birds be still.

Zoo let the day come on to spread
His kindly light above my head,
Wi' zights to zee, an' sounds to hear,
That still do cheer my thoughtvul mind;
Or let en goo, an' leäve behind
An' hour to stroll along the gleädes,
Where night do drown the beeches' sheädes,
On grasses' bleädes, when birds be still.

Vor when the night do lull the sound
O' cows a-bleärèn out in ground,
The sh'ill-vaïc'd dog do stan' an' bark
'Ithin the dark, bezide the road;
An' when noo cracklèn waggon's lwoad
Is in the leäne, the wind do bring
The merry peals that bells do ring
O ding-dong-ding, when birds be still.

Zoo teäke, vor me, the town a-drown'd,
'Ithin a storm o' rumblèn sound,
An' gi'e me vaïces that do speak
So soft an' meek, to souls alwone;
The brook a-gurglèn round a stwone,

An' birds o' day a-zingèn clear,
An' leaves, that I mid zit an' hear
A-rustlèn near, when birds be still.

RIDEN HWOME AT NIGHT.

Oh! no, I quite injaÿ'd the ride
   Behind wold Dobbin's heavy heels,
Wi' Jeäne a-prattlèn at my zide,
   Above our peäir o' spinnèn wheels,
As grey-rin'd ashes' swayèn tops
Did creak in moonlight in the copse,
Above the quiv'rèn grass, a-beät
By wind a-blowèn drough the geät.

If weary souls did want their sleep,
   They had a-zent vor sleep the night;
Vor vo'k that had a call to keep
   Awake, lik' us, there still wer light.
An' He that shut the sleepers' eyes,
A-waïtèn vor the zun to rise,
Ha' too much love to let em know
The ling'rèn night did goo so slow.

But if my wife did catch a zight
   O' zome queer pollard, or a post,
Poor soul! she took en in her fright
   To be a robber or a ghost.
A two-stump'd withy, wi' a head,
Mus' be a man wi' eärms a-spread;
An' foam o' water, round a rock,
Wer then a drownèn leädy's frock.

Zome staddle stwones to bear a mow,
   Wer dancèn veäries on the lag;
An' then a snow-white sheeted cow
   Could only be, she thought, their flag,

An owl a-vleèn drough the wood
Wer men on watch vor little good;
An' geätes a slam'd by wind, did goo,
She thought, to let a robber drough.

But after all, she lik'd the zight
   O' cows asleep in glitt'rèn dew;
An' brooks that gleam'd below the light,
   An' dim vield paths 'ithout a shoe.
An' gaïly talk'd bezide my ears,
A-laughèn off her needless fears:
Or had the childern uppermost
In mind, instead o' thief or ghost.

An' when our house, wi' open door,
   Did rumble hollow round our heads,
She heästen'd up to tother vloor,
   To zee the childern in their beds;
An' vound woone little head awry,
Wi' woone a-turn'd toward the sky;
An' wrung her hands ageän her breast,
A-smilèn at their happy rest.

ZUN-ZET.

Where the western zun, unclouded,
   Up above the grey hill-tops,
Did sheen drough ashes, lofty sh'ouded.
   On the turf bezide the copse,
     In zummer weather,
     We together,
     Sorrow-slightèn, work-vorgettèn.
   Gambol'd wi' the zun a-zetten.

There, by flow'ry bows o' bramble,
   Under hedge, in ash-tree sheädes,

ZUN-ZET.

The dun-heaïr'd ho'se did slowly ramble
  On the grasses' dewy bleädes,
    Zet free o' lwoads,
    An' stwony rwoads,
    Vorgetvul o' the lashes frettèn,
    Grazèn wi' the zun a-zettèn.

There wer rooks a-beätèn by us
  Drough the aïr, in a vlock,
An' there the lively blackbird, nigh us,
  On the meäple bough did rock,
    Wi' ringèn droat,
    Where zunlight smote
    The yollow boughs o' zunny hedges
    Over western hills' blue edges.

Waters, drough the meäds a-purlèn,
  Glissen'd in the evenèn's light,
An' smoke, above the town a-curlèn,
  Melted slowly out o' zight;
    An' there, in glooms
    Ov unzunn'd rooms,
    To zome, wi' idle sorrows frettèn,
    Zuns did set avore their zettèn.

We were out in geämes and reäces,
  Loud a-laughèn, wild in me'th,
Wi' windblown heäir, an' zunbrown'd feäces,
  Leäpen on the high-sky'd e'th,
    Avore the lights
    Wer tin'd o' nights,
    An' while the gossamer's light nettèn
    Sparkled to the zun a-zettèn.

SPRING.

Now the zunny aïr's a-blowèn
Softly over flowers a-growèn;
An' the sparklèn light do quiver
On the ivy-bough an' river;
Bleätèn lambs, wi' woolly feäces,
Now do play, a-runnèn reäces;
    An' the springèn
    Lark's a-zingèn,
Lik' a dot avore the cloud,
High above the ashes sh'oud.

Housèn, in the open brightness,
Now do sheen in spots o' whiteness;
Here an' there, on upland ledges,
In among the trees an' hedges,
Where, along by vlocks o' sparrows,
Chatt'rèn at the ploughman's harrows,
    Dousty rwoaded,
    Errand-lwoaded;
Jenny, though her cloak is thin,
Do wish en hwome upon the pin.

Zoo come along, noo longer heedvul
Ov the vier, leätely needvul,
Over grass o' slopèn leäzes,
Zingèn zongs in zunny breezes;
Out to work in copse, a-mootèn,
Where the primrwose is a-shootèn,
    An in gladness,
    Free o' sadness,
In the warmth o' Spring vorget
Leafless winter's cwold an' wet.

THE ZUMMER HEDGE.

As light do gleäre in ev'ry ground,
Wi' boughy hedges out a-round
A-climmèn up the slopèn brows
O' hills, in rows o' sheädy boughs:
The while the hawthorn buds do blow
As thick as stars, an' white as snow;
Or cream-white blossoms be a-spread
About the guelder-rwoses' head;
How cool's the sheäde, or warm's the lewth,
Bezide a zummer hedge in blooth.

When we've a-work'd drough longsome hours,
Till dew's a-dried vrom dazzlèn flow'rs,
The while the climmèn zun ha' glow'd
Drough mwore than half his daily road:
Then where the sheädes do slily pass
Athirt our veet upon the grass,
As we do rest by lofty ranks
Ov elems on the flow'ry banks;
How cool's the sheäde, or warm's the lewth,
Bezide a zummer hedge in blooth.

But oh! below woone hedge's zide
Our jay do come a-most to pride;
Out where the high-stemm'd trees do stand,
In row bezide our own free land,
An' where the wide-leav'd clote mid zwim
'Ithin our water's rushy rim:
An' raïn do vall, an' zuns do burn,
An' each in season, and in turn,
To cool the sheäde or warm the lewth
Ov our own zummer hedge in blooth.

How soft do sheäke the zummer hedge—
How soft do sway the zummer zedge—
How bright be zummer skies an' zun—
How bright the zummer brook do run;
An' feäir the flow'rs do bloom, to feäde
Behind the swaÿen mower's bleäde;
An' sweet be merry looks o' jaÿ,
By weäles an' pooks o' June's new haÿ,
Wi' smilèn age, an laughèn youth,
Bezide the zummer hedge in blooth.

THE WATER CROWVOOT.

O' SMALL-FEÄC'D flow'r that now dost bloom
To stud wi' white the shallow Frome,
An' leäve the clote to spread his flow'r
On darksome pools o' stwoneless Stour,
When sof'ly-rizèn aïrs do cool
The water in the sheenèn pool,
Thy beds o' snow-white buds do gleam
So feäir upon the sky-blue stream,
As whitest clouds, a-hangèn high
Avore the blueness o' the sky;
An' there, at hand, the thin-heäir'd cows,
In aïry sheädes o' withy boughs,
Or up bezide the mossy raïls,
Do stan' an' zwing their heavy taïls,
The while the ripplèn stream do flow
Below the dousty bridge's bow;
An' quiv'rèn water-gleams do mock
The weäves, upon the sheäded rock;
An' up athirt the copèn stwone
The laïtren bwoy do leän alwone,
A-watchèn, wi' a stedvast look,
The vallèn waters in the brook,

The while the zand o' time do run
An' leäve his errand still undone.
An' oh! as long's thy buds would gleam
Above the softly-slidèn stream,
While sparklèn zummer-brooks do run
Below the lofty-climèn zun,
I only wish that thou could'st stay
Vor noo man's harm, an' all men's jay.
But no, the waterman 'ull weäde
Thy water wi' his deadly bleäde,
To slay thee even in thy bloom,
Fair small-feäced flower o' the Frome.

THE LILAC.

Dear lilac-tree, a-spreadèn wide
Thy purple blooth on ev'ry zide,
As if the hollow sky did shed
Its blue upon thy flow'ry head;
Oh! whether I mid sheäre wi' thee
Thy open aïr, my bloomèn tree,
Or zee thy blossoms vrom the gloom,
'Ithin my zunless workèn-room,
My heart do leäp, but leäp wi' sighs,
At zight o' thee avore my eyes,
For when thy grey-blue head do sway
In cloudless light, 'tis Spring, 'tis May.

'Tis Spring, 'tis May, as May woonce shed
His glowèn light above thy head—
When thy green boughs, wi' bloomy tips,
Did sheäde my childern's laughèn lips;
A-screenèn vrom the noonday gleäre
Their rwosy cheäks an' glossy heäir;

The while their mother's needle sped,
Too quick vor zight, the snow-white thread,
Unless her han', wi' lovèn ceäre,
Did smooth their little heads o' heäir;

Or wi' a sheäke, tie up anew
Vor zome wild voot, a slippèn shoe;
An' I did leän bezide thy mound
Ageän the deäsy-dappled ground,
The while the woaken clock did tick
My hour o' rest away too quick,
An' call me off to work anew,
Wi' slowly-ringèn strokes, woone, two.

Zoo let me zee noo darksome cloud
Bedim to-day thy flow'ry sh'oud,
But let en bloom on ev'ry spray,
Drough all the days o' zunny May.

THE BLACKBIRD.

'Twer out at Penley I'd a-past
A zummer day that went too vast,
An' when the zettèn zun did spread
On western clouds a vi'ry red;
The elems' leafy limbs wer still
Above the gravel-bedded rill,
An' under en did warble sh'ill,
Avore the dusk, the blackbird.

An' there, in sheädes o' darksome yews,
Did vlee the maïdens on their tooes,
A-laughèn sh'ill wi' merry feäce
When we did vind their hidèn pleäce.

'Ithin the loose-bough'd ivy's gloom,
Or lofty lilac, vull in bloom,
Or hazzle-wrides that gi'ed em room
Below the zingèn blackbird.

Above our heads the rooks did vlee
To reach their nested elem-tree,
An' splashèn vish did rise to catch
The wheelèn gnots above the hatch;
An' there the miller went along,
A-smilèn, up the sheädy drong,
But yeet too deaf to hear the zong
A-zung us by the blackbird.

An' there the sh'illy-bubblèn brook
Did leäve behind his rocky nook,
To run drough meäds a-chill'd wi' dew,
Vrom hour to hour the whole night drough;
But still his murmurs wer a-drown'd
By vaïces that mid never sound
Ageän together on that ground,
Wi' whislèns o' the blackbird.

THE SLANTÈN LIGHT O' FALL.

AH! Jeäne, my maïd, I stood to you,
   When you wer christen'd, small an' light,
Wi' tiny eärms o' red an' blue,
   A-hangèn in your robe o' white.
We brought ye to the hallow'd stwone,
Vor Christ to teäke ye vor his own,
When harvest work wer all a-done,
An' time brought round October zun—
   The slantèn light o' Fall.

An' I can mind the wind wer rough,
   An' gather'd clouds, but brought noo storms,

An' you did nessle warm enough,
  'Ithin your smilèn mother's eärms.
The whindlèn grass did quiver light,
Among the stubble, feäded white,
An' if at times the zunlight broke
Upon the ground, or on the vo'k,
  'Twer slantèn light o' Fall.

An' when we brought ye drough the door
  O' Knapton Church, a child o' greäce,
There cluster'd round a'most a score
  O' vo'k to zee your tiny feäce.
An' there we all did veel so proud,
To zee an' op'nèn in the cloud,
An' then a stream o' light break drough,
A-sheenèn brightly down on you—
  The slantèn light o' Fall.

But now your time's a-come to stand
  In church, a-blushèn at my zide,
The while a bridegroom vrom my hand
  Ha' took ye vor his faïthvul bride.
Your christèn neäme we gi'd ye here,
When Fall did cool the weästèn year;
An' now, ageän, we brought ye drough
The doorway, wi' your surneäme new,
  In slantèn light o' Fall.

An' zoo vur, Jeäne, your life is feäir,
  An' God ha' been your steadvast friend,
An' mid ye have mwore jay than ceäre,
  Vor ever, till your journey's end.
An' I've a-watch'd ye on wi' pride,
But now I soon mus' leäve your zide,
Vor you ha' still life's spring-tide zun,
But my life, Jeäne, is now a-run
  To slantèn light o' Fall.

THISSLEDOWN.

The thissledown by wind's a-roll'd
   In Fall along the zunny plaïn,
Did catch the grass, but lose its hold,
   Or cling to bennets, but in vaïn.

But when it zwept along the grass,
   An' zunk below the hollow's edge,
It lay at rest while winds did pass
   Above the pit-bescreenèn ledge.

The plaïn ha' brightness wi' his strife,
   The pit is only dark at best,
There's pleasure in a worksome life,
   An' sloth is tiresome wi' its rest.

Zoo, then, I'd sooner beär my peärt,
   Ov all the trials vo'k do rue,
Than have a deadness o' the heart,
   Wi' nothèn mwore to veel or do.

THE MAY-TREE.

I've a-come by the May-tree all times o' the year,
   When leaves wer a-springèn,
   When vrost wer a-stingèn,
When cool-winded mornèn did show the hills clear.
When night wer bedimmèn the vields vur an' near.

When, in zummer, his head wer as white as a sheet,
   Wi' white buds a-zwellèn,
   An' blossom, sweet-smellèn,
While leaves wi' green leaves on his bough-zides did meet,
A-sheädèn the deäisies down under our veet.

When the zun, in the Fall, wer a-wanderèn wan,
    An' haws on his head
    Did sprinkle en red,
Or bright drops o' raïn wer a-hung loosely on,
To the tips o' the sprigs when the scud wer a-gone.

An' when, in the winter, the zun did goo low,
    An' keen win' did huffle,
    But never could ruffle
The hard vrozen feäce o' the water below,
His limbs wer a-fringed wi' the vrost or the snow.

LYDLINCH BELLS.

When skies wer peäle wi' twinklèn stars,
  An' whislèn aïr a-risèn keen;
An' birds did leäve the icy bars
  To vind, in woods, their mossy screen;
When vrozen grass, so white's a sheet,
Did scrunchy sharp below our veet,
An' water, that did sparkle red
At zunzet, wer a-vrozen dead;
The ringers then did spend an hour
A-ringèn changes up in tow'r;
Vor Lydlinch bells be good vor sound,
An' liked by all the naïghbours round.

An' while along the leafless boughs
O' ruslèn hedges, win's did pass,
An' orts ov haÿ, a-left by cows,
Did russle on the vrozen grass,
An' maïdens' païls, wi' all their work
A-done, did hang upon their vurk,
An' they, avore the fleämèn brand,
Did teäke their needle-work in hand,
The men did cheer their heart an hour
A-ringèn changes up in tow'r;

Vor Lydlinch bells be good vor sound,
An' liked by all the naïghbours round.

There sons did pull the bells that rung
Their mothers' weddèn peals avore,
The while their fathers led em young
An' blushèn vrom the churches door,
An' still did cheem, wi' happy sound,
As time did bring the Zundays round,
An' call em to the holy pleäce
Vor heav'nly gifts o' peace an' greäce;
An' vo'k did come, a-streamèn slow
Along below the trees in row,
While they, in merry peals, did sound
The bells vor all the naïghbours round.

An' when the bells, wi' changèn peal,
Did smite their own vo'ks window-peänes,
Their sof'en'd sound did often steal
Wi' west winds drough the Bagber leänes;
Or, as the win' did shift, mid goo
Where woody Stock do nessle lew,
Or where the risèn moon did light
The walls o' Thornhill on the height;
An' zoo, whatever time mid bring
To meäke their vive clear vaïces zing,
Still Lydlinch bells wer good vor sound,
An' liked by all the naïghbours round.

THE STAGE COACH.

Ah! when the wold vo'k went abroad
   They thought it vast enough,
If vow'r good ho'ses beät the road
   Avore the coach's ruf;
     An' there they zot,
     A-cwold or hot,

An' roll'd along the ground,
    While the whip did smack
    On the ho'ses' back,
An' the wheels went swiftly round, Good so's;
    The wheels went swiftly round.

Noo iron raïls did streak the land
  To keep the wheels in track.
The coachman turn'd his vow'r-in-hand,
  Out right, or left, an' back;
    An' he'd stop avore
    A man's own door,
To teäke en up or down:
    While the reïns vell slack
    On the ho'ses' back,
Till the wheels did rottle round ageän;
    Till the wheels did rottle round.

An' there, when wintry win' did blow,
  Athirt the plaïn an' hill,
An' the zun wer peäle above the snow,
  An' ice did stop the mill,
    They did laugh an' joke
    Wi' cwoat or cloke,
So warmly roun' em bound,
    While the whip did crack
    On the ho'ses' back,
An' the wheels did trundle round, d'ye know;
    The wheels did trundle round.

An' when the rumblèn coach did pass
  Where hufflèn winds did roar,
They'd stop to teäke a warmèn glass
  By the sign above the door;
    An' did laugh an' joke
    An' ax the vo'k

The miles they wer vrom town,
    Till the whip did crack
    On the ho'ses back,
An' the wheels did truckle roun', good vo'k ;
    The wheels did truckle roun'.

An' gaïly rod wold age or youth,
    When zummer light did vall
On woods in leaf, or trees in blooth,
    Or girt vo'ks parkzide wall.
        An' they thought they past
        The pleäces vast,
Along the dousty groun',
    When the whip did smack
    On the ho'ses' back,
An' the wheels spun swiftly roun'.   Them days
    The wheels spun swiftly roun'.

WAYFEAREN.

THE sky wer clear, the zunsheen glow'd
    On droopèn flowers drough the day,
As I did beät the dousty road
    Vrom hinder hills, a-feädèn gray ;
    Drough hollows up the hills,
    Vrom knaps along by mills,
Vrom mills by churches tow'rs, wi' bells
That twold the hours to woody dells.

An' when the windèn road do guide
    The thirsty vootman where mid flow
The water vrom a rock bezide
    His vootsteps, in a sheenèn bow ;
    The hand a-hollow'd up
    Do beät a goolden cup,
To catch an' drink it, bright an' cool,
A-vallèn light 'ithin the pool.

Zoo when, at last, I hung my head
   Wi' thirsty lips a-burnèn dry,
I come bezide a river-bed
   Where water flow'd so blue's the sky;
   An' there I meäde me up
   O' coltsvoot leaf a cup,
Where water vrom his lip o' gray,
Wer sweet to sip thik burnèn day.

But when our work is right, a jay
   Do come to bless us in its traïn,
An' hardships ha' zome good to pay
   The thoughtvul soul vor all their päin:
   The het do sweetèn sheäde,
   An' weary lim's ha' meäde
A bed o' slumber, still an' sound,
By woody hill or grassy mound.

An' while I zot in sweet delay
   Below an elem on a hill,
Where boughs a-halfway up did sway
   In sheädes o' lim's above em still,
   An' blue sky show'd between
   The flutt'rèn leäves o' green;
I woulden gi'e that gloom an' sheäde
Vor any room that weälth ha' meäde.

But oh! that vo'k that have the roads
   Where weary-vooted souls do pass,
Would leäve bezide the stwone vor lwoads,
   A little strip vor zummer grass;
   That when the stwones do bruise
   An' burn an' gall our tooes,
We then mid cool our veet on beds
O' wild-thyme sweet, or deäisy-heads.

THE LEANE.

They do zay that a travellèn chap
    Have a-put in the newspeäper now,
That the bit o' green ground on the knap
    Should be all a-took in vor the plough.
He do fancy 'tis easy to show
    That we can be but stunpolls at best,
Vor to leäve a green spot where a flower can grow,
    Or a voot-weary walker mid rest.
'Tis hedge-grubbèn, Thomas, an' ledge-grubbèn,
        Never a-done
While a sov'rèn mwore's to be won.

The road, he do zay, is so wide
    As 'tis wanted vor travellers' wheels,
As if all that did travel did ride
    An' did never get galls on their heels.
He would leäve sich a thin strip o' groun',
    That, if a man's veet in his shoes
Wer a-burnèn an' zore, why he coulden zit down
    But the wheels would run over his tooes.
Vor 'tis meäke money, Thomas, an' teäke money,
        What's zwold an' bought
Is all that is worthy o' thought.

Years agoo the leäne-zides did bear grass,
    Vor to pull wi' the geeses' red bills,
That did hiss at the vo'k that did pass,
    Or the bwoys that pick'd up their white quills.
But shortly, if vower or vive
    Ov our goslèns do creep vrom the agg,
They must mwope in the geärden, mwore dead than alive,
    In a coop, or a-tied by the lag.

Vor to catch at land, Thomas, an' snatch at land,
    Now is the plan;
Meäke money wherever you can.

The childern wull soon have noo pleäce
    Vor to play in, an' if they do grow,
They wull have a thin musheroom feäce,
    Wi' their bodies so sumple as dough.
But a man is a-meäde ov a child,
    An' his limbs do grow worksome by play;
An' if the young child's little body's a-spweil'd,
    Why, the man's wull the sooner decay.
But wealth is wo'th now mwore than health is wo'th;
    Let it all goo,
If't 'ull bring but a sov'rèn or two.

Vor to breed the young fox or the heäre,
    We can gi'e up whole eäcres o' ground,
But the greens be a-grudg'd, vor to rear
    Our young childern up healthy an' sound,
Why, there woont be a-left the next age
    A green spot where their veet can goo free;
An' the goocoo wull soon be committed to cage
    Vor a trespass in zomebody's tree.
Vor 'tis lockèn up, Thomas, an' blockèn up,
    Stranger or brother,
Men mussen come nigh woone another.

Woone day I went in at a geäte,
    Wi' my child, where an echo did sound,
An' the owner come up, an' did reäte
    Me as if I would car off his ground.
But his vield an' the grass wer-a-let,
    An' the damage that he could a-took
Wer at mwost that the while I did open the geäte
    I did rub roun' the eye on the hook.

But 'tis drevèn out, Thomas, an' hevèn out.
    Trample noo grounds,
Unless you be after the hounds.

Ah! the Squiër o' Culver-dell Hall
  Wer as diff'rent as light is vrom dark,
Wi' zome vo'k that, as evenèn did vall,
  Had a-broke drough long grass in his park;
Vor he went, wi' a smile, vor to meet
  Wi' the trespassers while they did pass,
An' he zaid, "I do fear you'll catch cwold in your veet,
  You've a-walk'd drough so much o' my grass."
His mild words, Thomas, cut em like swords, Thomas,
    Newly a-whet,
An' went vurder wi' them than a dreat.

THE RAILROAD.

I took a flight, awhile agoo,
Along the raïls, a stage or two,
An' while the heavy wheels did spin
An' rottle, wi' a deafnèn din,
In clouds o' steam, the zweepèn traïn
Did shoot along the hill-bound plaïn,
As sheädes o' birds in flight, do pass
Below em on the zunny grass.
An' as I zot, an' look'd abrode
On leänen land an' windèn road,
The ground a-spread along our flight
Did vlee behind us out o' zight;
The while the zun, our heav'nly guide,
Did ride on wi' us, zide by zide.
An' zoo, while time, vrom stage to stage,
Do car us on vrom youth to age,

The e'thly pleasures we do vind
Be soon a-met, an' left behind;
But God, beholdèn vrom above
Our lowly road, wi' yearnèn love,
Do keep bezide us, stage by stage,
Vrom be'th to youth, vrom youth to age.

THE RAILROAD.

An' while I went 'ithin a traïn,
A-ridèn on athirt the plaïn,
A-cleärèn swifter than a hound,
On twin-laid rails, the zwimmèn ground;
I cast my eyes 'ithin a park,
Upon a woak wi' grey-white bark,
An' while I kept his head my mark,
The rest did wheel around en.

An' when in life our love do cling
The clwosest round zome single thing,
We then do vind that all the rest
Do wheel roun' that, vor vu'st an' best;
Zoo while our life do last, mid nought
But what is good an' feäir be sought,
In word or deed, or heart or thought,
An' all the rest wheel round it.

SEATS.

When starbright maïdens be to zit
   In silken frocks, that they do wear,
The room mid have, as 'tis but fit,
   A han'some seat vor vo'k so feäir;
But we, in zun-dried vield an' wood,
   Ha' seats as good's a goolden chair.

SEATS.

Vor here, 'ithin the woody drong,
   A ribbèd elem-stem do lie,
A-vell'd in Spring, an' stratch'd along
   A bed o' grægles up knee-high,
A sheädy seat to rest, an' let
   The burnèn het o' noon goo by.

Or if you'd look, wi' wider scope,
   Out where the gray-tree'd plaïn do spread,
The ash bezide the zunny slope,
   Do sheäde a cool-aïr'd deäisy bed,
An' grassy seat, wi' spreadèn eaves
   O' rus'lèn leaves, above your head.

An' there the traïn mid come in zight,
   Too vur to hear a-rollèn by,
A·breathèn quick, in heästy flight,
   His breath o' tweil, avore the sky,
The while the waggon, wi' his lwoad,
   Do crawl the rwoad a-windèn nigh.

Or now theäse happy holiday
   Do let vo'k rest their weäry lim's,
An' lwoaded haÿ's a-hangèn gray,
   Above the waggon-wheels' dry rims,
The meäd ha' seats in weäles or pooks,
   By windèn brooks, wi' crumblèn brims.

Or if you'd gi'e your thoughtvul mind
   To yonder long-vorseäken hall,
Then teäke a stwonèn seat behind
   The ivy on the broken wall,
An' learn how e'thly wealth an' might
   Mid clim' their height, an' then mid **vall**.

SOUND O' WATER.

I BORN in town! oh no, my dawn
O' life broke here beside theäse lawn;
Not where pent aïr do roll along,
In darkness drough the wall-bound drong,
An' never bring the goo-coo's zong,
Nor sweets o' blossoms in the hedge,
Or bendèn rush, or sheenèn zedge,
  Or sounds o' flowèn water.

The aïr that I've a-breath'd did sheäke
The draps o' raïn upon the breäke,
An' bear aloft the swingèn lark,
An' huffle roun' the elem's bark,
In boughy grove, an' woody park,
An' brought us down the dewy dells,
The high-wound zongs o' nightingeäles,
  An' sounds o' flowèn water.

An' when the zun, wi' vi'ry rim,
'S a-zinkèn low, an' wearèn dim,
Here I, a-most too tired to stand,
Do leäve my work that's under hand
In pathless wood or oben land,
To rest 'ithin my thatchèn oves,
Wi' ruslèn win's in leafy groves,
  An' sounds o' flowèn water.

TREES BE COMPANY.

WHEN zummer's burnèn het's a-shed
Upon the droopèn grasses head,
A-drevèn under sheädy leaves
The workvo'k in their snow-white sleeves.

TREES BE COMPANY.

We then mid yearn to clim' the height,
   Where thorns be white, above the vern ;
An' aïr do turn the zunsheen's might
   To softer light too weak to burn—
     On woodless downs we mid be free,
     But lowland trees be company.

Though downs mid show a wider view
O' green a-reachèn into blue
Than roads a-windèn in the glen,
An' ringèn wi' the sounds o' men ;
The thissle's crown o' red an' blue
   In Fall's cwold dew do wither brown,
An' larks come down 'ithin the lew,
   As storms do brew, an' skies do frown—
     An' though the down do let us free,
     The lowland trees be company.

Where birds do zing, below the zun,
In trees above the blue-smok'd tun,
An' sheädes o' stems do overstratch
The mossy path 'ithin the hatch ;
If leaves be bright up over head,
   When May do shed its glitt'rèn light ;
Or, in the blight o' Fall, do spread
   A yollow bed avore our zight—
     Whatever season it mid be,
     The trees be always company.

When dusky night do nearly hide
The path along the hedge's zide,
An' dailight's hwomely sounds be still
But sounds o' water at the mill ;
Then if noo feäce we long'd to greet
   Could come to meet our lwonesome treäce
Or if noo peäce o' weary veet,

However fleet, could reach its pleäce—
However lwonesome we mid be,
The trees would still be company.

A PLEÄCE IN ZIGHT.

As I at work do look aroun'
Upon the groun' I have in view,
To yonder hills that still do rise
Avore the skies, wi' backs o' blue;
'Ithin the ridges that do vall
An' rise roun' Blackmwore lik' a wall,
'Tis yonder knap do teäke my zight
Vrom dawn till night, the mwost ov all.

An' there, in May, 'ithin the lewth
O' boughs in blooth, be sheädy walks,
An' cowslips up in yollow beds
Do hang their heads on downy stalks;
An' if the weather should be feäir
When I've a holiday to speäre,
I'll teäke the chance o' gettèn drough
An hour or two wi' zome vo'k there.

An' there I now can dimly zee
The elem-tree upon the mound,
An' there meäke out the high-bough'd grove
An' narrow drove by Redcliff ground;
An' there by trees a-risèn tall,
The glowèn zunlight now do vall,
Wi' shortest sheädes o' middle day,
Upon the gray wold house's wall.

An' I can zee avore the sky
A-risèn high the churches speer,
Wi' bells that I do goo to swing,
An' like to ring, an' like to hear;

An' if I've luck upon my zide,
They bells shall sound bwoth loud an' wide,
A peal above they slopes o' gray,
Zome merry day wi' Jeäne a bride.

GWAIN TO BROOKWELL.

At Easter, though the wind wer high,
We vound we had a zunny sky,
An' zoo wold Dobbin had to trudge
His dousty road by knap an' brudge,
An' jog, wi' hangèn vetterlocks
A-sheäkèn roun' his heavy hocks,
An' us, a lwoad not much too small,
A-ridèn out to Brookwell Hall;
An' there in doust vrom Dobbin's heels,
An' green light-waggon's vower wheels,
Our merry laughs did loudly sound,
In rollèn winds athirt the ground;
While sheenèn-ribbons' color'd streäks
Did flutter roun' the maïdens' cheäks,
As they did zit, wi' smilèn lips,
A-reachèn out their vinger-tips
Toward zome teäkèn pleäce or zight
That they did shew us, left or right;
An' woonce, when Jimmy tried to pleäce
A kiss on cousin Polly's feäce,
She push'd his hat, wi' wicked leers,
Right off above his two red ears,
An' there he roll'd along the groun'
Wi' spreadèn brim an' rounded crown,
An' vound, at last, a cowpon's brim,
An' launch'd hizzelf, to teäke a zwim;
An' there, as Jim did run to catch
His neäked noddle's bit o' thatch,

To zee his straïnèns an' his strides,
We laugh'd enough to split our zides.
At Harwood Farm we pass'd the land
That father's father had in hand,
An' there, in oben light did spread,
The very groun's his cows did tread,
An' there above the stwonèn tun
Avore the dazzlèn mornèn zun,
Wer still the rollèn smoke, the breath
A-breath'd vrom his wold house's he'th;
An' there did lie below the door,
The drashol' that his vootsteps wore;
But there his meäte an' he bwoth died,
Wi' hand in hand, an' zide by zide;
Between the seäme two peals a-rung,
Two Zundays, though they wer but young,
An' laid in sleep, their worksome hands,
At rest vrom tweil wi' house or lands.
Then vower childern laid their heads
At night upon their little beds,
An' never rose ageän below
A mother's love, or father's ho:
Dree little maïdens, small in feäce,
An' woone small bwoy, the fourth in pleäce.
Zoo when their heedvul father died,
He call'd his brother to his zide,
To meäke en stand, in hiz own stead,
His childern's guide, when he wer dead;
But still avore zix years brought round
The woodland goo-coo's zummer sound,
He weästed all their little store,
An' hardship drove em out o' door,
To tweil till tweilsome life should end,
'Ithout a single e'thly friend.
But soon wi' Harwood back behind,
An' out o' zight an' out o' mind,

We went a-rottlèn on, an' meäde
Our way along to Brookwell Sleäde;
An' then we vound ourselves draw nigh
The Leädy's Tow'r that rose on high,
An' seem'd a-comèn on to meet,
Wi' growèn height, wold Dobbin's veet.

BROOKWELL.

WELL, I do zay 'tis wo'th woone's while
To beät the doust a good six mile
To zee the pleäce the squier plann'd
At Brookwell, now a-meäde by hand;
Wi' oben lawn, an' grove, an' pon',
An' gravel-walks as cleän as bron;
An' grass a'most so soft to tread
As velvet-pile o' silken thread;
An' mounds wi' mæsh, an' rocks wi' flow'rs,
An' ivy-sheäded zummer bow'rs,
An' dribblèn water down below
The stwonèn archès lofty bow.
An' there do sound the watervall
Below a cavern's mæshy wall,
Where peäle-green light do struggle down
A leafy crevice at the crown.
An' there do gush the foamy bow
O' water, white as driven snow;
An' there, a zittèn all alwone,
A little maïd o' marble stwone
Do leän her little cheäk azide
Upon her lily han', an' bide
Bezide the vallèn stream to zee
Her pitcher vill'd avore her knee.
An' then the brook, a-rollèn dark
Below a leänèn yew-tree's bark,

Wi' playsome ripples that do run
A-flashèn to the western zun,
Do shoot, at last, wi' foamy shocks,
Athirt a ledge o' craggy rocks,
A-castèn in his heästy flight,
Upon the stwones a robe o' white;
An' then ageän do goo an' vall
Below a bridge's archèd wall,
Where vo'k agwaïn athirt do pass
Vow'r little bwoys a-cast in brass;
An' woone do hold an angler's wand,
Wi' steady hand, above the pond;
An' woone, a-pweïntèn to the stream
His little vinger-tip, do seem
A-showèn to his playmeätes' eyes,
Where he do zee the vishes rise;
An' woone ageän, wi' smilèn lips,
Do put a vish his han' do clips
'Ithin a basket, loosely tied
About his shoulder at his zide:
An' after that the fourth do stand
A-holdèn back his pretty hand
Behind his little ear, to drow
A stwone upon the stream below.
An' then the housèn, that be all
Sich pretty hwomes, vrom big to small,
A-lookèn south, do cluster round
A zunny ledge o' risèn ground,
Avore a wood, a-nestled warm,
In lewth ageän the northern storm,
Where smoke, a-wreathèn blue, do spread
Above the tuns o' dusky red,
An' window-peänes do glitter bright
Wi' burnèn streams o' zummer light,
Below the vine, a-traïn'd to hem
Their zides 'ithin his leafy stem,

An' rangle on, wi' flutt'rèn leaves,
Below the houses' thatchen eaves.
An' drough a lawn a-spread avore
The windows, an' the pworchèd door,
A path do wind 'ithin a hatch,
A-vastèn'd wi' a clickèn latch,
An' there up over ruf an' tun,
Do stan' the smooth-wall'd church o' stwone,
Wi' carvèd windows, thin an' tall,
A-reachèn up the lofty wall;
An' battlements, a-stannèn round
The tower, ninety veet vrom ground,
Vrom where a teäp'rèn speer do spring
So high's the mornèn lark do zing.
Zoo I do zay 'tis wo'th woone's while
To beät the doust a good six mile,
To zee the pleäce the squier plann'd
At Brookwell, now a-meäde by hand.

THE SHY MAN.

AH! good Meäster Gwillet, that you mid ha' know'd,
Wer a-bred up at Coomb, an' went little abroad;
An' if he got in among strangers, he velt
His poor heart in a twitter, an' ready to melt;
Or if, by ill luck, in his rambles, he met
Wi' zome maïdens a-titt'rèn, he burn'd wi' a het,
That shot all drough the lim's o'n, an' left a cwold zweat,
    The poor little chap wer so shy,
    He wer ready to drap, an' to die.

But at last 'twer the lot o' the poor little man
To vall deeply in love, as the best ov us can;
An' 'twer noo easy task vor a shy man to tell
Sich a dazzlèn feäir maïd that he loved her so well;

An' woone day when he met her, his knees nearly smote
Woone another, an' then wi' a struggle he bro't
A vew vords to his tongue, wi' some mwore in his droat.
    But she, 'ithout doubt, could soon vind
    Vrom two words that come out, zix behind.

Zoo at langth, when he vound her so smilèn an' kind,
Why he wrote her zome laïns, vor to tell her his mind,
Though 'twer then a hard task vor a man that wer shy,
To be married in church, wi' a crowd stannèn by.
But he twold her woone day, "I have housen an' lands,
We could marry by licence, if you don't like banns,"
An' he cover'd his eyes up wi' woone ov his han's,
    Vor his head seem'd to zwim as he spoke,
    An' the aïr look'd so dim as a smoke.

Well! he vound a good naïghbour to goo in his pleäce
Vor to buy the goold ring, vor he hadden the feäce.
An' when he went up vor to put in the banns,
He did sheäke in his lags, an' did sheäke in his han's.
Then they ax'd vor her neäme, an' her parish or town,
An' he gi'ed em a leaf, wi' her neäme a-wrote down;
Vor he coulden ha' twold em outright, vor a poun',
    Vor his tongue wer so weak an' so loose,
    When he wanted to speak 'twer noo use.

Zoo they went to be married, an' when they got there
All the vo'k wer a-gather'd as if 'twer a feäir,
An' he thought, though his pleäce mid be pleazèn to zome,
He could all but ha' wish'd that he hadden a-come.
The bride wer a-smilèn as fresh as a rwose,
An' when he come wi' her, an' show'd his poor nose,
All the little bwoys shouted, an' cried "There he goes,"
    "There he goes." Oh! vor his peärt he velt
    As if the poor heart o'n would melt.

An' when they stood up by the chancel together,
Oh! a man mid ha' knock'd en right down wi' a veather,
He did veel zoo asheäm'd that he thought he would rather
He wërden the bridegroom, but only the father.
But, though 'tis so funny to zee en so shy,
Yeet his mind is so lowly, his aïms be so high,
That to do a meän deed, or to tell woone a lie,
   You'd vind that he'd shun mwore by half,
   Than to stan' vor vo'ks fun, or their laugh.

THE WINTER'S WILLOW.

There Liddy zot bezide her cow,
   Upon her lowly seat, O;
A hood did overhang her brow,
   Her pail wer at her veet, O;
An' she wer kind, an' she wer feäir,
An' she wer young, an' free o' ceärc;
Vew winters had a-blow'd her heäir,
   Bezide the Winter's Willow.

She idden woone a-rear'd in town
   Where many a gaÿer lass, O,
Do trip a-smilèn up an' down,
   So peäle wi' smoke an' gas, O;
But here, in vields o' greäzèn herds,
Her väice ha' mingled sweetest words
Wi' evenèn cheärms o' busy birds,
   Bezide the Winter's Willow.

An' when, at last, wi' beätèn breast,
   I knock'd avore her door, O,
She ax'd me in to teäke the best
   O' pleäces on the vloor, O;

An' smilèn feäir avore my zight,
She blush'd bezide the yollow light
O' bleäzèn brands, while winds o' night
    Do sheäke the Winter's Willow.

An' if there's readship in her smile,
    She don't begrudge to speäre, O,
To zomebody, a little while,
    The empty woaken chair, O;
An' if I've luck upon my zide,
Why, I do think she'll be my bride
Avore the leaves ha' twice a-died
    Upon the Winter's Willow.

Above the coach-wheels' rollèn rims
    She never rose to ride, O,
Though she do zet her comely lim's
    Above the mare's white zide, O;
But don't become too proud to stoop
An' scrub her milkèn païl's white hoop,
Or zit a-milkèn where do droop,
    The wet-stemm'd Winter's Willow.

An' I've a cow or two in leäze,
    Along the river-zide, O,
An' pails to zet avore her knees,
    At dawn an' evenèn-tide, O;
An' there she still mid zit, an' look
Athirt upon the woody nook
Where vu'st I zeed her by the brook
    Bezide the Winter's Willow.

Zoo, who would heed the treeless down,
    A-beät by all the storms, O,
Or who would heed the busy town,
    Where vo'k do goo in zwarms, O;

If he wer in my house below
The elems, where the vier did glow
In Liddy's feäce, though winds did blow
   Ageän the Winter's Willow.

I KNOW WHO.

Aye, aye, vull rathe the zun mus' rise
To meäke us tired o' zunny skies,
A-sheenèn on the whole day drough,
From mornèn's dawn till evenèn's dew.
When trees be brown an' meäds be green,
An' skies be blue, an' streams do sheen,
An' thin-edg'd clouds be snowy white
Above the bluest hills in zight;
But I can let the daylight goo,
When I've a-met wi'—I know who.

In Spring I met her by a bed
O' laurels higher than her head;
The while a rwose hung white between
Her blushes an' the laurel's green;
An' then in Fall, I went along
The row of elems in the drong,
An' heärd her zing bezide the cows,
By yollow leaves o' meäple boughs;
But Fall or Spring is feäir to view
When day do bring me—I know who.

An' when, wi' wint'r a-comèn roun',
The purple he'th's a-feädèn brown,
An' hangèn vern's a-sheäkèn dead,
Bezide the hill's besheäded head:
An' black-wing'd rooks do glitter bright
Above my head, in peäler light;

'Then though the birds do still the glee
That sounded in the zummer tree,
My heart is light the winter drough,
In me'th at night, wi'—I know who.

JESSIE LEE.

Above the timber's bendèn sh'ouds,
    The western wind did softly blow ;
An' up avore the knap, the clouds
    Did ride as white as driven snow.
Vrom west to east the clouds did zwim
Wi' wind that plied the elem's lim' ;
Vrom west to east the stream did glide,
A-sheenèn wide, wi' windèn brim.

How feäir, I thought, avore the sky
    The slowly-zwimmèn clouds do look ;
How soft the win's a-streamèn by ;
    How bright do roll the weävy brook :
When there, a-passèn on my right,
A-walkèn slow, an' treadèn light,
Young Jessie Lee come by, an' there
Took all my ceäre, an' all my zight.

Vor lovely wer the looks her feäce
    Held up avore the western sky :
An' comely wer the steps her peäce
    Did meäke a-walkèn slowly by :
But I went east, wi' beätèn breast,
Wi' wind, an' cloud, an' brook, vor rest,
Wi' rest a-lost, vor Jessie gone
So lovely on, toward the west.

Blow on, O winds, athirt the hill;
  Zwim on, O clouds; O waters vall,
Down mæshy rocks, vrom mill to mill;
  I now can overlook ye all.
But roll, O zun, an' bring to me
My day, if such a day there be,
When zome dear path to my abode
Shall be the road o' Jessie Lee.

TRUE LOVE.

As evenèn aïr, in green-treed Spring,
Do sheäke the new-sprung pa'sley bed,
An' wither'd ash-tree keys do swing
An' vall a-flutt'rèn roun' our head:
There, while the birds do zing their zong
In bushes down the ash-tree drong,
Come Jessie Lee, vor sweet's the pleäce
Your vaïce an' feäce can meäke vor me.

Below the buddèn ashes' height
We there can linger in the lew,
While boughs, a-gilded by the light,
Do sheen avore the sky o' blue:
But there by zettèn zun, or moon
A-risèn, time wull vlee too soon
Wi' Jessie Lee, vor sweet's the pleäce
Her vaïce an' feäce can meäke vor me.

Down where the darksome brook do flow,
Below the bridge's archèd wall,
Wi' alders dark, a-leanèn low,
Above the gloomy watervall;
There I've a-led ye hwome at night,
Wi' noo feäce else 'ithin my zight

But yours so feäir, an' sweet's the pleäce
Your vaïce an' feäce ha' meäde me there.

An' oh! when other years do come,
An' zettèn zuns, wi' yollow gleäre,
Drough western window-peänes, at hwome,
Do light upon my evenèn chair:
While day do weäne, an' dew do vall,
Be wi' me then, or else in call,
As time do vlee, vor sweet's the pleäce
Your vaïce an' feäce do meäke vor me.

Ah! you do smile, a-thinkèn light
O' my true words, but never mind;
Smile on, smile on, but still your flight
Would leäve me little jay behind:
But let me not be zoo a-tried
Wi' you a-lost where I do bide,
O Jessie Lee, in any pleäce
Your vaïce an' feäce ha' blest vor me.

I'm sure that when a soul's a-brought
To this our life ov aïr an' land,
Woone mwore's a-mark'd in God's good thought,
To help, wi' love, his heart an' hand.
An' oh! if there should be in store
An angel here vor my poor door,
'Tis Jessie Lee, vor sweet's the pleäce
Her vaïce an' feäce can meäke vor me.

THE BEAN YIELD.

'Twer where the zun did warm the lewth,
An' win' did whiver in the sheäde,
The sweet-aïr'd beäns were out in blooth,
Down there 'ithin the elem gleäde;

THE BEAN VIELD.

A yollow-banded bee did come,
An' softly-pitch, wi' hushèn hum,
Upon a beän, an' there did sip,
Upon a swayèn blossom's lip:
An' there cried he, "Aye, I can zee,
This blossom's all a-zent vor me."

A-jilted up an' down, astride
Upon a lofty ho'se a-trot,
The meäster then come by wi' pride,
To zee the beäns that he'd a-got;
An' as he zot upon his ho'se,
The ho'se ageän did snort an' toss
His high-ear'd head, an' at the zight
Ov all the blossom, black an' white:
"Ah! ah!" thought he, the seäme's the bee,
"Theäse beäns be all a-zent vor me."

Zoo let the worold's riches breed
A strife o' claïms, wi' weak and strong,
Vor now what cause have I to heed
Who's in the right, or in the wrong;
Since there do come drough yonder hatch,
An' bloom below the house's thatch,
The best o' maïdens, an' do own
That she is mine, an' mine alwone:
Zoo I can zee that love do gi'e
The best ov all good gifts to me.

Vor whose be all the crops an' land
A-won an' lost, an' bought, an zwold
Or whose, a-roll'd vrom hand to hand,
The highest money that's a-twold?
Vrom man to man a passèn on,
'Tis here to-day, to-morrow gone.

But there's a blessèn high above
It all—a soul o' stedvast love :
Zoo let it vlee, if God do gi'e
Sweet Jessie vor a gift to me.

WOLD FRIENDS A-MET.

AYE, vull my heart's blood now do roll,
An' gay do rise my happy soul,
An' well they mid, vor here our veet
Avore woone vier ageän do meet ;
Vor you've avoun' my feäce, to greet
Wi' welcome words my startlèn ear.
An' who be you, but John o' Weer,
An' I, but William Wellburn.

Here, light a candle up, to shed
Mwore light upon a wold friend's head,
An' show the smile, his feäce woonce mwore
Ha' brought us vrom another shore.
An' I'll heave on a brand avore
The vier back, to meäke good cheer,
O' roarèn fleämes, vor John o' Weer
To chat wi' William Wellburn.

Aye, aye, it mid be true that zome,
When they do wander out vrom hwome,
Do leäve their nearest friends behind,
Bwoth out o' zight, an' out o' mind ;
But John an' I ha' ties to bind
Our souls together, vur or near,
For, who is he but John o' Weer,
An' I, but William Wellburn.

Look, there he is, with twinklèn eyes,
An' elbows down upon his thighs,

A-chucklèn low, wi' merry grin.
Though time ha' roughen'd up his chin,
'Tis still the seäme true soul 'ithin,
As woonce I know'd, when year by year,
Thik very chap, thik John o' Weer,
Did play wi' William Wellburn.

Come, John, come; don't be dead-alive
Here, reach us out your clust'r o' vive.
Oh! you be happy. Ees, but that
Woon't do till you can laugh an' chat.
Don't blinky, lik' a purrèn cat,
But leäp an' laugh, an' let vo'k hear
What's happen'd, min, that John o' Weer
Ha' met wi' William Wellburn.

Vor zome, wi' selfishness too strong
Vor love, do do each other wrong;
An' zome do wrangle an' divide
In hets ov anger, bred o' pride;
But who do think that time or tide
Can breed ill-will in friends so dear,
As William wer to John o' Weer,
An' John to William Wellburn?

If other vo'ks do gleen to zee
How lovèn an' how glad we be,
What, then, poor souls, they had but vew
Sich happy days, so long agoo,
As they that I've a-spent wi' you;
But they'd hold woone another dear,
If woone o' them wer John o' Weer,
An' tother William Wellburn.

FIFEHEAD.

'Twer where my fondest thoughts do light,
At Fifehead, while we spent the night;
The millwheel's restèn rim wer dry,
An' houn's held up their evenèn cry;
An' lofty, drough the midnight sky,
Above the vo'k, wi' heavy heads,
Asleep upon their darksome beds,
The stars wer all awake, John.

Noo birds o' day wer out to spread
Their wings above the gully's bed,
An' darkness roun' the elem-tree
'D a-still'd the charmy childern's glee.
All he'ths wer cwold but woone, where we
Wer gay, 'tis true, but gay an' wise,
An' laugh'd in light o' maïden's eyes,
That glissen'd wide awake, John.

An' when we all, lik' loosen'd hounds,
Broke out o' doors, wi' merry sounds,
Our friends among the playsome team,
All brought us gwäin so vur's the stream.
But Jeäne, that there, below a gleam
O' light, watch'd woone o's out o' zight;
Vor willènly, vor his "Good night,"
She'd longer bide awake, John.

An' while up *Leighs* we stepp'd along
Our grassy path, wi' joke an' zong,
There *Plumber*, wi' its woody ground,
O' slopèn knaps a-screen'd around,
Rose dim 'ithout a breath o' sound,
The wold abode o' squiers a-gone,
Though while they lay a-sleepèn on,
Their stars wer still awake, John.

IVY HALL.

If I've a-stream'd below a storm,
  An' not a-velt the raïn,
An' if I ever velt me warm,
  In snow upon the plaïn,
'Twer when, as evenèn skies wer dim,
An' vields below my eyes wer dim,
I went alwone at evenèn-fall,
Athirt the vields to Ivy Hall.

I voun' the wind upon the hill,
  Last night, a-roarèn loud,
An' rubbèn boughs a-creakèn sh'ill
  Upon the ashes' sh'oud;
But oh! the reelèn copse mid groan;
An' timber's lofty tops mid groan;
The hufflèn winds be music all,
Bezide my road to Ivy Hall.

A sheädy grove o' ribbèd woaks,
  Is Wootton's shelter'd nest,
An' woaks do keep the winter's strokes
  Vrom Knapton's evenèn rest.
An' woaks ageän wi' bossy stems,
An' elems wi' their mossy stems,
Do rise to screen the leafy wall
An' stwonèn ruf ov Ivy Hall.

The darksome clouds mid fling their sleet,
  An' vrost mid pinch me blue,
Or snow mid cling below my veet,
  An' hide my road vrom view.
The winter's only jaÿ ov heart,
An' storms do meäke me gaÿ ov heart,

When I do rest, at evenèn-fall,
Bezide the he'th ov Ivy Hall.

There leafy stems do clim' around
    The mossy stwonèn eaves;
An' there be window-zides a-bound
    Wi' quiv'rèn ivy-leaves.
But though the sky is dim 'ithout,
An' feäces mid be grim 'ithout,
Still I ha' smiles when I do call,
At evenèn-tide, at Ivy Hall.

FALSE FRIENDS-LIKE.

When I wer still a bwoy, an' mother's pride,
A bigger bwoy spoke up to me so kind-like,
"If you do like, I'll treat ye wi' a ride
In theäse wheel-barrow here." Zoo I wer blind-like
To what he had a-workèn in his mind-like,
An' mounted vor a passenger inside;
An' comèn to a puddle, perty wide,
He tipp'd me in, a-grinnèn back behind-like.
Zoo when a man do come to me so thick-like,
An' sheäke my hand, where woonce he pass'd me by,
An' tell me he would do me this or that,
I can't help thinkèn o' the big bwoy's trick-like.
An' then, vor all I can but wag my hat
An' thank en, I do veel a little shy.

THE BACHELOR.

No! I don't begrudge en his life,
    Nor his goold, nor his housen, nor lands;
Teäke all o't, an' gi'e me my wife,
    A wife's be the cheapest ov hands.

THE BACHELOR.

  Lie alwone! sigh alwone! die alwone!
   Then be vorgot.
 No! I be content wi' my lot.

Ah! where be the vingers so feäir,
 Vor to pat en so soft on the feäce,
To mend ev'ry stitch that do tear,
 An' keep ev'ry button in pleäce?
  Crack a-tore! brack a-tore! back a-tore!
   Buttons a-vled!
  Vor want ov a wife wi' her thread.

Ah! where is the sweet-perty head
 That do nod till he's gone out o' zight?
An' where be the two eärms a-spread,
 To show en he's welcome at night?
  Dine alwone! pine alwone! whine alwone!
   Oh! what a life!
  I'll have a friend in a wife.

An' when vrom a meetèn o' me'th
 Each husban' do leäd hwome his bride,
'Then he do slink hwome to his he'th,
 Wi' his eärm a-hung down his cwold zide.
  Slinkèn on! blinkèn on! thinkèn on!
   Gloomy an' glum;
  Nothèn but dullness to come.

An' when he do onlock his door,
 Do rumble as hollow's a drum,
An' the veäries a-hid roun' the vloor,
 Do grin vor to see en so glum.
  Keep alwone! sleep alwone! weep alwone!
   There let en bide,
  I'll have a wife at my zide.

But when he's a-laid on his bed
   In a zickness, O, what wull he do!
Vor the hands that would lift up his head,
   An' sheäke up his pillor anew.
      Ills to come! pills to come! bills to come!
         Noo soul to sheäre
     The trials the poor wratch must bear.

MARRIED PEÄIR'S LOVE WALK.

Come let's goo down the grove to-night;
The moon is up, 'tis all so light
As day, an' win' do blow enough
To sheäke the leaves, but tiddèn rough.
Come, Esther, teäke, vor wold time's seäke,
Your hooded cloke, that's on the pin,
An' wrap up warm, an' teäke my eärm,
You'll vind it better out than in.
Come, Etty dear; come out o' door,
An' teäke a sweetheart's walk woonce mwore.

How charmèn to our very souls,
Wer woonce your evenèn maiden strolls,
The while the zettèn zunlight dyed
Wi' red the beeches' western zide,
But back avore your vinger wore
The weddèn ring that's now so thin;
An' you did sheäre a mother's ceäre,
To watch an' call ye eärly in.
Come, Etty dear; come out o' door,
An' teäke a sweetheart's walk woonce mwore

An' then ageän, when you could slight
The clock a-strikèn leäte at night,
The while the moon, wi' risèn rim,
Did light the beeches' eastern lim'.

When I'd a-bound your vinger round
Wi' thik goold ring that's now so thin,
An' you had nwone but me alwone
To teäke ye leäte or eärly in.
Come, Etty dear; come out o' door,
An' teäke a sweetheart's walk woonce mwore.

But often when the western zide
O' trees did glow at evenèn-tide,
Or when the leäter moon did light
The beeches' eastern boughs at night,
An' in the grove, where vo'k did rove
The crumpled leaves did vlee an' spin,
You couldèn sheäre the pleasure there:
Your work or childern kept ye in.
Come, Etty dear, come out o' door,
An' teäke a sweetheart's walk woonce mwore.

But ceäres that zunk your oval chin
Ageän your bosom's lily skin,
Vor all they meäde our life so black,
Be now a-lost behind our back.
Zoo never mwope, in midst of hope,
To slight our blessèns would be sin.
Ha! ha! well done, now this is fun;
When you do like I'll bring ye in.
Here, Etty dear; here, out o' door,
We'll teäke a sweetheart's walk woonce mwore.

A WIFE A-PRAÏS'D.

'Twer May, but ev'ry leaf wer dry
All day below a sheenèn sky;
The zun did glow wi' yollow gleäre,
An' cowslips blow wi' yollow gleäre,

Wi' grægles' bells a-droopèn low,
An' bremble boughs a-stoopèn low;
While culvers in the trees did coo
　　Above the vallèn dew.

An' there, wi' heäir o' glossy black,
Bezide your neck an' down your back,
You rambled gay a-bloomèn feäir;
By boughs o' may a-bloomèn feäir;
An' while the birds did twitter nigh,
An' water weäves did glitter nigh,
You gather'd cowslips in the lew,
　　Below the vallèn dew.

An' now, while you've a-been my bride
As years o' flow'rs ha' bloom'd an' died,
Your smilèn feäce ha' been my jay;
Your soul o' greäce ha' been my jay;
An' wi' my evenèn rest a-come,
An' zunsheen to the west a-come,
I'm glad to teäke my road to you
　　Vrom vields o' vallèn dew.

An' when the raïn do wet the may,
A-bloomèn where we woonce did stray,
An' win' do blow along so vast,
An' streams do flow along so vast;
Ageän the storms so rough abroad,
An' angry tongues so gruff abroad,
The love that I do meet vrom you
　　Is lik' the vallèn dew.

An' you be sprack's a bee on wing,
In search ov honey in the Spring:
The dawn-red sky do meet ye up;
The birds vu'st cry do meet ye up;

An' wi' your feäce a-smilèn on,
An' busy hands a-tweilèn on,
You'll vind zome useful work to do
   Until the vallèn dew.

THE WIFE A-LOST.

Since I noo mwore do zee your feäce,
   Up steäirs or down below,
I'll zit me in the lwonesome pleäce,
   Where flat-bough'd beech do grow:
Below the beeches' bough, my love,
   Where you did never come,
An' I don't look to meet ye now,
   As I do look at hwome.

Since you noo mwore be at my zide,
   In walks in zummer het,
I'll goo alwone where mist do ride,
   Drough trees a-drippèn wet:
Below the raïn-wet bough, my love,
   Where you did never come,
An' I don't grieve to miss ye now,
   As I do grieve at home.

Since now bezide my dinner-bwoard
   Your vaïce do never sound,
I'll eat the bit I can avword,
   A-vield upon the ground;
Below the darksome bough, my love,
   Where you did never dine,
An' I don't grieve to miss ye now,
   As I at hwome do pine.

Since I do miss your vaïce an' feäce
    In prayer at eventide,
I'll pray wi' woone said vaïce vor greäce
    To goo where you do bide;
Above the tree an' bough, my love,
    Where you be gone avore,
An' be a-waïtèn vor me now,
    To come vor evermwore.

THE THORNS IN THE GEÄTE.

Ah! Meäster Collins overtook
Our knot o' vo'k a-stannèn still,
Last Zunday, up on Ivy Hill,
To zee how strong the corn did look.
An' he stay'd back awhile an' spoke
A vew kind words to all the vo'k,
Vor good or joke, an' wi' a smile
Begun a-playèn wi' a chile.

The zull, wi' iron zide awry,
Had long a-vurrow'd up the vield;
The heavy roller had a-wheel'd
It smooth vor showers vrom the sky;
The bird-bwoy's cry, a-risèn sh'ill,
An' clacker, had a-left the hill,
All bright but still, vor time alwone
To speed the work that we'd a-done.

Down drough the wind, a-blowèn keen,
Did gleäre the nearly cloudless sky,
An' corn in bleäde, up ancle-high,
'Ithin the geäte did quiver green;
An' in the geäte a-lock'd there stood
A prickly row o' thornèn wood

Vor vo'k vor food had done their best,
An' left to Spring to do the rest.

"The geäte," he cried, "a-seal'd wi' thorn
Vrom harmvul veet's a-left to hold
The bleäde a-springèn vrom the mwold,
While God do ripen it to corn.
An' zoo in life let us vulvil
Whatever is our Meäker's will,
An' then bide still, wi' peacevul breast,
While He do manage all the rest.

ANGELS BY THE DOOR.

OH! there be angels evermwore,
A-passèn onward by the door,
A-zent to teäke our jays, or come
To bring us zome—O Meärianne.
Though doors be shut, an' bars be stout,
Noo bolted door can keep em out;
But they wull leäve us ev'ry thing
They have to bring—My Meärianne.

An' zoo the days a-stealèn by,
Wi' zuns a-ridèn drough the sky,
Do bring us things to leäve us sad,
Or meäke us glad—O Meärianne.
The day that's mild, the day that's stern,
Do teäke, in stillness, each his turn;
An' evils at their worst mid mend,
Or even end—My Meärianne.

But still, if we can only bear
Wi' faïth an' love, our païn an' ceäre,
We shan't vind missèn jays a-lost,
Though we be crost—O Meärianne.

But all a-took to heav'n, an' stow'd
Where we can't weäste em on the road,
As we do wander to an' fro,
Down here below—My Meärianne.

But there be jays I'd soonest choose
To keep, vrom them that I must lose ;
Your workzome hands to help my tweil,
Your cheerful smile—O Meärianne.
The Zunday bells o' yonder tow'r,
The moonlight sheädes o' my own bow'r,
An' rest avore our vier-zide,
At evenèn-tide—My Meärianne.

VO'K A-COMÈN INTO CHURCH.

THE church do zeem a touchèn zight,
   When vo'k, a-comèn in at door,
   Do softly tread the long-aïl'd vloor
Below the pillar'd arches' height,
    Wi' bells a-pealèn,
    Vo'k a-kneelèn,
Hearts a-healèn, wi' the love
An' peäce a-zent em vrom above.

An' there, wi' mild an' thoughtvul feäce,
   Wi' downcast eyes, an' vaïces dum',
   The wold an' young do slowly come,
An' teäke in stillness each his pleäce,
    A-zinkèn slowly,
    Kneelèn lowly,
Seekèn holy thoughts alwone,
In pray'r avore their Meäker's throne.

An' there be sons in youthvul pride,
   An' fathers weak wi' years an' païn,
   An' daughters in their mother's traïn,
The tall wi' smaller at their zide;
     Heads in murnèn
     Never turnèn,
Cheäks a-burnèn, wi' the het
O' youth, an' eyes noo tears do wet.

There friends do settle, zide by zide,
   The knower speechless to the known;
   Their vaïce is there vor God alwone
To flesh an' blood their tongues be tied.
     Grief a-wringèn,
     Jaÿ a-zingèn,
Pray'r a-bringèn welcome rest
So softly to the troubled breast.

WOONE RULE.

An' while I zot, wi' thoughtvul mind,
Up where the lwonesome Coombs do wind,
An' watch'd the little gully slide
So crookèd to the river-zide;
I thought how wrong the Stour did zeem
To roll along his ramblèn stream,
A-runnèn wide the left o' south,
To vind his mouth, the right-hand zide.

But though his stream do teäke, at mill,
An' eastward bend by Newton Hill,
An' goo to lay his welcome boon
O' daïly water round Hammoon,

An' then wind off ageän, to run
By Blanvord, to the noonday zun,
'Tis only bound by woone rule all,
An' that's to vall down steepest ground.

An' zoo, I thought, as we do bend
Our way drough life, to reach our end,
Our God ha' gi'ed us, vrom our youth,
Woone rule to be our guide—His truth.
An' zoo wi' that, though we mid teäke
Wide rambles vor our callèns' seäke,
What is, is best, we needen fear,
An' we shall steer to happy rest.

GOOD MEÄSTER COLLINS.

Aye, Meäster Collins wer a-blest
Wi' greäce, an' now's a-gone to rest;
An' though his heart did beät so meek
'S a little child's, when he did speak,
The godly wisdom ov his tongue
Wer dew o' greäce to wold an' young.

'Twer woonce, upon a zummer's tide,
I zot at Brookwell by his zide,
Avore the leäke, upon the rocks,
Above the water's idle shocks,
As little playsome weäves did zwim
Ageän the water's windy brim,
Out where the lofty tower o' stwone
Did stan' to years o' wind an' zun;
An' where the zwellèn pillars bore
A pworch above the heavy door,
Wi' sister sheädes a-reachèn cool
Athirt the stwones an' sparklèn pool.

I spoke zome word that meäde en smile,
O' girt vo'k's wealth an' poor vo'k's tweil,
As if I pin'd, vor want ov greäce,
To have a lord's or squier's pleäce.
"No, no," he zaid, "what God do zend
Is best vor all o's in the end,
An' all that we do need the mwost
Do come to us wi' leäst o' cost;—
Why, who could live upon the e'th
'Ithout God's gift ov air vor breath?
Or who could bide below the zun
If water didden rise an' run?
An' who could work below the skies
If zun an' moon did never rise?
Zoo aïr an' water, an' the light,
Be higher gifts, a-reckon'd right,
Than all the goold the darksome clay
Can ever yield to zunny day:
But then the aïr is roun' our heads,
Abroad by day, or on our beds;
Where land do gi'e us room to bide,
Or seas do spread vor ships to ride;
An' He do zend his waters free,
Vrom clouds to lands, vrom lands to sea;
An' mornèn light do blush an' glow,
'Ithout our tweil—'ithout our ho.

"Zoo let us never pine, in sin,
Vor gifts that bèn't the best to win;
The heaps o' goold that zome mid pile,
Wi' sleepless nights an' peaceless tweil;
Or manor that mid reach so wide
As Blackmwore is vrom zide to zide,
Or kingly sway, wi' life or death,
Vor helpless childern ov the e'th:

Vor theäse ben't gifts, as He do know,
That He in love should vu'st bestow;
Or else we should have had our sheäre
O'm all wi' little tweil or ceäre.

"Ov all His choicest gifts, His cry
Is, 'Come, ye moneyless, and buy.'
Zoo blest is he that can but lift
His prayer vor a happy gift."

HERRENSTON.

Zoo then the leädy an' the squier,
   At Chris'mas, gather'd girt an' small,
Vor me'th, avore their roarèn vier,
   An' roun' their bwoard, 'ithin the hall;
An' there, in glitt'rèn rows, between
The roun'-rimm'd pleätes, our knives did sheen,
   Wi' frothy eäle, an' cup an' can,
   Vor maïd an' man, at Herrenston.

An' there the jeints o' beef did stand,
   Lik' cliffs o' rock, in goodly row;
Where woone mid quarry till his hand
   Did tire, an' meäke but little show;
An' after we'd a-took our seat,
An' greäce had been a-zaid vor meat,
   We zet to work, an' zoo begun
   Our feäst an' fun at Herrenston.

An' mothers there, bezide the bwoards,
   Wi' little childern in their laps,
Did stoop, wi' lovèn looks an' words,
   An' veed em up wi' bits an' draps;

An' smilèn husbands went in quest
O' what their wives did like the best;
　An' you'd ha' zeed a happy zight,
　　Thik merry night, at Herrenston.

An' then the band, wi' each his leaf
　O' notes, above us at the zide,
Play'd up the praïse ov England's beef
　An' vill'd our hearts wi' English pride;
An' leafy chaïns o' garlands hung,
Wi' dazzlèn stripes o' flags, that swung
　　Above us, in a bleäze o' light,
　　Thik happy night, at Herrenston.

An' then the clerk, avore the vier,
　Begun to lead, wi' smilèn feäce,
A carol, wi' the Monkton quire,
　That rung drough all the crowded pleäce.
An' dins' o' words an' laughter broke
In merry peals drough clouds o' smoke;
　　Vor hardly wer there woone that spoke,
　　But pass'd a joke, at Herrenston.

Then man an' maïd stood up by twos,
　In rows, drough passage, out to door,
An' gaïly beät, wi' nimble shoes,
　A dance upon the stwonèn floor.
But who is worthy vor to tell,
If she that then did bear the bell,
　　Wer woone o' Monkton, or o' Ceäme,
　　Or zome sweet neäme ov Herrenston.

Zoo peace betide the girt vo'k's land,
　When they can stoop, wi' kindly smile,
An' teäke a poor man by the hand,
　An' cheer en in his daily tweil.

An' oh! mid He that's vur above
The highest here, reward their love,
   An' gi'e their happy souls, drough greäce,
  A higher pleäce than Herrenston.

OUT AT PLOUGH.

Though cool avore the sheenèn sky
Do vall the sheädes below the copse,
The timber-trees, a-reachèn high,
Ha' zunsheen on their lofty tops,
Where yonder land's a-lyèn plow'd,
An' red, below the snow-white cloud,
An' vlocks o' pitchèn rooks do vwold
Their wings to walk upon the mwold,
    While floods be low,
      An' buds do grow,
        An' aïr do blow, a-broad, O.

But though the aïr is cwold below
The creakèn copses' darksome screen,
The truest sheäde do only show
How strong the warmer zun do sheen;
An' even times o' grief an' païn,
Ha' good a-comèn in their traïn,
An' 'tis but happiness do mark
The sheädes o' sorrow out so dark.
    As tweils be sad,
      Or smiles be glad,
        Or times be bad, at hwome, O.

An' there the zunny land do lie
Below the hangèn, in the lew,
Wi' vurrows now a-crumblèn dry,
Below the plowman's dousty shoe;

An' there the bwoy do whissel sh'ill,
Below the skylark's merry bill,
Where primrwose beds do deck the zides
O' banks below the meäple wrides.
    As trees be bright
      Wi' bees in flight,
        An' weather's bright, abroad, O.

An' there, as sheenèn wheels do spin
Vull speed along the dousty rwoad,
He can but stan', an' wish 'ithin
His mind to be their happy lwoad,
That he mid gaïly ride, an' goo
To towns the rwoad mid teäke en drough,
An' zee, for woonce, the zights behind
The bluest hills his eyes can vind,
    O' towns, an' tow'rs,
      An' downs, an' flow'rs,
        In zunny hours, abroad, O.

But still, vor all the weather's feäir,
Below a cloudless sky o' blue,
The bwoy at plough do little ceäre
How vast the brightest day mid goo;
Vor he'd be glad to zee the zun
A-zettèn, wi' his work a-done,
That he, at hwome, mid still injaÿ
His happy bit ov evenèn plaÿ,
    So light's a lark
      Till night is dark,
        While dogs do bark, at hwome, O.

THE BWOAT.

Where cows did slowly seek the brink
O' *Stour*, drough zunburnt grass, to drink;
Wi' vishèn float, that there did zink
    An' rise, I zot as in a dream.
The dazzlèn zun did cast his light
On hedge-row blossom, snowy white,
Though nothèn yet did come in zight,
    A-stirrèn on the strayèn stream;

Till, out by sheädy rocks there show'd,
A bwoat along his foamy road,
Wi' thik feäir maïd at mill, a-row'd
    Wi' Jeäne behind her brother's oars.
An' steätely as a queen o' vo'k,
She zot wi' floatèn scarlet cloak,
An' comèn on, at ev'ry stroke,
    Between my withy-sheäded shores.

The broken stream did idly try
To show her sheäpe a-ridèn by,
The rushes brown-bloom'd stems did ply,
    As if they bow'd to her by will.
The rings o' water, wi' a sock,
Did break upon the mossy rock,
An' gi'e my beätèn heart a shock,
    Above my float's up-leapèn quill.

Then, lik' a cloud below the skies,
A-drifted off, wi' less'nèn size,
An' lost, she floated vrom my eyes,
    Where down below the stream did wind;
An' left the quiet weäves woonce mwore
To zink to rest, a sky-blue'd vloor,
Wi' all so still's the clote they bore,
    Aye, all but my own ruffled mind.

THE PLEÄCE OUR OWN AGEÄN.

Well! thanks to you, my faïthful Jeäne,
So worksome wi' your head an' hand,
We seäved enough to get ageän
My poor vorefather's plot o' land.
'Twer folly lost, an' cunnèn got,
What should ha' come to me by lot.
But let that goo; 'tis well the land
Is come to hand, by be'th or not.

An' there the brook, a-windèn round
The parrick zide, do run below
The grey-stwon'd bridge wi' gurglèn sound,
A-sheäded by the arches' bow;
Where former days the wold brown meäre.
Wi' father on her back, did wear
Wi' heavy shoes the grav'ly leäne,
An' sheäke her meäne o' yollor heäir.

An' many zummers there ha' glow'd,
To shrink the brook in bubblèn shoals,
An' warm the doust upon the road,
Below the trav'ller's burnèn zoles.
An' zome ha' zent us to our bed
In grief, an' zome in jaÿ ha' vled;
But vew ha' come wi' happier light
Than what's now bright, above our head.

The brook did peärt, zome years agoo,
Our Grenley meäds vrom Knapton's Ridge;
But now you know, between the two,
A-road's a-meäde by Grenley Bridge.
Zoo why should we shrink back at zight
Ov hindrances we ought to slight?
A hearty will, wi' God our friend,
Will gain its end, if 'tis but right.

Eclogue.

John an' Thomas.

THOMAS.

How b'ye, then, John, to-night; an' how
Be times a-waggèn on w' ye now?
I can't help slackenèn my peäce
When I do come along your pleäce,
To zee what crops your bit o' groun'
Do bear ye all the zummer roun'.
'Tis true you don't get fruit nor blooth,
'Ithin the glassèn houses' lewth;
But if a man can rear a crop
Where win' do blow an' raïn can drop,
Do seem to come, below your hand,
As fine as any in the land.

JOHN.

Well, there, the geärden stuff an' flow'rs
Don't leäve me many idle hours;
But still, though I mid plant or zow,
'Tis Woone above do meäke it grow.

THOMAS.

Aye, aye, that's true, but still your strip
O' groun' do show good workmanship:
You've onions there nine inches round,
An' turmits that would waïgh a pound;
An' cabbage wi' its hard white head,
An' teäties in their dousty bed,
An' carrots big an' straïght enough
Vor any show o' geärden stuff;
An' trees ov apples, red-skinn'd balls,
An' purple plums upon the walls,

An' peas an' beäns; bezides a store
O' heärbs vor ev'ry païn an' zore.

JOHN.

An' over hedge the win's a-heärd,
A-ruslèn drough my barley's beard;
An' swayen wheat do overspread
Zix ridges in a sheet o' red;
An' then there's woone thing I do call
The girtest handiness ov all:
My ground is here at hand, avore
My eyes, as I do stand at door;
An' zoo I've never any need
To goo a mile to pull a weed.

THOMAS.

No, sure, a miël shoulden stratch
Between woone's geärden an' woone's hatch.
A man would like his house to stand
Bezide his little bit o' land.

JOHN.

Ees. When woone's groun' vor geärden stuff
Is roun' below the house's ruf,
Then woone can spend upon woone's land
Odd minutes that mid lie on hand,
The while, wi' night a-comèn on,
The red west sky's a-wearèn wan;
Or while woone's wife, wi' busy hands,
Avore her vier o' burnèn brands,
Do put, as best she can avword,
Her bit o' dinner on the bwoard.
An' here, when I do teäke my road,
At breakfast-time, agwaïn abrode,
Why, I can zee if any plot
O' groun' do want a hand or not;
An' bid my childern, when there's need,
To draw a reäke or pull a weed,

Or heal young beäns or peas in line,
Or tie em up wi' rods an' twine,
Or peel a kindly withy white
To hold a droopèn flow'r upright.

THOMAS.

No. Bits o' time can zeldom come
To much on groun' a mile vrom hwome
A man at hwome should have in view
The jobs his childern's hands can do;
An' groun' abrode mid teäke em all
Beyond their mother's zight an' call,
To get a zoakèn in a storm,
Or vall, i' may be, into harm.

JOHN.

Ees. Geärden groun', as I've a-zed,
Is better near woone's bwoard an' bed.

PENTRIDGE BY THE RIVER.

PENTRIDGE!— oh! my heart's a-zwellèn
Vull o' jay wi' vo'k a-tellèn
   Any news o' thik wold pleäce,
An' the boughy hedges round it,
An' the river that do bound it
   Wi' his dark but glis'nèn feäce.
Vor there's noo land, on either hand,
To me lik' Pentridge by the river.

Be there any leaves to quiver
On the aspen by the river?
   Doo he sheäde the water still,
Where the rushes be a-growèn,
Where the sullen Stour's a-flowèn
   Drough the meäds vrom mill to mill?
Vor if a tree wer dear to me,
Oh! 'twer thik aspen by the river.

There, in eegrass new a-shootèn,
I did run on even vootèn,
　Happy, over new-mow'd land;
Or did zing wi' zingèn drushes
While I plaïted, out o' rushes,
　Little baskets vor my hand;
Bezide the clote that there did float,
Wi' yollow blossoms, on the river.

When the western zun's a vallèn,
What sh'ill vaïce is now a-callèn
　Hwome the deäiry to the païls;
Who do dreve em on, a-flingèn
Wide-bow'd horns, or slowly zwingèn
　Right an' left their tufty taïls?
As they do goo a-huddled drough
The geäte a-leädèn up vrom river.

Bleäded grass is now a-shootèn
Where the vloor wer woonce our vootèn,
　While the hall wer still in pleäce.
Stwones be looser in the wallèn;
Hollow trees be nearer vallèn;
　Ev'ry thing ha' chang'd its feäce.
But still the neäme do bide the seäme—
'Tis Pentridge—Pentridge by the river.

WHEAT.

IN brown-leav'd Fall the wheat a-left
　'Ithin its darksome bed,
Where all the creakèn roller's heft
　Seal'd down its lowly head,
Sprung sheäkèn drough the crumblèn mwold,
　Green-yollow, vrom below,
An' bent its bleädes, a-glitt'rèn cwold,
　At last in winter snow.

Zoo luck betide
The upland zide,
Where wheat do wride,
In corn-vields wide,
By crowns o' Do'set Downs, O.

An' while the screamèn bird-bwoy shook
  Wi' little zun-burnt hand,
His clacker at the bright-wing'd rook,
  About the zeeded land;
His meäster there did come an' stop
  His bridle-champèn meäre,
Wi' thankvul heart, to zee his crop
  A-comèn up so feäir.
    As there awhile
    By geäte or stile,
    He gi'ed the chile
    A cheerèn smile,
By crowns o' Do'set Downs, O.

At last, wi' eärs o' darksome red,
  The yollow stalks did ply,
A-swayèn slow, so heavy's lead,
  In aïr a-blowèn by;
An' then the busy reapers laid
  In row their russlèn grips,
An' sheäves, a-leänèn head by head,
  Did meäke the stitches tips.
    Zoo food's a-vound,
    A-comèn round,
    Vrom zeed in ground,
    To sheaves a-bound,
By crowns o' Do'set Downs, O.

An' now the wheat, in lofty lwoads,
  Above the meäres' broad backs,
Do ride along the cracklèn rwoads,
  Or dousty waggon-tracks.

An' there, mid every busy pick,
   Ha' work enough to do;
An' where, avore, we built woone rick,
   Mid theäse year gi'e us two;
      Wi' God our friend,
      An' wealth to spend,
      Vor zome good end,
      That times mid mend,
In towns, an' Do'set Downs, O.

Zoo let the merry thatcher veel
   Fine weather on his brow,
As he, in happy work, do kneel
   Up roun' the new-built mow,
That now do zwell in sich a size,
   An' rise to sich a height,
That, oh! the miller's wistful eyes
   Do sparkle at the zight.
      An' long mid stand,
      A happy band,
      To till the land,
      Wi' head an' hand,
By crowns o' Do'set Downs, O.

THE MEÄD IN JUNE.

AH! how the looks o' sky an' ground
Do change wi' months a-stealèn round,
When northern winds, by starry night,
Do stop in ice the river's flight;
Or brooks in winter raïns do zwell,
Lik' rollèn seas athirt the dell;
Or trickle thin in zummer-tide;
Among the mossy stwones half dried;
But still, below the zun or moon,
The feärest vield's the meäd in June.

An' I must own, my heart do beät
Wi' pride avore my own blue geäte,
Where I can bid the steätely tree
Be cast, at langth, avore my knee;
An' clover red, an' deäzies feaïr,
An' gil'cups wi' their yollow gleäre,
Be all a-match'd avore my zight
By wheelèn buttervlees in flight,
The while the burnèn zun at noon
Do sheen upon my meäd in June.

An' there do zing the swingèn lark
So gaÿ's above the finest park,
An' day do sheäde my trees as true
As any steätely avenue;
An' show'ry clouds o' Spring do pass
To shed their raïn on my young grass,
An' aïr do blow the whole day long,
To bring me breath, an' teäke my zong,
An' I do miss noo needvul boon
A-gi'ed to other meäds in June.

An' when the bloomèn rwose do ride
Upon the boughy hedge's zide,
We haymeäkers, in snow-white sleeves,
Do work in sheädes o' quiv'rèn leaves,
In afternoon, a-liftèn high
Our reäkes avore the viery sky,
A-reäken up the haÿ a-dried
By day, in lwongsome weäles, to bide
In chilly dew below the moon,
O' shorten'd nights in zultry June.

An' there the brook do softly flow
Along, a-bendèn in a bow,

An' vish, wi' zides o' zilver-white,
Do flash vrom shoals a dazzlèn light;
An' alders by the water's edge,
Do sheäde the ribbon-bleäded zedge,
An' where, below the withy's head,
The zwimmèn clote-leaves be a-spread,
The angler is a-zot at noon
Upon the flow'ry bank in June.

Vor all the aiër that do bring
My little meäd the breath o' Spring,
By day an' night's a-flowèn wide
Above all other vields bezide;
Vor all the zun above my ground
'S a-zent vor all the naighbours round,
An' raïn do vall, an' streams do flow,
Vor lands above, an' lands below,
My bit o' meäd is God's own boon,
To me alwone, vrom June to June.

EARLY RISÈN.

The aïr to gi'e your cheäks a hue
O' rwosy red, so feaïr to view,
Is what do sheäke the grass-bleädes gray
At breäk o' day, in mornèn dew;
Vor vo'k that will be rathe abrode,
Will meet wi' health upon their road.

But bidèn up till dead o' night,
When han's o' clocks do stan' upright,
By candle-light, do soon consume
The feäce's bloom, an' turn it white.
An' light a-cast vrom midnight skies
Do blunt the sparklèn ov the eyes.

Vor health do weäke vrom nightly dreams
Below the mornèn's eärly beams,
An' leäve the dead-aïr'd houses' eaves,
Vor quiv'rèn leaves, an' bubblèn streams,
A-glitt'rèn brightly to the view,
Below a sky o' cloudless blue.

ZELLEN WOONE'S HONEY TO BUY ZOME'HAT SWEET.

Why, his heart's lik' a popple, so hard as a stwone,
   Vor 'tis money, an' money's his ho,
An' to handle an' reckon it up vor his own,
   Is the best o' the jays he do know.
Why, vor money he'd gi'e up his lags an' be leäme,
   Or would peärt wi' his zight an' be blind,
Or would lose vo'k's good will, vor to have a bad neäme,
   Or his peace, an' have trouble o' mind.
But wi' ev'ry good thing that his meänness mid bring,
     He'd pay vor his money,
An' only zell honey to buy zome'hat sweet.

He did whisper to me, "You do know that you stood
   By the Squier, wi' the vote that you had,
You could ax en to help ye to zome'hat as good,
   Or to vind a good pleäce vor your lad."
"Aye, aye, but if I wer beholdèn vor bread
   To another," I zaid, "I should bind
All my body an' soul to the nod of his head,
   An' gi'e up all my freedom o' mind."
An' then, if my païn wer a-zet wi' my gaïn,
     I should pay vor my money,
An' only zell honey to buy zome'hat sweet.

Then, if my bit o' brook that do wind so vur round,
　Wer but his, why, he'd straïghten his bed,
An' the wold stunpole woak that do stan' in my ground,
　Shoudden long sheäde the grass wi' his head.
But if I do vind jaÿ where the leaves be a-shook
　On the limbs, wi' their sheädes on the grass,
Or below, in the bow o' the withy-bound nook,
　That the rock-washèn water do pass,
Then wi' they jaÿs a-vled an' zome goold in their stead,
　　I should paÿ vor my money,
An' only zell honey to buy zome'hat sweet.

No, be my lot good work, wi' the lungs well in piaÿ,
　An' good rest when the body do tire,
Vor the mind a good conscience, wi' hope or wi' jaÿ,
　Vor the body, good lewth, an' good vire,
There's noo good o' goold, but to buy what 'ull meäke
　Vor our happiness here among men;
An' who would gi'e happiness up vor the seäke
　O' zome money to buy it ageän?
Vor 'twould seem to the eyes ov a man that is wise,
　　Lik' money vor money,
Or zellèn woone's honey to buy zome'hat sweet.

DOBBIN DEAD.

Thomas (1) *an' John* (2) *a-ta'èn o't.*

2. I do veel vor ye, Thomas, vor I be a-feär'd
　You've a-lost your wold meäre then, by what I've a-heärd.

1. Ees, my meäre is a-gone, an' the cart's in the shed
　Wi' his wheelbonds a-rustèn, an' I'm out o' bread;
Vor what be my han's vor to eärn me a croust,
　Wi' noo meäre's vower legs vor to trample the doust.

2. Well, how did it happen? He vell vrom the brim
　Ov a cliff, as the teäle is, an' broke ev'ry lim'.

1. Why, I gi'ed en his run, an' he shook his wold meäne,
    An' he rambled a-veedèn in Westergap Leäne;
    An' there he must needs goo a-riggèn, an' crope
    Vor a vew bleädes o' grass up the wo'st o' the slope;
    Though I should ha' thought his wold head would ha' know'd
    That vor stiff lags, lik' his, the best pleäce wer the road.

2. An' you hadden a-kept en so short, he must clim',
    Lik' a gwoat, vor a bleäde, at the risk ov a lim'.

1. Noo, but there, I'm a-twold, he did clim' an' did slide,
    An' did screäpe, an' did slip, on the shelvèn bank-zide,
    An' at length lost his vootèn, an' roll'd vrom the top,
    Down, thump, kick, an' higgledly, piggledly, flop.

2. Dear me, that is bad! I do veel vor your loss,
    Vor a vew years agoo, Thomas, I lost my ho'se.

1. How wer't? If I heärd it, I now ha' vorgot;
    Wer the poor thing bewitch'd or a-pweison'd, or what?

2. He wer out, an' a-meäkèn his way to the brink
    O' the stream at the end o' Church Leäne, vor to drink;
    An' he met wi' zome yew-twigs the men had a-cast
    Vrom the yew-tree, in churchyard, the road that he past.
    He wer pweison'd. (1.) O dear, 'tis a hard loss to bear,
    Vor a tranter's whole bread is a-lost wi' his meäre;
    But ov all churches' yew-trees, I never zet eyes
    On a tree that would come up to thik woone vor size.

2. Noo, 'tis long years agone, but do linger as clear
    In my mind though as if I'd a-heärd it to year.
    When King George wer in Do'set, an' show'd us his feäce
    By our very own doors, at our very own pleäce,
    That he look'd at thik yew-tree, an' nodded his head,
    An' he zaid,—an' I'll tell ye the words that he zaid :—
    " I'll be bound, if you'll sarch my dominions all drough,
    That you woon't vind the fellow to thik there wold yew."

HAPPINESS.

Ah! you do seem to think the ground,
Where happiness is best a-vound,
Is where the high-peäl'd park do reach
Wi' elem-rows, or clumps o' beech,
Or where the coach do stand avore
The twelve-tunn'd house's lofty door,
Or men can ride behin' their hounds
Vor miles athirt their own wide grounds,
   An' seldom wi' the lowly;
Upon the green that we do tread,
Below the welsh-nut's wide-limb'd head,
Or grass where apple trees do spread?
No, so's; no, no: not high nor low:
'Tis where the heart is holy.

'Tis true its veet mid tread the vloor,
'Ithin the marble-pillar'd door,
Where day do cast, in high-ruf'd halls,
His light drough lofty window'd walls;
An' wax-white han's do never tire
Wi' strokes ov heavy work vor hire,
An' all that money can avword
Do lwoad the zilver-brighten'd bwoard;
   Or mid be wi' the lowly,
Where turf's a-smwoderèn avore
The back, to warm the stwonèn vloor,
An' love's at hwome 'ithin the door?
No, so's; no, no; not high nor low:
   'Tis where the heart is holy.

An' ceäre can come 'ithin a ring
O' sworded guards, to smite a king.

Though he mid hold 'ithin his hands
The zwarmèn vo'k o' many lands;
Or goo in drough the iron-geäte
Avore the house o' lofty steäte;
Or reach the miser that do smile
A-buildèn up his goolden pile;
 Or else mid smite the lowly,
That have noo pow'r to loose or bind
Another's body, or his mind,
But only hands to help mankind.
If there is rest 'ithin the breast,
 'Tis where the heart is holy.

GRUFFMOODY GRIM.

AYE, a sad life his wife must ha' led,
Vor so snappish he's leätely a-come,
That there's nothèn but anger or dread
Where he is, abroad or at hwome;
He do wreak all his spite on the bwones
O' whatever do vlee, or do crawl;
He do quarrel wi' stocks, an' wi' stwones,
An' the raïn, if do hold up or vall;
There is nothèn vrom mornèn till night
Do come right to Gruffmoody Grim.

Woone night, in his anger, he zwore
At the vier, that didden burn free:
An' he het zome o't out on the vloor,
Vor a vlanker it cast on his knee.
Then he kicked it vor burnèn the child,
An' het it among the cat's heaïrs;
An' then beät the cat, a-run wild,
Wi' a spark on her back up the steaïrs:
Vor even the vier an' fleäme
Be to bleäme wi' Gruffmoody Grim.

GRUFFMOODY GRIM.

Then he snarl'd at the tea in his cup,
Vor 'twer all a-got cwold in the pot,
But 'twer woo'se when his wife vill'd it up
Vrom the vier, vor 'twer then scaldèn hot;
Then he growl'd that the bread wer sich stuff
As noo hammer in parish could crack,
An' flung down the knife in a huff;
Vor the edge o'n wer thicker'n the back.
Vor beäkers an' meäkers o' tools
Be all fools wi' Gruffmoody Grim.

Oone day as he vish'd at the brook,
He flung up, wi' a quick-handed knack,
His long line, an' his high-vleèn hook
Wer a-hitch'd in zome briars at his back.
Then he zwore at the brembles, an' prick'd
His beäre hand, as he pull'd the hook free;
An' ageän, in a rage, as he kick'd
At the briars, wer a-scratch'd on the knee.
An' he wish'd ev'ry bremble an' briar
Wer o' vier, did Gruffmoody Grim.

Oh! he's welcome, vor me, to breed dread
Wherever his sheäde mid alight,
An' to live wi' noo me'th round his head,
An' noo feäce wi' a smile in his zight;
But let vo'k be all merry an' zing
At the he'th where my own logs do burn,
An' let anger's wild vist never swing
In where I have a door on his durn;
Vor I'll be a happier man,
While I can, than Gruffmoody Grim.

To zit down by the vier at night,
Is my jay—vor I woon't call it pride,—
Wi' a brand on the bricks, all alight,
An' a pile o' zome mwore at the zide.
Then tell me o' zome'hat that's droll,

x

An' I'll laugh till my two zides do eäche
Or o' naïghbours in sorrow o' soul,
An' I'll tweil all the night vor their seäke;
An' show that to teäke things amiss
Idden bliss, to Gruffmoody Grim.

An' then let my child clim' my lag,
An' I'll lift en, wi' love, to my chin;
Or my maïd come an' coax me to bag
Vor a frock, an' a frock she shall win;
Or, then if my wife do meäke light
O' whatever the bwoys mid ha' broke,
It wull seem but so small in my zight,
As a leaf a-het down vrom a woak
An' not meäke me ceäper an' froth
Vull o' wrath, lik' Gruffmoody Grim.

THE TURN O' THE DAYS.

O THE wings o' the rook wer a-glitterèn bright,
As he wheel'd on above, in the zun's evenèn light,
An' noo snow wer a-left, but in patches o' white,
   On the hill at the turn o' the days.
An' along on the slope wer the beäre-timber'd copse,
Wi' the dry wood a-sheäkèn, wi' red-twiggèd tops.
Vor the dry-flowèn wind, had a-blow'd off the drops
   O' the raïn, at the turn o' the days.

There the stream did run on, in the sheäde o' the hill,
So smooth in his flowèn, as if he stood still,
An' bright wi' the skylight, did slide to the mill,
   By the meäds, at the turn o' the days.
An' up by the copse, down along the hill brow,
Wer vurrows a-cut down, by men out at plough,
So straïght as the zunbeams, a-shot drough the bough
   O' the tree at the turn o' the days.

Then the boomèn wold clock in the tower did mark
His vive hours, avore the cool evenèn wer dark,
An' ivy did glitter a-clung round the bark
　　O' the tree, at the turn o' the days.
An' womèn a-fraïd o' the road in the night,
Wer a-heästenèn on to reach hwome by the light,
A-castèn long sheädes on the road, a-dried white,
　　Down the hill, at the turn o' the days.

The father an' mother did walk out to view
The moss-bedded snow-drop, a-sprung in the lew,
An' hear if the birds wer a-zingèn anew,
　　In the boughs, at the turn o' the days.
An' young vo'k a-laughèn wi' smooth glossy feäce,
Did hie over vields, wi' a light-vooted peäce,
To friends where the tow'r did betoken a pleäce
　　Among trees, at the turn o' the days.

THE SPARROW CLUB.

Last night the merry farmers' sons,
　　Vrom biggest down to leäst, min,
Gi'ed in the work of all their guns,
　　An' had their sparrow feäst, min.
An' who vor woone good merry soul
　　Should goo to sheäre their me'th, min,
But Gammon Gay, a chap so droll,
　　He'd meäke ye laugh to death, min.

Vor heads o' sparrows they've a-shot
　　They'll have a prize in cwein, min,
That is, if they can meäke their scot,
　　Or else they'll pay a fine, min.
An' all the money they can teäke
　　'S a-gather'd up there-right, min,

An' spent in meat an' drink, to meäke
　　A supper vor the night, min.

Zoo when they took away the cloth,
　　In middle of their din, min,
An' cups o' eäle begun to froth,
　　Below their merry chin, min.
An' when the zong, by turn or chaïce,
　　Went roun' vrom tongue to tongue, min,
Then Gammon pitch'd his merry vaïce,
　　An' here's the zong he zung, min.

Zong.

If you'll but let your clackers rest
　　Vrom jabberèn an' hootèn,
I'll teäke my turn, an' do my best,
　　To zing o' sparrow shootèn.
Since every woone mus' pitch his key,
　　An' zing a zong, in coo'se, lads,
Why sparrow heads shall be to-day
　　The heads o' my discoo'se, lads.

We'll zend abroad our viery haïl
　　Till ev'ry foe's a-vled, lads,
An' though the rogues mid all turn taïl,
　　We'll quickly show their head, lads.
In corn, or out on oben ground,
　　In bush, or up in tree, lads,
If we don't kill em, I'll be bound,
　　We'll meäke their veathers vlee, lads.

Zoo let the belted spwortsmen brag
　　When they've a-won a neäme, so's,
That they do vind, or they do bag,
　　Zoo many head o' geäme, so's:

Vor when our cwein is woonce a-won,
   By heads o' sundry sizes,
Why, who can slight what we've a-done?
   We've all a-won *head* prizes.

Then teäke a drap vor harmless fun,
   But not enough to quarrel;
Though where a man do like the gun,
   He can't but need the barrel.
O' goodly feäre, avore we'll start,
   We'll zit an' teäke our vill, min;
Our supper-bill can be but short,
   'Tis but a sparrow-bill, min.

GAMMONY GAŸ.

OH! thik Gammony Gaÿ is so droll,
That if he's at hwome by the he'th,
Or wi' vo'k out o' door, he's the soul
O' the meetèn vor antics an' me'th;
He do cast off the thoughts ov ill luck
As the water's a-shot vrom a duck;
He do zing where his naïghbours would cry—
He do laugh where the rest o's would sigh:
Noo other's so merry o' feäce,
In the pleäce, as Gammony Gaÿ.

An' o' workèn days, Oh! he do wear
Such a funny roun' hat,—you mid know't—
Wi' a brim all a-strout roun' his heäir,
An' his glissenèn eyes down below't:
An' a cwoat wi' broad skirts that do vlee
In the wind ov his walk, round his knee;
An' a peäir o' girt pockets lik' bags,
That do swing an' do bob at his lags
While me'th do walk out drough the pleäce,
In the feäce o' Gammony Gaÿ.

An' if he do goo over groun'
Wi' noo soul vor to greet wi' his words,
The feäce o'n do look up an' down,
An' round en so quick as a bird's;
An' if he do vall in wi' vo'k,
Why, tidden vor want ov a joke,
If he don't zend em on vrom the pleäce
Wi' a smile or a grin on their feäce:
An' the young wi' the wold have a-heärd
A kind word vrom Gammony Gaÿ.

An' when he do whissel or hum,
'Ithout thinkèn o' what he's a-doèn,
He'll beät his own lags vor a drum,
An' bob his gaÿ head to the tuèn;
An' then you mid zee, 'etween whiles,
His feäce all alive wi' his smiles,
An' his gaÿ-breathèn bozom do rise,
An' his me'th do sheen out ov his eyes:
An' at last to have praïse or have bleäme,
Is the seäme to Gammony Gaÿ.

When he drove his wold cart out, an' broke
The nut o' the wheel at a butt,
There wer "woo'se things," he cried, wi' a joke,
"To grieve at than crackèn a nut."
An' when he tipp'd over a lwoad
Ov his reed-sheaves woone day on the rwoad,
Then he spet in his han's, out o' sleeves,
An' whissel'd, an' flung up his sheaves,
As very vew others can wag,
Eärm or lag, but Gammony Gaÿ.

He wer wi' us woone night when the band
Wer a-come vor to gi'e us a hop,
An' he pull'd Grammer out by the hand
All down drough the dance vrom the top;

An' Grammer did hobble an' squall,
Wi' Gammon a-leädèn the ball;
While Gammon did sheäke up his knee
An' his voot, an' zing "Diddle-ee-dee!"
An' we laugh'd ourzelves all out o' breath
At the me'th o' Gammony Gaÿ.

When our tun wer' o' vier he rod
Out to help us, an' meäde us sich fun,
Vor he clomb up to dreve in a wad
O' wet thorns, to the he'th, vrom the tun;
An' there he did stamp wi' his voot,
To push down the thorns an' the zoot,
Till at last down the chimney's black wall
Went the wad, an' poor Gammon an' all:
An' seäfe on the he'th, wi' a grin
On his chin pitch'd Gammony Gaÿ.

All the house-dogs do waggle their taïls,
If they do but catch zight ov his feäce;
An' the ho'ses do look over rails,
An' do whicker to zee'n at the pleäce;
An' he'll always bestow a good word
On a cat or a whisselèn bird;
An' even if culvers do coo,
Or an owl is a-cryèn "Hoo, hoo,"
Where he is, there's always a joke
To be spoke, by Gammony Gaÿ.

THE HEARE.

(Dree o'm a-ta'kèn o't.)

(1) There be the greyhounds! lo'k! an' there's the heäre!
(2) What houn's, the squier's, Thomas? where, then, where?

(1) Why, out in Ash Hill, near the barn, behind
　　Thik tree. (3) The pollard? (1) Pollard! no, b'ye blind?
(2) There, I do zee em over-right thik cow.
(3) The red woone? (1) No, a mile beyand her now.
(3) Oh! there's the heäre, a-meäkèn for the drong.
(2) My goodness! How the dogs do zweep along,
　　A-pokèn out their pweinted noses' tips.
(3) He can't allow hizzelf much time vor slips!
(1) They'll hab'en, after all, I'll bet a crown.
(2) Done vor a crown. They woon't! He's gwäin to groun'.
(3) He is! (1) He idden! (3) Ah! 'tis well his tooes
　　Ha' got noo corns, inside o' hobnaïl shoes.
(1) He's geäme a-runnèn too. Why, he do mwore
　　Than eärn his life. (3) His life wer his avore.
(1) There, now the dogs wull turn en. (2) No! He's right.
(1) He idden! (2) Ees he is! (3) He's out o' zight.
(1) Aye, aye. His mettle wull be well a-tried
　　Agwaïn down Verny Hill, o' tother zide.
　　They'll have en there. (3) O no! a vew good hops
　　Wull teäke en on to Knapton Lower Copse.
(2) An' that's a meesh that he've a-took avore.
(3) Ees, that's his hwome. (1) He'll never reach his door.
(2) He wull. (1) He woon't. (3) Now, hark, d'ye heär em now?
(2) O! here's a bwoy a-come athirt the brow
　　O' Knapton Hill. We'll ax en. (1) Here, my bwoy!
　　Can'st tell us where's the heäre? (4) He's got awoy.
(2) Ees, got awoy, in coo'se, I never zeed
　　A heäre a-scotèn on wi' half his speed.
(1) Why, there, the dogs be wold, an' half a-done.
　　They can't catch anything wi' lags to run.
(2) Vrom vu'st to last they had but little chance
　　O' catchèn o'n. (3) They had a perty dance.
(1) No, catch en, no! I little thought they would;
　　He know'd his road too well to Knapton Wood.
(3) No! no! I wish the squier would let me feäre
　　On rabbits till his hounds do catch thik heäre.

NANNY GILL.

AH! they wer times, when Nanny Gill
Went so'jerèn ageänst her will,
Back when the King come down to view
His ho'se an' voot, in red an' blue,
   An' they did march in rows,
   An' wheel in lines an' bows,
   Below the King's own nose;
An' guns did pwoint, an' swords did gleäre,
A-fightèn foes that werden there.

Poor Nanny Gill did goo to zell
In town her glitt'rèn macarel,
A-pack'd wi' ceäre, in even lots,
A-ho'seback in a peäir o' pots.
   An' zoo when she did ride
   Between her panniers wide,
   Red-cloked in all her pride,
Why, who but she, an' who but broke
The road avore her scarlet cloke!

But Nanny's ho'se that she did ride,
Woonce carr'd a sword ageän his zide,
An' had, to prick en into rank,
A so'jer's spurs ageän his flank;
   An' zoo, when he got zight
   O' swords a-gleamèn bright,
   An' men agwaïn to fight,
He set his eyes athirt the ground,
An' prick'd his ears to catch the sound.

Then Nanny gi'ed his zide a kick,
An' het en wi' her limber stick:

But suddenly a horn did sound,
An' zend the ho'semen on vull bound;
  An' her ho'se at the zight
  Went after em, vull flight,
  Wi' Nanny in a fright,
A-pullèn, wi' a scream an' grin,
Her wold brown raïns to hold en in.

But no! he went away vull bound,
As vast as he could tear the ground,
An' took, in line, a so'jer's pleäce,
Vor Nanny's cloke an' frighten'd feäce;
  While vo'k did laugh an' shout
  To zee her cloke stream out,
  As she did wheel about,
A-cryèn, "Oh! la! dear!" in fright,
The while her ho'se did play sham fight.

MOONLIGHT ON THE DOOR.

A-swaÿèn slow, the poplar's head,
  Above the slopèn thatch did ply,
The while the midnight moon did shed
  His light below the spangled sky.
An' there the road did reach avore
  The hatch, all vootless down the hill;
  An' hands, a-tired by day, wer still,
Wi' moonlight on the door.

A-boomèn deep, did slowly sound
  The bell, a-tellèn middle night;
The while the quiv'rèn ivy, round
  The tree, did sheäke in softest light.

But vootless wer the stwone avore
   The house where I, the maïden's guest,
   At evenèn, woonce did zit at rest
By moonlight on the door.

Though till the dawn, where night's a-meäde
   The day, the laughèn crowds be gay,
Let evenèn zink wi' quiet sheäde,
   Where I do hold my little sway.
An' childern dear to my heart's core,
   A-sleep wi' little heavèn breast,
That pank'd by day in play, do rest
Wi' moonlight on the door.

But still 'tis good, woonce now an' then.
   To rove where moonlight on the land
Do show in vaïn, vor heedless men,
   The road, the vield, the work in hand.
When curtains be a-hung avore
   The glitt'rèn windows, snowy white,
   An' vine-leaf sheädes do sheäke in light
O' moonlight on the door.

MY LOVE'S GUARDIAN ANGEL.

As in the cool-aïr'd road I come by,
               —in the night,
Under the moon-clim'd height o' the sky,
               —in the night,
There by the lime's broad lim's as I stay'd,
Dark in the moonlight, bough's sheädows play'd
Up on the window-glass that did keep
Lew vrom the wind, my true love asleep,
               —in the night.

While in the grey-wall'd height o' the tow'r,
               —in the night,

Sounded the midnight bell wi' the hour,
                    —in the night,
There lo! a bright-heäir'd angel that shed
Light vrom her white robe's zilvery thread,
Put her vore-vinger up vor to meäke
Silence around lest sleepers mid weäke,
                    —in the night.
"Oh! then," I whisper'd, do I behold
                    —in the night.
Linda, my true-love, here in the cwold,
                    —in the night?"
"No," she meäde answer, "you do misteäke:
She is asleep, but I that do weäke,
Here be on watch, an' angel a-blest,
Over her slumber while she do rest,
                    —in the night."

"Zee how the winds, while here by the bough,
                    —in the night,
They do pass on, don't smite on her brow,
                    in the night;
Zee how the cloud-sheädes naïseless do zweep
Over the house-top where she's asleep.
You, too, goo by, in times that be near,
You too, as I, mid speak in her ear
                    —in the night."

LEEBURN MILL.

Ov all the meäds wi' shoals an' pools,
Where streams did sheäke the limber zedge,
An' milkèn vo'k did teäke their stools,
In evenèn zun-light under hedge:
Ov all the wears the brook did vill,
Or all the hatches where a sheet

O' foam did leäp below woone's veet,
The pleäce vor me wer Leeburn Mill.

An' while below the mossy wheel
All day the foamèn stream did roar,
An' up in mill the floatèn meal
Did pitch upon the sheäkèn vloor.
We then could vind but vew han's still,
Or veet a-restèn off the ground,
An' seldom hear the merry sound
O' geämes a-play'd at Leeburn Mill.

But when they let the stream goo free,
Bezide the drippèn wheel at rest,
An' leaves upon the poplar-tree
Wer dark avore the glowèn west;
An' when the clock, a-ringèn sh'ill,
Did slowly beät zome evenèn hour,
Oh! then 'ithin the leafy bow'r
Our tongues did run at Leeburn Mill.

An' when November's win' did blow,
Wi' hufflèn storms along the plaïn,
An' blacken'd leaves did lie below
The neäked tree, a-zoak'd wi' raïn,
I werden at a loss to vill
The darkest hour o' raïny skies,
If I did vind avore my eyes
The feäces down at Leeburn Mill.

PRAISE O' DO'SET.

We Do'set, though we mid be hwomely,
  Be'nt asheäm'd to own our pleäce;
An' we've zome women not uncomely;
  Nor asheäm'd to show their feäce:

We've a meäd or two wo'th mowèn,
We've an ox or two wo'th showèn,
    In the village,
    At the tillage,
Come along an' you shall vind
That Do'set men don't sheäme their kind.
    Friend an' wife,
    Fathers, mothers, sisters, brothers,
    Happy, happy, be their life!
    Vor Do'set dear,
    Then gi'e woone cheer;
    D'ye hear? woone cheer!

If you in Do'set be a-roamèn,
  An' ha' business at a farm,
Then woont ye zee your eäle a-foamèn!
  Or your cider down to warm?
Woont ye have brown bread a-put ye,
An' some vinny cheese a-cut ye?
    Butter?—rolls o't!
    Cream?—why bowls o't!
Woont ye have, in short, your vill,
A-gi'ed wi' a right good will?
    Friend an' wife,
    Fathers, mothers, sisters, brothers
    Happy, happy, be their life!
    Vor Do'set dear,
    Then gi'e woone cheer;
    D'ye hear? woone cheer!

An' woont ye have vor ev'ry shillèn,
  Shillèn's wo'th at any shop,
Though Do'set chaps be up to zellèn,
  An' can meäke a tidy swop?
Use em well, they'll use you better;
In good turns they woont be debtor.

   An' so comely,
   An' so hwomely,
Be the maïdens, if your son
Took woone o'm, then you'd cry " Well done!"
   Friend an' wife,
    Fathers, mothers, sisters, brothers,
     Happy, happy, be their life!
    Vor Do'set dear,
    Then gi'e woone cheer;
    D'ye hear? woone cheer!

 If you do zee our good men travel,
  Down a-voot, or on their meäres,
Along the windèn leänes o' gravel,
  To the markets or the feäirs,—
Though their ho'ses cwoats be ragged,
'Though the men be muddy-laggèd,
   Be they roughish,
   Be they gruffish,
They be sound, an' they will stand
By what is right wi' heart an' hand.
   Friend an' wife,
    Fathers, mothers, sisters, brothers,
     Happy, happy, be their life!
    Vor Do'set dear,
    Then gi'e woone cheer;
    D'ye hear? woone cheer!

POEMS OF RURAL LIFE.

THIRD COLLECTION.

Y

WOONE SMILE MWORE.

O! MEÁRY, when the zun went down,
   Woone night in Spring, wi' vi'ry rim,
Behind thik nap wi' woody crown,
   An' left your smilèn feäce so dim;
Your little sister there, inside,
   Wi' bellows on her little knee,
Did blow the vier, a-glearèn wide
   Drough window-peänes, that I could zee,—
As you did stan' wi' me, avore
The house, a-peärten,—woone smile mwore.

The chatt'rèn birds, a-risèn high,
   An' zinkèn low, did swiftly vlee
Vrom shrinkèn moss, a-growèn dry,
   Upon the leänèn apple tree.
An' there the dog, a-whippèn wide
   His heäiry tail, an' comèn near,
Did fondly lay ageän your zide
   His coal-black nose an' russet ear:
To win what I'd a-won avore,
Vrom your gay feäce, his woone smile mwore.

An' while your mother bustled sprack,
   A-gettèn supper out in hall,
An' cast her sheäde, a-whiv'rèn black
   Avore the vier, upon the wall;
Your brother come, wi' easy peäce,
   In drough the slammèn geäte, along

The path, wi' healthy-bloomèn feäce,
   A-whis'lèn shrill his last new zong ;
An' when he come avore the door,
He met vrom you his woone smile mwore.

Now you that wer the daughter there,
   Be mother on a husband's vloor,
An' mid ye meet wi' less o' ceäre
   Than what your hearty mother bore ,
An' if abroad I have to rue
   The bitter tongue, or wrongvul deed,
Mid I come hwome to sheäre wi' you
   What's needvul free o' pinchèn need :
An' vind that you ha' still in store,
My evenèn meal, an' woone smile mwore.

THE ECHO.

About the tow'r an' churchyard wall,
   Out nearly overright our door,
A tongue ov wind did always call
   Whatever we did call avore.
The vaïce did mock our neämes, our cheers,
   Our merry laughs, our hands' loud claps,
An' mother's call "Come, come, my dears"
                         —*my dears;*
   Or "Do as I do bid, bad chaps"
                         —*bad chaps.*

An' when o' Zundays on the green,
   In frocks an' cwoats as gay as new,
We walk'd wi' shoes a-meäde to sheen
   So black an' bright's a vull-ripe slooe

We then did hear the tongue ov aïr
   A-mockèn mother's vaïce so thin,
"Come, now the bell do goo vor pray'r"
                         —vor pray'r;
"'Tis time to goo to church; come in"
                         —come in.

The night when little Anne, that died,
   Begun to zickèn, back in May,
An' she, at dusk ov evenèn-tide,
   Wer out wi' others at their play,
Within the churchyard that do keep
   Her little bed, the vaïce o' thin
Dark aïr, mock'd mother's call "To sleep"
                         —to sleep;
"'Tis bed time now, my love, come in"
                         —come in.

An' when our Jeäne come out so smart
   A-married, an' we help'd her in
To Henry's newly-painted cart,
   The while the wheels begun to spin,
An' her gay nods, vor all she smil'd,
   Did sheäke a tear-drop vrom each eye,
The vaïce mock'd mother's call, "Dear child"
                         —dear child;
"God bless ye evermwore; good bye"
                         —good bye.

VULL A MAN.

No, I'm a man, I'm vull a man,
You beät my manhood, if you can.
You'll be a man if you can teäke
All steätes that household life do meäke.

The love-toss'd child, a-croodlèn loud,
　The bwoy a-screamèn wild in play,
The tall grown youth a-steppèn proud,
　The father staïd, the house's stay.
　　No; I can boast if others can,
　　　I'm vull a man.

A young-cheäk'd mother's tears mid vall,
When woone a-lost, not half man-tall,
Vrom little hand, a-called vrom play,
Do leäve noo tool, but drop a tay,
An' die avore he's father-free
　To sheäpe his life by his own plan;
An' vull an angel he shall be,
　But here on e'th not vull a man,
　　No; I could boast if others can,
　　　I'm vull a man.

I woonce, a child, wer father-fed,
An' I've a-vound my childern bread;
My eärm, a sister's trusty crook,
Is now a faïthvul wife's own hook;
An' I've a-gone where vo'k did zend,
　An' gone upon my own free mind,
An' of'en at my own wits' end.
　A-led o' God while I wer blind.
　　No; I could boast if others can
　　　I'm vull a man.

An' still, ov all my tweil ha' won,
My lovèn maïd an' merry son,
Though each in turn's a jay an' ceäre,
'Ve a-had, an' still shall have, their sheäre;
An' then, if God should bless their lives,
　Why I mid zend vrom son to son

My life, right on drough men an' wives,
　　As long, good now, as time do run.
　　No; I could boast if others can,
　　　I'm vull a man.

NAIGHBOUR PLAŸMEÄTES.

O JAŸ betide the dear wold mill,
　　My naïghbour plaÿmeätes' happy hwome,
Wi' rollèn wheel, an' leäpèn foam,
　　Below the overhangèn hill,
　　　Where, wide an' slow,
　　　The stream did flow,
An' flags did grow, an' lightly vlee
Below the grey-leav'd withy tree,
While clack, clack, clack, vrom hour to hour,
Wi' whirlèn stwone, an' streamèn flour,
Did goo the mill by cloty Stour.

An' there in geämes by evenèn skies,
　　When Meäry zot her down to rest,
The broach upon her pankèn breast,
　　Did quickly vall an' lightly rise,
　　　While swans did zwim
　　　In steätely trim.
An' swifts did skim the water, bright
Wi' whirlèn froth, in western light;
An' clack, clack, clack, that happy hour,
Wi' whirlèn stwone, an' streamèn flour,
Did goo the mill by cloty Stour.

Now mortery jeints, in streaks o' white,
　　Along the geärdèn wall do show
In May, an' cherry boughs do blow,
　　Wi' bloomèn tutties, snowy white,

       Where rollèn round,
       Wi' rumblèn sound,
The wheel woonce drown'd the vaïce so dear
To me. I faïn would goo to hear
The clack, clack, clack, vor woone short hour,
Wi' whirlèn stwone, an' streamèn flour,
Bezide the mill on cloty Stour.

But should I vind a-heavèn now
   Her breast wi' aïr o' thik dear pleäce?
Or zee dark locks by such a brow,
   Or het o' play on such a feäce?
      No! She's now staïd,
      An' where she play'd,
There's noo such maïd that now ha' took
The pleäce that she ha' long vorsook,
Though clack, clack, clack, vrom hour to hour,
Wi' whirlèn stwone an' streamèn flour,
Do goo the mill by cloty Stour.

An' still the pulley rwope do heist
   The wheat vrom red-wheeled waggon beds,
An' ho'ses there wi' lwoads of grist,
   Do stand an' toss their heavy heads;
      But on the vloor,
      Or at the door,
Do show noo mwore the kindly feäce
Her father show'd about the pleäce,
As clack, clack, clack, vrom hour to hour,
Wi' whirlèn stwone, an' streamèn flour,
Did goo his mill by cloty Stour.

THE LARK.

As I, below the mornèn sky,
   Wer out a workèn in the lew
O' black-stemm'd thorns, a-springèn high,
   Avore the worold-boundèn blue,
A-reäkèn, under woak tree boughs,
The orts a-left behin' by cows.

Above the grey-grow'd thistle rings,
   An' deäisy-buds, the lark, in flight,
Did zing a-loft, wi' flappèn wings,
   Tho' mwore in heärèn than in zight;
The while my bwoys, in playvul me'th,
Did run till they wer out o' breath.

Then woone, wi' han'-besheäded eyes,
   A-stoppèn still, as he did run,
Look'd up to zee the lark arise
   A-zingèn to the high-gone zun;
The while his brother look'd below
Vor what the groun' mid have to show.

Zoo woone did watch above his head
   The bird his hands could never teäke;
An' woone, below, where he did tread,
   Vound out the nest within the breäke;
But, aggs be only woonce a-vound,
An' uncaught larks ageän mid sound.

THE TWO CHURCHES.

A HAPPY day, a happy year,
A zummer Zunday, dazzlèn ciear,
I went athirt vrom Lea to Noke.
To goo to church wi' Fanny's vo'k:

The sky o' blue did only show
A cloud or two, so white as snow,
An' aïr did sway, wi' softest strokes,
The eltrot roun' the dark-bough'd woaks.
O day o' rest when bells do toll!
O day a-blest to ev'ry soul!
How sweet the zwells o' Zunday bells.

An' on the cowslip-knap at Creech,
Below the grove o' steätely beech,
I heärd two tow'rs a-cheemèn clear,
Vrom woone I went, to woone drew near,
As they did call, by flow'ry ground,
The bright-shod veet vrom housen round,
A-drownèn wi' their holy call,
The goocoo an' the water-vall.
Die off, O bells o' my dear pleäce,
Ring out, O bells avore my feäce,
Vull sweet your zwells, O ding-dong bells.

Ah! then vor things that time did bring
My kinsvo'k, *Lea* had bells to ring;
An' then, ageän, vor what bevell
My wife's, why *Noke* church had a bell;
But soon wi' hopevul lives a-bound
In woone, we had woone tower's sound,
Vor our high jays all vive bells rung,
Our losses had woone iron tongue.
Oh! ring all round, an' never mwoän
So deep an' slow woone bell alwone.
Vor sweet your swells o' vive clear bells.

WOAK HILL.

When sycamore leaves wer a-spreadèn,
    Green-ruddy, in hedges,
Bezide the red doust o' the ridges,
    A-dried at Woak Hill;

I packed up my goods all a-sheenèn
    Wi' long years o' handlèn,
On dousty red wheels ov a waggon,
    To ride at Woak Hill.

The brown thatchen ruf o' the dwellèn,
    I then wer a-leävèn,
Had shelter'd the sleek head o' Meäry,
    My bride at Woak Hill.

But now vor zome years, her light voot-vall
    'S a-lost vrom the vloorèn.
Too soon vor my jäy an' my childern,
    She died at Woak Hill.

But still I do think that, in soul,
    She do hover about us;
To ho vor her motherless childern,
    Her pride at Woak Hill.

Zoo—lest she should tell me hereafter
    I stole off 'ithout her,
An' left her, uncall'd at house-ridden,
    To bide at Woak Hill—

I call'd her so fondly, wi' lippèns
    All soundless to others,
An' took her wi' aïr-reachèn hand,
    To my zide at Woak Hill.

On the road I did look round, a-talkèn
        To light at my shoulder,
An' then led her in at the door-way,
        Miles wide vrom Woak Hill.

An' that's why vo'k thought, vor a season,
        My mind wer a-wandrèn
Wi' sorrow, when I wer so sorely
        A-tried at Woak Hill.

But no; that my Meäry mid never
        Behold herzelf slighted,
I wanted to think that I guided
        My guide vrom Wóak Hill.

THE HEDGER.

Upon the hedge theäse bank did bear,
  Wi' lwonesome thought untwold in words,
I woonce did work, wi' noo sound there
  But my own strokes, an' chirpèn birds;
As down the west the zun went wan,
An' days brought on our Zunday's rest,
When sounds o' cheemèn bells did vill
The aïr, an' hook an' axe wer still.

Along the wold town-path vo'k went,
  An' met unknown, or friend wi' friend,
The maïd her busy mother zent,
  The mother wi' noo maïd to zend;
An' in the light the gleäzier's glass,
As he did pass, wer dazzlèn bright,
Or woone went by wi' down-cast head,
A wrapp'd in blackness vor the dead.

An' then the bank, wi' risèn back,
   That's now a-most a-troddèn down,
Bore thorns wi' rind o' sheeny black,
   An' meäple stems o' ribby brown;
An' in the lewth o' theäse tree heads,
Wer primrwose beds a-sprung in blooth,
An' here a geäte, a-slammèn to,
Did let the slow-wheel'd plough roll drough.

Ov all that then went by, but vew
   Be now a-left behine', to beät
The mornèn flow'rs or evenèn dew,
   Or slam the woakèn vive-bar'd geäte;
But woone, my wife, so litty-stepp'd,
That have a-kept my path o' life,
Wi' her vew errands on the road,
Where woonce she bore her mother's lwoad.

IN THE SPRING.

My love is the maïd ov all maïdens,
   Though all mid be comely,
Her skin's lik' the jessamy blossom
   A-spread in the Spring.

Her smile is so sweet as a beäby's
   Young smile on his mother,
Her eyes be as bright as the dew drop
   A-shed in the Spring.

O grey-leafy pinks o' the geärden,
   Now bear her sweet blossoms;
Now deck wi' a rwose-bud, O briar,
   Her head in the Spring.

O light-rollèn wind blow me hither,
    The väice ov her talkèn,
Or bring vrom her veet the light doust,
    She do tread in the Spring.

O zun, meäke the gil'cups all glitter,
    In goold all around her;
An' meäke o' the deäisys' white flowers
    A bed in the Spring.

O whissle gäy birds, up bezide her,
    In drong-way, an' woodlands,
O zing, swingèn lark, now the clouds,
    Be a-vled in the Spring.

An' who, you mid ax, be my praïses
    A-meäkèn so much o',
An' oh! 'tis the maïd I'm a-hopèn
    To wed in the Spring.

THE FLOOD IN SPRING.

LAST night below the elem in the lew
    Bright the sky did gleam
On water blue, while aïr did softly blow
    On the flowèn stream,
An' there wer gil'cups' buds untwold,
An' deäisies that begun to vwold
Their low-stemm'd blossoms vrom my zight
Ageän the night, an' evenèn's cwold.

But, oh! so cwold below the darksome cloud
    Soon the night-wind roar'd,
Wi' raïny storms that zent the zwollèn streams
    Over ev'ry vword.

The while the drippèn tow'r did tell
The hour, wi' storm-be-smother'd bell,
An' over ev'ry flower's bud
Roll'd on the flood, 'ithin the dell.

But when the zun arose, an' lik' a rwose
    Shone the mornèn sky;
An' roun' the woak, the wind a-blowèn weak,
    Softly whiver'd by.
Though drown'd wer still the deäisy bed
Below the flood, its feäce instead
O' flow'ry grown', below our shoes
Show'd feäirest views o' skies o'er head.

An' zoo to try if all our faïth is true
    Jay mid end in tears,
An' hope, woonce feäir, mid saddèn into fear,
    Here in e'thly years.
But He that tried our soul do know
To meäke us good amends, an' show
Instead o' things a-took away,
Some higher jay that He'll bestow.

COMEN HWOME.

As clouds did ride wi' heästy flight.
An' woods did swäy upon the height,
An' bleädes o' grass did sheäke, below
The hedge-row bremble's swingèn bow,
I come back hwome where winds did zwell,
    In whirls along the woody gleädes,
    On primrwose beds, in windy sheädes,
To Burnley's dark-tree'd dell.

There hills do screen the timber's bough,
The trees do screen the leäze's brow,
The timber-sheäded leäze do bear
A beäten path that we do wear.
The path do stripe the leäze's zide,
   To willows at the river's edge.
   Where hufflèn winds did sheäke the zedge,
An' sparklèn weäves did glide.

An' where the river, bend by bend,
Do dräin our meäd, an' mark its end,
The hangèn leäze do teäke our cows,
An' trees do sheäde em wi' their boughs,
An' I the quicker beät the road,
   To zee a-comèn into view,
   Still greener vrom the sky-line's blue,
Wold Burnley our abode.

GRAMMER A-CRIPPLED.

"The zunny copse ha' birds to zing,
   The leäze ha' cows to low,
The elem trees ha' rooks on wing,
   The meäds a brook to flow,
But I can walk noo mwore, to pass
   The drashel out abrode,
To wear a path in theäse year's grass
   Or tread the wheelworn road,"
Cried Grammer, "then adieu,
   O runnèn brooks,
   An' vleèn rooks,
I can't come out to you.
If 'tis God's will, why then 'tis well,
That I should bide 'ithin a wall."

An' then the childern, wild wi' fun,
  An' loud wi' jaÿvul sounds,
Sprung in an' cried, "We had a run,
  A-playèn heäre an' hounds;
But oh! the cowslips where we stopt
  In Maÿcreech, on the knap!"
An' vrom their little han's each dropt
  Some cowslips in her lap.
Cried Grammer, "Only zee!
    I can't teäke strolls,
    An' little souls
Would bring the vields to me.
Since 'tis God's will, an' mus' be well
That I should bide 'ithin a wall."

"Oh! there be prison walls to hold
  The han's o' lawless crimes,
An' there be walls arear'd vor wold
  An' zick in tryèn times;
But oh! though low mid slant my ruf,
  Though hard my lot mid be,
Though dry mid come my daily lwoaf,
  Mid mercy leäve me free!"
Cried Grammer, "Or adieu
    To jaÿ; O grounds,
    An' bird's gaÿ sounds
If I mus' gi'e up you,
Although 'tis well, in God's good will,
That I should bide 'ithin a wall."

"Oh! then," we answer'd, "never fret,
  If we shall be a-blest,
We'll work vull hard drough het an' wet
  To keep your heart at rest:
To woaken chair's vor you to vill,
  For you shall glow the coal,

An' when the win' do whissle sh'ill
  We'll screen it vrom your poll."
Cried Grammer, " God is true.
    I can't but feel
    He smote to heal
My wounded heart in you ;
An' zoo 'tis well, if 'tis His will,
That I be here 'ithin a wall."

THE CASTLE RUINS.

A HAPPY day at Whitsuntide,
  As soon's the zun begun to vall,
We all stroll'd up the steep hill-zide
  To Meldon, girt an' small;
Out where the castle wall stood high
A-mwoldrèn to the zunny sky.

An' there wi' Jenny took a stroll
  Her youngest sister, Poll, so gay,
Bezide John Hind, ah ! merry soul,
  An' mid her wedlock fay ;
An' at our zides did play an' run
My little maïd an' smaller son.

Above the beäten mwold upsprung
  The driven doust, a-spreadèn light,
An' on the new-leav'd thorn, a-hung,
  Wer wool a-quiv'rèn white ;
An' corn, a sheenèn bright, did bow,
On slopèn Meldon's zunny brow.

There, down the rufless wall did glow
  The zun upon the grassy vloor,
An' weakly-wandrèn winds did blow,
  Unhinder'd by a door ;

An' smokeless now avore the zun
Did stan' the ivy-girded tun.

My bwoy did watch the daws' bright wings
   A-flappèn vrom their ivy bow'rs;
My wife did watch my maïd's light springs,
   Out here an' there vor flow'rs;
And John did zee noo tow'rs, the pleäce
Vor him had only Polly's feäce.

An' there, of all that pried about
   The walls, I overlook'd em best,
An' what o' that? Why, I meäde out
   Noo mwore than all the rest:
That there wer woonce the nest of zome
That wer a-gone avore we come.

When woonce above the tun the smoke
   Did wreathy blue among the trees,
An' down below, the livèn vo'k,
   Did tweil as brisk as bees;
Or zit wi' weary knees, the while
The sky wer lightless to their tweil.

Eclogue.

JOHN, JEALOUS AT SHROTON FEÄIR.

Jeäne; her Brother; John, her Sweetheart; and Rackettèn Joe

JEÄNE.

I'M thankvul I be out o' that
Thick crowd, an' not asquot quite flat.
That ever we should plunge in where the vo'k do drunge
So tight's the cheese-wring on the veät!

I've sca'ce a thing a-left in pleäce.
'Tis all a-tore vrom pin an' leäce.
My bonnet's like a wad, a-beät up to a dod,
An' all my heäir's about my feäce.

HER BROTHER.

Here, come an' zit out here a bit,
An' put yourzelf to rights.

JOHN.

No, Jeäne; no, no! Now you don't show
The very wo'st o' plights.

HER BROTHER.

Come, come, there's little harm adone;
Your hoops be out so roun's the zun.

JOHN.

An' there's your bonnet back in sheäpe.

HER BROTHER.

An' there's your pin, and there's your ceäpe.

JOHN.

An' there your curls do match, an' there
'S the vittiest maïd in all the feäir.

JEÄNE.

Now look, an' tell us who's a-spied
Vrom Sturminster, or Manston zide.

HER BROTHER.

There's rantèn Joe! How he do stalk,
An' zwang his whip, an' laugh, an' talk!

JOHN.

An' how his head do wag, avore his steppèn lag.
Jist like a pigeon's in a walk!

HER BROTHER.

Heigh! there, then, Joey, ben't we proud

JEÄNE.
He can't hear you among the crowd.

HER BROTHER.
Why, no, the thunder peals do drown the sound o' wheels.
His own pipe is a-pitched too loud.
What, you here too?

RACKETÈN JOE.
    Yes, Sir, to you.
All o' me that's a-left.

JEÄNE.
A body plump's a goodish lump
Where reämes ha' such a heft.

JOHN.
Who lost his crown a-racèn?

RACKETÈN JOE.
    Who?
Zome silly chap abackèn you.
Well, now, an' how do vo'k treat Jeäne?

JEÄNE.
Why not wi' feärèns.

RACKETÈN JOE.
    What d'ye meän,
When I've a-brought ye such a bunch
O' theäse nice ginger-nuts to crunch?
An' here, John, here! you teäke a vew.

JOHN.
No, keep em all vor Jeäne an' you!

RACKETÈN JOE.
Well, Jeäne, an' when d'ye meän to come
An' call on me, then, up at hwome.
You han't a-come athirt, since I'd my voot a-hurt,
A-slippèn vrom the tree I clomb.

JEÄNE.

Well, if so be that you be stout
On voot ageän, you'll vind me out.

JOHN.

Aye, better chaps woont goo, not many steps vor you,
If you do hawk yourzelf about.

RACKETÈN JOE.

Wull John, come too?

JOHN.

     No, thanks to you.
Two's company, dree's nwone.

HER BROTHER.

There don't be stung by his mad tongue,
'Tis nothèn else but fun.

JEANE.

There, what d'ye think o' my new ceäpe?

JOHN.

Why, think that 'tis an ugly sheäpe.

JEÄNE.

Then you should buy me, now theäse feäir,
A mwore becomèn woone to wear.

JOHN.

I buy your ceäpe! No; Joe wull screäpe
Up dibs enough to buy your ceäpe.
As things do look, to meäke you fine
Is long Joe's business mwore than mine.

JEÄNE.

Lauk, John, the mwore that you do pout
The mwore he'll glēne.

JOHN.

     A yelpèn lout.

EARLY PLAŸMEÄTE.

AFTER many long years had a-run,
   The while I wer a-gone vrom the pleäce,
I come back to the vields, where the zun
   Ov her childhood did show me her feäce.
There her father, years wolder, did stoop.
   An' her brother, wer now a-grow'd staïd,
An' the apple tree lower did droop.
   Out in the orcha'd where we had a-plaÿ'd,
There wer zome things a-seemèn the seäme,
   But Meäry's a-married awaÿ.

There wer two little childern a-zent,
   Wi' a message to me, oh! so feaïr
As the mother that they did zoo ment,
   When in childhood she plaÿ'd wi' me there.
Zoo they twold me that if I would come
   Down to Coomb, I should zee a wold friend,
Vor a plaÿmeäte o' mine wer at hwome,
   An' would staÿ till another week's end.
At the dear pworchèd door, could I dare
   To zee Meäry a-married awaÿ!

On the flower-not, now all a-trod
   Stwony hard, the green grass wer a-spread,
An' the long-slighted woodbine did nod
   Vrom the wall, wi' a loose-hangèn head.
An' the martin's clay nest wer a-hung
   Up below the brown oves, in the dry,
An' the rooks had a-rock'd broods o' young
   On the elems below the Maÿ sky;
But the bud on the bed, coulden bide,
   Wi' young Meäry a-married awaÿ.

There the copse-wood, a-grow'd to a height,
    Wer a-vell'd, an' the primrwose in blooth,
Among chips on the ground a-turn'd white,
    Wer a-quiv'rèn, all beäre ov his lewth.
The green moss wer a-spread on the thatch,
    That I left yollow reed, an' avore
The small green, there did swing a new hatch,
    Vor to let me walk into the door.
Oh! the rook did still rock o'er the rick,
    But wi' Meäry a-married away.

PICKEN O' SCROFF.

Oh! the wood wer a-vell'd in the copse,
    An' the moss-bedded primrwose did blow;
An' vrom tall-stemmèd trees' leafless tops,
    There did lie but slight sheädes down below.
An' the sky wer a-showèn, in drough
By the tree-stems, the deepest o' blue,
Wi' a light that did vall on an' off
The dry ground, a-strew'd over wi' scroff.

There the hedge that wer leätely so high,
    Wer a-plush'd, an' along by the zide,
Where the waggon 'd a-haul'd the wood by,
    There did reach the deep wheelrouts, a-dried.
An' the groun' wi' the sticks wer bespread,
Zome a-cut off alive, an' zome dead.
An' vor burnèn, well wo'th reäkèn off,
By the childern a-pickèn o' scroff.

In the tree-studded leäze, where the woak
    Wer a-spreadèn his head out around,
There the scrags that the wind had a-broke,
    Wer a-lyèn about on the ground

Or the childern, wi' little red hands,
Wer a-tyèn em up in their bands;
Vor noo squier or farmer turn'd off
Little childern a-pickèn o' scroff.

There wer woone bloomèn child wi' a cloak
  On her shoulders, as green as the ground;
An' another, as gray as the woak,
  Wi' a bwoy in a brown frock, a-brown'd.
An' woone got up, in play, vor to taït,
On a woak-limb, a-growèn out straïght.
But she soon wer a-taited down off,
By her meätes out a-pickèn o' scroff.

When they childern do grow to staïd vo'k,
  An' goo out in the worold, all wide
Vrom the copse, an' the zummerleäze woak,
  Where at last all their elders ha' died,
They wull then vind it touchèn to bring,
To their minds, the sweet springs o' their spring,
Back avore the new vo'k did turn off
The poor childern a-pickèn o' scroff.

GOOD NIGHT.

WHILE down the meäds wound slow,
  Water vor green-wheel'd mills,
Over the streams bright bow,
  Win' come vrom dark-back'd hills.
Birds on the win' shot along down steep
Slopes, wi' a swift-swung zweep.
Dim weän'd the red streak'd west.
Lim'-weary souls "Good-rest."

Up on the plough'd hill brow,
   Still wer the zull's wheel'd beam,
Still wer the red-wheel'd plough,
   Free o' the strong limb'd team,
Still wer the shop that the smith meäde ring,
Dark where the sparks did spring;
Low shot the zun's last beams.
Lim'-weary souls " Good dreams."

Where I vrom dark bank-sheädes
   Turn'd up the west hill road,
Where all the green grass bleädes
   Under the zunlight glow'd.
Startled I met, as the zunbeams play'd
Light, wi' a zunsmote maïd,
Come vor my day's last zight.
Zun-brighten'd maïd " Good night."

WENT HWOME.

Upon the slope, the hedge did bound
The vield wi' blossom-whited zide,
An' charlock patches, yollow-dyed,
Did reach along the white-soil'd ground;
An' vo'k, a-comèn up vrom meäd,
   Brought gil'cup meal upon the shoe;
Or went on where the road did leäd,
   Wi' smeechy doust from heel to tooe.
As noon did smite, wi' burnèn light,
The road so white, to Meldonley.

An' I did tramp the zun-dried ground,
By hedge-climb'd hills, a-spread wi' flow'rs,
An' watershootèn dells, an' tow'rs,
By elem-trees a-hemm'd all round,

To zee a vew wold friends, about
   Wold Meldon, where I still ha' zome,
That bid me speed as I come out,
   An' now ha' bid me welcome hwome,
As I did goo, while skies wer blue,
Vrom view to view, to Meldonley.

An' there wer timber'd knaps, that show'd
Cool sheädes, vor rest, on grassy ground,
An' thatch-brow'd windows, flower-bound,
Where I could wish wer my abode.
I pass'd the maïd avore the spring,
   An' shepherd by the thornèn tree;
An' heärd the merry dréver zing,
   But met noo kith or kin to me,
Till I come down, vrom Meldon's crown
To rufs o' brown, at Meldonley.

THE HOLLOW WOAK.

The woaken tree, so hollow now,
   To souls ov other times wer sound,
An' reach'd on ev'ry zide a bough
   Above their heads, a-gather'd round,
      But zome light veet
      That here did meet
In friendship sweet, vor rest or jaÿ,
Shall be a-miss'd another Maÿ.

My childern here, in plaÿvul pride
   Did zit 'ithin his wooden walls,
A-mentèn steätely vo'k inside
   O' castle towers an' lofty halls.
      But now the vloor
      An' mossy door

That woonce they wore would be too small
To teäke em in, so big an' tall.

Theäse year do show, wi' snow-white cloud,
   An' deäsies in a sprinkled bed,
An' green-bough birds a-whislèn loud,
   The looks o' zummer days a-vled ;
      An' grass do grow,
      An' men do mow,
An' all do show the wold times' feäce
Wi' new things in the wold things' pleäce.

CHILDERN'S CHILDERN.

OH ! if my ling'rèn life should run,
   Drough years a-reckoned ten by ten,
Below the never-tirèn zun,
   Till beäbes ageän be wives an' men ;
An' stillest deafness should ha' bound
My ears, at last, vrom ev'ry sound ;
Though still my eyes in that sweet light,
Should have the zight o' sky an' ground :
      Would then my steäte
      In time so leäte,
Be jay or païn, be païn or jay?

When Zunday then, a-weänèn dim,
   As theäse that now's a-clwosèn still,
Mid lose the zun's down-zinkèn rim,
   In light behind the vier-bound hill ;
An' when the bells' last peal's a-rung,
An' I mid zee the wold an' young
A-vlockèn by, but shoulden hear,
However near, a voot or tongue :

   Mid zuch a zight,
   In that soft light
Be jay or païn, be païn or jay.

If I should zee among em all,
 In merry youth, a-glidèn by,
My son's bwold son, a-grown man-tall,
 Or daughter's daughter, woman-high;
An' she mid smile wi' your good feäce,
Or she mid walk your comely peäce,
But seem, although a-chattèn loud,
So dumb's a cloud, in that bright pleäce:
   Would youth so feäir,
   A-passèn there,
Be jay or païn, be päin or jay.

'Tis seldom strangth or comeliness
 Do leäve us long. The house do show
Men's sons wi' mwore, as they ha' less,
 An' daughters brisk, vor mothers slow.
A dawn do clear the night's dim sky,
Woone star do zink, an' woone goo high,
An' livèn gifts o' youth do vall,
Vrom girt to small, but never die:
   An' should I view,
   What God mid do,
Wi' jay or païn, wi' païn or jay?

THE RWOSE IN THE DARK.

IN zummer, leäte at evenèn tide,
 I zot to spend a moonless hour
'Ithin the window, wi' the zide
 A-bound wi' rwoses out in flow'r,
Bezide the bow'r, vorsook o' birds,
An' listen'd to my true-love's words.

A-risèn to her comely height,
   She push'd the swingèn ceäsement round;
And I could hear, beyond my zight,
   The win'-blow'd beech-tree softly sound,
On higher ground, a-swayèn slow,
On drough my happy hour below.

An' tho' the darkness then did hide
   The dewy rwose's blushèn bloom,
He still did cast sweet aïr inside
   To Jeäne, a-chattèn in the room;
An' though the gloom did hide her feäce,
Her words did bind me to the pleäce.

An' there, while she, wi' runnèn tongue,
   Did talk unzeen 'ithin the hall,
I thought her like the rwose that flung
   His sweetness vrom his darken'd ball,
'Ithout the wall, an' sweet's the zight
Ov her bright feäce by mornèn light.

COME.

Wull ye come in eärly Spring,
Come at Easter, or in May?
Or when Whitsuntide mid bring
Longer light to show your way?
Wull ye come, if you be true,
Vor to quicken love anew.
Wull ye call in Spring or Fall?
Come now soon by zun or moon?
      Wull ye come?

Come wi' vaïce to vaïce the while
All their words be sweet to hear;
Come that feäce to feäce mid smile,
While their smiles do seem so dear;

Come within the year to seek
Woone you have sought woonce a week?
Come while flow'rs be on the bow'rs,
And the bird o' zong's a-heärd.
      Wùll ye come?

Ees come *to* ye, an' come *vor* ye, is my word,
      I wull come.

ZUMMER WINDS.

Let me work, but mid noo tie
Hold me vrom the oben sky,
When zummer winds, in playsome flight,
Do blow on vields in noon-day light,
Or ruslèn trees, in twilight night.
      Sweet's a stroll,
By flow'ry knowl, or blue-feäced pool
That zummer win's do ruffle cool.

When the moon's broad light do vill
Plaïns, a-sheenèn down the hill;
A-glitterèn on window glass,
O then, while zummer win's do pass
The rippled brook, an' swayèn grass,
      Sweet's a walk,
Where we do talk, wi' feäces bright,
In whispers in the peacevul night.

When the swayèn men do mow
Flow'ry grass, wi' zweepèn blow,
In het a-most enough to dry
The flat-spread clote-leaf that do lie
Upon the stream a-stealèn by,
      Sweet's their rest,
Upon the breast o' knap or mound
Out where the goocoo's vaïce do sound.

Where the sleek-heäir'd maïd do zit
Out o' door to zew or knit,
Below the elem where the spring
'S a-runnèn, an' the road do bring
The people by to hear her zing,
    On the green,
Where she's a-zeen, an' she can zee,
O gay is she below the tree.

Come, O zummer wind, an' bring
Sounds o' birds as they do zing,
An' bring the smell o' bloomèn may,
An' bring the smell o' new-mow'd hay;
Come fan my feäce as I do stray,
    Fan the heäir
O' Jessie feäir; fan her cool,
By the weäves o' stream or pool.

THE NEÄME LETTERS.

WHEN high-flown larks wer on the wing,
A warm-aïr'd holiday in Spring,
We stroll'd, 'ithout a ceäre or frown,
   Up roun' the down at Meldonley;
An' where the hawthorn-tree did stand
Alwone, but still wi' mwore at hand,
We zot wi' sheädes o' clouds on high
   A-flittèn by, at Meldonley.

An' there, the while the tree did sheäde
Their gigglèn heads, my knife's keen bleäde
Carved out, in turf avore my knee,
   J. L., *T. D., at Meldonley.

THE NEÄME LETTERS.

'Twer Jessie Lee J. L. did meän,
T. D. did stan' vor Thomas Deäne;
The "L" I scratch'd but slight, vor he
　　Mid soon be D, at Meldonley.

An' when the vields o' wheat did spread
Vrom hedge to hedge in sheets o' red.
An' bennets wer a-sheäkèn brown,
　　Upon the down at Meldonley,
We stroll'd ageän along the hill,
An' at the hawthorn-tree stood still,
To zee J. L. vor Jessie Lee,
　　An' my T. D., at Meldonley.

The grey-poll'd bennet-stems did hem
Each half-hid letter's zunken rim,
By leädy's-vingers that did spread
　　In yollow red, at Meldonley.
An' heärebells there wi' light blue bell
Shook soundless on the letter L,
To ment the bells when L vor Lee
　　Become a D at Meldonley.

Vor Jessie, now my wife, do strive
Wi' me in life, an' we do thrive;
Two sleek-heäired meäres do sprackly pull
　　My waggon vull, at Meldonley;
An' small-hoof'd sheep, in vleeces white,
Wi' quickly-pankèn zides, do bite
My thymy grass, a-mark'd vor me
　　In black, **T.D.**, at Meldonley.

THE NEW HOUSE A-GETTÈN WOLD.

AH! when our wedded life begun,
   Theäse clean-wall'd house of ours wer new;
Wi' thatch as yollor as the zun
   Avore the cloudless sky o' blue;
The sky o' blue that then did bound
The blue-hilled worold's flow'ry ground.

An' we've a-vound it weather-brown'd,
   As Spring-tide blossoms oben'd white,
Or Fall did shed, on zunburnt ground,
   Red apples from their leafy height:
Their leafy height, that Winter soon
Left leafless to the cool-feäced moon.

An' raïn-bred moss ha' staïn'd wi' green
   The smooth-feäced wall's white-morter'd streaks,
The while our childern zot between
   Our seats avore the fleäme's red peaks:
The fleäme's red peaks, till axan white
Did quench em vor the long-sleep'd night.

The bloom that woonce did overspread
   Your rounded cheäk, as time went by,
A-shrinkèn to a patch o' red,
   Did feäde so soft's the evenèn sky:
The evenèn sky, my faithful wife,
O' days as feäir's our happy life.

ZUNDAY.

IN zummer, when the sheädes do creep
   Below the Zunday steeple, round
The mossy stwones, that love cut deep
   Wi' neämes that tongues noo mwore do sound,

The leäne do lose the stalkèn team,
   An' dry-rimm'd waggon-wheels be still,
An' hills do roll their down-shot stream
   Below the restèn wheel at mill.
O holy day, when tweil do ceäse,
Sweet day o' rest an' greäce an' peäce!

The eegrass, vor a while unwrung
   By hoof or shoe, 's a sheenèn bright,
An' clover flowers be a-sprung
   On new-mow'd knaps in beds o' white,
An' sweet wild rwoses, up among
   The hedge-row boughs, do yield their smells,
To aïer that do bear along
   The loud-rung peals o' Zunday bells,
Upon the day o' days the best,
The day o' greäce an' peäce an' rest.

By brightshod veet, in peäir an' peäir,
   Wi' comely steps the road's a-took
To church, an' work-free han's do beär
   Woone's walkèn stick or sister's book;
An' there the bloomèn niece do come
   To zee her aunt, in all her best;
Or married daughter do bring hwome
   Her vu'st sweet child upon her breast,
As she do seek the holy pleäce,
The day o' rest an' peäce an' greäce.

THE PILLAR'D GEÄTE.

As I come by, zome years agoo,
   A-burnt below a sky o' blue,
'Ithin the pillar'd geäte there zung
   A vaïce a-soundèn sweet an' young,

'That meäde me veel awhile to zwim
In weäves o' jay to hear its hymn;
Vor all the zinger, angel-bright,
Wer then a-hidden vrom my zight,
    An' I wer then too low
To seek a meäte to match my steäte
'Ithin the lofty-pillar'd geäte,
Wi' stwonèn balls upon the walls:
    Oh, no! my heart, no, no.

Another time as I come by
The house, below a dark-blue sky.
The pillar'd geäte wer oben wide,
An' who should be a-show'd inside,
But she, the comely maïd whose hymn
Woonce meäde my giddy braïn to zwim,
A-zittèn in the sheäde to zew,
A-clad in robes as white as snow.
    What then? could I so low
Look out a meäte ov higher steäte
So gay 'ithin a pillar'd geäte,
Wi' high walls round the smooth-mow'd ground?
    Oh, no! my heart, no, no.

Long years stole by, a-glidèn slow,
Wi' winter cwold an' zummer glow,
An' she wer then a widow, clad
In grey; but comely, though so sad;
Her husband, heartless to his bride,
Spent all her store an' wealth, an' died,
Though she noo mwore could now rejaïce,
Yet sweet did sound her zongless vaïce.
    But had she, in her woe,
The higher steäte she had o' leäte
'Ithin the lofty pillar'd geäte,
Wi' stwonèn balls upon the walls?
    Oh, no! my heart, no, no.

But while she vell, my Meäker's greäce
Led me to teäke a higher pleäce,
An' lighten'd up my mind wi' lore,
An' bless'd me wi' a worldly store;
But still noo winsome feäce or vaïce,
Had ever been my wedded chaïce;
An' then I thought, why do I mwope
Alwone without a jaÿ or hope?
    Would she still think me low?
Or scorn a meäte, in my feäir steäte,
In here 'ithin a pillar'd geäte,
A happy pleäce wi' her kind feäce?
    Oh, no! my hope, no, no.

I don't stand out 'tis only feäte
Do gi'e to each his wedded meäte;
But eet there's woone above the rest,
That every soul can like the best.
An' my wold love's a-kindled new,
An' my wold dream's a-come out true;
But while I had noo soul to sheäre
My good an' ill, an' jäy an ceäre,
    Should I have bliss below,
In gleämèn pleäte an' lofty steäte
'Ithin the lofty pillar'd geäte,
Wi' feäirest flow'rs, an' ponds an' tow'rs?
    Oh, no! my heart, no, no.

ZUMMER STREAM.

AH! then the grassy-meäded Maÿ
Did warm the passèn year, an' gleam
Upon the yellow-grounded stream,
That still by beech-tree sheädes do straÿ.

The light o' weäves, a-runnèn there,
   Did play on leaves up over head,
An' vishes sceäly zides did gleäre,
   A-dartèn on the shallow bed,
An' like the stream a-slidèn on,
My zun out-measur'd time's agone.

There by the path, in grass knee-high,
Wer buttervlees in giddy flight,
All white above the deäisies white,
Or blue below the deep blue sky.
Then glowèn warm wer ev'ry brow,
O' maïd, or man, in zummer het,
An' warm did glow the cheäks I met
That time, noo mwore to meet em now.
As brooks, a-slidèn on their bed,
My season-measur'd time's a-vled.

Vrom yonder window, in the thatch,
Did sound the maïdens' merry words,
As I did stand, by zingèn birds,
Bezide the elem-sheäded hatch.
'Tis good to come back to the pleäce,
   Back to the time, to goo noo mwore;
'Tis good to meet the younger feäce
   A-mentèn others here avore.
As streams do glide by green mead-grass,
My zummer-brighten'd years do pass.

LINDA DEÄNE.

THE bright-tunn'd house, a-risèn proud,
Stood high avore a zummer cloud,
An' windy sheädes o' tow'rs did vall
Upon the many-window'd wall;

An' on the grassy terrace, bright
Wi' white-bloom'd zummer's deaïsy beds,
An' snow-white lilies noddèn heads,
Sweet Linda Deäne did walk in white;
But ah! avore too high a door,
Wer Linda Deäne ov Ellendon.

When sparklèn brooks an' grassy ground,
By keen-aïr'd Winter's vrost wer bound,
An' star-bright snow did streak the forms
O' beäre-lim'd trees in darksome storms,
Sweet Linda Deäne did lightly glide,
Wi' snow-white robe an' rwosy feäce,
Upon the smooth-vloor'd hall, to treäce
The merry dance o' Chris'mas tide;
But oh! not mine be balls so fine
As Linda Deäne's at Ellendon.

Sweet Linda Deäne do match the skies
Wi' sheenèn blue o' glisnèn eyes,
An' feaïrest blossoms do but show
Her forehead's white, an' feäce's glow;
But there's a winsome jay above,
The brightest hues ov e'th an' skies.
The dearest zight o' many eyes,
Would be the smile o' Linda's love;
But high above my lowly love
Is Linda Deäne ov Ellendon.

Eclogue.

COME AND ZEE US IN THE ZUMMER.

John; William; William's Bwoy; and William's Maïd at Feäir.

JOHN.
Zoo here be your childern, a-sheären
Your feäir-day, an' each wi' a feäirèn.

WILLIAM.
Aye, well, there's noo peace 'ithout comèn
To stannèn an' show, in the zummer.

JOHN.
An' how is your Jeäne? still as merry
As ever, wi' cheäks lik' a cherry?

WILLIAM.
Still merry, but beauty's as feädesome
'S the raïn's glowèn bow in the zummer.

JOHN.
Well now, I do hope we shall vind ye
Come soon, wi' your childern behind ye,
To Stowe, while o' bwoth zides o' hedges,
The zunsheen do glow in the zummer.

WILLIAM.
Well, aye, when the mowèn is over,
An' ee-grass do whiten wi' clover.
A man's a-tired out, vor much walken,
The while he do mow in the zummer.

WILLIAM'S BWOY.

I'll goo, an' we'll zet up a wicket,
An' have a good innèns at cricket;
An' teäke a good plounce in the water,
Where clote-leaves do grow in the zummer.

WILLIAM'S MAID.

I'll goo, an' we'll play "Thread the needle"
Or "Huntèn the slipper," or wheedle
Young Jemmy to fiddle, an' reely
So brisk to an' fro in the zummer.

JOHN.

An' Jeäne. Mind you don't come 'ithout her,
My wife is a-thinkèn about her;
At our house she'll find she's as welcome
'S the rwose that do blow in the zummer.

LINDENORE.

At Lindenore upon the steep,
    Bezide the trees a-reachèn high,
The while their lower limbs do zweep
    The river-stream a-flowèn by;
By grægle bells in beds o' blue,
Below the tree-stems in the lew,
Calm aïr do vind the rwose-bound door,
Ov Ellen Dare o' Lindenore.

An' there noo foam do hiss avore
    Swift bwoats, wi' water-plowèn keels,
An' there noo broad high-road's a-wore
    By vur-brought trav'lers' cracklèn wheels;

Noo crowd's a-passèn to and fro,
Upon the bridge's high-sprung bow:
An' vew but I do seek the door
Ov Ellen Dare o' Lindenore.

Vor there the town, wi' zun-bright walls,
  Do sheen vur off, by hills o' grey,
An' town-vo'k ha' but seldom calls
  O' business there, from day to day:
But Ellen didden leäve her ruf
To be admir'd, an' that's enough—
Vor I've a-vound 'ithin her door,
Feäir Ellen Dare o' Lindenore.

ME'TH BELOW THE TREE.

O when theäse elems' crooked boughs,
A'most too thin to sheäde the cows,
Did slowly swing above the grass
As winds o' Spring did softly pass,
An' zunlight show'd the shiftèn sheäde,
While youthful me'th wi' laughter loud,
Did twist his lim's among the crowd
Down there below; up there above
Wer bright-ey'd me'th below the tree.

Down there the merry vo'k did vill
The stwonèn doorway, now so still;
An' zome did joke, wi' ceäsement wide,
Wi' other vo'k a-stood outside,
Wi' words that head by head did heed.
Below blue sky an' blue-smok'd tun,
'Twer jay to zee an' hear their fun,
But sweeter jay up here above
Wi' bright-ey'd me'th below the tree.

Now unknown veet do beät the vloor,
An' unknown han's do shut the door,
An' unknown men do ride abrode,
An' hwome ageän on thik wold road,
Drough geätes all now a-hung anew.
Noo mind but mine ageän can call
Wold feäces back around the wall,
Down there below, or here above,
Wi' bright-ey'd me'th below the tree.

Aye, pride mid seek the crowded pleäce
To show his head an' frownèn feäce,
An' pleasure vlee, wi' goold in hand,
Vor zights to zee vrom land to land,
Where winds do blow on seas o' blue :—
Noo wealth wer mine to travel wide
Vor jaÿ, wi' Pleasure or wi' Pride :
My happiness wer here above
The feäst, wi' me'th below the tree.

The wild rwose now do hang in zight,
To mornèn zun an' evenèn light,
The bird do whissle in the gloom,
Avore the thissle out in bloom,
But here alwone the tree do leän.
The twig that woonce did whiver there
Is now a limb a-wither'd beäre:
Zoo I do miss the sheäde above
My head, an' me'th below the tree.

TREAT WELL YOUR WIFE.

No, no, good Meäster Collins cried,
Why you've a good wife at your zide ;
Zoo do believe the heart is true
That gi'ed up all bezide vor you,

An' still beheäve as you begun
To seek the love that you've a-won
    When woonce in dewy June,
In hours o' hope soft eyes did flash,
Each bright below his sheädy lash,
    A-glisnèn to the moon.

Think how her girlhood met noo ceäre
To peäle the bloom her feäce did weär,
An' how her glossy temple prest
Her pillow down, in still-feäced rest,
While sheädes o' window bars did vall
In moonlight on the gloomy wall,
    In cool-aïr'd nights o' June ;
The while her lids, wi' bendèn streäks
O' lashes, met above her cheäks,
    A-bloomèn to the moon.

Think how she left her childhood's pleäce,.
An' only sister's long-known feäce,
An' brother's jokes so much a-miss'd,
An' mother's cheäk, the last a-kiss'd;
An' how she lighted down avore
Her new abode, a husband's door,
    Your weddèn night in June ;
Wi' heart that beät wi' hope an' fear,
While on each eye-lash hung a tear,
    A-glisnèn to the moon.

Think how her father zot all dum',
A-thinkèn on her, back at hwome,
The while grey axan gather'd thick,
On dyèn embers, on the brick ;
An' how her mother look'd abrode,
Drough window, down the moon-bright road,

Thik cloudless night o' June,
Wi' tears upon her lashes big
As raïn-drops on a slender twig,
    A-glisnèn to the moon.

Zoo don't zit thoughtless at your cup
An' keep your wife a-wäitèn up,
The while the clock's a-tickèn slow
The chilly hours o' vrost an' snow,
Until the zinkèn candle's light
Is out avore her drowsy sight,
    A-dimm'd wi' grief too soon;
A-leävèn there alwone to murn
The feädèn cheäk that woonce did burn,
    A-bloomèn to the moon.

THE CHILD AN' THE MOWERS.

O, AYE! they had woone child bezide,
    An' a finer your eyes never met,
'Twer a dear little fellow that died
    In the zummer that come wi' such het;
By the mowers, too thoughtless in fun,
    He wer then a-zent off vrom our eyes,
Vrom the light ov the dew-dryèn zun,—
    Aye! vrom days under blue-hollow'd skies.

He went out to the mowers in meäd,
    When the zun wer a-rose to his height,
An' the men wer a-swingèn the sneäd,
    Wi' their eärms in white sleeves, left an' right;
An' out there, as they rested at noon,
    O! they drench'd en vrom eäle-horns too deep,
Till his thoughts wer a-drown'd in a swoon;
    Aye! his life wer a-smother'd in sleep.

Then they laid en there-right on the ground,
    On a grass-heap, a-zweltrèn wi' het,
Wi' his heäir all a-wetted around
    His young feäce, wi' the big drops o' zweat;
In his little left palm he'd a-zet,
    Wi' his right hand, his vore-vinger's tip,
As for zome'hat he wouden vorget,—
    Aye! zome thought that he wouden let slip.

Then they took en in hwome to his bed,
    An' he rose vrom his pillow noo mwore,
Vor the curls on his sleek little head
    To be blown by the wind out o' door.
Vor he died while the häy russled grey
    On the staddle so leätely begun:
Lik' the mown-grass a-dried by the day,—
    Aye! the zwath-flow'r's a-killed by the zun.

THE LOVE CHILD.

WHERE the bridge out at Woodley did stride,
    Wi' his wide arches' cool sheäded bow,
Up above the clear brook that did slide
    By the popples, befoam'd white as snow:
As the gilcups did quiver among
    The white deäisies, a-spread in a sheet.
There a quick-trippèn maïd come along,—
    Aye, a girl wi' her light-steppèn veet.

An' she cried "I do pray, is the road
    Out to Lincham on here, by the meäd?"
An' "oh! ees," I meäde answer, an' show'd
    Her the way it would turn an' would leäd:
"Goo along by the beech in the nook,
    Where the childern do play in the cool,
To the steppèn stwones over the brook,—
    Aye, the grey blocks o' rock at the pool."

"Then you don't seem a-born an' a-bred,"
    I spoke up, "at a place here about;"
An' she answer'd wi' cheäks up so red
    As a pi'ny but leäte a-come out,
"No, I liv'd wi' my uncle that died
    Back in Eäpril, an' now I'm a-come
Here to Ham, to my mother, to bide,—
    Aye, to her house to vind a new hwome."

I'm asheämed that I wanted to know
    Any mwore of her childhood or life,
But then, why should so feäir a child grow
    Where noo father did bide wi' his wife;
Then wi' blushes of zunrisèn morn,
    She replied "that it midden be known,
"Oh! they zent me away to be born,—*
    Aye, they hid me when zome would be shown."

Oh! it meäde me a'most teary-ey'd,
    An' I vound I a'most could ha' groan'd—
What! so winnèn, an' still cast a-zide—
    What! so lovely, an' not to be own'd;
Oh! a God-gift a-treated wi' scorn,
    Oh! a child that a squier should own;
An' to zend her away to be born!—
    Aye, to hide her where others be shown!

HAWTHORN DOWN.

ALL up the down's cool brow
    I work'd in noontide's gleäre,
On where the slow-wheel'd plow
    'D a-wore the grass half bare.

---

* Words once spoken to the writer.

An' gil'cups quiver'd quick,
   As aïr did pass,
An' deäisies huddled thick
   Among the grass.

The while my eärms did swing
   Wi' work I had on hand,
The quick-wing'd lark did zing
   Above the green-tree'd land,
An' bwoys below me chafed
   The dog vor fun,
An' he, vor all they laef'd,
   Did meäke em run.

The south zide o' the hill,
   My own tun-smoke rose blue,—
In North Coomb, near the mill,
   My mother's wer in view—
Where woonce her vier vor all
   Ov us did burn,
As I have childern small
   Round mine in turn.

An' zoo I still wull cheer
   Her life wi' my small store,
As she do drop a tear
   Bezide her lwonesome door.
The love that I do owe
   Her ruf, I'll pay,
An' then zit down below
   My own wi' jay.

OBEN VIELDS.

Well, you mid keep the town an' street,
Wi' grassless stwones to beät your veet,
An' zunless windows where your brows
Be never cooled by swayèn boughs;
An' let me end, as I begun,
My days in oben aïr an' zun,
Where zummer win's a-blowèn sweet,
Wi' blooth o' trees as white's a sheet;
Or swayèn boughs, a-bendèn low
Wi' rip'nèn apples in a row,
An' we a-risèn rathe do meet
The bright'nèn dawn wi' dewy veet,
An' leäve, at night, the vootless groves,
To rest 'ithin our thatchen oves.
An' here our childern still do bruise
The deäisy buds wi' tiny shoes,
As we did meet avore em, free
Vrom ceäre, in play below the tree.
An' there in me'th their lively eyes
Do glissen to the zunny skies,
As aïr do blow, wi' leäzy peäce
To cool, in sheäde, their burnèn feäce.
Where leaves o' spreadèn docks do hide
The zawpit's timber-lwoaded zide,
An' trees do lie, wi' scraggy limbs,
Among the deäisy's crimson rims.
An' they, so proud, wi' eärms a-spread
To keep their balance good, do tread
Wi' ceäreful steps o' tiny zoles
The narrow zides o' trees an' poles.
An' zoo I'll leäve vor your light veet
The peävement o' the zunless street,
While I do end, as I begun,
My days in oben aïr an' zun.

WHAT JOHN WER A-TELLÈN HIS MIS'ESS OUT IN THE CORN GROUND.

Ah! mam! you woonce come here the while
   The zun, long years agoo, did shed
His het upon the wheat in hile,
   Wi' yollow hau'm an' ears o' red,
Wi' little shoes too thin vor walks
   Upon the scratchèn stubble-stalks;
You hardly reach'd wi' glossy head,
   The vore wheel's top o' dousty red.
How time's a-vled! How years do vlee!

An' there you went an' zot inzide
   A hile, in aïr a-streamèn cool,
As if 'ithin a room, vull wide
   An' high, you zot to guide an' rule.
You leäz'd about the stubbly land,
   An' soon vill'd up your small left hand
Wi' ruddy ears your right hand vound,
   An' trail'd the stalks along the ground.
How time's a-gone! How years do goo!

Then in the waggon you did teäke
   A ride, an' as the wheels vell down
Vrom ridge to vurrow, they did sheäke
   On your small head your poppy crown,
An' now your little maïd, a dear,
   Your childhood's very daps, is here,
Zoo let her stay, that her young feäce
   Mid put a former year in pleäce.
How time do run! How years do roll

SHEÄDES.

Come here an' zit a while below
   Theäse tower, grey and ivy-bound,
In sheäde, the while the zun do glow
   So hot upon the flow'ry ground;
     An' winds in flight,
     Do briskly smite
The blossoms bright, upon the gleäde,
But never stir the sleepèn sheäde.

As when you stood upon the brink
   O' yonder brook, wi' back-zunn'd head,
Your zunny-grounded sheäde did zink
   Upon the water's grav'lly bed,
     Where weäves could zweep
     Away, or keep,
The gravel heap that they'd a-meäde,
But never wash away the sheäde.

An' zoo, when you can woonce vulvil
   What's feäir, a-tried by heaven's light,
Why never fear that evil will
   Can meäke a wrong o' your good right.
     The right wull stand,
     Vor all man's hand,
Till streams on zand, an' wind in gleädes,
Can zweep away the zuncast sheädes.

TIMES O' YEAR.

Here did swäy the eltrot flow'rs,
   When the hours o' night wer vew,
An' the zun, wi' eärly beams

Brighten'd streams, an' dried the dew,
An' the goocoo there did greet
Passers by wi' dousty veet.

There the milkmaïd hung her brow
By the cow, a-sheenèn red;
An' the dog, wi' upward looks,
Watch'd the rooks above his head,
An' the brook, vrom bow to bow,
Here went swift, an' there wer slow.

Now the cwolder-blowèn blast,
Here do cast vrom elems' heads
Feäded leaves, a-whirlèn round,
Down to ground, in yollow beds,
Ruslèn under milkers' shoes,
When the day do dry the dews.

Soon shall grass, a-vrosted bright,
Glisten white instead o' green,
An' the wind shall smite the cows,
Where the boughs be now their screen.
Things do change as years do vlee;
What ha' years in store vor me?

Eclogue.

RACKETÈN JOE.

Racketèn Joe; his Sister; his Cousin Fanny; and the Dog.

RACKETÈN JOE.

HEIGH! heigh! here. Who's about?

HIS SISTER.

Oh! lauk! Here's Joe, a rantèn lout,
A-meäkèn his wild randy-rout.

RACKETÈN JOE.

Heigh! Fanny! How d'ye do? (*slaps her.*)

FANNY.

Oh! fie; why all the woo'se vor you
A-slappèn o' me, black an' blue,
My back!

HIS SISTER.

A whack! you loose-eärm'd chap,
To gi'e your cousin sich a slap!

FANNY.

I'll pull the heäir o'n, I do vow;

HIS SISTER.

I'll pull the ears o'n. There.

THE DOG.

Wowh! wow!

FANNY.

A-comèn up the drong,
How he did smack his leather thong,
A-zingèn, as he thought, a zong;

HIS SISTER.

An' there the pigs did scote
Azide, in fright, wi' squeakèn droat,
Wi' geese a pitchèn up a note.
Look there.

FANNY.

His chair!

HIS SISTER.
      He thump'd en down,
As if he'd het en into ground.
RACKETÈN JOE.
Heigh! heigh! Look here! the vier is out.
HIS SISTER.
How he do knock the tongs about!
FANNY.
Now theäre's his whip-nob, plum
Upon the teäble vor a drum;
HIS SISTER.
An' there's a dent so big's your thumb.
RACKETÈN JOE.
My hat's awore so quaer.
HIS SISTER.
'Tis quaer enough, but not wi' wear;
But dabs an' dashes he do bear.
RACKETÈN JOE.
The zow!
HIS SISTER.
  What now?
RACKETÈN JOE.
      She's in the plot.
A-routèn up the flower knot.
Ho! Towzer! Here, rout out the zow,
Heigh! here, hie at her. Tiss!
THE DOG.
      Wowh! wow!
HIS SISTER.
How he do rant and roar,
An' stump an' stamp about the vloor,
An' swing, an' slap, an' slam the door!

He don't put down a thing,
But he do dab, an' dash, an' ding
It down, till all the house do ring.
RACKETÈN JOE.
She's out.
FANNY.
Noo doubt.
HIS SISTER.
Athirt the bank,
Look! how the dog an' he do pank.
FANNY.
Staÿ out, an' heed her now an' then,
To zee she don't come in ageän.

ZUMMER AN' WINTER.

WHEN I led by zummer streams
　The pride o' Lea, as naïghbours thought her,
While the zun, wi' evenèn beams,
　Did cast our sheädes athirt the water;
　　Winds a-blowèn,
　　Streams a-flowèn,
　　Skies a-glowèn,
Tokens ov my jaÿ zoo fleetèn,
Heighten'd it, that happy meetèn.

Then, when maïd an' man took pleäces,
　Gaÿ in winter's Chris'mas dances,
Showèn in their merry feäces
　Kindly smiles an' glisnèn glances:
　　Stars a-winkèn,
　　Day a-shrinkèn,
　　Sheädes a-zinkèn,
Brought anew the happy meetèn,
That did meake the night too fleetèn.

TO ME.

At night, as drough the meād I took my way,
In aïr a-sweeten'd by the new-meäde hay,
A stream a-vallèn down a rock did sound,
Though out o' zight wer foam an' stwone to me.

Behind the knap, above the gloomy copse,
The wind did russle in the trees' high tops,
Though evenèn darkness, an' the risèn hill,
Kept all the quiv'rèn leaves unshown to me,

Within the copse, below the zunless sky,
I heärd a nightèngeäle, a-warblèn high
Her lwoansome zong, a-hidden vrom my zight,
An' showèn nothèn but her mwoan to me.

An' by a house, where rwoses hung avore
The thatch-brow'd window, an' the oben door,
I heärd the merry words, an' hearty laugh
O' zome feäir maid, as eet unknown to me.

High over head the white-rimm'd clouds went on,
Wi' woone a-comèn up, vor woone a-gone;
An' feäir they floated in their sky-back'd flight,
But still they never meäde a sound to me.

An' there the miller, down the stream did float
Wi' all his childern, in his white-sail'd bwoat,
Vur off, beyond the stragglèn cows in meäd,
But zent noo vaïce, athirt the ground, to me.

An' then a buttervlee, in zultry light,
A-wheelèn on about me, vier-bright,
Did show the gayest colors to my eye,
But still did bring noo vaïce around to me.

I met the merry laugher on the down,
Bezide her mother, on the path to town,
An' oh! her sheäpe wer comely to the zight,
But wordless then wer she a-vound to me.

Zoo, sweet ov unzeen things mid be sound,
An' feäir to zight mid soundless things be vound,
But I've the laugh to hear, an' feäce to zee,
Vor they be now my own, a-bound to me.

TWO AN' TWO.

The zun, O Jessie, while his feäce do rise
   In vi'ry skies, a-shedden out his light
On yollow corn a-weäven down below
   His yollow glow, is gaÿ avore the zight.
     By two an' two,
       How goodly things do goo,
   A-matchen woone another to fulvill
    The goodness ov their Meäker's will.

How bright the spreaden water in the lew
   Do catch the blue, a-sheenen vrom the sky;
How true the grass do teäke the dewy bead
   That it do need, while dousty roads be dry.
     By peäir an' peäir
      Each thing's a-meäde to sheäre
   The good another can bestow,
    In wisdom's work down here below.

The lowest lim's o' trees do seldom grow
   A-spread too low to gi'e the cows a sheäde;
The aïr's to bear the bird, the bird's to rise;
   Vor light the eyes, vor eyes the light's a-meäde.

'Tis gi'e an' teäke,
An' woone vor others' seäke;
In peäirs a-worken out their ends,
Though men be foes that should be friends.

THE LEW O' THE RICK.

At eventide the wind wer loud
　By trees an' tuns above woone's head,
An' all the sky wer woone dark cloud,
　Vor all it had noo raïn to shed;
An' as the darkness gather'd thick,
I zot me down below a rick,
Where straws upon the win' did ride
Wi' giddy flights, along my zide,
Though unmolestèn me a-restèn,
　　Where I lay 'ithin the lew.

My wife's bright vier indoors did cast
　Its fleäme upon the window peänes
That screen'd her teäble, while the blast
　Vled on in music down the leänes;
An' as I zot in vaïceless thought
Ov other zummer-tides, that brought
The sheenèn grass below the lark,
Or left their ricks a-wearèn dark,
My childern voun' me, an' come roun' me,
　　Where I lay 'ithin the lew.

The rick that then did keep me lew
　Would be a-gone another Fall,
An' I, in zome years, in a vew,
　Mid leäve the childern, big or small;

But He that meäde the wind, an' meäde
The lewth, an' zent wi' het the sheäde,
Can keep my childern, all alwone
O' under me, an' though vull grown
Or little lispers, wi' their whispers,
    There a-lyèn in the lew.

THE WIND IN WOONE'S FEÄCE.

There lovely Jenny past,
  While the blast did blow
On over Ashknowle Hill
  To the mill below;
A-blinkèn quick, wi' lashes long,
  Above her cheäks o' red,
Ageän the wind, a-beätèn strong,
  Upon her droopèn head.

Oh! let dry win' blow bleäk,
  On her cheäk so heäle,
But let noo raïn-shot chill
  Meäke her ill an' peäle;
Vor healthy is the breath the blast
  Upon the hill do yield,
An' healthy is the light a cast
  Vrom lofty sky to yield.

An' mid noo sorrow-pang
  Ever hang a tear
Upon the dark lash-heäir
  Ov my feäirest dear;
An' mid noo unkind deed o' mine
  Spweil what my love mid gaïn,
Nor meäke my merry Jenny pine
  At last wi' dim-ey'd païn.

TOKENS

Green mwold on zummer bars do show
  That they've a-dripp'd in Winter wet;
The hoof-worn ring o' groun' below
  The tree, do tell o' storms or het;
The trees in rank along a ledge
Do show where woonce did bloom a hedge;
An' where the vurrow-marks do stripe
The down, the wheat woonce rustled ripe.
Each mark ov things a-gone vrom view—
To eyezight's woone, to soulzight two.

The grass ageän the mwoldrèn door
  'S a tóken sad o' vo'k a-gone,
An' where the house, bwoth wall an' vloor,
  'S a-lost, the well mid linger on.
What tokens, then, could Meäry gi'e
Thät she'd a-liv'd, an' liv'd vor me,
But things a-done vor thought an' view?
Good things that nwone ageän can do,
An' every work her love ha' wrought,
To eyezight's woone, but two to thought.

TWEIL.

The rick ov our last zummer's haulèn
  Now vrom grey's a-feäded dark,
An' off the barken raïl's a-vallèn,
  Day by day, the rottèn bark.—
But short's the time our works do stand,
So feäir's we put em out ov hand.
Vor time a-passèn, wet an' dry,
Do spweïl em wi' his changèn sky,

The while wi' strivèn hope, we men,
   Though a-ruèn time's undoèn,
Still do tweil an' tweil ageän.

In wall-zide sheädes, by leafy bowers,
   Underneath the swayèn tree,
O' leäte, as round the bloomèn flowers,
   Lowly humm'd the giddy bee,
My children's small left voot did smite
Their tiny speäde, the while the right
Did trample on a deäisy head,
Bezïde the flower's dousty bed,
An' though their work wer idle then,
   They a-smilèn, an' a-tweilèn,
Still did work an' work ageän.

Now their little limbs be stronger,
   Deeper now their vaïce do sound;
An' their little veet be longer,
   An' do tread on other ground;
An' rust is on the little bleädes
   Ov all the broken-hafted speädes,
An' flow'rs that wer my hope an' pride
Ha' long agoo a-bloom'd an' died,
But still as I did leäbor then
   Vor love ov all them childern small,
Zoo now I'll tweil an' tweil ageän.

When the smokeless tun's a-growèn
   Cwold as dew below the stars,
An' when the vier noo mwore's a-glowèn
   Red between the window bars,
We then do lay our weary heads
In peace upon their nightly beds,
An' gi'e woone sock, wi' heavèn breast,
An' then breathe soft the breath o' rest,

Till day do call the sons o' men
   Vrom night-sleep's blackness, vull o' sprackness,
Out abroad to tweil ageän.

Where the vaïce o' the winds is mildest,
   In the plaïn, their stroke is keen;
Where their dreatnèn vaïce is wildest,
   In the grove, the grove's our screen.
An' where the worold in their strife
Do dreatèn mwost our tweilsome life,
Why there Almighty ceäre mid cast
A better screen ageän the blast.
Zoo I woon't live in fear o' men,
   But, man-neglected, God-directed,
Still wull tweil an' tweil ageän.

FANCY.

IN stillness we ha' words to hear,
   An' sheäpes to zee in darkest night,
An' tongues a-lost can haïl us near,
   An' souls a-gone can smile in zight;
When Fancy now do wander back
   To years a-spent, an' bring to mind
   Zome happy tide a-left behind
In' weästèn life's slow-beatèn track.

When feädèn leaves do drip wi' raïn,
   Our thoughts can ramble in the dry;
When Winter win' do zweep the plaïn
   We still can have a zunny sky.
Vor though our limbs be winter-wrung,
   We still can zee, wi' Fancy's eyes,
   The brightest looks ov e'th an' skies,
That we did know when we wer young.

In païn our thoughts can pass to eäse,
　　In work our souls can be at play,
An' leäve behind the chilly leäse
　　Vor warm-aïr'd meäds o' new mow'd hay.
When we do vlee in Fancy's flight
　　Vrom daily ills avore our feäce,
　　An' linger in zome happy pleäce
Ov mè'th an' smiles, an' warmth an' light.

THE BROKEN HEART.

News o' grief had overteäken
Dark-ey'd Fanny, now vorseäken;
There she zot, wi' breast a-heavèn,
While vrom zide to zide, wi' grievèn,
Vell her head, wi' tears a-creepèn
Down her cheäks, in bitter weepèn.
There wer still the ribbon-bow
She tied avore he hour ov woe,
An' there wer still the han's that tied it
　　　　Hangèn white,
　　　　　Or wringèn tight,
In ceäre that drown'd all ceäre bezide it.

When a man, wi' heartless slightèn,
Mid become a maïden's blightèn,
He mid ceärlessly vorseäke her,
But must answer to her Meäker;
He mid slight, wi' selfish blindness,
All her deeds o' lovèn-kindness,
God wull waïgh em wi' the slightèn
That mid be her love's requitèn;
He do look on each deceiver,
　　　　He do know
　　　　　What weight o' woe
Do breäk the heart ov ev'ry griever.

EVENÈN LIGHT.

The while I took my bit o' rest,
  Below my house's eastern sheäde,
  The things that stood in vield an' gleäde
Wer bright in zunsheen vrom the west.
  There bright wer east-ward mound an' wall,
  An' bright wer trees, arisèn tall,
An' bright did break 'ithin the brook,
  Down rocks, the watervall.

There deep 'ithin my pworches bow
  Did hang my heavy woaken door,
  An' in beyond en, on the vloor,
The evenèn dusk did gather slow;
  But bright did gleäre the twinklèn spwokes
  O' runnèn carriage wheels, as vo'ks
Out east did ride along the road,
  Bezide the low-bough'd woaks,

An' I'd a-lost the zun vrom view,
  Until ageän his feäce mid rise,
  A-sheenèn vrom the eastern skies
To brighten up the rwose-borne dew;
  But still his lingrèn light did gi'e
  My heart a touchèn jay, to zee
His beams a-shed, wi' stratchèn sheäde,
  On east-ward wall an' tree.

When jay, a-zent me vrom above,
  Vrom my sad heart is now agone,
  An' others be a-walkèn on,
Amid the light ov Heavèn's love,
  Oh! then vor lovèn-kindness seäke,
  Mid I rejäice that zome do teäke
My hopes a-gone, until ageän
  My happy dawn do breäk.

VIELDS BY WATERVALLS.

When our downcast looks be smileless,
    Under others' wrongs an' slightèns,
When our daily deeds be guileless,
    An' do meet unkind requitèns,
You can meäke us zome amends
Vor wrongs o' foes, an' slights o' friends;—
O flow'ry-gleäded, timber-sheäded
Vields by flowèn watervalls!

Here be softest aïrs a-blowèn
    Drough the boughs, wi' zingèn drushes,
Up above the streams, a-flowèn
    Under willows, on by rushes.
Here below the bright-zunn'd sky
The dew-bespangled flow'rs do dry,
In woody-zided, stream-divided
Vields by flowèn watervalls.

Waters, wi' their giddy rollèns;
    Breezes wi' their playsome wooèns;
Here do heal, in soft consolèns,
    Hearts a-wrung wi' man's wrong doèns.
Day do come to us as gay
As to a king ov widest sway,
In deäisy-whitèn'd, gil'cup-brightèn'd
Vields by flowèn watervalls.

Zome feäir buds mid outlive blightèns,
    Zome sweet hopes mid outlive sorrow,
After days of wrongs an' slightèns
    There mid break a happy morrow.
We mid have noo e'thly love;
But God's love-tokens vrom above
Here mid meet us, here mid greet us,
In the vields by watervalls.

THE WHEEL ROUTS.

'Tis true I brought noo fortune hwome
   Wi' Jenny, vor her honey-moon,
But still a goodish hansel come
   Behind her perty soon,
Vor stick, an' dish, an' spoon, all vell
To Jeäne, vrom Aunt o' Camwy dell.

Zoo all the lot o' stuff a-tied
   Upon the plow, a tidy tod,
On gravel-crunchèn wheels did ride,
   Wi' ho'ses, iron-shod,
That, as their heads did nod, my whip
Did guide along wi' lightsome flip.

An' there it rod 'ithin the rwope,
   Astraïn'd athirt, an' straïn'd along,
Down Thornhay's evenèn-lighted slope
   An' up the beech-tree drong;
Where wheels a-bound so strong, cut out
On either zide a deep-zunk rout.

An' when at Fall the trees wer brown,
   Above the bennet-bearèn land,
When beech-leaves slowly whiver'd down,
   By evenèn winds a-fann'd;
The routs wer each a band o' red,
A-vill'd by drifted beech-leaves dead.

An' when, in Winter's leafless light,
   The keener eastern wind did blow,
An' scatter down, avore my zight,
   A chilly cwoat o' snow;
The routs ageän did show vull bright,
In two long streaks o' glitt'rèn white.

But when, upon our weddèn night,
   The cart's light wheels, a-rollèn round,
Brought Jenny hwome, they run too light
   To mark the yieldèn ground;
Or welcome would be vound a peäir
O' green-vill'd routs a-runnèn there.

Zoo let me never bring 'ithin
   My dwellèn what's a-won by wrong,
An' can't come in 'ithout a sin;
   Vor only zee how long
The waggon marks in drong, did show
Wi' leaves, wi' grass, wi' groun' wi' snow.

NANNY'S NEW ABODE.

Now day by day, at lofty height,
   O zummer noons, the burnèn zun
've a-show'd avore our eastward zight,
   The sky-blue zide ov Hameldon,
An' shone ageän, on new-mow'd ground,
   Wi' haÿ a-piled up grey in pook,
An' down on leäzes, bennet-brown'd,
   An' wheat a-vell avore the hook;
Till, under elems tall,
   The leaves do lie on leänèn lands,
In leäter light o' Fall.

An' last year, we did zee the red
   O' dawn vrom Ash-knap's thatchen oves,
An' walk on crumpled leaves a-laid
   In grassy rook-trees' timber'd groves,
Now, here, the cooler days do shrink
   To vewer hours o' zunny sky,
While zedge, a-weävèn by the brink
   O' shallow brooks, do slowly die.

An' on the timber tall,
　　The boughs, half beäre, do bend above
The bulgèn banks in Fall.

There, we'd a spring o' water near,
　　Here, water's deep in wink-draïn'd wells,
The church 'tis true, is nigh out here,
　　Too nigh wi' vive loud-boomèn bells.
There, naïghbours wer vull wide a-spread,
　　But vo'k be here too clwose a-stow'd.
Vor childern now do stun woone's head,
　　Wi' naïsy play bezide the road,
Where big so well as small,
　　The little lad, an' lump'rèn lout,
Do leäp an' laugh theäse Fall.

LEAVES A-VALLÈN.

There the ash-tree leaves do vall
　　In the wind a-blowèn cwolder,
An' my childern, tall or small,
　　Since last Fall be woone year wolder.
Woone year wolder, woone year dearer,
　　Till when they do leave my he'th,
I shall be noo mwore a hearer
　　O' their vaïces or their me'th.

There dead ash leaves be a-toss'd
　　In the wind, a-blowèn stronger,
An' our life-time, since we lost
　　Souls we lov'd, is woone year longer.
Woone year longer, woone year wider,
　　Vrom the friends that death ha' tcok,
As the hours do teäke the rider
　　Vrom the hand that last he shook.

No. If he do ride at night
   Vrom the zide the zun went under,
Woone hour vrom his western light
   Needen meäke woone hour asunder;
Woone hour onward, woone hour nigher
   To the hopeful eastern skies,
Where his mornèn rim o' vier
   Soon ageän shall meet his eyes.

Leaves be now a-scatter'd round
   In the wind, a-blowèn bleaker,
An' if we do walk the ground
   Wi' our life-strangth woone year weaker.
Woone year weaker, woone year nigher
   To the pleäce where we shall vind
Woone that's deathless vor the dier,
   Voremost they that dropp'd behind.

LIZZIE.

O Lizzie is so mild o' mind,
   Vor ever kind, an' ever true;
A-smilèn, while her lids do rise
   To show her eyes as bright as dew.
An' comely do she look at night,
A-dancèn in her skirt o' white,
An' blushèn wi' a rwose o' red
   Bezide her glossy head.

Feäir is the rwose o' blushèn hue,
   Behung wi' dew, in mornèn's hour,
Feäir is the rwose, so sweet below
   The noontide glow, bezide the bow'r.
Vull feäir, an' eet I'd rather zee
The rwose a-gather'd off the tree,
An' bloomèn still with blossom red,
   By Lizzie's glossy head.

Mid peace droughout her e'thly day,
  Betide her way, to happy rest,
An' mid she, all her weanèn life,
  Or maïd or wife, be loved and blest.
Though I mid never zing anew
To neäme the maïd so feäir an' true,
A-blushèn, wi' a rwose o' red,
Bezide her glossy head.

BLESSENS A-LEFT.

Lik' souls a-toss'd at sea I bore
  Sad strokes o' trial, shock by shock,
An' now, lik' souls a-cast ashore
  To rest upon the beäten rock,
I still do seem to hear the sound
O' weäves that drove me vrom my track,
An' zee my strugglèn hopes a-drown'd,
An' all my jays a-floated back.
By storms a-toss'd, I'll gi'e God praïse,
Wi' much a-lost I still ha' jays.
My peace is rest, my faïth is hope,
An' freedom's my unbounded scope.

Vor faïth mid blunt the sting o' fear,
  An' peace the pangs ov ills a-vound,
An' freedom vlee vrom evils near,
  Wi' wings to vwold on other ground.
Wi' much a-lost, my loss is small,
Vor though ov e'thly goods bereft,
A thousand times well worth em all
Be they good blessèns now a-left.
What e'th do own, to e'th mid vall,
But what's my own my own I'll call,
My faïth, an' peäce, the gifts o' greäce,
An' freedom still to shift my pleäce.

When I've a-had a tree to screen
   My meal-rest vrom the high zunn'd-sky,
Or ivy-holdèn wall between
   My head an' win's a-rustlèn by,
I had noo call vor han's to bring
Their seäv'ry daïnties at my nod,
But stoop'd a-drinkèn vrom the spring,
An' took my meal, wi' thanks to God,
Wi' faïth to keep me free o' dread,
An' peäce to sleep wi' steadvast head,
An' freedom's hands, an' veet unbound
To woone man's work, or woone seäme ground.

FALL TIME.

THE gather'd clouds, a-hangèn low,
   Do meäke the woody ridge look dim;
An' raïn-vill'd streams do brisker flow,
   Arisèn higher to their brim.
In the tree, vrom lim' to lim',
       Leaves do drop
Vrom the top, all slowly down,
Yollow, to the gloomy groun'.

The rick's a-tipp'd an' weather-brown'd,
   An' thatch'd wi' zedge a-dried an' dead;
An' orcha'd apples, red half round,
   Have all a-happer'd down, a-shed
Underneath the trees' wide head.
      Ladders long,
Rong by rong, to clim' the tall
Trees, be hung upon the wall.

The crumpled leaves be now a-shed
   In mornèn winds a-blowèn keen;
When they wer green the moss wer dead,
   Now they be dead the moss is green.

Low the evenèn zun do sheen
    By the boughs,
Where the cows do swing their tails
Over the merry milkers' pails.

FALL.

Now the yollow zun, a-runnèn
    Daily round a smaller bow,
Still wi' cloudless sky's a-zunnèn
    All the sheenèn land below.
    Vewer blossoms now do blow,
But the fruit's a-showèn
    Reds an' blues, an' purple hues,
By the leaves a-glowèn.

Now the childern be a-pryèn
    Roun' the berried bremble-bow,
Zome a-laughèn, woone a-cryèn
    Vor the slent her frock do show.
    Bwoys be out a-pullèn low
Slooe-boughs, or a-runnèn
    Where, on zides of hazzle-wrides,
Nuts do hang a-zunnèn.

Where do reach roun' wheat-ricks yollow
    Oves o' thatch, in long-drawn ring,
There, by stubbly hump an' hollow,
    Russet-dappled dogs do spring.
    Soon my apple-trees wull fling
Bloomèn balls below em,
    That shall hide, on ev'ry zide
Ground where we do drow em.

THE ZILVER-WEED.

The zilver-weed upon the green,
    Out where my sons an' daughters play'd,
Had never time to bloom between
    The litty steps o' bwoy an' maïd.
But rwose-trees down along the wall,
    That then wer all the maïden's ceäre,
An' all a-trimm'd an' traïn'd, did bear
    Their bloomèn buds vrom Spring to Fall.

But now the zilver leaves do show
    To zummer day their goolden crown,
Wi' noo swift shoe-zoles' litty blow,
    In merry play to beät em down.
An' where vor years zome busy hand
    Did traïn the rwoses wide an' high :
Now woone by woone the trees do die,
    An' vew of all the row do stand.

THE WIDOW'S HOUSE.

I went hwome in the dead o' the night,
    When the vields wer all empty o' vo'k,
An' the tuns at their cool-winded height
    Wer all dark, an' all cwold 'ithout smoke ;
An' the heads o' the trees that I pass'd
    Wer a-swayèn wi' low-ruslèn sound,
An' the doust wer a-whirl'd wi' the blast,
    Aye, a smeech wi' the wind on the ground.

Then I come by the young widow's hatch,
    Down below the wold elem's tall head,
But noo vinger did lift up the latch,
    Vor the vo'k wer so still as the dead ;

But inside, to a tree a-meäde vast,
   Wer the childern's light swing, a-hung low,
An' a-rock'd by the brisk-blowèn blast,
   Aye, a-swung by the win' to an' fro.

Vor the childern, wi' pillow-borne head,
   Had vorgotten their swing on the lawn,
An' their father, asleep wi' the dead,
   Had vorgotten his work at the dawn;
An' their mother, a vew stilly hours,
   Had vorgotten where he sleept so sound,
Where the wind wer a-sheakèn the flow'rs,
   Aye, the blast the feäir buds on the ground.

Oh! the moon, wi' his peäle lighted skies,
   Have his sorrowless sleepers below.
But by day to the zun they must rise
   To their true lives o' tweil an' ov ho.
Then the childern wull rise to their fun,
   An' their mother mwore sorrow to veel,
While the aïr is a-warm'd by the zun,
   Aye, the win' by the day's vi'ry wheel.

THE CHILD'S GREÄVE.

AVORE the time when zuns went down
On zummer's green a-turn'd to brown,
When sheädes o' swayèn wheat-eärs vell
Upon the scarlet pimpernel;
The while you still mid goo, an' vind
   'Ithin the geärden's mossy wall,
   Sweet blossoms, low or risèn tall,
To meäke a tutty to your mind,
In churchyard heav'd, wi' grassy breast,
The greäve-mound ov a beäby's rest.

An' when a high day broke, to call
A throng 'ithin the churchyard wall,
The mother brought, wi' thoughtvul mind,
The feäirest buds her eyes could vind,
To trim the little greäve, an' show
    To other souls her love an' loss,
    An' meäde a Seävior's little cross
O' brightest flow'rs that then did blow,
A-droppèn tears a-sheenèn bright,
Among the dew, in mornèn light.

An' woone sweet bud her han' did pleäce
Up where did droop the Seävior's feäce;
An' two she zet a-bloomèn bright,
Where reach'd His hands o' left an' right;
Two mwore feäir blossoms, crimson dyed,
    Did mark the pleäces ov his veet,
    An' woone did lie, a-smellèn sweet,
Up where the spear did wound the zide
Ov Him that is the life ov all
Greäve sleepers, whether big or small.

The mother that in faïth could zee
The Seävior on the high cross tree
Mid be a-vound a-grievèn sore,
But not to grieve vor evermwore,
Vor He shall show her faïthvul mind,
    His chaïce is all that she should choose,
    An' love that here do grieve to lose,
Shall be, above, a jaÿ to vind,
Wi' Him that evermwore shall keep
The souls that He do lay asleep.

WENT VROM HWOME.

THE stream-be-wander'd dell did spread
    Vrom height to woody height,
An' meäds did lie, a grassy bed,
    Vor elem-sheädèn light.
The milkmaïd by her white-horn'd cow,
    Wi' païl so white as snow,
Did zing below the elem bough
    A-swayèn to an' fro.

An' there the evenèn's low-shot light
    Did smite the high tree-tops,
An' rabbits vrom the grass, in fright,
    Did leäp 'ithin the copse.
An' there the shepherd wi' his crook,
    An' dog bezide his knee,
Went whisslèn by, in aïr that shook
    The ivy on the tree.

An' on the hill, ahead, wer bars
    A-showèn dark on high,
Avore, as eet, the evenèn stars
    Did twinkle in the sky,
An' then the last sweet evenèn-tide
    That my long sheäde vell there,
I went down Brindon's thymy zide,
    To my last sleep at Ware.

THE FANCY FEÄIR AT MAÏDEN NEWTON.

THE Frome, wi' ever-water'd brink,
Do run where shelvèn hills do zink
Wi' housen all a-cluster'd roun'
The parish tow'rs below the down.

THE FANCY FFÄIR AT MAÏDEN NEWTON.

An' now, vor woonce, at leäst, ov all
The pleäcen where the stream do vall,
There's woone that zome to-day mid vind,
Wi' things a-suited to their mind.
   An' that's out where the Fancy Feäir
   Is on at Maïden Newton.

An' vo'k, a-smarten'd up, wull hop
Out here, as ev'ry traïn do stop,
Vrom up the line, a longish ride,
An' down along the river-zide.
An' zome do beät, wi' heels an' tooes,
The leänes an' paths, in nimble shoes,
An' bring, bezides, a biggish knot,
Ov all their childern that can trot,
   A-vlockèn where the Fancy Feäir
   Is here at Maïden Newton.

If you should goo, to-day, avore
A *Chilfrome* house or *Downfrome* door,
Or *Frampton's* park-zide row, or look
Drough quiet *Wraxall's* slopy nook,
Or elbow-streeted *Catt'stock*, down
By *Castlehill's* cwold-winded crown,
An' zee if vo'k be all at hwome,
You'd vind em out—they be a-come
   Out hither, where the Fancy Feäir
   Is on at Maïden Newton.

Come, young men, come, an' here you'll vind
A gift to please a maïden's mind;
Come, husbands, here be gifts to please
Your wives, an' meäke em smile vor days;
Come, so's, an' buy at Fancy Feäir
A keepseäke vor your friends elsewhere;

You can't but stop an' spend a cwein
Wi' leädies that ha' goods so fine;
    An' all to meake, vor childern's seäke,
    The School at Maïden Newton.

THINGS DO COME ROUND.

Above the leafless hazzle-wride
  The wind-drove raïn did quickly vall,
An' on the meäple's ribby zide
  Did hang the raïn-drops quiv'rèn ball;
Out where the brook o' foamy yollow
Roll'd along the meäd's deep hollow,
An' noo birds wer out to beät,
Wi' flappèn wings, the vleèn wet
O' zunless clouds on flow'rless ground.
How time do bring the seasons round!

The moss, a-beät vrom trees, did lie
  Upon the ground in ashen droves,
An' western wind did huffle high,
  Above the sheds' quick-drippèn oves.
An' where the ruslèn straw did sound
  So dry, a-shelter'd in the lew,
I staïed alwone, an' weather-bound,
  An' thought on times, long years agoo.
Wi' water-floods on flow'rless ground.
How time do bring the seasons round!

We then, in childhood play, did seem
  In work o' men to teäke a peärt,
A-drevèn on our wild bwoy team,
  Or lwoadèn o' the tiny cart.
Or, on our little refters, spread
The zedgen ruf above our head,

But couden tell, as now we can,
Where each would goo to tweil a man.
O jays a-lost, an' jays a-vound,
How Providence do bring things round!

Where woonce along the sky o' blue
   The zun went roun' his longsome bow,
An' brighten'd, to my soul, the view
   About our little farm below.
There I did play the merry geäme,
   Wi' childern ev'ry holitide,
But couden tell the vaïce or neäme
   That time would vind to be my bride.
O hwome a-left, O wife a-vound,
How Providence do bring things round!

An' when I took my manhood's pleäce,
   A husband to a wife's true vow,
I never thought by neäme or feäce
   O' childern that be round me now.
An' now they all do grow vrom small,
Drough life's feäir sheäpes to big an' tall,
I still be blind to God's good plan,
To pleäce em out as wife, or man.
O thread o' love by God unwound,
How He in time do bring things round;

ZUMMER THOUGHTS IN WINTER TIME.

WELL, aye, last evenèn, as I shook
My locks ov hay by Leecombe brook,
The yollow zun did weakly glance
Upon the winter meäd askance,
A-castèn out my narrow sheäde
   Athirt the brook, an' on the meäd.

The while ageän my lwonesome ears
Did russle weatherbeäten spears,
Below the withy's leafless head
That overhung the river's bed;
I there did think o' days that dried
The new-mow'd grass o' zummer-tide,
When white-sleev'd mowers' whetted bleädes
Rung sh'ill along the green-bough'd gleädes,
An' maïdens gay, wi' playsome chaps,
A-zot wi' dinners in their laps,
Did talk wi' merry words that rung
Around the ring, vrom tongue to tongue;
An' welcome, when the leaves ha' died,
Be zummer thoughts in winter-tide.

I'M OUT O' DOOR.

I'M out, when, in the Winter's blast,
  The zun, a-runnèn lowly round,
Do mark the sheädes the hedge do cast
  At noon, in hoarvrost, on the ground.
I'm out when snow's a-lyèn white
  In keen-aïr'd vields that I do pass,
An' moonbeams, vrom above, do smite
  On ice an' sleeper's window-glass.
     I'm out o' door,
     When win' do zweep,
     By hangèn steep,
     Or hollow deep,
          At Lindenore.

O welcome is the lewth a-vound
  By rustlèn copse, or ivied bank,
Or by the hay-rick, weather-brown'd
  By barken-grass, a-springèn rank;

Or where the waggon, vrom the team
  A-freed, is well a-housed vrom wet,
An' on the dousty cart-house beam
  Do hang the cobweb's white-lin'd net.
    While storms do roar,
      An' win' do zweep,
      By hangèn steep, -
      Or hollow deep,
        At Lindenore.

An' when a good day's work 's a-done
  An' I do rest, the while a squall
Do rumble in the hollow tun,
  An' ivy-stems do whip the wall.
Then in the house do sound about
  My ears, dear vaïces vull or thin,
A prayèn vor the souls vur out
  At sea, an' cry wi' bibb'rèn chin—
    Oh! shut the door.
      What soul can sleep,
      Upon the deep,
      When storms do zweep
        At Lindenore.

GRIEF AN' GLADNESS.

"Can all be still, when win's do blow?
  Look down the grove an' zee
  The boughs a-swingèn on the tree,
An' beäten weäves below.
Zee how the tweilèn vo'k do bend
  Upon their windward track,
Wi' ev'ry string, an' garment's end,
  A-flutt'rèn at their back."

2 D

I cried, wi' sorrow sore a-tried,
An' hung, wi' Jenny at my zide,
  My head upon my breast.
Wi' strokes o' grief so hard to bear,
  'Tis hard vor souls to rest.

Can all be dull, when zuns do glow?
  Oh! no; look down the grove,
  Where zides o' trees be bright above;
An' weäves do sheen below;
An' neäked stems o' wood in hedge
  Do gleäm in streäks o' light,
An' rocks do gleäre upon the ledge
  O' yonder zunny height,
"No, Jeäne, wi' trials now withdrawn,
Lik' darkness at a happy dawn."
  I cried, "Noo mwore despair;
Wi' our lost peace ageän a-vound,
  'Tis wrong to harbour ceäre."

SLIDÈN.

When wind wer keen.
Where ivy-green
Did clwosely wind
Roun' woak-tree rind,
  An' ice shone bright,
An' meäds wer white, wi' thin-spread snow
  Then on the pond, a-spreadèn wide,
  We bwoys did zweep along the slide,
A-strikèn on in merry row.

  There ruddy-feäced,
  In busy heäste,

SLIDÈN.

    We all did wag
    A spankèn lag,
    To win good speed,
When we, straïght-knee'd, wi' foreright tooes,
  Should shoot along the slipp'ry track,
  Wi' grindèn sound, a-gettèn slack,
The slower went our clumpèn shoes.

    Vor zome slow chap,
    Did teäke mishap,
    As he did veel
    His hinder heel
    A-het a thump,
Wi' zome big lump, o' voot an' shoe.
  Down vell the voremost wi' a squall,
  An' down the next went wi' a sprawl,
An' down went all the laughèn crew.

    As to an' fro,
    In merry row,
    We all went round
    On ice, on ground
    The maïdens nigh
A-stannèn shy, did zee us slide,
  An' in their eäprons small, did vwold
  Their little hands, a-got red-cwold,
Or slide on ice o' two veet wide.

    By leafless copse,
    An' beäre tree-tops,
    An' zun's low beams,
    An' ice-boun' streams,
    An' vrost-boun' mill,
A-stannèn still. Come wind, blow on,
  An' gi'e the bwoys, this Chris'mas tide,
  The glitt'rèn ice to meäke a slide,
As we had our slide, years agone.

LWONESOMENESS.

As I do zew, wi' nimble hand,
    In here avore the window's light,
How still do all the housegear stand
    Around my lwonesome zight.
How still do all the housegear stand
Since Willie now 've a-left the land.

The rwose-tree's window-sheäden bow
    Do hang in leaf, an' win'-blow'd flow'rs,
Avore my lwonesome eyes do show
    Theäse bright November hours.
Avore my lwonesome eyes do show
Wi' nwone but I to zee em blow.

The sheädes o' leafy buds, avore
    The peänes, do sheäke upon the glass,
An' stir in light upon the vloor,
    Where now vew veet do pass,
An' stir in light upon the vloor,
Where there's a-stirrèn nothèn mwore.

This win' mid dreve upon the maïn,
    My brother's ship, a-plowèn foam,
But not bring mother, cwold, nor raïn,
    At her now happy hwome.
But not bring mother, cwold, nor raïn,
Where she is out o' pain.

Zoo now that I'm a-mwopèn dumb,
    A-keepèn father's house, do you
Come of'en wi' your work vrom hwome,
    Vor company. Now do.
Come of'en wi' your work vrom hwome,
Up here a-while. Do come.

A SNOWY NIGHT.

'Twer at night, an' a keen win' did blow
    Vrom the east under peäle-twinklèn stars,
All a-zweepèn along the white snow;
    On the groun', on the trees, on the bars,
Vrom the hedge where the win' russled drough,
    There a light-russlèn snow-doust did vall;
An' noo pleäce wer a-vound that wer lew,
    But the shed, or the ivy-hung wall.

Then I knock'd at the wold passage door
    Wi' the win'-driven snow on my locks;
Till, a-comèn along the cwold vloor,
    There my Jenny soon answer'd my knocks.
Then the wind, by the door a-swung wide,
    Flung some snow in her clear-bloomèn feäce,
An' she blink'd wi' her head all a-zide,
    An' a-chucklèn, went back to her pleäce.

An' in there, as we zot roun' the brands,
    Though the talkers wer maïnly the men,
Bloomèn Jeäne, wi' her work in her hands,
    Did put in a good word now an' then.
An' when I took my leave, though so bleäk
    Wer the weather, she went to the door,
Wi' a smile, an' a blush on the cheäk
    That the snow had a-smitten avore.

THE YEAR-CLOCK.

We zot bezide the leäfy wall,
Upon the bench at evenfall,
While aunt led off our minds vrom ceäre
Wi' veäiry teäles, I can't tell where:

An' vound us woone among her stock
O' feäbles, o' the girt Year-clock.
His feäce wer blue's the zummer skies,
An' wide's the zight o' lookèn eyes,
For hands, a zun wi' glowèn feäce,
An' peäler moon wi' swifter peäce,
Did wheel by stars o' twinklèn light,
By bright-wall'd day, an' dark-treed night;
An' down upon the high-sky'd land,
A-reachèn wide, on either hand,
Wer hill an' dell wi' win'-swaÿ'd trees,
An' lights a-zweepèn over seas,
An' gleamèn cliffs, an' bright-wall'd tow'rs,
Wi' sheädes a-markèn on the hours;
An' as the feäce, a-rollèn round,
Brought comely sheäpes along the ground,
The Spring did come in winsome steäte
Below a glowèn raïnbow geäte;
An' fan wi' aïr a-blowèn weak,
Her glossy heäir, an' rwosy cheäk,
As she did shed vrom oben hand,
The leäpèn zeed on vurrow'd land;
The while the rook, wi' heästy flight,
A-floatèn in the glowèn light,
Did bear avore her glossy breast
A stick to build her lofty nest,
An' strong-limb'd Tweil, wi' steady hands,
Did guide along the vallow lands
The heavy zull, wi' bright-sheär'd beam,
Avore the weäry oxen team.
Wi' Spring a-gone there come behind
Sweet Zummer, jaÿ ov ev'ry mind,
Wi' feäce a-beamèn to beguile
Our weäry souls ov ev'ry tweil.
While birds did warble in the dell
In softest aïr o' sweetest smell;

THE YEAR-CLOCK.

An' she, so winsome-feäir did vwold
Her comely limbs in green an' goold,
An' wear a rwosy wreath, wi' studs
O' berries green, an' new-born buds,
A-fring'd in colours vier-bright,
Wi' sheäpes o' buttervlees in flight.
When Zummer went, the next ov all
Did come the sheäpe o' brown-feäc'd Fall,
A-smilèn in a comely gown
O' green, a-shot wi' yellow-brown,
A-border'd wi' a goolden stripe
O' fringe, a-meäde o' corn-ears ripe,
An' up ageän her comely zide,
Upon her rounded eärm, did ride
A perty basket, all a-twin'd
O' slender stems wi' leaves an' rind,
A-vill'd wi' fruit the trees did shed,
All ripe, in purple, goold, an' red;
An' busy Leäbor there did come
A-zingèn zongs ov harvest hwome,
An' red-ear'd dogs did briskly run
Roun' cheervul Leisure wi' his gun,
Or stan' an' mark, wi' stedvast zight,
The speckled pa'tridge rise in flight.
An' next ageän to mild-feäc'd Fall
Did come peäle Winter, last ov all,
A-bendèn down, in thoughtvul mood,
Her head 'ithin a snow-white hood
A-deck'd wi' icy-jewels, bright
An' cwold as twinklèn stars o' night;
An' there wer weary Leäbor, slack
O' veet to keep her vrozen track,
A-lookèn off, wi' wistful eyes,
To reefs o' smoke, that there did rise
A-meltèn to the peäle-feäc'd zun,
Above the houses' lofty tun.

An' there the girt Year-clock did goo
By day an' night, vor ever true,
Wi' mighty wheels a-rollèn round
'Ithout a beät, 'ithout a sound.

NOT GOO HWOME TO-NIGHT.

No, no, why you've noo wife at hwome
Abidèn up till you do come,
Zoo leäve your hat upon the pin,
Vor I'm your waïter. Here's your inn,
Wi' chair to rest, an' bed to roost;
You have but little work to do
This vrosty time at hwome in mill,
Your vrozen wheel's a-stannèn still,
The sleepèn ice woont grind vor you.
No, no, you woont goo hwome to-night,
Good Robin White, o' Craglin mill.

As I come by, to-day, where stood
Wi' neäked trees, the purple wood,
The scarlet hunter's ho'ses veet
Tore up the sheäkèn ground, wind-fleet,
Wi' reachèn heads, an' paukèn hides;
The while the flat-wing'd rooks in vlock,
Did zwim a-sheenèn at their height;
But your good river, since last night,
Wer all a-vroze so still's a rock.
No, no, you woont goo hwome to-night,
Good Robin White, o' Craglin mill.

Zee how the hufflèn win' do blow,
A-whirlèn down the giddy snow:
Zee how the sky's a-weärèn dim,
Behind the elem's neäked lim'.

NOT GOO HWOME TO NIGHT.

That there do leän above the leäne;
Zoo teäke your pleäce bezide the dogs,
An' sip a drop o' hwome-brew'd eäle,
An' zing your zong or tell your teäle,
While I do baït the vier wi' logs.
No, no, you woont goo hwome to-night,
Good Robin White, o' Craglin mill.

Your meäre's in steäble wi' her hocks
In straw above her vetterlocks,
A-reachèn up her meäney neck,
An' pullèn down good haÿ vrom reck,
A-meäkèn slight o' snow an' sleet;
She don't want you upon her back,
To vall upon the slippery stwones
On Hollyhill, an' break your bwones,
Or miss, in snow, her hidden track.
No, no, you woont goo hwome to-night,
Good Robin White, o' Craglin mill.

Here, Jenny, come pull out your key
An' hansel, wi' zome tidy tea,
The zilver pot that we do owe
To your prize butter at the show,
An' put zome bread upon the bwoard.
Ah! he do smile; now that 'ull do,
He'll staÿ. Here, Polly, bring a light,
We'll have a happy hour to-night,
I'm thankvul we be in the lew.
No, no, he woont goo hwome to-night,
Not Robin White, o' Craglin mill.

THE HUMSTRUM.

Why woonce, at Chris'mas-tide, avore
The wold year wer a-reckon'd out,
The humstrums here did come about,
A-soundèn up at ev'ry door.
But now a bow do never screäpe
   A humstrum, any where all round,
An' zome can't tell a humstrum's sheäpe,
   An' never heärd his jinglèn sound.
As *ing-an-ing* did ring the string,
As *ang-an-ang* the wires did clang.

The strings a-tighten'd lik' to crack
Athirt the canister's tin zide,
Did reach, a glitt'rèn, zide by zide,
Above the humstrum's hollow back.
An' there the bwoy, wi' bended stick,
   A-strung wi' heäir, to meäke a bow,
Did dreve his elbow, light'nèn quick,
   Athirt the strings from high to low.
As *ing-an-ing* did ring the string,
As *ang-an-ang* the wires did clang.

The mother there did stan' an' hush
Her child, to hear the jinglèn sound,
The merry maïd, a-scrubbèn round
Her white-steäv'd païl, did stop her brush.
The mis'ess there, vor wold time's seäke,
   Had gifts to gi'e, and smiles to show,
An' meäster, too, did stan' an' sheäke
   His two broad zides, a-chucklèn low,
While *ing-an-ing* did ring the string,
While *ang-an-ang* the wires did clang.

The players' pockets wer a-strout,
Wi' wold brown pence, a-rottlèn in,
Their zwangèn bags did soon begin,
Wi' brocks an' scraps, to plim well out.
The childern all did run an' poke
   Their heads vrom hatch or door, an' shout
A-runnèn back to wolder vo'k.
   Why, here! the humstrums be about!
As *ing-an-ing* did ring the string,
As *ang-an-ang* the wires did clang.

SHAFTESBURY FEÄIR.

When hillborne Paladore did show
So bright to me down miles below.
As woonce the zun, a-rollèn west,
Did brighten up his hill's high breast.
Wi' walls a-lookèn dazzlèn white,
Or yollow, on the grey-topp'd height
Of Paladore, as peäle day wore
      Away so feäir.
Oh! how I wish'd that I wer there.

The pleäce wer too vur off to spy
The livèn vo'k a-passèn by;
The vo'k too vur vor aïr to bring
The words that they did speak or zing.
All dum' to me wer each abode,
An' empty wer the down-hill road
Vrom Paladore, as peäle day wore
      Away so feäir;
But how I wish'd that I wer there.

But when I clomb the lofty ground
Where livèn veet an' tongues did sound,

At feäir, bezide your bloomèn feäce,
The pertiest in all the pleäce,
As you did look, wi' eyes as blue
As yonder southern hills in view,
Vrom Paladore—O Polly dear,
     Wi' you up there,
How merry then wer I at feäir.

Since vu'st I trod thik steep hill-zide
My grievèn soul 'v a-been a-tried
Wi' païn, an' loss o' worldly geär,
An' souls a-gone I wanted near;
But you be here to goo up still,
An' look to Blackmwore vrom the hill
O' Paladore. Zoo, Polly dear,
     We'll goo up there,
An' spend an hour or two at feäir.

The wold brown meäre's a-brought vrom grass,
An' rubb'd an' cwomb'd so bright as glass;
An' now we'll hitch her in, an' start
To feäir upon the new green cart,
An' teäke our little Poll between
Our zides, as proud's a little queen,
To Paladore. Aye, Poll a dear,
     Vor now 'tis feäir,
An' she's a-longèn to goo there.

While Paladore, on watch, do strain
Her eyes to Blackmwore's blue-hill'd pläin,
While Duncliffe is the traveller's mark,
Or cloty Stour's a-rollèn dark;
Or while our bells do call, vor greäce,
The vo'k avore their Seävior's feäce,
Mid Paladore, an' Poll a dear,
     Vor ever know
O' peäce an' plenty down below.

THE BEÄTEN PATH.

The beäten path where vo'k do meet
    A-comèn on vrom vur an' near;
How many errands had the veet
    That wore en out along so clear!
Where eegrass bleädes be green in meäd,
    Where bennets up the leäze be brown,
An' where the timber bridge do leäd
    Athirt the cloty brook to town,
Along the path by mile an' mile,
Athirt the vield, an' brook, an' stile,

There runnèn childern's hearty laugh
    Do come an' vlee along—win' swift:
The wold man's glossy-knobbèd staff
    Do help his veet so hard to lift;
The maïd do bear her basket by,
    A-hangèn at her breäthèn zide;
An' ceäreless young men, straïght an' spry,
    Do whissle hwome at eventide,
Along the path, a-reachèn by
Below tall trees an' oben sky.

There woone do goo to jay a-head;
    Another's jay's behind his back.
There woone his vu'st long mile do tread,
    An' woone the last ov all his track.
An' woone mid end a hopevul road,
    Wi' hopeless grief a-teäkèn on,
As he that leätely vrom abroad
    Come hwome to seek his love a-gone,
Noo mwore to tread, wi' comely eäse,
The beäten path athirt the leäze.

In tweilsome hardships, year by year,
    He drough the worold wander'd wide,
Still bent, in mind, both vur an' near
    To come an' meäke his love his bride.
An' passèn here drough evenèn dew
    He heästen'd, happy, to her door,
But vound the wold vo'k only two,
    Wi' noo mwore vootsteps on the vloor,
To walk ageän below the skies,
Where beäten paths do vall an' rise;

Vor she wer gone vrom e'thly eyes
    To be a-kept in darksome sleep,
Until the good ageän do rise
    A-jay to souls they left to weep.
The rwose wer doust that bound her brow;
    The moth did eat her Zunday ceäpe;
Her frock wer out o' fashion now;
    Her shoes wer dried up out o' sheäpe—
The shoes that woonce did glitter black
Along the leäzes beäten track.

RUTH A-RIDÈN.

Ov all the roads that ever bridge
    Did bear athirt a river's feäce,
Or ho'ses up an' down the ridge
    Did wear to doust at ev'ry peäce,
I'll teäke the Stalton leäne to tread,
By banks wi' primrwose-beds bespread,
An' steätely elems over head,
    Where Ruth do come a-ridèn.

An' I would rise when vields be grey
    Wi' mornèn dew, avore 'tis dry,
An' beät the doust droughout the day
    To bluest hills ov all the sky;

If there, avore the dusk o' night,
The evenèn zun, a-sheenèn bright,
Would pay my leäbors wi' the zight
    O' Ruth—o' Ruth a-ridèn.

Her healthy feäce is rwosy feäir,
  She's comely in her gaït an' lim',
An' sweet's the smile her feäce do wear,
  Below her cap's well-rounded brim;
An' while her skirt's a-spreädèn wide,
In vwolds upon the ho'se's zide,
He'll toss his head, an' snort wi' pride,
    To trot wi' Ruth a-ridèn.

An' as her ho'se's rottlèn peäce
  Do slacken till his veet do beät
A slower trot, an' till her feäce
  Do bloom avore the tollman's geäte;
Oh! he'd be glad to oben wide
His high-back'd geäte, an' stand azide,
A-givèn up his toll wi' pride,
    Vor zight o' Ruth a-ridèn.

An' oh! that Ruth could be my bride,
  An' I had ho'ses at my will,
That I mid teäke her by my zide,
  A-ridèn over dell an' hill;
I'd zet wi' pride her litty tooe
'Ithin a stirrup, sheenèn new,
An' leäve all other jays to goo
    Along wi' Ruth a-ridèn.

If maïdens that be weäk an' peäle
  A-mwopèn in the house's sheäde,
Would wish to be so blithe and heäle
  As you did zee young Ruth a-meäde;

Then, though the zummer zun mid glow,
Or though the Winter win' mid blow,
They'd leäp upon the saddle's bow,
   An' goo, lik' Ruth, a-ridèn.

While evenèn light do sof'ly gild
   The moss upon the elem's bark,
Avore the zingèn bird's a-still'd,
   Or woods be dim, or day is dark,
Wi' quiv'rèn grass avore his breast,
In cowslip beds, do lie at rest,
The ho'se that now do goo the best
   Wi' rwosy Ruth a-ridèn.

BEAUTY UNDECKED.

THE grass mid sheen when wat'ry beäds
O' dew do glitter on the meäds,
An' thorns be bright when quiv'rèn studs
O' raïn do hang upon their buds—
As jewels be a-meäde by art
To zet the plaïnest vo'k off smart

But sheäkèn ivy on its tree,
An' low-bough'd laurel at our knee,
Be bright all däy, without the gleäre,
O' drops that duller leäves mid weär—
As Jeäne is feäir to look upon
In plaïnest gear that she can don.

MY LOVE IS GOOD.

MY love is good, my love is feäir,
   She's comely to behold, O,
In ev'rything that she do wear,
   Altho' 'tis new or wold, O.

MY LOVE IS GOOD.

My heart do leäp to see her walk,
  So straïght do step her veet, O,
My tongue is dum' to hear her talk,
  Her vaïce do sound so sweet, O.
The flow'ry groun' wi' floor o' green
Do bear but vew, so good an' true.

When she do zit, then she do seem
  The feäirest to my zight, O,
Till she do stan' an' I do deem,
  She's feäirest at her height, O.
An' she do seem 'ithin a room
  The feäirest on a floor, O,
Till I ageän do zee her bloom
  Still feäirer out o' door, O.
Where flow'ry groun' wi' floor o' green
Do bear but vew, so good an' true.

An' when the deäisies be a-press'd
  Below her vootsteps waïght, O,
Do seem as if she look'd the best
  Ov all in walkèn gaït, O.
Till I do zee her zit upright
  Behind the ho'ses neck, O,
A-holdèn wi' the raïn so tight
  His tossèn head in check, O,
Where flow'ry groun' wi' floor o' green
Do bear but vew, so good an' true.

I wish I had my own free land
  To keep a ho'se to ride, O,
I wish I had a ho'se in hand
  To ride en at her zide, O.
Vor if I wer as high in rank
  As any duke or lord, O,

Or had the goold the richest bank
   Can shovel from his horde, O,
I'd love her still, if even then
She wer a leäser in a glen.

HEEDLESS O' MY LOVE.

OH! I vu'st know'd o' my true love,
   As the bright moon up above,
Though her brightness wer my pleasure,
   She wer heedless o' my love.
Tho' 'twer all gay to my eyes,
Where her feäir feäce did arise,
She noo mwore thought upon my thoughts,
   Than the high moon in the skies.

Oh! I vu'st heärd her a-zingèn,
   As a sweet bird on a tree,
Though her zingèn wer my pleasure,
   'Twer noo zong she zung to me.
Though her sweet vaïce that wer nigh,
Meäde my wild heart to beat high,
She noo mwore thought upon my thoughts,
   Than the birds would passers by.

Oh! I vu'st know'd her a-weepèn,
   As a raïn-dimm'd mornèn sky,
Though her teär-draps dimm'd her blushes,
   They wer noo draps I could dry.
Ev'ry bright tear that did roll,
Wer a keen païn to my soul,
But noo heärt's pang she did then veel,
   Wer vor my words to console.

But the wold times be a-vanish'd,
   An' my true love is my bride,

An' her kind heart have a-meäde her.
   As an angel at my zide;
I've her best smiles that mid play,
I've her me'th when she is gay,
When her tear-draps be a-rollèn,
I can now wipe em away.

THE DO'SET MILITIA.

Hurrah! my lads, vor Do'set men!
A-muster'd here in red ageän;
All welcome to your ranks, a-spread
Up zide to zide, to stand, or wheel,
An' welcome to your files, to head
The steady march wi' tooe to heel;
Welcome to marches slow or quick!
Welcome to gath'rèns thin or thick;
God speed the Colonel on the hill,*
An' Mrs Bingham,† off o' drill.

When you've a-handled well your lock,
An' flung about your rifle stock
Vrom han' to shoulder, up an' down;
When you've a-lwoaded an' a-vired,
Till you do come back into town,
Wi' all your loppèn limbs a-tired,
An' you be dry an' burnèn hot,
Why here's your tea an' coffee pot
At Mister Greenèn's penny till,
Wi' Mrs Bingham off o' drill.

Last year John Hinley's mother cried,
"Why my bwoy John is quite my pride:

---

* Poundbury, Dorchester, the drill ground.

† The colonel's wife, who opened a room with a coffee-stall, and entertainments for the men off drill.

Vor he've a-been so good to-year,
An' han't a-mell'd wi' any squabbles,
An' han't a-drown'd his wits in beer,
An' han't a-been in any hobbles.
I never thought he'd turn out bad,
He always wer so good a lad;
But now I'm sure he's better still,
Drough Mrs Bingham, off o' drill."

Jeäne Hart, that's Joey Duntley's chaice,
Do praise en up wi' her sweet vaïce,
Vor he's so strait's a hollyhock
(Vew hollyhocks be up so tall),
An' he do come so true's the clock
To Mrs Bingham's coffee-stall;
An' Jeäne do write, an' brag o' Joe
To teäke the young recruits in tow,
An' try, vor all their good, to bring em,
A-come from drill, to Mrs Bingham.

God speed the Colonel, toppèn high,
An' officers wi' sworded thigh,
An' all the sargeants that do bawl
All day enough to split their droats,
An' all the corporals, and all
The band a-playèn up their notes,
An' all the men vrom vur an' near,
We'll gi'e em all a hearty cheer,
An' then another cheerèn still
Vor Mrs Bingham, off o' drill.

A DO'SET SALE.

WITH A MISTAKE.

(Thomas and Mr Auctioneer.)

T. Well here, then, Mister auctioneer,
  Be theäse the virs, I bought, out here?

A. The firs, the fir-poles, you bought? Who?
  'Twas *furze,* not *firs,* I sold to you.

T. I bid vor *virs,* and not vor *vuzzen,*
  Vor vir-poles, as I thought, two dozen.

A. Two dozen faggots, and I took
  Your bidding for them. Here's the book.

T. I wont have what I diddèn buy.
  I don't want *vuzzen,* now. Not I.
  Why *firs* an' *furze* do sound the seäme.
  Why don't ye gi'e a thing his neäme?
  Aye, *firs* and *furze !* Why, who can tell
  Which 'tis that you do meän to zell?
  No, no, be kind enough to call
  Em *virs,* and *vuzzen,* then, that's all.

DON'T CEÄRE.

At the feäst, I do mind very well, all the vo'ks
  Wer a-took in a happerèn storm,
But we chaps took the maïdens, an' kept em wi' clokes
  Under shelter, all dry an' all warm;
An' to my lot vell Jeäne, that's my bride,
That did titter, a-hung at my zide;
Zaid her aunt, " Why the vo'k 'ull talk finely o' you,"
An', cried she, " I don't ceäre if they do."

When the time o' the feäst wer ageän a-come round,
    An' the vo'k wer a-gather'd woonce mwore,
Why she guess'd if she went there, she'd soon be a-vound
    An' a-took seäfely hwome to her door.
Zaid her mother, " 'Tis sure to be wet."
Zaid her cousin, " 'T'ull raïn by zunzet."
Zaid her aunt, "Why the clouds there do look black an' blue,"
An' zaid she, " I don't ceäre if they do."

An' at last, when she own'd I mid meäke her my bride,
    Vor to help me, an' sheäre all my lot,
An' wi' faïthvulness keep all her life at my zide,
    Though my way mid be happy or not.
Zaid her naïghbours, " Why wedlock's a clog,
An' a wife's a-tied up lik' a dog."
Zaid her aunt, " You'll vind trials enough vor to rue,"
An', zaid she, " I don't ceäre if I do."

Now she's married, an' still in the midst ov her tweils
    She's as happy's the daylight is long,
She do goo out abroad wi' her feäce vull o' smiles,
    An' do work in the house wi' a zong.
An', zays woone, " She don't grieve, you can tell."
Zays another, " Why, don't she look well ! "
Zays her aunt, " Why the young vo'k do envy you two,"
An', zays she, " I don't ceäre if they do."

Now vor me I can zing in my business abrode,
    Though the storm do beät down on my poll,
There's a wife-brighten'd vier at the end o' my road,
    An' her love vor the jay o' my soul.
Out o' door I wi' rogues mid be tried :
Out o' door be brow-beäten wi' pride ;
Men mid scowl out o' door, if my wife is but true—
Let em scowl, " I don't ceäre if they do."

CHANGES.

By time's a-brought the mornèn light,
   By time the light do weäne;
By time's a-brought the young man's might,
   By time his might do weäne;
The Winter snow do whitèn grass,
The zummer flow'rs do brightèn grass,
Vor zome things we do lose wi' païn,
We've mwore that mid be jaÿ to gain,
An' my dear life do seem the seäme
      While at my zide
      There still do bide
Your welcome feäce an' hwomely neäme.

Wi' ev'ry day that woonce come on
   I had to choose a jaÿ,
Wi' many that be since a-gone
   I had to lose a jaÿ.
Drough longsome years a-wanderèn,
Drough lwonesome rest a-ponderèn,
Woone peaceful daytime wer a-bro't
To heal the heart another smote;
But my dear life do seem the seäme
      While I can hear,
      A-soundèn near,
Your answ'rèn vaïce an' long-call'd neäme.

An' oh! that hope, when life do dawn,
   Should rise to light our waÿ,
An' then, wi' weänèn het withdrawn,
   Should soon benight our waÿ.
Whatever mid beval me still,
Wherever chance mid call me still,

Though leäte my evenèn tweil mid cease,
An' though my night mid lose its peace,
My life will seem to me the seäme
    While you do sheäre
    My daily ceäre,
An' answer to your long-call'd neäme.

KINDNESS.

GOOD Meäster Collins heärd woone day
A man a-talkèn, that did zay
It woulden answer to be kind,
He thought, to vo'k o' grov'lèn mind,
Vor they would only teäke it wrong,
That you be weak an' they be strong.
"No," cried the goodman, "never mind,
Let vo'k be thankless,—you be kind;
Don't do your good for e'thly ends
At man's own call vor man's amends.
Though souls befriended should remaïn
As thankless as the sea vor raïn,
On them the good's a-lost 'tis true,
But never can be lost to you.
Look on the cool-feäced moon at night
Wi' light-vull ring, at utmost height,
A-castèn down, in gleamèn strokes,
His beams upon the dim-bough'd woaks,
To show the cliff a-risèn steep,
To show the stream a-vallèn deep,
To show where windèn roads do leäd,
An' prickly thorns do ward the meäd.
While sheädes o' boughs do flutter dark
Upon the woak-trees' moon-bright bark,
There in the lewth, below the hill,
The nightèngeäle, wi' ringèn bill,

Do zing among the soft-aïr'd groves,
While up below the house's oves
The maïd, a-lookèn vrom her room
Drough window, in her youthvul bloom,
Do listen, wi' white ears among
Her glossy heäirlocks, to the zong.
If, then, the while the moon do light
The lwonesome zinger o' the night,
His cwold-beam'd light do seem to show
The prowlèn owls the mouse below.
What then? Because an evil will,
Ov his sweet good, mid meäke zome ill,
Shall all his feäce be kept behind
The dark-brow'd hills to leäve us blind?"

WITHSTANDERS.

When weakness now do strive wi' might
   In struggles ov an e'thly trial,
Might mid overcome the right,
   An' truth be turn'd by might's denial;
Withstanders we ha' mwost to feär,
If selfishness do wring us here,
Be souls a-holdèn in their hand,
The might an' riches o' the land.

But when the wicked, now so strong,
   Shall stan' vor judgment, peäle as ashes,
By the souls that rued their wrong,
   Wi' tears a-hangèn on their lashes—
Then withstanders they shall deäre
The leäst ov all to meet wi' there,
Mid be the helpless souls that now
Below their wrongvul might mid bow.

Sweet childern o' the dead, bereft
  Ov all their goods by guile an' forgèn;
Souls o' driven sleäves that left
  Their weäry limbs a-mark'd by scourgèn;
They that God ha' call'd to die
Vor truth ageän the worold's lie,
An' they that groan'd an' cried in vaïn,
A-bound by foes' unrighteous chaïn.

The maïd that selfish craft led on
  To sin, an' left wi' hope a-blighted;
Starvèn workmen, thin an' wan,
  Wi' hopeless leäbour ill requited;
Souls a-wrong'd, an' call'd to vill
Wi' dread, the men that us'd em ill.
When might shall yield to right as pliant
As a dwarf avore a giant.

When there, at last, the good shall glow
  In starbright bodies lik' their Seäviour,
Vor all their flesh noo mwore mid show,
  The marks o' man's unkind beheäviour:
Wi' speechless tongue, an' burnèn cheak,
The strong shall bow avore the weäk,
An' vind that helplessness, wi' right,
Is strong beyond all e'thly might.

DANIEL DWITHEN, THE WISE CHAP.

DAN DWITHEN wer the chap to show
His naïghbours mwore than they did know,
Vor he could zee, wi' half a thought,
What zome could hardly be a-taught;
  An' he had never any doubt
Whatever 'twer, but he did know't,
An' had a-reach'd the bottom o't,
  Or soon could meäke it out.

DANIEL DWITHEN, THE WISE CHAP.

Wi' narrow feäce, an' nose so thin
That light a'most shone drough the skin,
As he did talk, wi' his red peäir
O' lips, an' his vull eyes did steäre,
    What nippy looks friend Daniel wore,
An' how he smiled as he did bring
Such reasons vor to clear a thing,
    As dather'd vo'k the mwore!

When woonce there come along the road
At night, zome show-vo'k, wi' a lwoad
Ov half the wild outlandïsh things
That crawl'd, or went wi' veet, or wings;
    Their elephant, to stratch his knees,
Walk'd up the road-zide turf, an' left
His tracks a-zunk wi' all his heft
    As big's a vinny cheese.

An' zoo next mornèn zome vo'k vound
The girt round tracks upon the ground,
An' view'd em all wi' stedvast eyes,
An' wi' their vingers spann'd their size,
    An' took their depth below the brink:
An' whether they mid be the tracks
O' things wi' witches on their backs,
    Or what, they coulden think.

At last friend Dan come up, an' brought
His wit to help their dizzy thought,
An' lookèn on an' off the ea'th,
He cried, a-drawèn a vull breath,
    Why, I do know; what, can't ye zee 't?
I'll bet a shillèn 'twer a deer
Broke out o' park, an' sprung on here,
    Wi' quoits upon his veet.

TURNÈN THINGS OFF.

Upzides wi' Polly! no, he'd vind
That Poll would soon leäve him behind.
To turn things off! oh! she's too quick
To be a-caught by ev'ry trick.
Woone day our Jimmy stole down steäirs
On merry Polly unaweäres,
The while her nimble tongue did run
A-tellèn, all alive wi' fun,
To sister Anne, how Simon Heäre
Did hanker after her at feäir.
"He left," cried Polly, "cousin Jeäne,
An' kept wi' us all down the leäne,
An' which way ever we did leäd
He vollow'd over hill an' meäd;
An' wi' his head o' shaggy heäir,
An' sleek brown cwoat that he do weäre,
An' collar that did reach so high
'S his two red ears, or perty nigh,
He swung his täil, wi' steps o' pride,
Back right an' left, vrom zide to zide,
A-walkèn on, wi' heavy strides
A half behind, an' half upzides."
"Who's that?" cried Jimmy, all agog;
An' thought he had her now han'-pat,
"That's Simon Heäre," but no, "Who's that?
Cried she at woonce, "Why Uncle's dog,
Wi' what have you a-been misled
I wonder. Tell me what I zaid."
Woone evenèn as she zot bezide
The wall the ranglèn vine do hide,
A-prattlèn on, as she did zend
Her needle, at her vinger's end.

On drough the work she had in hand,
Zome bran-new thing that she'd a-plann'd,
Jim overheärd her talk ageän
O' Robin Hine, ov Ivy Leäne,
"Oh! no, what he!" she cried in scorn,
"I woulden gie a penny vor'n;
The best ov him's outzide in view;
His cwoat is gay enough, 'tis true,
But then the wold vo'k didden bring
En up to know a single thing,
An' as vor zingèn,—what do seem
His zingèn's nothèn but a scream."
"So ho!" cried Jim, "Who's that, then, Meäry,
That you be now a-talkèn o'?"
He thought to catch her then, but, no,
Cried Polly, "Oh! why Jeäne's caneäry,
Wi' what have you a-been misled,
I wonder. Tell me what I zaid."

THE GIANTS IN TREÄDES.

Gramfer's Feäble.

(How the steam engine come about.)

Vier, Aïr, E'th, Water, wer a-meäde
Good workers, each o'm in his treäde,
An' *Aïr* an' *Water*, wer a-match
   Vor woone another in a mill;
The giant *Water* at a hatch,
   An' *Aïr* on the windmill hill.
Zoo then, when *Water* had a-meäde
Zome money, *Aïr* begrudg'd his treäde,
An' come by, unaweäres woone night,
   An' vound en at his own mill-head,
An' cast upon en, iron-tight,

An icy cwoat so stiff as lead.
An' there he wer so good as dead
Vor grindèn any corn vor bread.
Then *Water* cried to *Vier*, "Alack!
    Look, here be I, so stiff's a log,
Thik fellor *Air* do keep me back
    Vrom grindèn. I can't wag a cog.
If I, dear *Vier*, did ever souse
Your nimble body on a house,
When you wer on your merry pranks
Wi' thatch or refters, beams or planks,
Vorgi'e me, do, in pity's neäme,
Vor 'twerden I that wer to bleäme,
I never wagg'd, though I be'nt cringèn,
Till men did dreve me wi' their engine.
Do zet me free vrom theäse cwold jacket,
Vor I myzelf shall never crack it."
"Well come," cried *Vier*, " My vo'k ha' meäde
An engine that 'ull work your treäde.
If *E'th* is only in the mood,
While I do work, to gi'e me food,
I'll help ye, an' I'll meäke your skill
A match vor Mister *Air's* wold mill."
"What food," cried *E'th*, "'ull suit your bwoard?"
"Oh! trust me, I be'nt over nice,"
    Cried *Vier*, " an' I can eat a slice
Ov any thing you can avword."
" I've lots," cried *E'th*, " ov coal an' wood."
"Ah! that's the stuff," cried *Vier*, " that's good."
    Zoo *Vier* at woonce to *Water* cried,
" Here, *Water*, here, you get inside
    O' theäse girt bwoiler. Then I'll show
How I can help ye down below,
An' when my work shall woonce begin
You'll be a thousand times so strong,
An' be a thousand times so long

An' big as when you vu'st got in.
An' I wull meäke, as sure as death,
Thik fellor *Air* to vind me breath,
An' you shall grind, an' pull, an' dreve,
An' zaw, an' drash, an' pump, an' heave,
An' get vrom *Aïr*, in time, I'll lay
A pound, the drevèn ships at sea."
An' zoo 'tis good to zee that might
Wull help a man a-wrong'd, to right.

THE LITTLE WOROLD.

My hwome wer on the timber'd ground
O' Duncombe, wi' the hills a-bound :
Where vew from other peärts did come,
An' vew did travel vur from hwome,
An' small the worold I did know ;
But then, what had it to bestow
But Fanny Deäne so good an' feäir?
'Twer wide enough if she wer there.

In our deep hollow where the zun
Did eärly leäve the smoky tun,
An' all the meäds a-growèn dim,
Below the hill wi' zunny rim ;
Oh! small the land the hills did bound,
But there did walk upon the ground
Young Fanny Deäne so good an' feäir :
'Twer wide enough if she wer there.

O' leäte upon the misty plaïn
I staÿ'd vor shelter vrom the raïn,
Where sharp-leav'd ashes' heads did twist
In hufflèn wind, an' driftèn mist,

An' small the worold I could zee;
But then it had below the tree
My Fanny Deäne so good an' feäir :
'Twer wide enough if she wer there.

An' I've a house wi' thatchen ridge,
Below the elems by the bridge :
Wi' small-peän'd windows, that do look
Upon a knap, an' ramblèn brook;
An' small's my house, my ruf is low,
But then who mid it have to show
But Fanny Deäne so good an' feäir?
'Tis fine enough if peace is there.

BAD NEWS.

I DO mind when there broke bitter tidèns,
    Woone day, on their ears,
An' their souls wer a-smote wi' a stroke
As the lightnèn do vall on the woak,
An' the things that wer bright all around em
    Seem'd dim drough their tears.

Then unheeded wer things in their vingers,
    Their grief wer their all.
All unheeded wer zongs o' the birds,
All unheeded the child's perty words,
All unheeded the kitten a-rollèn
    The white-threaded ball.

Oh! vor their minds the daylight around em
    Had nothèn to show.
Though it brighten'd their tears as they vell,
An' did sheen on their lips that did tell,
In their vaïces all thrillèn an' mwoansome,
    O' nothèn but woe.

But they vound that, by Heavenly mercy,
    The news werden true;
An' they shook, wi' low laughter, as quick
As a drum when his blows do vall thick,
An' wer eärnest in words o' thanksgivèn,
    Vor mercies anew.

THE TURNSTILE.

AH! sad wer we as we did peäce
The wold church road, wi' downcast feäce,
The while the bells, that mwoan'd so deep
Above our child a-left asleep,
Wer now a-zingèn all alive
Wi' tother bells to meäke the vive.
But up at woone pleäce we come by,
'Twer hard to keep woone's two eyes dry:
On Steän-cliff road, 'ithin the drong,
Up where, as vo'k do pass along,
The turnèn stile, a-painted white,
Do sheen by day an' show by night.
Vor always there, as we did goo
To church, thik stile did let us drough,
Wi' spreadèn eärms that wheel'd to guide
Us each in turn to tother zide.
An' vu'st ov all the train he took
My wife, wi' winsome gaït an' look;
An' then zent on my little maïd,
A-skippèn onward, overjay'd
To reach ageän the pleäce o' pride,
Her comely mother's left han' zide.
An' then, a-wheelèn roun', he took
On me, 'ithin his third white nook.
An' in the fourth, a-sheäkèn wild,
He zent us on our giddy child.

2 F

But eesterday he guided slow
My downcast Jenny, vull o' woe,
An' then my little maïd in black,
A-walkèn softly on her track;
An' after he'd a-turn'd ageän,
To let me goo along the leäne,
He had noo little bwoy to vill
His last white eärms, an' they stood still.

THE BETTER VOR ZEÈN O' YOU.

'TWER good what Meäster Collins spoke
O' spite to two poor spitevul vo'k,
When woone twold tother o' the two
" I be never the better vor zeèn o' you."
If soul to soul, as Christians should,
Would always try to do zome good,
" How vew," he cried, " would zee our feäce
A-brighten'd up wi' smiles o' greäce,
An' tell us, or could tell us true,
I be never the better vor zeèn o' you."

A man mus' be in evil ceäse
To live 'ithin a land o' greäce,
Wi' nothèn that a soul can read
O' goodness in his word or deed;
To still a breast a-heav'd wi' sighs,
Or dry the tears o' weepèn eyes;
To stay a vist that spite ha' wrung,
Or cool the het ov anger's tongue:
Or bless, or help, or gi'e, or lend;
Or to the friendless stand a friend,
An' zoo that all could tell en true,
" I be never the better vor zeèn o' you."

Oh! no, mid all o's try to spend
Our passèn time to zome good end,
An' zoo vrom day to day teäke heed,
By mind, an' han', by word or deed;
To lessen evil, and increase
The growth o' righteousness an' peäce,
A-speakèn words o' lovèn-kindness,
Openèn the eyes o' blindness;
Helpèn helpless striver's weakness,
Cheerèn hopeless grievers' meekness,
Meäkèn friends at every meetèn,
Veel the happier vor their greetèn;
Zoo that vew could tell us true,
"I be never the better vor zeèn o' you."
No, let us even try to win
Zome little good vrom sons o' sin,
An' let their evils warn us back
Vrom teäkèn on their hopeless track,
Where we mid zee so clear's the zun
That harm a-done is harm a-won,
An' we mid cry an' tell em true,
"I be even the better vor zeèn o' you."

PITY.

Good Meäster Collins! aye, how mild he spoke
Woone day o' Mercy to zome cruel vo'k.
"No, no. Have Mercy on a helpless head,
An' don't be cruel to a zoul," he zaid.
"When Babylon's king woonce cast 'ithin
    The viery furnace, in his spite,
The vetter'd souls whose only sin
    Wer prayer to the God o' might,
He vound a fourth, 'ithout a neäme,
A-walkèn wi' em in the fleäme.

An' zoo, whenever we mid hurt,
   Vrom spite, or vrom disdaïn,
A brother's soul, or meäke en smert
   Wi' keen an' needless païn,
Another that we midden know
Is always wi' en in his woe.
Vor you do know our Lord ha' cried,
"By faïth my bretheren do bide
In me the livèn vine,
   As branches in a livèn tree;
Whatever you've a-done to mine
   Is all a-done to me.
Oh! when the new-born child, the e'th's new guest,
Do lie an' heave his little breast,
In pillow'd sleep, wi' sweetest breath
O' sinless days drough rwosy lips a-drawn;
Then, if a han' can smite en in his dawn
O' life to darksome death,
Oh! where can Pity ever vwold
   Her wings o' swiftness vrom their holy flight,
To leäve a heart o' flesh an' blood so cwold
   At such a tonchèn zight?
An' zoo mid meek-soul'd Pity still
Be zent to check our evil will,
An' keep the helpless soul from woe,
   An' hold the hardened heart vrom **sin**,
Vor they that can but mercy show
   Shall all their Father's mercy **win**."

JOHN BLOOM IN LON'ON.

(All true.)

JOHN BLOOM he wer a jolly soul,
    A grinder o' the best o' meal,
Bezide a river that did roll,
    Vrom week to week, to push his wheel.
His flour wer all a-meäde o' wheat ;
An' fit for bread that vo'k mid eat ;
Vor he would starve avore he'd cheat.
" 'Tis pure," woone woman cried ;
" Aye, sure," woone mwore replied ;
" You'll vind it nice.   Buy woonce, buy twice,"
    Cried worthy Bloom the miller.

Athirt the chest he wer so wide
    As two or dree ov me or you.
An' wider still vrom zide to zide,
    An' I do think still thicker drough.
Vall down, he couldn, he did lie
When he wer up on-zide so high
As up on-end or perty nigh.
" Meäke room," woone naïghbour cried ;
" 'Tis Bloom," woone mwore replied ;
" Good morn t'ye all, bwoth girt an' small,"
    Cried worthy Bloom the miller.

Noo stings o' conscience ever broke
    His rest, a-twitèn o'n wi' wrong,
Zoo he did sleep till mornèn broke,
    An' birds did call en wi' their zong.
But he did love a harmless joke,
An' love his evenèn whiff o' smoke,
A-zittèn in his cheäir o' woak.

"Your cup," his daughter cried;
"Vill'd up," his wife replied;
"Aye, aye; a drap avore my nap,"
　Cried worthy Bloom the miller.

When Lon'on vok did meäke a show
　O' their girt glassen house woone year,
An' people went, bwoth high an' low,
　To zee the zight, vrom vur an' near,
"O well," cried Bloom, "why I've a right
So well's the rest to zee the zight;
I'll goo, an' teäke the rail outright."
"Your feäre," the booker cried;
"There, there," good Bloom replied;
"Why this June het do meäke woone zweat,"
　Cried worthy Bloom the miller,

Then up the guard did whissle sh'ill,
　An' then the engine pank'd a-blast,
An' rottled on so loud's a mill,
　Avore the traïn, vrom slow to vast.
An' oh! at last how they did spank
By cuttèn deep, an' high-cast bank
The while their iron ho'se did pank.
"Do whizzy," woone o'm cried;
"I'm dizzy," woone replied;
"Aye, here's the road to hawl a lwoad,"
　Cried worthy Bloom the miller.

In Lon'on John zent out to call
　A tidy trap, that he mid ride
To zee the glassen house, an' all
　The lot o' things a-stow'd inside.
"Here, Boots, come here," cried he, "I'll dab
A sixpence in your han' to nab
Down street a tidy little cab."

"A feäre," the boots then cried;
"I'm there," the man replied.
"The glassen pleäce, your quickest peäce,"
Cried worthy Bloom the miller.

 The steps went down wi' rottlèn slap,
  The zwingèn door went open wide:
 Wide? no; vor when the worthy chap
  Stepp'd up to teäke his pleäce inside,
Breast-foremost, he wer twice too wide
Vor thik there door. An' then he tried
To edge in woone an' tother zide.
"'Twont do," the drever cried;
"Can't goo," good Bloom replied;
"That you should bring theäse vooty thing!"
Cried worthy Bloom the miller.

 "Come," cried the drever. "Pay your feäre
  You'll teäke up all my time, good man."
"Well," answer'd Bloom, "to meäke that square,
  You teäke up me, then, if you can."
"I come at call," the man did nod.
"What then?" cried Bloom, "I han't a-rod,
An' can't in thik there hodmadod."
"Girt lump," the drever cried;
"Small stump," good Bloom replied;
"A little mite, to meäke so light,
 O' jolly Bloom the miller."

 "You'd best be off now perty quick,"
  Cried Bloom, "an' vind a lighter lwoad,
 Or else I'll vetch my voot, an' kick
  The vooty thing athirt the road."
"Who is the man?" they cried, "meäke room,"
"A halfstarv'd Do'set man," cried Bloom;

" You be ? " another cried ;
" Hee ! Hee ! " woone mwore replied.
" Aye, shrunk so thin, to bwone an' skin,"
  Cried worthy Bloom the miller.

A LOT O' MAÏDENS A-RUNNÈN THE VIELDS.*

" Come on. Be sprack, a-laggèn back."
" Oh ! be there any cows to hook ? "
" Lauk she's afraïd, a silly maïd,"
  Cows? No, the cows be down by brook.
" O here then, oh ! here is a lot."
" A lot o' what ? what is it ? what ? "
" Why blackberries, as thick
  As ever they can stick."
" I've dewberries, oh ! twice
  As good as they ; so nice."
" Look here. Theäse boughs be all but blue
  Wi' snags."
          " Oh ! gi'e me down a vew."
" Come here, oh ! do but look."
" What's that ? what is it now ? "
" Why nuts a-slippèn shell."
" Hee ! hee ! pull down the bough."
" I wish I had a crook."
" There zome o'm be a-vell."
  (*One sings*)
          " I wish I was on Bimport Hill
  I would zit down and cry my vill."
" Hee ! hee ! there's Jenny zomewhere nigh,
  A-zingèn that she'd like to cry."

---

* The idea, though but little of the substance, of this poem, will be found in a little Italian poem called *Caccia*, written by Franco Sacchetti.

(*Jenny sings*)
"I would zit down and cry my vill
Until my tears would dreve a mill."
"Oh! here's an ugly crawlèn thing,
   A sneäke." "A slooworm; he wont sting."
"Hee! hee! how she did squal an' hop,
   A-spinnèn roun' so quick's a top."
"Look here, oh! quick, be quick."
"What is it? what then? where?"
"A rabbit." "No, a heäre."
"Ooh! ooh! the thorns do prick,"
"How he did scote along the ground
   As if he wer avore a hound."
"Now mind the thistles." "Hee, hee, hee,
   Why they be knapweeds."
"No." "They be."
"I've zome'hat in my shoe."
"Zit down, an' sheäke it out."
"Oh! emmets, oh! ooh, ooh,
   A-crawlèn all about."
"What bird is that, O harken, hush.
   How sweetly he do zing."
"A nightingeäle." "La! no, a drush."
"Oh! here's a funny thing."
"Oh! how the bull do hook,
   An' bleäre, an' fling the dirt."
"Oh! wont he come athirt?"
"No, he's beyond the brook."
"O lauk! a hornet rose
   Up clwose avore my nose."
"Oh! what wer that so white
   Rush'd out o' thik tree's top?"
"An owl." "How I did hop,
   How I do sheäke wi' fright."
"A musheroom." "O lau!

A twoadstool! Pwoison! Augh."
'What's that, a mouse?"
"O no,
Teäke ceäre, why 'tis a shrow."
" Be sure dont let en come
  An' run athirt your shoe
  He'll meäke your voot so numb
  That you wont veel a tooe."*
"Oh! what wer that so loud
  A-rumblèn?"   "Why a clap
  O' thunder. Here's a cloud
  O' raïn. I veel a drap."
" A thunderstorm. Do raïn.
  Run hwome wi' might an' main."
" Hee! hee! oh! there's a drop
  A-trickled down my back. Hee! hee!"
" My head's as wet's a mop."
" Oh! thunder," "there's a crack. Oh! Oh!"
" Oh! I've a-got the stitch, Oh!"
" Oh! I've a-lost my shoe, Oh!"
" There's Fanny into ditch, Oh!"
" I'm wet all drough an' drough, Oh!"

* The folklore is, that if a shrew-mouse run over a person's foot, it will lame him.

A LIST

OF

SOME DORSET WORDS

WITH A FEW HINTS ON DORSET WORD-SHAPES.

THE MAIN SOUNDS.

1. *ee* in beet.
2. *e* in Dorset (a sound between 1 and 3.)
3. *a* in mate.
4. *i* in birth.
5. *a* in father.
6. *aw* in awe.
7. *o* in dote.
8. *oo* in rood.

In Dorset words which are forms of book-English ones, the Dorset words differ from the others mainly by Grimm's law, that "likes shift into likes," and I have given a few hints by which the putting of an English heading for the Dorset one will give the English word. If the reader is posed by *dreaten*, he may try for *dr*, *thr*, which will bring out *threaten* See *Dr* under D.

A.

a in father, and *au* in daughter are, in "Blackmore," often *a* = 3. So king Alfred gives a legacy to his *yldsta dehter*—oldest daehter. *a* is a fore-eking to participes of a fore time, as *a-vound*; also for the Anglo-Saxon *an*, *in* or *on*, as *a-huntèn* for *an huntunge*.

ai, *aÿ* (5, 1), Maid, Maÿ.

(*Note*— The numbers (as 5, 1) refer to the foregiven table.)

ag, often for *eg*, as bag, agg, beg, egg.

Anewst, } very near, or nearly.
Anighst, }
A'r a, ever a, as.
A'r a dog, ever a dog.
Amper, pus.
A'r'n, e'er a one.
A-stooded (as a waggon), with wheels sunk fast into rotten ground.
A-stogged, } with feet stuck fast in
A-stocked, } clay.
A-strout, stiff stretched.
A-thirt, athwart (*th* soft).
A-vore, afore, before.
Ax, ask.
Axan, ashes (of fire).
A-zew, dry, milkless.

B.

Backbran' (*brand*), } A big brand or block of wood
Backbron' (*brond*), } put on the back of the fire.

Ballywrag, scold.

Bandy, a long stick with a bent end to beat abroad cow-dung.
Barken, } a stack-yard or cow-
Barton, } yard.
Bavèn, a faggot of long brushwood.
Beä'nhan' (1, 3, 5), bear in hand, uphold or maintain, as an opinion or otherwise.
Beät (1, 4), *up*, to beat one's way up.
Bennets, flower-stalks of grass.
Be'th, birth.
Bibber, to shake with cold.
[This is a Friesic and not an Anglo-Saxon form of the word, and Halbertsma, in his " Lexicon Frisicum," gives it, among others, as a token that Frisians came into Wessex with the Saxons. *See* Eltrot.]
Bissen, thou bist not.
Bittle, a beetle.
Blatch, black stuff; smut.
Blather, a bladder.
Bleàre (1, 3), to low as a cow.
Blind-buck o' Davy, blindman's buff.
Bloodywarrior, the ruddy Stock gilliflower.
Blooèns, blossoms.
Blooth, blossom in the main.
Bluevinny, blue mouldy.
Brack, a breach.
" Neither brack nor crack in it."
Bran', a brand.
Brantèn, brazen-faced.
Bring-gwain (Bring-going), to bring one on his way.
Brocks, broken pieces (as of food).
Bron', a brand.
Bruckly, Bruckle, brittle.
Bundle, to bound off; go away quickly.
Bu'st, burst.

C.

Caddle, a muddle; a puzzling plight amid untoward things, such that a man knows not what to do first.
Car, to carry.
Cassen, casn, canst not.
Chanker, a wide chink.
Charlick, charlock, field-mustard; *Sinapis arvensis.*
Charm, a noise as of many voices.
Choor, a chare, a (weekly) job as of house work.
Chuck, to throw underhanded to a point, or for a catch.
Clack, } a bird-clacker;
Clacker, } a bird-boy's clacking tool, to fray away birds; also the tongue.
Clavy, } the mantel-shelf.
Clavy-bwoard, }
Clèden, cleavers, goosegrass; *Galium aparine.*
Clips, to clasp.
Clitty, clingy.
Clocks, ornaments on the ankles of stockings.
Clom', clomb, climbed.
Clote, the yellow water-lily; *Nuphar lutea.*
Clout, a blow with the flat hand.
Clum, to handle clumsily.
Cluster o' vive (cluster of five), the fist or hand with its five fingers; wording taken from a cluster of nuts.
Cockle, Cuckle, the bur of the burdock.
Cockleshell, snail shell.
Colepexy, to glean the few apples left on the tree after intaking.
Coll (7), to embrace the neck.
Conker, the hip, or hep; the fruit of the briar.
Cothe, coath (*th* soft), a disease of sheep, the plaice or flook, a flat worm *Distoma nepaticum* in the stomach.
Cou'den, could not.
Coussen, } *coosn*, couldest not.
Coossen, }
Craze, to crack a little.
Critch, a big pitcher.
Crock, an iron cooking-pot.
Croodle, to crow softly.
Croop, } to bend down the
Croopy-down, } body; to stoop very low.
Crope, crept.
Crowshell, shell of the fresh-water mussel, as taken out of the river for food by crows.
Cubby-hole, } between the father's
Cubby-house, } knees.

Culver, the wood pigeon.
Cutty, Cut, the kittywren.
Cwein,
Cwoïn, } (4, 1) coin.
Cwoffer (8, 4, 4), a coffer.

D.

Dadder, dather, dudder, to maze or bewilder.
Dag, childag, a chilblain.
Dake, to ding or push forth.
Daps, the very likeness, as that of a cast from the same mould.
Dather, see *Dadder*.
Dent, a dint.
Dewberry, a big kind of blackberry.
Dibs, coins; but truly, the small knee bones of a sheep used in the game of Dibs.
Didden (didn), did not.
Do, the *o*, when not under a strain of voice, is (4) as *e* in 'the man' or as *e* in the French *le*.
Dod, a dump.
Dogs, andirons.
Don, to put on.
Doust, dust.
dr for *thr* in some words, as Drash, thresh.
Drashel, threshold.
Dreaten, threaten.
Dree, three.
Dringe, Drunge, to throng; push as in a throng.
Droat, throat.
Drong, throng; also a narrow way.
Drough, through.
Drow, throw.
Drub, throb.
Drush, thrush.
Drust, thrust.
Drean, Drène (2), to drawl.
Drève (2), drive.
Duck, a darkening, dusk.
Dumbledore, the humble bee.
Dummet, dusk.
Dunch, dull of hearing, or mind.
Dunch-nettle, the dead nettle, *Lamium*.
Dunch-pudden, pudding of bare dough.

Dungpot, a dungcart.
Dunt, to blunten as an edge or pain.
Durns, the side posts of a door.

E

long itself alone has mostly the Dorset sound (2.)
eä (1, 4) for *ea*, with the *a* unsounded as lead, mead, leäd, meäd.
eä (1, 3) for the long *a*, 3, as in lade, made, leäde, meäde.
ea of one sound (2) as meat.
e is put in before *s* after *st*, as nestes, nests, vistes, fists.
The two sundry soundings of *ea* 2 and 3 do not go by our spelling *ea* for both, but have come from earlier forms of the words.
After a roof letter it may stay as it is, a roof letter, as madden, madd'n; rotten, rott'n. So with *en* for him, tell en, tell'n.
The *en* sometimes at the end of words means not, as bisse'n, bist not; coust'en, cous'n, could'st not; I didd'n, I did not; diss'n, didst not; hadd'n, had not; muss'n, must not; midd'n, mid not; should'n, should not; 'tis'n, 'tis not; would'n, would not.
en—not *èn*—in Dorset, as well as in book English, as an ending of some kinds of words often, in running talk, loses the *e*, and in some cases shifts into a sound of the kind of the one close before it. After a lip-letter it becomes a lip-letter *m*, as Rub en, Rub-him; rub'n, rub'm; oven, ov'm; open, op'n op'm, in Dorset mostly oben, ob'n, ob'm. So after *f*, deafen, deaf'n, deaf'm, heaven, heav'n, heav'm, in Dorset sometimes heab'm. zeven, zeb'n, zeb'm. After a throat-letter it becomes a throat one, *ng*, as token, tok'n, tok'ng.

ē (2).
Eegrass, aftermath.
Eltrot, Eltroot, cowparsley (*Myrrhis*). [Elt is Freisic, robustus,

vegetus, as cowparsley is among other kinds.] *See* Bibber.
Emmet, an ant.
Emmetbut, an anthill.
En, him; A.-Saxon, *hine*.
En, for ing, zingèn, singing.
Eve, to become wet as a cold stone floor from thickened steam in some weather.
Evet, eft, newt.
Exe, an axle.

F

Fakket, a faggot.
Fall, autumn; to fall down is *vall*.
Faÿ (5, 1) to speed, succeed.
Feäst (1, 4), a village wake or festival; *festa*.
Flag, a water plant.
Flinders, flying pieces of a body smashed; "Hit it all to flinders."
Flounce, a flying fall as into water.
Flout, a flinging, or blow of one.
Flush, fledged.
Footy, unhandily little.

G

Gally, to frighten, fray.
Gee, jee, to go, fit, speed.
Giddygander, the meadow orchis.
Gil'cup, gilt cup, the buttercup.
Girt, great.
Glēne (2), to smile sneeringly.
Glutch, to swallow.
Gnang, to mock one with jaw waggings, and noisy sounds.
Gnot, a gnat.
Goo, go.
Coocoo flower, *Cardamine pratensis*.
Goodnow, goodn'er, good neighbour; my good friend; "No, no; not I, goodnow;" "No, no; not I, my good friend."
Coolden chain, the laburnum.
Gout, an underground gutter.
Grægle, } the wild hyacinth,
Greygle, } *Hyacinthus nonscriptus*.
Gramfer, grandfather.
Ground-ash, an ash stick that springs from the ground, and so is tough;
"Ground the pick," to put the stem of it on the ground, to raise a pitch of hay.
Gwoad (8, 4), a goad.

H

Hacker, a hoe.
Hagrod, hagridden in sleep, if not under the nightmare.
Haïn (5, 1), to fence in ground or shut up a field for mowing.
Ha'me, see *Hau'm*.
Hangèn, sloping ground.
Hansel, } a hand gift.
Handsel, }
Hansel, } to use a new thing for the
Handsel, } first time.
Happer, to hop up as hailstones or rain-drops from ground or pavement in a hard storm, or as downshaken apples; to fall so hard as to hop up at falling.
Haps, a hasp.
Ha'skim, halfskim cheese of milk skimmed only once.
Hassen, hast not.
Haum, } the hollow stalks of
Haulm, } plants. *Tātie haum*,
Hulm, } potatoe stalks.
Hatch, a low wicket or half door.
Haÿmeäkèn, haymaking.

The steps of haymaking by hand, in the rich meadow lands of Blackmore, ere machines were brought into the field, were these:—The grass being mown, and lying in *swath*, it was (1) *tedded*, spread evenly over the ground; (2) it was *turned* to dry the under side; (3) it was in the evening raked up into *rollers*, each roller of the grass of the stretch of one rake, and the rollers were sometimes put up into hay cocks; (4) in the morning the rollers were cast abroad into *pa'sels* (parcels) or broad lists, with clear ground between each two; (5) the parcels were turned, and when dry they were pushed up into *weäles* (weales) or long ridges; and, with a fear of rain, the weales were put up into *pooks*, or big peaked heaps; the waggon (often called the *plow*) came along between two weäles or rows of pooks, with two loaders, and a pitcher on each side pitched up to them the hay of his side, while two women raked after plow, or raked up the leavings of the pitchers, who stepped back from time to time to take it from them.

GLOSSARY.

Hazen, to forebode.
Hazzle, hazel.
Heal (2), hide, to cover.
Heal pease, to hoe up the earth on them.
Hean (1, 4), a haft, handle.
Heft, weight.
Herence, hence.
Here right, here on the spot, etc.
Het, heat, also a heat in running.
Het, to hit.
Heth, a hearth, a heath.
Hick, to hop on one leg.
Hidelock,) a hiding place. "He is
Hidlock,) in hidelock." He is absconded.
Hidybuck, hide-and-seek, the game.
Hile of Sheaves, ten, 4 against 4 in a ridge, and 1 at each end.
Ho, to feel misgiving care.
Hodmadod, a little dod or dump; in some parts of England a snail.
Holm, ho'me, holly.
Hook, to gore as a cow.
Honeyzuck, honeysuckle.
Ho'se-tinger, the dragon-fly, *Libellula*. Horse does not mean a horse, but is an adjective meaning coarse or big of its kind, as in horse-radish, or horse-chesnut; most likely the old form of the word gave name to the horse as the big beast where there was not an elephant or other greater one. The dragon-fly is, in some parts, called the "tanging ether" or tanging adder, from *tang*, a long thin body, and a sting. Very few Dorset folk believe that the dragon-fly stings horses any more than that the horse eats horse-brambles or horse-mushrooms.
Hud, a pod, a hood-like thing.
Ho'se, hoss, a board on which a ditcher may stand in a wet ditch.
Huadick (hoodock), a fingerstall.
Hull, a pod, a hollow thing.
Humbuz, a notched strip of lath, swung round on a string, and humming or buzzing.
Humstrum, a rude, home-made musical instrument, now given up.

J.

Jack-o'-lent, a man-like scarecrow.
The true Jack-o'-lent was, as we learn from Taylor, the water poet, a ragged, lean-like figure which went as a token of Lent, in olden times, in Lent processions.
Jist, just.
Jut, to nudge or jog quickly.

K.

Kag, a keg.
Kapple cow, a cow with a white muzzle.
Kern, to grow into fruit.
Ketch,) to thicken or harden from
Katch,) thinness, as melted fat.
Kecks,) a stem of the hemlock or
Kex,) cowparsley.
Keys, (2), the seed vessels of the sycamore.
Kid, a pod, as of the pea.
Kittyboots, low uplaced boots, a little more than ancle high.
Knap, a hillock, a head, or knob, (2.) a knob-like bud, as of the potatoe. "The teaties be out in knap."

L.

Laiter (5, 1), one run of laying of a hen.
Lean (1, 4), to lean.
Leane (1, 3), a lane.
Lease (1, 4), to glean.
Lease (1, 4),) an unmown field,
Leaze,) stocked through the Spring and Summer.
Leer, Leery, empty.
Lence, a loan, a lending.
Levers, Livers, the corn flag.
Lew, sheltered from cold wind.
Lewth, lewness.
Libbets, loose-hanging rags.
Limber, limp.
Linch, Linchet, a ledge on a hill-side.
Litsome, lightsome, gay.
Litty, light and brisk of body.
Lo't (7), loft, an upper floor.
Lowl, to loll loosely.

Lumper, a loose step.

M.

Maesh (2), *Mesh*, (Blackmore) moss, also a hole or run of a hare, fox, or other wild animal.
Mammet, an image, scarecrow.
Marrels, *Merrels*, The game of nine men's morris.
Mawn, mān, (5) a kind of basket.
Meàden (1, 4), stinking chamomile.
Ment (2), to imitate, be like.
Mēsh, (2) moss.
Mid, might.
Miff, a slight feud, a tiff.
Min (2), observe. You must know.
Mither ho, come hither. A call to a horse on the road.
Moot, the bottom and roots of a felled tree.
More, a root, taproot.
Muggy, misty, damp (weather).

N.

Na'r a, never a (man).
Nar'n, never a one.
N'eet, not yet.
Nēsh (2), soft.
Nesthooden, a hooding over a bird's nest, as a wren's.
Netlèns, a food of a pig's inwards tied in knots.
Never'stide, never at all.
Nicky, a very small fagot of sticks.
Nippy, hungry, catchy.
Nitch, a big fagot of wood; a load; a fagot of wood which custom allows a hedger to carry home at night.
Not (hnot or knot), hornless.
Nother, neither (adverb).
Nunch, a nog or knob of food.
Nut (of a wheel), the stock or nave.

O.

O', of.
O'm (2), of em, them.
O'n (2), of him.
O's (2), of us.
Orts, leavings of hay put out in little heaps in the fields for the cows.
Over-right, opposite.
Oves, eaves.

P.

Paladore, a traditional name of Shaftesbury, the British *Caer Paladr*, said by British history to have been founded by *Rhun Paladr-bras*, 'Rhun of the stout spear.'
Pank, pant.
Par, to shut up close; confine.
Parrick, a small enclosed field; a paddock—but paddock was an old word for a toad or frog.
Pa'sels, parcels. See Haÿmeakèn.
Peärt (1, 4), pert; lively.
Peaze, *Peeze* (2), to ooze.
Peewit, the lapwing.
Pitch. See Haÿmeakèn.
Plesh, (2) *Plush* (a hedge), to lay it.
  To cut the stems half off and peg them down on the bank where they sprout upward.
  To plush, shear, and trim a hedge are sundry handlings of it.
Plim, to swell up.
Plock, a hard block of wood.
Plow, a waggon, often so called.
  The plough or plow for ploughing is the Zull.
Plounce, a strong plunge.
Pluffy, plump.
Pont, to hit a fish or fruit, so as to bring on a rotting.
Pooks. See Haÿmeakèn.
Popple, a pebble.
Praise (5, 1), prize, to put forth or tell to others a pain or ailing. "I had a risèn on my eärm, but I didden *praise* it," say anything about it.
Pummy, pomice.
  ps for *sp* in clasp, claps; hasp, haps; wasp, waps.

Q.

Quaer, queer.

Quag, a quaking bog.
Quar, a quarry.
Quarrel, a square window pane.
Quid, a cud.
Quirk, to grunt with the breath without the voice.

R.

R, at the head of a word, is strongly breathed, as *Hr* in Anglo-Saxon, as *Hhrong*, the rong of a ladder.
R is given in Dorset by a rolling of the tongue back under the roof.
For *or*, as an ending sometimes given before a free breathing, or *h*, try *ow*,—*hollor*, hollow.
R before *s*, *st*, and *th* often goes out, as bu'st, burst; ve'ss, verse; be'th, birth; cu'st, curst; fwo'ce, force; me'th, mirth.
Raft, to rouse, excite.
Rake, to reek.
Ram, Rammish, rank of smell.
Rammil, raw milk (cheese), of unskimmed milk.
Ramsclaws, the creeping crowfoot. *Ranunculus repens*.
Randy, a merry uproar or meeting.
Rangle, to range or reach about.
Rathe, early; whence rather.
Ratch, to stretch.
Readship, criterion, counsel.
Reämes, (1, 3) skeleton, frame.
Reän (1, 4), to reach in greedily in eating.
Reaves, a frame of little rongs on the side of a waggon.
Reed (2), wheat hulm drawn for thatching.
Reely, to dance a reel.
Reem, to stretch, broaden.
Rick, a stack.
Rig, to climb about.
Rivel, shrivel; to wrinkle up.
Robin Hood, The Red campion.
Roller (6, 4). See Haÿmeakèn.
A Roller was also a little roll ot wool from the card of a woolcomber.
Rottlepenny, the yellow rattle. *Rhinanthus Crista-galli*.
Rouet, a rough tuft of grass.

S

Sammy, soft, a soft head; simpleton.
Sar, to serve or give food to (cattle).
Sarch, to search.
Scrag, a crooked branch of a tree.
Scraggle, to screw scramly about (of a man), to screw the limbs scramly as from rheumatism.
Scram, distorted, awry.
Scroff, bits of small wood or chips, as from windfalls or hedge plushing.
Scroop, to skreak lowly as new shoes or a gate hinge.
Scote, to shoot along fast in running.
Scud, a sudden or short down-shooting of rain, a shower.
Scwo'ce, chop or exchange.
Settle, a long bench with a high planken back.
Shard, a small gap in a hedge.
Sharps, shafts of a waggon.
Shatten, shalt not.
Shroud (trees), to cut off branches.
Sheeted cow, with a broad white band round her body.
Shoulden (*Shoodn*), should not.
Shrow,
Sh'ow, }the shrew mouse.
Sh'ow-crop,
Skim, } grass; to cut off rank
Skimmy, } tuffs, or rouets.
Slait, (5, 1) *Slite*, a slade, or sheep run.
Slent, a tear in clothes.
Slidder, to slide about.
Slim, sly.
Sloo, sloe.
Slooworm, the slow-worm.
Smame, to smear.
Smeech, a cloud of dust.
Smert, to smart; pain.
Snabble, to snap up quickly.
Snags, small pea-big sloes, also stumps.
Sneäd (1, 4), a scythe stem.
Snoatch, to breathe loudly through the nose.
Snoff, a snuff of a candle.
Sock, a short loud sigh.
Spur (*dung*), to cast it abroad.

Squaïl (5, 1), to fling something at a bird or ought else.
Squot, to flatten by a blow.
Sowel,
Zowel, } a hurdle stake.
Sparbill,
Sparrabill, } a kind of shoe nail.
Spars, forked sticks used in thatching.
Speäker (1, 4), a long spike of wood to bear the hedger's nitch on his shoulder.
Spears,
Speers, } the stalks of reed grass.
Spik, spike, lavender.
Sprack, active.
Sprethe (2), to chap as of the skin, from cold.
Spry, springy in leaping, or limb work.
Staddle, a bed or frame for ricks.
Staïd (5, 1), steady, oldish.
Stannèns, stalls in a fair or market.
Steän (1, 4) (a road), to lay it in stone.
Steärt (1, 4), a tail or outsticking thing.
Stout, the cowfly, *Tabanus*.
Stitch (of corn), a conical pile of sheaves.
Strawèn, a strewing. All the potatoes of one mother potatoe.
Strawmote, a straw or stalk.
Strent, a long slent or tear.
Streech, an outstretching (as of a rake in raking); a-strout stretched out stiffly like frozen linen.
Stubbard, a kind of apple.
Stunpoll (7), stone head, blockhead; also an old tree almost dead.

T

th is soft (as *th* in thee), as a heading of these words:—thatch, thief, thik, thimble, thin, think, thumb.
Tack, a shelf on a wall.
Taffle, to tangle, as grass or corn beaten down by storms.
Taït, to play at see-saw.
Tamy (3, 1), *tammy* (5, 1), tough, that may be drawn out in strings, as rich toasted cheese.
Teäve, (1, 3), to reach about strongly as in work or a struggle.
Teery, Tewly, weak of growth.
Tewly, weakly.
Theäse, this or these.
Theasum (1, 4), these.
Tidden (tidn), it is not.
Tilty, touchy, irritable.
Timmersome, restless.
Tine, to kindle, also to fence in ground.
Tistytosty, a toss ball of cowslip blooms.
To-year, this year (as to-day.)
Tranter, a common carrier.
Trendel, a shallow tub.
Tump, a little mound.
Tun, the top of tne chimney above the roof ridge.
Tut (work), piecework.
Tutty, a nosegay.
Tweil, (4, 1) toil.
Twite, to twit reproach.

U.

Unheal, uncover, unroof.

V

v is taken for *f* as the heading of some purely English words, as vall, fall, vind, find.
Veag, Vēg (2), a strong fit of anger.
Vern, fern.
Ve'se, vess, a verse.
Vinny cheese, cheese with fen or blue-mould.
Vitty, nice in appearance.
Vlanker, a flake of fire.
Vlee, fly.
Vo'k, folk.
Vooty, unhandily little.
Vuz, Vuzzen, furze, gorse.

W

wo (8, 4), for the long o, 7, as bwold, bold; cwold, cold.
Wag, to stir.

GLOSSARY.

Wagwanton, quaking grass.
Wease, (1, 4) a pad or wreath for the head under a milkpail.
Weäle (1, 3), a ridge of dried hay; see *Haymeaken*.
Welshnut, a walnut.
Werden, were not or was not.
Wevet, a spider's web.
Whindlen, weakly, small of growth.
Whicker, to neigh.
Whiver, to hover, quiver.
Whog, go off; to a horse.
Whur, to fling overhanded.
Wi', with.
Widdicks, withes or small brushwood.
Wink, a winch; crank of a well.
Withwind, the bindweed.
Wont, a mole.
Wops, wasp.
ps, not *sp*, in Anglo-Saxon, and now in Holstein.
Wotshed, } wet-footed.
Wetshod, }
Wride, to spread out in growth.
Wride, the set of stems or stalks from one root or grain of corn.
Writh, a small wreath of tough wands, to link hurdles to the sowels (stakes).
Wrix, wreathed or wattle work, as a fence.

Y

Yop, yelp.

Z

z for *s* as a heading of some, not all, pure Saxon words, nor for *s* of inbrought foreign words.
Zand, sand.
Zennit, } seven night; "This day
Zennight, } zennit."
Zew, *azew*, milkless.
Zoo, so.
Zive, a scythe.
Zull a plough to plough ground.
Zwath, a swath.

Turnbull & Spears, Printers.